CHILDREN'S RIGHTS AND CHILDREN'S DEVELOPMENT

FAMILIES, LAW, AND SOCIETY SERIES

General Editors: Nancy E. Dowd and Robin A. Lenhardt

Masculinities and the Law: A Multidimensional Approach
Edited by Frank Rudy Cooper and Ann C. McGinley

Justice for Kids: Keeping Kids Out of the Juvenile Justice System
Edited by Nancy E. Dowd

The New Kinship: Constructing Donor-Conceived Families
Naomi Cahn

What Is Parenthood? Contemporary Debates about the Family
Edited by Linda C. McClain and Daniel Cere

The Marriage Buyout: The Troubled Trajectory of U.S. Alimony Law
Cynthia Lee Starnes

A New Juvenile Justice System: Total Reform for a Broken System
Edited by Nancy E. Dowd

Children, Sexuality, and the Law
Edited by Sasha M. Coupet and Ellen Marrus

Divorced from Reality: Rethinking Family Dispute Resolution
Jane C. Murphy and Jana B. Singer

In Our Hands: The Struggle for U.S. Child Care Policy
Elizabeth Palley and Corey S. Shdaimah

Ending Zero Tolerance: The Crisis of Absolute School Discipline
Derek W. Black

The Poverty Industry: The Exploitation of America's Most Vulnerable Citizens
Daniel L. Hatcher

The Politicization of Safety: Critical Perspectives on Domestic Violence Responses
Edited by Jane K. Stoever

Blaming Mothers: American Law and the Risks to Children's Health
Linda C. Fentiman

The Ecology of Childhood: How Our Changing World Threatens Children's Rights
Barbara Bennett Woodhouse

Living Apart Together: Legal Protections for a New Form of Family
Cynthia Grant Bowman

Social Parenthood in Comparative Perspective
Edited by Clare Huntington, Courtney G. Joslin, and Christiane von Bary

The End of Family Court: How Abolishing the Court Brings Justice to Children and Families
Jane M. Spinak

The Architecture of Desire: How the Law Shapes Interracial Intimacy and Perpetuates Inequality
Solangel Maldonado

Children's Rights and Children's Development: An Integrated Approach
Edited by Jonathan Todres and Ursula Kilkelly

Children's Rights and Children's Development

An Integrated Approach

Edited by

Jonathan Todres *and* Ursula Kilkelly

NEW YORK UNIVERSITY PRESS
New York, New York

NEW YORK UNIVERSITY PRESS
New York
www.nyupress.org

Library of Congress Cataloging-in-Publication Data
Names: Todres, Jonathan, editor. | Kilkelly, Ursula, editor.
Title: Children's rights and children's development : an integrated approach / edited by Jonathan Todres and Ursula Kilkelly.
Description: New York, New York : New York University Press, 2025. |
Series: Families, law, and society | Includes bibliographical referencesand index.
Identifiers: LCCN 2024006501 (print) | LCCN 2024006502 (ebook) |
ISBN 9781479825486 (hardback) | ISBN 9781479825493 (ebook) |
ISBN 9781479825509 (ebook other)
Subjects: LCSH: Children—Legal status, laws, etc. | Children's rights. |
Child development—Law and legislation. | Children (International law)
Classification: LCC K639 .C4823 2025 (print) | LCC K639 (ebook) |
DDC342.08/772—dc23/eng/20240209
LC record available at https://lccn.loc.gov/2024006501
LC ebook record available at https://lccn.loc.gov/2024006502

This book is printed on acid-free paper, and its binding materials are chosen for strength and durability. We strive to use environmentally responsible suppliers and materials to the greatest extent possible in publishing our books.

Manufactured in the United States of America

10 9 8 7 6 5 4 3 2 1

Also available as an ebook

CONTENTS

Introduction

JONATHAN TODRES AND URSULA KILKELLY

The UN Convention on the Rights of the Child, the most widely accepted human rights treaty in history, defines a child as every human being below the age of eighteen years (Article 1). Despite the widespread acceptance of this definition, it is equally clear that "children" by definition are not a homogeneous group; they experience diverse cultures and backgrounds and have unique lived experiences for a whole range of complex reasons. Children are also distinguished by their age and stage of development, as their capacity to exercise their rights evolves throughout childhood. It is readily apparent, for instance, that babies have very different needs and interests from adolescents. Moreover, even young and older children can be distinguished from one another in relation to their maturity, how they exercise their rights, and the contexts in which they seek to do so. Yet, while there have important advances in law and policy since the adoption of the Convention on the Rights of the Child (CRC) in 1989, acknowledging how children differ from adults, there has been significantly less progress in law and policy domains with regard to recognizing the diversity and developmental nature of childhood.[1]

The CRC makes no distinction between children of different ages and stages of development, recognizing all children as rights holders and equally worthy of dignity and respect. This approach is consistent with the foundational concept of human rights that rights are inherent in all individuals.[2] At the same time, reading through the CRC, it is clear that certain provisions will resonate more clearly with children of particular stages of development. For instance, the right to play may apply more commonly to younger children, while the provisions relating to children in conflict with the law typically apply to older children. While there is merit in the CRC's uniform approach—where children's rights appear to apply equally to all children at all stages of development—this approach could be said to be unhelpful insofar as it ignores the relevance of children's development to the exercise of their rights. Certainly, as attention shifts more and more to the implementation of the CRC and children's rights more generally, a greater granularity in the understanding of children's development is necessary to achieve full implementation of children's rights.

Although developmental differences are acknowledged in the children's rights literature, they are rarely engaged with in any depth. For example, scholars frequently note that provisions like Article 12 of the CRC—which affirms children's right to be heard on matters that affect them—apply to all children, but relatively few focus on its application to young children.[3] The literature rarely addresses what participation rights mean in the specific contexts of early childhood or middle childhood, with little analysis, for example, of how this and other provisions of the CRC might differ in application to a five-year-old compared with a fifteen-year-old. Even less consideration is given to what steps duty bearers—notably governments—should take to ensure the implementation of children's rights law in developmentally appropriate ways for children of all ages. At the same time, there is little engagement with children's rights in the developmental literature, and few scholars in the field of child development engage with or draw on rights analysis in their work. Despite the common concern for children's lives, their care, education, and well-being, these two fields correspond infrequently.[4]

And yet, there would appear to be much to be gained in the understanding of children's rights to consider them through a developmental lens and vice versa. In particular, deeper engagement with the stages of childhood can help to further unpack what rights mean, and how they apply, to children of various ages and stages of development. At the same time, applying the rights perspective to child development can also extend the reach of this field, connecting it to the international legal framework with greater effect and channeling development science findings to law and policy domains. More generally, encouraging dialogue across disciplines and approaches has genuine potential to advance children's rights, knowing that with greater awareness comes greater understanding and, ultimately, greater implementation of children's rights. At the basis of this edited collection, therefore, is the belief that intentionally connecting children's rights and child development can yield benefits for both fields, leading to their mutual advancement. More importantly, it is our view that bringing the two fields together in dialogue can help to develop law, policies, and programs that better support the rights and healthy development of all children.

The aim of this collection is thus to advance children's rights through interdisciplinary dialogue between the child development and children's rights communities that seeks to identify and explore their common and distinctive themes and issues. In particular, this book seeks to engage child development and children's rights scholars in analyses of the issues at play, from each perspective, during the principal stages of childhood. This very precise objective required the collection to have a unique structure, and to this end, the book is divided into three main parts, according to early childhood, middle childhood, and late childhood or adolescence. Each part begins with a chapter that sets out the current development literature relevant to that stage of development. These are written by experts in their respective fields, in chapters that seek to establish a baseline of empirical knowledge on children's development in that life stage. As we discuss further in the conclusion, it is important to recognize that science is continually evolving, and in this regard, the three chapters on child development map what we currently know about the science of child development, revealing how scientific understanding has advanced since the adoption of the CRC more than three decades ago. In mapping the science, these development chapters—by Iheoma U. Iruka (on early childhood), Josephine Grant (middle childhood), and Joanna Williams (adolescence)—aim to anchor the discussion of children's rights at each stage in evidence-based research, helping to elucidate children's general needs, development, and capacities during that stage of childhood.

The second chapter in each part reflects on that literature and considers the key children's rights issues pertinent to that stage of development. These chapters are written by children's rights authors who each present their perspective on the application of children's rights law to that developmental stage. To facilitate comparisons across the stages of childhood, the authors of these chapters—Meredith Johnson Harbach (early childhood), Aoife Daly and Amy Walsh (middle childhood), and Stephanie Rap (adolescence)—have focused, in particular, on four main areas of children's rights: child participation; the best interests of the child; health and education; and protection from harm. This common approach is designed to help produce insights across the parts into the different ways children's rights operate at various stages of development (for example, how participation rights operate in early childhood versus adolescence in both the home and public sphere, how health rights play out in middle childhood versus adolescence, and so on). They also provide readers with an opportunity to evaluate and compare how children's rights are implemented or should be implemented at each developmental stage.

Each part then concludes with a look at selected contemporary issues in children's rights, in chapters—by Caralyn Blaisdell and E. Kay M. Tisdall (early childhood), Noam Peleg and Sheila Varadan (middle childhood), and Yanghee Lee and Sangwon Kim (adolescence)—that seek to explore, from a more critical perspective, some thematic issues or challenges relevant to children's rights in that stage. This third chapter also addresses some of the cross-cutting rights issues at each stage of development. In contrast to the second chapter for each stage of childhood, which starts with specific rights and examines how they apply to and are realized in that stage of childhood, these "contemporary children's rights issues" chapters examine prominent issues that implicate a range of children's rights, tapping into some very current issues—like climate justice and the digital environment—that present challenges from both development and children's rights perspectives.

The final two chapters, in part 4 of this volume, stand outside the stage-specific structure of the core of the book. The first—by Charlene Choi, Jonathan Todres, and Clara Paul—is an analysis of the literature on children's participation in research, designed to go some way to addressing the gap in the project with respect to the views and perspectives of children themselves. In particular, this chapter seeks to summarize research in each stage of childhood that engages with children themselves, making the case for greater participation of children in research. The second, and the concluding, chapter in part 4, by the book's editors, seeks to elucidate and bring together some of the key themes of the book, highlighting the messages that emerge from an exercise that aims to bridge the divide across development and children's rights research. This concluding chapter presents some new perspectives and novel themes from the literature, highlighting some areas worthy of further research.

Although collectively the six children's rights chapters and the final two chapters cover a breadth of issues, we appreciate that no single volume can address every children's rights issue faced by children around the world. As we write, children are experiencing extremely grave violations of their rights through war and conflict, and hunger, poverty, and inequality continue to present major barriers to the implementation of the CRC. Many of these barriers, such as poverty, are particularly pronounced in the Global South, though all of these issues are present in all countries. While much more must be done to address these systemic and existential challenges to children's rights, especially for the most vulnerable children, we approach this volume from the perspective that advances in children's rights, through inquiries such as this, have the potential to benefit children's enjoyment of their rights in all communities and countries.

It is our aim that this volume will provide a roadmap for scholars, students, and advocates seeking to understand how children's rights law applies more specifically to early childhood, middle childhood, and adolescence, identifying some novel perspectives on how child development relates to and informs our understanding of children's rights. In addition, we hope the volume will be of value to scholars and students of child development who are looking to better understand the rights-based approach to such issues and to identify opportunities to connect child development science with law and policy affecting children. In presenting the material in a structured way, we hope to make the volume accessible to specialists and students in both fields, supporting both interdisciplinary and comparative perspectives.

We recognize that this book's structure gives more attention to infusing child development science into the children's rights domain as compared to a more equitable two-way dialogue. This is shaped, in part, by our own backgrounds in children's rights. However, our aim ultimately is to bring these two fields together to inspire a new, integrated field of study. In this way, we see this volume as an invitation to scholars and professionals in both fields to take up the questions raised here and build on our ambitions to bring the two fields together.

In undertaking the first integrated, thematic analysis of children's rights and child development, we experienced inevitable, unanticipated challenges and discoveries especially as we sought to forge a more nuanced, developmentally responsive approach to the implementation of children's rights law. In this respect, the chapters in this volume revealed some challenges for children's rights law and for law more generally when viewed from a child development lens. For instance, while evidence-based research on child development emphasizes precision and caution in expressing findings, law necessarily speaks in broader, often general terms. For example, law frequently uses the term "children" on a specific issue, even though the vast majority of the individuals affected might be infants, toddlers, or even adolescents. While the generality of the language used is important to ensure that less typical cases are not excluded from protection from various laws, this lack of precision, from a child development perspective, nonetheless increases the challenge of developing law and policy on children's rights that is specific to children's stage of development. At the same time, and conversely, the child development literature also recognizes that development and maturation occur differently in different children, suggesting that we must provide flexibility for individualized trajectories in children's development. Yet that flexibility sometimes pushes up against law's need for bright-line rules, to ensure greater clarity ex ante.[5]

In these and other respects, which we explore in greater depth in the conclusion, this project was more complex than originally conceived and was only brought to fruition by the willingness of the authors to embrace a more challenging structure than most edited collections require. We are grateful to them all for the persistence and patience they showed in supporting the project to completion in a way that, we hope, opens rather than closes discussion of the myriad issues on which the book touches. Ultimately, we believe that building bridges between the two disciplines has the potential to support advances in both fields and to lead to more effective research that can support the development and implementation of law, policies, and programs that help ensure the rights and healthy development of all children.

NOTES

1 See generally Jonathan Todres and Shani King, eds., *The Oxford Handbook of Children's Rights Law* (New York: Oxford University Press, 2020); Ursula Kilkelly and Ton Liefaard, eds., *International Human Rights of Children* (New York: Springer, 2019).

2 Jonathan Todres, "Confronting Categorical Exclusions Based on Age: The Rights of Children and Youth," *Harvard Human Rights Journal* 36 (2023): 283–298.

3 See Priscilla Alderson, *Young Children's Rights: Exploring Beliefs, Principles and Practice*, 2nd ed. (London: Jessica Kingsley, 2008).

4 See Emily Buss, "What the Law Should (and Should Not) Learn from Child Development Research," *Hofstra Law Review* 38 (2009): 13–68.

5 Todres, "Confronting Categorical Exclusions Based on Age."

PART I

Early Childhood

1

Early Childhood Development

IHEOMA U. IRUKA

I. Introduction

Science is clear about the importance of the first few years of life, generally ranging from birth through age eight. The early periods of life, especially the first two thousand days, are crucial for setting the foundation for healthy physical, cognitive, language, social, emotional, mental, and moral development. Recent consensus publications, such as from the National Academies of Sciences, Engineering, and Medicine (NASEM) and the United Nations Children's Fund (UNICEF), have identified early development concepts relevant to implementing and realizing children's rights.[1] While attention often focuses on the period after children are born, evidence indicates the importance of also attending to the prenatal period, which is a time of huge neurobiological development. For example, during the first trimester of pregnancy, there is initial wiring of the brain, and organogenesis occurs when the earliest-born neurons regulate organ (e.g., heart, lungs, gastrointestinal tract) functions. In the second trimester, the brain is developing the capacity to regulate the sympathetic and parasympathetic nervous systems—that is, the "fight or flight" and "rest and digest" responses. "By the second and third trimesters, sensory systems are connected from the periphery to the brain's cerebral cortex—the most complex part of the brain with the greatest neuronal diversity, which processes complex information from all of the senses."[2]

After children are born, their environments and interactions further accelerate neurocognitive processes such as language, conceptualization, emotional control, and motor control. Global indicators of children's well-being and opportunities to thrive indicate a crisis of massive proportion, with many children living in extreme poverty with housing insecurity and limited access to nutritional food, health care, and early learning opportunities, probably leading to premature death and other social, developmental, cognitive, and economic challenges over the life course.[3] Unfortunately, opportunities to thrive are not evenly available due to complex sociocultural and sociopolitical dynamics that create systemic inequities based on an individual's "country, community or family of origin, their gender, race or ethnicity and other factors."[4] Other factors likely to impact children's development include war, pandemic-related effects, climate change, and changing technology. The goal of this chapter is to provide insights into the critical developmental change occurring during this sensitive period and identify key factors that promote healthy development in the early years.

II. Critical Domains and Influencers during Early Childhood

To ensure the healthy development of children, it is critical to articulate the desired outcomes. Healthy child outcomes include physical health and safety (i.e., ability to thrive, survive, and be free from injury and physical and sexual maltreatment), emotional and behavioral competence (i.e., a positive sense of self; the ability to cope with stressful situations, temper emotional arousal, overcome fears, and accept disappointments and frustrations), social competence (i.e., the ability to get along and respect others; prosocial behavior such as empathy, cooperation, sharing, and perspective taking), and cognitive competence (i.e., skills in language and communication, as well as reading, writing, mathematics, and problem-solving).[5] In the early years, these skills and competencies are interrelated. More importantly, these early outcomes set the foundation for later skills, competencies, and outcomes in the adolescent period and beyond.

A. Neurobiological-Environment Interaction

It is important to acknowledge some key scientific and technological advancements that have occurred over the past two decades about early development, especially as it concerns brain and neurobiological development, such as the plasticity of the brain. This advancement in science and methodology is critical to better understanding processes occurring from conception through early childhood. Some of these critical advances noted in the NASEM reports include the following developments:

- Cost-effective methods for capturing whole genome sequences have helped to identify genetic variation in such areas as stress activation, physiological maturation, and the termination of the sensitive periods.
- Advances have occurred in methods to identify the consequences of differences in how, where, and when specific genes are expressed, such as how individuals' DNA is expressed and changed due to factors such as nutrition, environmental toxicants, and stressors (i.e., epigenetic).
- The study of transcriptomics, a method used to identify how particular genes are expressed over time, in specific types of cells, and under specific circumstances, has led to understanding how the expression of genes responsible for producing thousands of neuron types in the brain during the first trimester turns off as development continues to allow for other types of brain architecture to occur.
- Advancement in neuroimaging has helped a new understanding of the brain connectome, which defines the breadth and complexity of circuits that relay information between ensembles of neurons.
- Investment by federal agencies and foundations has resulted in substantial growth in longitudinal child development research data to facilitate the examination of changes across development within individuals and subgroup differences in within-person changes over time.[6]

These advances in scientific technology and methodology have provided more information about the various stages of early childhood development. For instance, prenatal development is "marked by a unique relationship between the mother, the fetus, and a transient organ, the placenta," which "has been shown by current genomic, cell biological, and physiological evidence to be an active partner in fetal development and influenced by maternal health."[7] Thus, maternal high stress, nutrient status, or exposure to toxicants during this prenatal period can alter placental cell gene expression and function, which can impact the fetus's organ development and maturation.[8] Emerging evidence also indicates that these adverse experiences (e.g., high stress, exposure to environmental toxicants, substance use) during the prenatal period mean that it is a sensitive period for intergenerational transmission of adverse maternal experiences, making children vulnerable to adverse birthing outcomes, cognitive deficiency, and future risk for chronic disease.[9] Thus, when talking about early childhood development, the conception period must also be paid attention.

Evidence indicates that complex development from biological to cognition is happening during the early years, which is highly influenced by context, including family cohesion, health care, healthy living conditions, economic and food security, and early care and education. In the next sections, we discuss some key features of the early child development period, including the neurobiological-environment interaction and contexts critical to children's early development.

Children's health, development, and learning are shaped by interactions in the human body's molecular, cellular, and organ systems with the family, neighborhood, and culture children are experiencing. These interactions set the stage for children's long-term social, emotional, behavioral, and health outcomes. Major physiological systems, such as the immune system, develop rapidly in pregnancy and early childhood. Similarly, "because the brain is massively complex, with billions of neurons and trillions of connections, at least 85 percent of the genome is expressed at various times and locations during [early] development."[10] For instance, the visual and auditory cortex in the brain begins to develop before children are born and peaks at two months. The receptive language and speech production areas, also called the angular gyrus and Broca's area, also begin right before birth and peak at seven to eight months, in contrast to the prefrontal cortex, or areas where higher cognitive functions occur, which peaks around two to three years.

B. Key Domains of Development during Early Childhood

While the early childhood period is a time of great neurobiological, social, and cognitive growth, there are core domains during this sensitive period, including self-regulation, communication, and social competence. During the early years, particular capacities are developing that set the foundation for later development and function.

1. SELF-REGULATION

In the early years, children transition from learning to regulating their emotions and behavior, with growing self-regulation, transitioning from a period of helplessness to self-control and independence.[11] During the prenatal period, while children are in the womb, they are dependent on their mother's body, for everything from getting nutrition to regulating their body temperature. This dependence on the caregiver, especially the mother, continues after birth, with mothers helping children to develop their internal and external regulatory systems, such as their wake-sleep cycles, which are critical for neurobiological development. During infancy, children are also learning to regulate their signals, such as the way they cry to draw attention to particular needs, like hunger, pain, or irritability.

Emotion regulation is another aspect of early development where children begin to develop and understand different emotional states, from joy and anger to fear. Early emotional development provides the foundation for psychosocial well-being and mental health. "Throughout early childhood, other brain regions (especially in the frontal neocortex) progressively mature and become interconnected with these early-developing brain regions to contribute to the development of more accurate emotion appraisals, growing capacities for emotion self-regulation, complex emotional blends, and other developing features of mature emotional experience."[12] Children's emotional development varies based on different factors, from their sociocultural context (e.g., how and when emotions are expressed) to their temperament (e.g., adaptive, anxious, withdrawn). That is, children's temperament, which is biologically based, could vary in their emotionality, activity, sociability, and shyness. For instance, children who are reticent or withdrawn are likely to be fearful in response to new challenges or stimuli compared to those with adaptive temperaments, influencing their self-regulatory capacity.[13] Thus, children's emotional regulation goes through a range of development, from not easily regulated in infancy to a stage in which children are able to talk about and become aware of and be able to regulate their emotions by preschool age.[14] Children with emotional regulatory capacities can more easily manage their frustration and disappointment and also relate to others in many social contexts (e.g., environment, child care). Parents* and other caregivers are critical in developing children's emotional regulation by helping them monitor, understand, and provide strategies for recognition and management.

Similar to emotion regulation, effortful control—one component of executive function—is also accelerating from infancy through early childhood. "Executive function is an umbrella term used to refer to a variety of interdependent skills that are necessary for purposeful, goal-directed activity, such as learning to hold a crayon and scribble on paper, string beads, or hand a cup of juice to a friend without spilling."[15] Executive function entails the ability to inhibit prepotent responses (e.g., not eating the candy when placed in front of the child), flexibility, planning, and self-regulation. Executive function begins to develop in infancy, such as infants being able to predict a sequence of events (e.g., shifting gaze to expected sequence), engage in goal-directed behaviors (e.g., moving an obstacle in the way of a toy), and demonstrate emerging self-control (e.g., complying with requests). It is, however, critical to recognize the interrelatedness and interconnectivity between executive function and self-regulatory skills, with success in one area accelerating the skill in another area. Relationships with others influence the development of these capacities with caregivers and others critical to providing appropriate experiences, scaffolding, and support to help children go from dependence to independence. However, there is a need to recognize biological-based factors that can impede health regulatory skills, leading to conduct problems, attention deficits, depressive and anxiety disorders, and other psychological problems of childhood, as well as a need to recognize cultural value and expectations of self-regulation, which require more research.

2. LANGUAGE DEVELOPMENT

The early years are a sensitive period of language development bolstered by varied forms of communication, ranging from crying as a baby to get a response from the environment, namely, the caregiver, to communication in which one is able to reason and problem solve.[16] Children begin to communicate the first day of their life, with almost all children

*We use the term "parent" as an inclusive term to describe the primary caregiver(s) regardless of a biological relationship with the child.

learning to talk without explicit instruction, though some children may require intervention. Evidence suggests a general universal process of learning one's native language that is similar across languages, beginning with distinguishing the full range of sounds in one's language, learning that words can be composed of smaller parts, and beginning to build meaningful phrases and sentences. Specifically, children's language content is the same; that is, "Children note the appearance and disappearance of objects, their properties, locations, and owners and comment on the actions done to and by objects and people. . . . Second, the words in these short sentences are consistently ordered in ways that mirror adult word orders (e.g., 'drink juice,' 'Mommy give')."[17]

The early child development period is particularly sensitive for language development, as well as intellectual growth (i.e., cognitive development), when children notice causal sequences (e.g., there is a noise that follows when a toy is dropped). Current evidence suggests that exposure to a language in the early years results in greater proficiency in that language than does late exposure.[18] As found with multilingual learners and those who are learning a second language, exposure to the second language after the early childhood period often results in it being difficult to master some aspects of language, such as morphology. While studies point to parent input as a major driver in children's vocabulary, there are other sources of language inputs that require more attention, including genetics. Although science has substantiated that certain language development processes are critical in the early years, such as morphology and grammar, not all language skills are age dependent, and children can catch up over time (e.g., vocabulary). Furthermore, not only is socioeconomic status found to be a predictor of later language and reading achievement, but current evidence also "suggests that young children's academic attainments may be even more susceptible to the negative influence of poverty than is the case for older children."[19] Language impairments can also hamper early language, especially if early intervention is not provided to address language deficits. However, there is no evidence of a magic bullet that can accelerate language, intelligence, or learning (e.g., listening to classic music in utero, toy, app); rather, the key is to ensure that children are consistently exposed to high-quality elaborative conversation in natural settings through diverse ways, from talking and storytelling to reading books.[20]

3. SOCIAL DEVELOPMENT

Peer relationships and other social skills, such as empathy and cooperation, are other capacities that develop during the early years. One key way peer relationships and other social and cognitive skills develop is through play. While in infancy, children seem to be less interested in playing with others, and there is an indication that this may be due to the sociocultural context and children's cognitive ability, with some children beginning to seek peer relationships by six to nine months.[21] By toddlerhood, children begin to transition from mere watching to becoming focused on intentional play that may involve mimicking or sharing toys with other peers. By the age of five, children's play with others goes beyond props to pretend play, which is influenced by their language and cognitive development. Researchers have found that children with secure attachments with parents are more likely to have stronger social competence with peers compared to those who have insecure attachments.[22] In fact, insecurely attached children are likely to be more hostile and aggressive, which may make them more likely to have conflicts with peers. Child temperament also has an impact on their socialization with peers. Children displaying early aggressive behaviors or conduct problems when engaging with peers may be at risk for later problems. Beyond parents ensuring a sensitive attachment with their child, they are also instrumental in providing opportunities for their children to engage in healthy peer relationships, monitoring their children's interactions with peers, and providing assistance in negotiating appropriate behaviors with peers.[23]

There are instances when more intervention may be needed to support children to develop skills to engage with peers, such as a child with a disability. Children with disabilities, depending on the nature of their disability, may not have the cognitive or language skills to interact fully with their peers or may have sensory or psychomotor challenges that hinder interactions with peers.[24] In addition, while some studies indicate that childhood abuse and exposure to other early adversities are likely to contribute to early problems, more studies are needed to identify key factors that impact children's social development and effective ways to support this key developmental milestone.[25]

C. Influencers of Child Development in the Early Years

There is a complex interplay between neurobiology and the environment that influences children's early development.[26] For instance, a disadvantaged environment can lead to poor feeding practices and iron deficiency, which can lead to decreased brain iron and delayed neuromaturation and stress vulnerability, which could lead to poor early outcomes. Similarly, a disadvantaged environment can impact parenting, limiting enriching opportunities for child development and learning, which can lead to poor early outcomes. Thus, there is a need to attend to multiple contexts in the early years that can facilitate or disrupt children's healthy development during the sensitive period, including poverty, childhood adversity, parenting, and early childhood development programs.

1. POVERTY

Many children across the globe experience childhood poverty. For instance, an estimated 333 million children—one out of every six children globally—live in extreme poverty, defined as less than $2.15 per day.[27] By 2030, nine out of ten children in extreme poverty will live in sub-Saharan Africa. Furthermore, 46 percent of children in Latin America live in poverty.[28]

In the United States, the childhood poverty level has dropped from 16.0 percent in 2020 to 15.3 percent in 2021. While childhood poverty has declined over the past decade, it is still felt unevenly by certain racial groups. More than 25 percent of Black children (about 2.8 million children) and 24 percent of Hispanic children (about 4.5 million children) are living in poverty, compared to 11.4 percent of White children (about 4.2 million children) and 15.1 percent of Asian children (approximately 659,000 children).[29]

Poverty affects the developing brain and cognitive outcomes, including areas that control memory, emotion, cognitive functioning, and language and literacy. Other consequences of family poverty are its impact on parents' access to resources to meet their own or children's needs in creating a safe, healthy, and enriching learning environment. Poverty is disruptive on many levels and reduces children's feeling of agency and safety because they are probably living in precarious situations that make them vulnerable to social, economic, and environmental conditions, including climate change. "[Poverty] affects very real aspects of [children's] lives—including whether they can attend school, be well nourished or have access to health care, safe drinking water and sanitation," which can be particularly detrimental at a time when children's brains and bodies are growing.[30] For example, in Latin America and the Caribbean, 4.8 million children are affected by chronic malnutrition; only six out of every ten children attend early education; 240,000 children are in residential institutions, and 10 percent of them are under the age of three; three out of every ten children live in precarious housing; and eighty-two million people do not have access to basic sanitation.[31]

Direct impacts of poverty on the development of children in early childhood have been identified. Hannah Strauß and colleagues examined the influence of early childhood poverty experiences on the cognitive outcomes of children in Mauritius at ages three, eleven, and seventeen years old.[32] They found that socioeconomic deprivation and chronic malnutrition impair early childhood functioning and predict a deterioration in cognitive outcomes over time. They concluded that interventions tackling poverty and malnutrition should be gender sensitive and focus on children during infancy. The effects of early childhood poverty also expand to adulthood, with Gary Evans and colleagues finding that poverty from birth to age nine was associated with reduced adult inhibitory control and worse working memory, though these effects are also partially explained by these children's later experiences in adolescence (lower levels of maternal sensitivity and chronic physiological stress).[33] Poverty may also affect children's health, with studies, for example, finding that poverty in very early childhood is associated with increases in early adult hypertension, arthritis, and limitations on activities of daily living.[34]

2. RACISM AND DISCRIMINATION

Similar to the complex and compounding nature of poverty on children's early development, racism and systemic inequities have been found to negatively impact the optimal health and social and emotional development of children during this critical period. Institutional racism (also called "structural" and "systemic" racism) and experiences of discrimination impact the health, well-being, and learning of children and the adults who care for them.[35] This can play out in a variety of ways, including limiting access to financial and material resources, services, and support that promote learning and well-being and long-term health, stability, and positive life outcomes. While much of the research on racial stress trauma has focused on older-age youth and children, studies have shown how experiences of racism and discrimination contribute to higher allostatic load, contributing to adverse birth outcomes and low birth weight and simultaneously can impact parents' mental health, limiting responsive and nurturing interactions necessary to support children's early cognitive, language, and socioemotional development.[36]

Racism has been implicated in the wealth gap, with white households in the United States having eight to ten times more wealth compared to Hispanic and Black households.[37] Considering the critical period of the first few years of life, it is expected that children who have access to wealth are more likely to experience optimal environments compared to children with less wealth. It is, however, important that research begins to recognize other forms of wealth that are valuable to children's healthy development, such as cultural wealth and strengths (e.g., language spoken, cultural norms and traditions), especially for communities that have been denied access to health care and education (e.g., Black and immigrant communities). These other forms of wealth can be capitalized on, for example, in the home and early childhood education, to promote strong outcomes for children.[38] Wealth with regard to culture, family, and community relationships will give children in early childhood strong attachments and will, in turn, serve as protective factors during this critical period of cognitive, language, and social development.

There are numerous ways that racism—from cultural, systemic, interpersonal, and internalized to vicarious—impacts the well-being of children in early childhood, directly and indirectly.[39] As noted by Jack Shonkoff and colleagues, cultural racism is "an ideology grounded in white supremacy that is deeply embedded in the language, symbols, media and taken-for-granted assumptions of the larger society."[40] Cultural racism can be seen in early childhood inequities that lead to racial disparities in suspension and expulsion rates, health systems inequities that lead to delayed diagnosis and treatment starting in early childhood, and criminal justice systems that see Black people as subhuman and menacing even when engaged in benign activities (e.g., shopping, traveling, driving, birdwatching), which are experiences that could hinder the parent-child relationship. Moreover, child development social identity theory has shown that normative expectations about others emerge in early childhood and contribute to prejudicial attitudes.[41] Marginalized children will therefore be treated prejudicially from early childhood, and children can start developing these attitudes at a young age. Michael Rizzo and colleagues' study with four-year-old children suggests that the emergence of racial bias in early childhood is predicted by children's foundational beliefs about the social world (i.e., beliefs that frame the shape and scope of future conceptual acquisitions).[42] For example, by age three, children's beliefs that interracial friendships are valued promotes their willingness to play with peers from different racial backgrounds, and the same is true for the contrary.[43] It is therefore imperative to have policies and programs that ensure that children in early childhood do not suffer from negative racist treatment but also that they benefit from ongoing interventions that target children's normative beliefs and explanatory beliefs about racial inequalities.[44]

One aspect of children's early development that is often ignored is their positive sense of self (i.e., racial and cultural identity), which begins in the early childhood period and lays the foundation for how children see and experience the world. For many racially and ethnically minoritized children, their positive sense of self and racial identity is challenged due to the colonial context that devastated the culture, language, and heritage of many communities. For example, Rakeeta Smallwood and colleagues find that colonization had devastating impacts on Indigenous people across the globe, from New Zealand to the US, akin to genocide.[45]

These false and negative narratives about certain communities could have a detrimental impact on children's self-esteem and self-worth, which begin developing in the early years. The lingering effects of colonialism have an impact on the sense of self and lived experiences of people whose families experienced colonialism, apartheid, and enslavement.[46] For example, research points to mental health challenges that US Black children experience from the daily negative assault of their race, culture, and personhood, making them vulnerable to internalized oppression that could have a devastating impact.[47] Seth Oppong argues that decolonizing early childhood development and care will improve self-perceptions and self-awareness of children in early childhood, and he proposes an implementation architecture that can be put in place for the successful implementation of decolonized early childhood development and care services in Africa.[48] Decolonizing the early childhood system requires leadership that is committed to centering the relevant knowledge of the community and ensuring that it is aligned with community values, such as what outcomes and skills matter for children's healthy development and school success and what education, skills, and training education professionals need to support children's development and learning.

3. ADVERSE CHILDHOOD EXPERIENCES

Brain and physiological systems develop simultaneously with the environment. The early childhood years are a critical sensitive period of development when adverse experiences could change the course of neurobiological and socio-behavioral development and have lifelong consequences. Similar to the brain, the physiological system, such as the immune system, can be disrupted by early adversity, with lifelong consequences. Although children are vulnerable to adversities throughout their life course, the early years are especially sensitive because they lay the foundation for healthy immunological development. It is often prevalent and day-to-day adverse events occurring in early childhood that have a lasting influence on the life course.[49] Adverse Childhood Experiences (ACEs)—such as psychological, physical, or sexual abuse; violence against the mother; living with household members who were substance abusers, mentally ill or suicidal, or ever imprisoned; and directly or indirectly experiencing discrimination—can disrupt child functioning and well-being. Early ACEs can lead to increased risk of developmental difficulties, affecting cognitive and emotional adjustment.[50] In the groundbreaking work of Vincent Felitti and colleagues, they found a graded relationship between the number of ACEs and adult risky behaviors (e.g., alcoholism, drug abuse, suicide attempt, smoking) and adult diseases (e.g., ischemic heart disease, cancer, chronic lung disease, liver disease).[51] The links between ACEs and adult behaviors and outcomes are probably due to disruption to children's regulation, impairing development and functioning over the life course.[52]

Research has also shown the links between experiences in early childhood and brain and physiological development. Negative early childhood experiences have been found to cause fundamental changes in several regions of the human brain, including the hippocampus (affecting learning and memory) and the prefrontal cortex (affecting executive functions such as decision-making and problem-solving).[53] Research found that children under six years old from the United States who had experienced ACEs were more likely to experience poor health and developmental outcomes.[54] For example, environments of maternal or paternal stress during infancy or preschool years were found to influence DNA methylation over developmental time, evidencing the temporally remote correlates of early adverse experiences on the human epigenome and its regulatory role in the expression of specific genes.[55] This suggests that epigenetic variation may constitute a biological "memory" of early life experiences and, in particular, of adverse experiences.[56] Thus, there is a need to attend to the lifelong consequences of being exposed to ACEs in early childhood.[57] While studies are still emerging about the prevalence of ACEs across the globe, researchers note that adversities, in particular adversities that occur in early childhood, are likely to impact the cognitive and regulatory processes, which have implications for early and later outcomes. For children who may experience multiple traumas and inequities, there is probably a compounded stressor on their functioning and overall development. However, caution should be taken linking ACEs to later outcomes when considering the cross-sectional nature and measurement approaches currently used to measure and assess the link between childhood trauma and life outcomes, as there may be unmeasured factors.[58]

4. PARENT AND FAMILY ENVIRONMENT

Children's chances of survival during the early childhood period are dependent on the maternal environment. Ensuring quality nutrition and access to health care and limiting chronic stressors, infection, toxicants, drugs, and alcohol will increase healthy birth and the developmental trajectory.[59] Ensuring access to a promotive environment during both the prenatal period and early childhood years ensures that the gene expressions occur in a typical fashion rather than altered due to adverse environments (i.e., epigenetic process).[60]

While maternal mortality rates decreased between 2000 to 2015, the rates have stalled between 2016 to 2020, especially in Western Europe and North America.[61] Nevertheless, maternal mortality remains a global crisis, especially in West, Central, and sub-Saharan Africa.[62] There are also disparities within countries, such as the United States, where American Indian/Alaska Native and Black women and birthing people are more likely to die from pregnancy-related causes or during childbirth than are White women.[63]

The causes of maternal mortality are due to complex and interrelated factors that vary across countries and regions, including discriminatory and inequitable practices and policies that lead to a lack of or poor health infrastructure, limited access to essential services and healthy conditions, and exposure to infectious diseases such as pneumonia, diarrhea, and malaria and to chronic stressors. Maternal mortality has a consequential impact on children's development during a sensitive period when children begin to attach and bond with their primary caregiver, primarily their mother, which sets the foundation for subsequent relationships and provides a sense of security for healthy development.[64] The National Research Council (NRC) has noted that maternal mortality and morbidity have various effects on children (as well as on families, households, communities, and society). The NRC report notes that for children, maternal mortality may lead to death, with children who lose their mothers more likely to die before the age of five; have poor health, such as illness, injury, malnutrition, and poor hygiene; experience psychological challenges, such as depression and other problems; and have increased social challenges, such as isolation, reduced education, and limited parental supervision and care.[65] The effects of maternal mortality on families and households, such as poor health of surviving household members or social isolation and changes in care for children, and on communities and societies, such as an increased number of one-parent households and orphans or grief and loss of community cohesion, can also negatively affect children's healthy development.

The parent-child relationship and attachment are also critical building blocks during the early childhood period, as they set the stage for children's other relationships and outcomes and can serve as a protective factor and buffer for children's healthy development. Parental practices and the home environment set the stage for children's health, development, and competencies. Although the parent-child relationship is significant throughout life, it is especially critical in the first years of life, when children depend on their primary caregivers for physical, emotional, and social protection. For example, parents and caregivers are necessary to ensure that children receive adequate nutrition for optimal physical development. These relationships also set the stage for future relationships. A secure parent-child attachment, the emotional bond that typically forms between infants and caregivers from the time of birth, supports children's curiosity and exploration of unfamiliar stimuli and environments.[66] These secure parent-child attachments are essential for both children and parents, reducing stress when positive or creating stress when less than optimal. Supportive relationships between the child and the adults in their life are essential to serving as protective factors and a buffer against adverse outcomes due to toxic stress. Unfortunately, the parent-child attachment may be placed at risk due to parental stress and trauma from emotional, social, and economic adversity. For example, studies indicate that abuse and neglect or unexpected separation (e.g., child welfare involvement) could impact a secure attachment, leading to insecure or disorganized attachment.[67] Some studies also point to child temperament that may make parent-child bonding challenging.[68]

The parent-child relationship can negatively affect young children's healthy development. There is growing evidence that children exposed to early adverse parenting in family contexts show neurodevelopmental alterations that increase risk for cognitive and emotional maladjustment.[69] Insecure parent-child attachment behavior, and particularly disorganized/controlling attachment, measured at preschool and early school age was typically associated with higher ratings of externalizing and internalizing symptoms.[70] Daniel Shaw and colleagues also found links (varying by sex of the child) between an increase in family stress for children at one and two years old and behavior problems at age three, echoing previous studies that associated an increase in family stress with an increase in behavior problems with preschool and school-age children.[71] The parent-child relationship can also affect children's physical development. For example, Shihong Wang and colleagues' research indicates that adolescents with prolonged parent-child separation have higher acceleration in functional aging and replicative senescence of cells.[72] However, the study also showed that children who had been separated from their parents in early childhood but regained stable parental care during adolescence did not experience this, pointing to the fact that pubertal development presents an opportunity to buffer the adverse biological effects that a child may have suffered in early childhood.[73] This shows that a strong and positive parent-child relationship can be a protective factor for children's healthy development. Studies have shown that features, such as parental sensitivity, affect attunement, and the use of mental state language with the child in the child-parent interaction in the first years of life, are of crucial importance to predict and support children's positive social-emotional development.[74] Moreover, based on a US study of children under six years old, Erica Webster found that, when comparing children who had experienced the same number of ACEs, children who were reported showing affection to their parent had decreased risk for health and developmental difficulties compared with children who were not.[75] Programs supporting families with young children, especially for those experiencing ACEs, should focus on enhancing quality of attachment between the parent and the child.[76] They should ensure that all families receive adequate support, which may prevent ACEs from occurring as well as limit their negative lifelong effects.[77] Parents who are experiencing stress should be identified and supported, which will help improve the mental health of children in early childhood.[78]

5. EARLY CHILDHOOD DEVELOPMENT (ECD)

Experiences across environmental contexts, including home, community, and early childhood development (ECD) settings, coupled with children's biological makeup, play a significant role in early development. Some of the interactions and adversities are seen with how poverty impacts children's ability to access quality community programs and essential resources, such as nutritious food, safe housing, safe drinking water, and enriching ECD programs. This section uses ECD to illustrate how children's experiences in early childhood can affect their trajectories, both positively and negatively.

Global data indicate that less than half of children in many countries have access to ECD programs.[79] About fifty-eight million primary-school-age children (usually between ages five and eleven and encompassing the early childhood period between birth and age eight) are not in school.[80] Although there has been an improvement in primary-age children attending school, more than 50 percent of the world's primary-age children who do not attend school live in sub-Saharan Africa (thirty-three million children).[81]

There is an increase in the number of children under the age of five likely to be in an ECD program or an out-of-home care arrangement. Claire Blewitt and colleagues found that children who were exposed to a universal social and emotional learning intervention at ages two to six showed significant improvements in social and emotional competence, behavioral self-regulation, emotional and behavioral problems, and early learning outcomes.[82] This finding highlights early childhood as a crucial moment for children's social, emotional, and cognitive development and the benefits of social and emotional learning programs for younger children.[83]

Although ECD programs have positive outcomes for children, there is a need to address the quality of such programs. For example, in the United States, there is a consistent pattern with many programs being low quality, especially those serving Black children and other minoritized children (e.g., Hispanic, American Indian/Alaska Native) and children from poor households.[84] While data from 2011–2013 showed that over half of Black children were eligible for Head Start (a federal program that provides comprehensive ECD services for children from low-income households) when the average was 43 percent for all children in the country, three out of four Black children are likely to be in ECD programs rated as low to moderate quality.[85] It is noteworthy that ECD is more segregated than are kindergarten and first grade in the United States, highlighting that children in early childhood are especially vulnerable to suffering from inequities in the education system.[86] Black and Hispanic children are more likely to be in low-quality and segregated schools, which means they will have fewer academic and enriching resources and courses and well-trained and supported education leaders and teachers. Because of the social nature of learning, in particular for children in early childhood, segregated learning experiences affect children's development, as they do not benefit from a unique heterogeneous and stimulating learning environment.[87] Furthermore, in the United States, Black and Native American children and children with a disability are further harmed in ECD settings by the disproportionate use of exclusionary practices such as suspension, expulsion, and use of physical restraint, starting in early childhood, which are likely to place children on a negative trajectory over time.[88] As illustrated earlier, these experiences of emotional and physical harm negatively affect young children's development, with regard to their brain, physiological, emotional, or psychosocial development.

Attending high-quality ECD programs is beneficial and a promotive factor for children. In fact, the quality of early childhood education and care directly affects child development.[89] Thus, conversely, one can assume that low-quality ECD programs are likely to be detrimental for children's healthy development by putting them at risk of physical harm, emotional distress, poor self-regulation, and lower academic achievement.[90] Poor quality of care in early childhood settings is a key contributor to toxic stress, a clear risk factor in early childhood development. Megan Gunnar and Bonny Donzella have emphasized the importance of variations in the quality of care to changes in newborns' cortisol levels (stress responses). They concluded that sensitive and responsive caregiving diminished newborns' high cortisol responsivity. Such caregiving also made children anticipate that adults will protect them and therefore improved their ability to cope with stress.[91]

Numerous studies and reports point to some promising avenues to ensure high-quality ECD programming.[92] Because of the importance of ECD for children's development, with regard to the development of cognitive and emotional abilities, ECD programs should promote both children's cognition and emotionality. Regarding children under two years old, Carmen Dalli and colleagues recommend that high-quality early childhood settings should be low-stress environments where children experience responsive caregiving attuned to their cues. These environments should actively avoid toxic stress or be able to buffer children through such stress. Adults working with children in these settings should understand the impact of their actions on children's development and receive the necessary training.[93]

To address systemic inequalities in ECD programming, the report *Start with Equity: Dismantling Systemic Racism in Early Childhood Education* recommends the equitable distribution of funds to address historical and contemporary gaps for programs serving children of color, children living in poverty, children with disabilities, and dual/multilingual learners. The report also calls for access to early intervention identification and support; adequate pay for teachers; culturally responsive curricula, assessment, and teaching pedagogy; and quality improvement systems that address inequities.[94]

III. Conclusion

Given the timing of much neurobiological, social, and cognitive development during the early childhood period, there is much resilience and flexibility in children's capacities to flourish. At the same time, biological and environmental factors can delay or impede the development of critical processes, such as language and social interaction, which set the foundation for future developmental process. Ensuring the well-being of children in early childhood is essential to avoid developmental consequences that can be detrimental to their present and future health, life, and happiness. Children's overall well-being, including their physical, emotional, social, and mental health, in the early years sets the foundation for their educational and life success by allowing them to regulate and critically examine their knowledge and beliefs, which then impact their behavior.

Children in early childhood are exposed to numerous influences that harm their health and well-being, including racism, poverty, and war. When occurring in early childhood, these adverse experiences affect children's brain, physiological, psychosocial, and emotional development and are likely to have lasting effects throughout their lives. Science is clear that for children to thrive, we must attend to their development in utero and after birth, such as through prenatal care and access to healthy nutrition during pregnancy. This requires centering children's sense of safety and, more importantly, their healthy development by ensuring access to essential resources, including safe and nutritious food, housing, health care, child care, and the right to start well. This is especially important for racially minoritized populations and those living in low-income countries and communities where children live in extreme poverty and deprivation. Given the history of racism and colonialism in the world, the burden and blame must not be solely placed on these minoritized communities, countries, and continents. Still, a global response is necessary that places well-being of children in early childhood at the forefront of international policies.

After children are provided with the essential resources, they must be fully supported to thrive. Families and other adults are critical to ensuring that children are thriving, in particular considering the importance of the parent-child relationship for children in early childhood. The community and macrosystems, including labor, education, housing, and human services, are necessary to ensure that communities and families can create promotive conditions for children in early childhood to thrive and excel. Specifically, their physical, mental, and emotional health must be intentionally attended to in a holistic manner that recognizes how historical and contemporary policies may impact children to be healthy and prepared for school and life. Approaches should ensure that children in early childhood are exposed to as few ACEs as possible and that they are provided with the care and support they need for their healthy development, both in the home and in educational settings. Policies must promote and foster a positive and caring parent-child relationship, which can serve as a protective factor against the negative effects of ACEs. They should also support families and communities to ensure that their young children do not live in poverty and suffer from harms.

Furthermore, health, wealth, and education are inextricably interconnected with wealthier countries, which are likely to be healthier and more educated based on national markers. However, efforts to promote children's health, wealth, and education must recognize the importance of centering their cultural knowledge and practices (e.g., materials used in the learning process, connection of land and water to learning, storytelling/oral narratives). For too long, health, wealth, and education have been Eurocentric and based on a white-supremacy lens, limiting the health, wealth, and education that meet the cultural needs of minoritized communities and populations. Thus, there must be early screening (coupled with services when warranted) to address delays in children's physical, mental, and emotional outcomes. To support children's families and communities to ensure that children experience as few adverse experiences as possible in early childhood, there is also a need to promote asset development through many mechanisms such as through microloans and financing, community development grants, land and home-ownership transfer, and much more. Ensuring educational excellence requires that quality child care and early child education be made available and accessible to all children on an equal basis and that it be led by well paid and trained teachers who are in safe and healthy learning environments that promote children's holistic development, from their language and cognition to their self-identity, starting from their earliest years.

Finally, children of all ages deserve the right to have a voice and agency. However, that does not always occur when children are placed in vulnerable positions, whether through removal from family, suspension and expulsion, corporal punishment, or deep poverty. Many children are often forced to be in spaces or have experiences where their identities, religion, and cultures are viewed as substandard and treated not with recognition but with oppression. For example, as children worldwide are increasingly attending early childhood education settings, research has shown that marginalized children have access to services of a lesser quality than others. This increases their risk of exposure to stress and adverse experiences and minimizes the likelihood that they will receive sensitive and responsive caregiving and benefit from higher educational attainments. Their communities are relegated to limited investment and opportunities, which impacts their families' well-being and stability. Their culture, language, and customs are invisible, devastatingly affecting children's sense of self and import. There is a need to ensure that community built and supported institutions, such as cultural and religious places and organizations and schools, are uplifted and preserved. There is also a need to honor the home language by ensuring that at least one teacher or staff communicates in children's home language and that there are adequate materials that represent the child's community and home. As normative expectations emerge at a young age, such efforts should start in early childhood, to foster children's sense of self, self-worth, and happiness and to promote inclusion, cultivating early learning skills that are critical for later learning and achievement.[95]

ACKNOWLEDGMENTS

Special thanks to Clara Paul for providing some insights for this chapter.

NOTES

1 National Academies of Sciences, Engineering, and Medicine (NASEM), *A Roadmap to Reducing Child Poverty* (Washington, DC: National Academies Press,

2019); United Nations Children's Fund (UNICEF), "The State of the World's Children: A Fair Chance for Every Child," 2016, www.unicef.org.

2 NASEM, *Roadmap to Reducing Child Poverty*, 104.

3 Alberto Minujin and Shailen Nandy, eds., *Global Child Poverty and Well-Being: Measurement, Concepts, Policy and Action* (Chicago: Policy, 2012).

4 UNICEF, "State of the World's Children," 7.

5 NASEM, *Parenting Matters: Supporting Parents of Children Ages 0–8* (Washington, DC: National Academies Press, 2016).

6 NASEM, *Vibrant and Healthy Kids: Aligning Science, Practice, and Policy to Advance Health Equity* (Washington, DC: National Academies Press, 2019).

7 Ibid., 90.

8 Annika Thorsell and Daniel Nätt, "Maternal Stress and Diet May Influence Affective Behavior and Stress-Response in Offspring via Epigenetic Regulation of Central Peptidergic Function," *Environmental Epigenetics* 2, no. 3 (August 2016): 6; Mary E. Coussons-Read, "Effects of Prenatal Stress on Pregnancy and Human Development: Mechanisms and Pathways," *Obstetric Medicine* 6, no. 2 (June 2013): 52–57.

9 Elysia Poggi Davis and Angela J. Narayan, "Pregnancy as a Period of Risk, Adaptation, and Resilience for Mothers and Infants," *Development and Psychopathology* 32, no. 5 (December 2020): 1625–1639.

10 NASEM, *Vibrant and Healthy Kids*, 99.

11 National Research Council and Institute of Medicine, *From Neurons to Neighborhoods: The Science of Early Childhood Development* (Washington, DC: National Academies Press, 2000).

12 Ibid., 106.

13 Mary K. Rothbart and John E. Bates, "Temperament," in *Handbook of Child Psychology*, vol. 3, *Social, Emotional, and Personality Development*, ed. William Damon, Nancy Eisenbeg, and Richard M. Lerner (New York: Wiley, 1998), 105–176.

14 Ross A. Thompson, "Emotion Regulation: A Theme in Search of Definition," *Monographs of the Society for Research in Child Development* 59, nos. 2–3 (1994): 25–52.

15 National Research Council and Institute of Medicine, *From Neurons to Neighborhoods*, 116.

16 Ibid.

17 Ibid., 127.

18 Dorthe Bleses, Guido Makransky, Philip S. Dale, Anders Højen, and Burcak Aktürk Ari, "Early Productive Vocabulary Predicts Academic Achievement 10 Years Later," *Applied Psycholinguistics* 37, no. 6 (March 2016): 1461–1476; Nicole Gardner-Neblett and Iheoma U. Iruka, "Oral Narrative Skills: Explaining the Language-Emergent Literacy Link by Race/Ethnicity and SES," *Developmental Psychology* 51, no. 7 (July 2015): 889–904.

19 National Research Council and Institute of Medicine, *From Neurons to Neighborhoods*, 162.

20 NASEM, *Parenting Matters*.

21 Deborah Lowe Vandell, Kathy Shores Wilson, and Nola R. Buchanan, "Peer Interaction in the First Year of Life: An Examination of Its Structure, Content, and Sensitivity to Toys," *Child Development* 51, no. 2 (June 1980): 481–488; Xinyin Chen, "Culture and Early Socio-emotional Development," *Encyclopedia on Early Childhood Development*, July 2023, www.child-encyclopedia.com.

22 Ashley M. Groh, R. M. Pasco Fearon, Marinus H. van Ijzendoorn, Marian J. Bakermans-Kranenburg, and Glenn I. Roisman, "Attachment in the Early Life Course: Meta-analytic Evidence for Its Role in Socioemotional Development," *Child Developmental Perspective* 11, no. 1 (November 2016): 70–76.

23 Amanda Sheffield Morris, Erin L. Ratliff, Kelly T. Cosgrove, and Laurence Steinberg, "We Know Even More Things: A Decade Review of Parenting Research," *Journal of Research on Adolescence* 31, no. 4 (December 2021): 870–888; Kenneth H. Rubin, Rosemary S. L. Mills, and Linda Rose-Krasnor, "Maternal Beliefs and Children's Social Competence," in *Social Competence in Developmental Perspective*, ed. Barry H. Schneider, Grazia Attili, Jacqueline Nadel, and Roger P. Weissberg (Boston: Kluwer Academic, 1989), 313–331.

24 Coral Kemp, Yuriko Kishida, Mark Carter, and Naomi Sweller, "The Effect of Activity Type on the Engagement and Interaction of Young Children with Disabilities in Inclusive Childcare Settings," *Early Childhood Research Quarterly* 28, no. 1 (2013): 134–143.

25 Emalee G. Flaherty, Richard Thompson, Howard Dubowitz, Elizabeth M. Harvey, Diana J. English, Laura J. Proctor, and Desmond K. Runyan, "Adverse Childhood Experiences and Child Health in Early Adolescence," *JAMA Pediatrics* 167, no. 7 (July 2013): 622–629; Abdulaziz Al Odhayani, William J. Watson, and Lindsay Watson, "Behavioural Consequences of Child Abuse," *Canadian Family Physician* 59, no. 8 (August 2013): 831–836.

26 Jennifer Delima and Graham Vimpani, "The Neurobiological Effects of Childhood Maltreatment: An Often Overlooked Narrative Related to the Long-Term Effects of Early Childhood Trauma?," *Family Matters* 89 (2011): 42–52. https://search.informit.org.

27 UNICEF, "Children Bearing Brunt of Stalled Progress on Extreme Poverty Reduction Worldwide," September 11, 2023, www.unicef.org; see also UNICEF, "State of the World's Children," 73.

28 UNICEF, "Children in Latin America and the Caribbean 2020: Regional Overview on the Situation of Children and Adolescents," December 2020, www.unicef.org.

29 Zachary Parolin, Sophie Collyer, and Megan A. Curran, "Absence of Monthly Child Tax Credit Leads to 3.7 Million More Children in Poverty in January 2022," *Poverty and Social Policy Brief* (Columbia Center on Poverty and Social Policy) 6, no. 2 (February 17, 2022): 1–5.

30 UNICEF, "State of the World's Children," 69.

31 Ibid.

32 Hannah Strauß, Peter Venables, and Marcel Zentner, "Associations between Early Childhood Poverty and Cognitive Functioning throughout Childhood and Adolescence: A 14-Year Prospective Longitudinal Analysis of the Mauritius Child Health Project," *PLoS ONE* 18, no. 2 (February 2023): e0278618.

33 Gary W. Evans, Martha J. Farah, and Daniel A. Hackman, "Early Childhood Poverty and Adult Executive Functioning: Distinct, Mediating Pathways for Different Domains of Executive Functioning," *Developmental Science* 24, no. 5 (September 2021): e13084.

34 Kathleen M. Ziol-Guest, Greg J. Duncan, Ariel Kalil, and W. Thomas Boyce, "Early Childhood Poverty, Immune-Mediated Disease Processes, and Adult Productivity," *Proceedings of the National Academy of Sciences of the United States of America* 109 (October 2012): 17289–17293.

35 Iheoma U. Iruka, Nicole Gardner-Neblett, Nicole A. Telfer, Nneka Ibekwe-Okafor, Stephanie M. Curenton, Jacqueline Sims, Amber B. Sansbury, and Enrique W. Neblett, "Effects of Racism on Child Development: Advancing Antiracist Developmental Science," *Annual Review of Developmental Psychology* 4, no. 1 (December 2022).

36 Anders Larrabee Sonderlund, Antoinette Schoenthaler, and Trine Thilsing, "The Association between Maternal Experiences of Interpersonal Discrimination and Adverse Birth Outcomes: A Systematic Review of the Evidence," *International Journal of Environmental Research and Public Health* 18, no. 4 (February 2021): 1465; Nia J. Heard-Garris, M. Cale, and Linda Camaj, "Transmitting Trauma: A Systematic Review of Vicarious Racism and Child Health," *Social Science & Medicine* 199 (February 2018): 230–240.

37 Neil Bennett, Donald Hays, and Briana Sullivan, "Wealth Inequality in the U.S. by Household Type: 2019 Data Shows Baby Boomers Nearly 9 Times Wealthier than Millennials," US Census Bureau, August 1, 2022, www.census.gov.

38 Elizabeth Pungello Bruno and Iheoma U. Iruka, "Reexamining the Carolina Abecedarian Project Using an Antiracist Perspective: Implications for Early Care and Education Research," *Early Childhood Research Quarterly* 58 (2022): 165–176.

39 Iruka et al., "Effects of Racism on Child Development."

40 Jack P. Shonkoff, Natalie Slopen, and David R. Williams, "Early Childhood Adversity, Toxic Stress, and the Impacts of Racism on the Foundations of Health," *Annual Review of Public Health* 42, no. 1 (2022): 119.

41 Melanie Killen, Kathryn M. Yee, and Martin D. Ruck, "Social and Racial Justice as Fundamental Goals for the Field of Human Development," *Human Development* 65 (December 2021): 257–269; Drew Nesdale, "Social Identity Processes and Children's Ethnic Prejudice," in *The Development of the Social Self*, ed. Mark Bennett and Fabio Sani (New York: Taylor and Francis, 2004), 219–246; Drew Nesdale, "Peer Group Rejection and Children's Intergroup Prejudice," in *Intergroup Attitudes and Relations in Childhood through Adulthood*, ed. Sheri R. Levy and Melanie Killen (New York: Oxford University Press, 2008), 32–46.

42 Michael T. Rizzo, Emily R. Green, Yarrow Dunham, Emile Bruneau, and Marjorie Rhodes, "Beliefs about Social Norms and Racial Inequalities Predict Variation in the Early Development of Racial Bias," *Developmental Science* 25, no. 2 (March 2022): e13170.

43 Frances E. Aboud, Morton J. Mendelson, and Kelly T. Purdy, "Cross-Race Peer Relations and Friendship Quality," *International Journal of Behavioral Development* 27, no. 2 (March 2003): 165–173; Dominic Abrams, Adam Rutland, and Lindsey Cameron, "The Development of Subjective Group Dynamics: Children's Judgments of Normative and Deviant In-Group and Out-Group Individuals," *Child Development* 74, no. 6 (2003): 1840–1856; Drew Nesdale, Anne Maass, Kevin Durkin, and Judith Griffiths, "Group Norms, Threat, and Children's Racial Prejudice," *Child Development* 76, no. 3 (2005): 652–663.

44 Rizzo et al., "Beliefs about Social Norms and Racial Inequalities."

45 Rakeeta Smallwood, Cindy Woods, Tamara Power, and Kim Usher, "Understanding the Impact of Historical Trauma Due to Colonization on the Health and Well-Being of Indigenous Young Peoples: A Systematic Scoping Review," *Journal of Transcultural Nursing* 32, no. 1 (January 2021): 59–68.

46 Seth Oppong, "Raising a New Generation in a Postcolonial Era through Decolonised Early Childhood Development and Care Services," *Contemporary Issues in Early Childhood* 23, no. 2 (November 2020): 182–197.

47 E. J. R. David, Tiera M. Schroeder, and Jessicaanne Fernandez, "Internalized Racism: A Systematic Review of the Psychological Literature on Racism's Most Insidious Consequence," *Journal of Social Issues* 75, no. 4 (September 2019): 1057–1086; Iruka et al., "Effects of Racism on Child Development."

48 Oppong, "Raising a New Generation in a Postcolonial Era."

49 Mark M. Kishiyama, W. Thomas Boyce, Amy M. Jimenez, Lee M. Perry, and Robert T. Knight, "Socioeconomic Disparities Affect Prefrontal Function in Children," *Journal of Cognitive Neuroscience* 21, no. 6 (June 2009): 1106–1115; Marilyn J. Essex, W. Thomas Boyce, Clyde Hertzman, Lucia L. Lam, Jeffrey M. Armstrong, Sarah M. A. Neumann, and Michael S. Kobor, "Epigenetic Vestiges of Early Developmental Adversity: Childhood Stress Exposure and DNA Methylation in Adolescence," *Child Development* 84, no. 1 (2013): 58–75.

50 Johanna Bick and Charles A. Nelson, "Early Adverse Experiences and the Developing Brain," *Neuropsychopharmacol* 41, no. 1 (January 2016): 177–196.

51 Vincent J. Felitti, Robert F. Anda, Dale Nordenberg, David F. Williamson, Alison M. Spitz, Valerie Edwards, Mary P. Koss, and James S. Marks, "Relationship of Childhood Abuse and Household Dysfunction to Many of Leading Causes of Death in Adults: The Adverse Childhood Experiences (ACE) Study," *American Journal of Prevention Medicine* 14, no. 4 (May 1998): 245–258.

52 NASEM, *Vibrant and Healthy Kids.*

53 Charles A. Nelson, "The Effects of Early Life Adversity on Brain and Behavioral Development," BrainFacts.org, October 1, 2012, www.brainfacts.org.

54 Erica M. Webster, "The Impact of Adverse Childhood Experiences on Health and Development in Young Children," *Global Pediatric Health* 9 (February 2022): 2333794X221078708.
55 Essex et al., "Epigenetic Vestiges of Early Developmental Adversity."
56 Ibid.
57 Jeong-Kyun Choi, Dan Wang, and Aurora P. Jackson, "Adverse Experiences in Early Childhood and Their Longitudinal Impact on Later Behavioral Problems of Children Living in Poverty," *Child Abuse & Neglect* 98 (December 2019): 104181.
58 Andrea Danese, "Annual Research Review: Rethinking Childhood Trauma—New Research Directions for Measurement, Study Design and Analytical Strategies," *Journal of Child Psychology and Psychiatry* 61, no. 3 (November 2019): 236–250.
59 Michael C. Lu, Milton Kotelchuck, Vijaya Hogan, Loretta Jones, Kynna Wright, and Neal Halfon, "Closing the Black-White Gap in Birth Outcomes: A Life-Course Approach," *Ethnicity & Disease* 20 (2010): S2-62–76.
60 NASEM, *Vibrant and Healthy Kids.*
61 Ibid.; World Health Organization, UNICEF, UN Population Fund (UNFPA), World Bank Group, and United Nations, *Trends in Maternal Mortality 2000 to 2020: Estimates by WHO, UNICEF, UNFPA, World Bank Group and UNDESA/Population Division* (Geneva: World Health Organization, 2023), www.who.int.
62 UNICEF, "State of the World's Children."
63 Gianna Melillo, "Racial Disparities Persist in Maternal Morbidity, Mortality and Infant Health," *American Journal of Managed Care*, June 13, 2020, www.ajmc.com.
64 Jay Belsky and R. M. Pasco Fearon, "Early Attachment Security, Subsequent Maternal Sensitivity, and Later Child Development: Does Continuity in Development Depend upon Continuity of Caregiving?," *Attachment & Human Development* 4, no. 3 (December 2002): 361–387.
65 National Research Council, *The Consequences of Maternal Morbidity and Maternal Mortality: Report of a Workshop*, ed. Holly A. Reed, Marjorie A. Koblinsky, and W. Henry Mosley (Washington, DC: National Academies Press, 2000).
66 Teresa Jacobsen and Volker Hofmann, "Children's Attachment Representations: Longitudinal Relations to School Behavior and Academic Competency in Middle Childhood and Adolescence," *Developmental Psychology* 33, no. 4 (1997): 703–710; L. Alan Sroufe, "Attachment and Development: A Prospective, Longitudinal Study from Birth to Adulthood," *Attachment & Human Development* 7, no. 4 (August 2006): 349–367.
67 Pehr Granqvist, L. Alan Sroufe, Mary Dozier, Erik Hesse, Miriam Steele, Marinus van Ijzendoorn, Judith Solomon, et al., "Disorganized Attachment in Infancy: A Review of the Phenomenon and Its Implications for Clinicians and Policy-Makers." *Attachment & Human Development* 19, no. 6 (December 2017): 534–558; Sheree L. Toth and Jody T. Manly, "Developmental Consequences of Child Abuse and Neglect: Implications for Intervention," *Child Development Perspectives* 13, no. 1 (December 2018): 59–64.

68 Carolyn Webster-Stratton and Sheila M. Eyberg, "Child Temperament: Relationship with Child Behavior Problems and Parent-Child Interactions," *Journal of Clinical Child Psychology* 11, no. 2 (1982): 123–129; Sanghag Kim and Grazyna Kochanska, "Child Temperament Moderates Effects of Parent-Child Mutuality on Self-Regulation: A Relationship-Based Path for Emotionally Negative Infants," *Child Development* 83, no. 4 (June 2012): 1275–1289.

69 Bick and Nelson, "Early Adverse Experiences and the Developing Brain."

70 Shaylea D. Badovinac, Rebecca Pillai Riddell, Audrey-Ann Deneault, Jodi Martin, Jean-François Bureau, and Monica C. O'Neill, "Associations between Early Childhood Parent-Child Attachment and Internalizing/Externalizing Symptoms: A Systematic Review and Narrative Synthesis," *Marriage & Family Review* 57, no. 7 (March 2021): 573–620; R. Pasco Fearon, Marian J. Bakermans-Kranenburg, Marinus H. van Ijzendoorn, Anne-Marie Lapsley, and Glenn I Roisman, "The Significance of Insecure Attachment and Disorganization in the Development of Children's Externalizing Behavior: A Meta-analytic Study," *Child Development* 81, no. 2 (March 2010): 435–456; Ashley M. Groh, Glenn I. Roisman, Marinus H. van Ijzendoorn, Marian J. Bakermans-Kranenburg, and R. Pasco Fearon, "The Significance of Insecure and Disorganized Attachment for Children's Internalizing Symptoms: A Meta-analytic Study," *Child Development* 83, no. 2 (January 2012): 591–610.

71 Daniel S. Shaw, Joan I. Vondra, Katherine Dowdell Hommerding, Kate Keenan, and Marija Dunn, "Chronic Family Adversity and Early Child Behavior Problems: A Longitudinal Study of Low Income Families," *Journal of Child Psychology and Psychiatry* 35, no. 6 (September 1994): 1109–1122; Bernd Blanz, Martin H. Schmidt, and Günter Esser, "Familial Adversities and Child Psychiatric Disorders," *Journal of Child Psychiatry and Psychology* 32, no. 6 (September 1991): 939–950; Michael Rutter, Antony Cox, Celia Tupling, Michael Berger, and William Yule, "Attainment and Adjustment in Two Geographical Areas: I. The Prevalence of Psychiatric Disorder," *British Journal of Psychiatry* 126, no. 6 (June 1975): 493–509; Daniel S. Shaw and Robert E. Emery, "Chronic Family Adversity and School-Age Children's Adjustment," *Journal of the American Academy of Child and Adolescent Psychiatry* 27, no. 2 (March 1988): 200–206; Naomi Richman, James Eric Stevenson, and Philip Jeremy Graham, *Pre-school to School: A Behavioural Study* (London: Academic, 1982).

72 Shihong Wang, Xudong Zhao, Yue Yu, Fangbiao Tao, Deyun Liu, and Ying Sun, "Prolonged Rather than Early Childhood Parent-Child Separation Predicts Change in Molecular Markers of Cellular Aging: A Consideration of the Role of Adolescence," *Journal of Youth and Adolescence* 52, no. 1 (January 2023): 165–176.

73 Ibid.

74 Elizabeth Meins, *Security of Attachment and the Social Development of Cognition* (London: Psychology, 1997); Maria Legerstee and Jean Varghese, "The Role of Maternal Affect Mirroring on Social Expectancies in Three-Month-Old Infants," *Child Development* 72, no. 5 (2001): 1301–1313; Ozlem Bekar, Miriam Steele, Rebecca

Shahmoon-Shanok, and Howard Steele, "Mothers' Mental State Talk and Preschool Children's Social-Behavioral Functioning: A Multidimensional Account," *Journal of Infant, Child, and Adolescent Psychotherapy* 17, no. 2 (2018): 119–133; Douglas K. Symons, Kristin-Lee M. Fossum, and T. B. Kate Collins, "A Longitudinal Study of Belief and Desire State Discourse during Mother-Child Play and Later False Belief Understanding," *Social Development* 15, no. 4 (October 2006): 676–692; Elizabeth Meins, Charles Fernyhough, Bronia Arnott, Susan R. Leekam, and Marc de Rosnay, "Mind-Mindedness and Theory of Mind: Mediating Roles of Language and Perspectival Symbolic Play," *Child Development* 84, no. 5 (2013): 1777–1790; Silja Martikainen, Mirjam Kalland, Tanja Linnavalli, Kaisamari Kostilainen, Metsämarja Aittokoski, Jyrki Reunamo, Zoi Vasileiou, and Mari Tervaniemi, "Supporting Social-Emotional Development in Early Childhood Education and Care—A Randomized Parallel Group Trial Evaluating the Impact of Two Different Interventions," *Scandinavian Journal of Educational Research*, April 27, 2023.

75 Webster, "Impact of Adverse Childhood Experiences."

76 Ibid.

77 Hayley Pierce, Melissa S. Jones, Hannah Shoaf, and Mackenzie Heim, "Early Adverse Childhood Experiences and Positive Functioning during Adolescence," *Journal of Youth and Adolescence* 52 (2023): 913–930.

78 Nayantara Hattangadi, Katherine T. Cost, Catherine S. Birken, Cornelia M. Borkhoff, Jonathon L. Maguire, Peter Szatmari, and Alice Charach, "Parenting Stress during Infancy Is a Risk Factor for Mental Health Problems in 3-Year-Old Children," *BMC Public Health* 20 (November 2020).

79 Abbie Raikes, Nirmala Rao, Hirokazu Yoshikawa, Caroline Cohrssen, Jere Behrman, Claudia Cappa, Amanda Devercelli, et al., "Global Tracking of Access and Quality in Early Childhood Care and Education," *International Journal of Child Care and Education Policy* 17, no. 1 (2023): 14.

80 Max Roser, "Access to Basic Education: Almost 60 Million Children of Primary School Age Are Not in School," Our World in Data, November 2, 2021, https://ourworldindata.org.

81 Ibid.

82 Claire Blewitt, Matthew Fuller-Tyszkiewicz, Andrea Nolan, Heidi Bergmeier, David Vicary, Terry Huang, Paul McCabe, Tracey McKay, and Helen Skouteris, "Social and Emotional Learning Associated with Universal Curriculum-Based Interventions in Early Childhood Education and Care Centers: A Systematic Review and Meta-analysis," *Journal of the American Medical Association* 1, no. 8 (December 2018): e185727.

83 Ibid.

84 Milagros Nores and W. Steven Barnett, "Access to High Quality Early Care and Education: Readiness and Opportunity Gaps in America," National Institute for Early Education Research, May 2014, https://nieer.org.

85 Stephanie Schmit and Christina Walker, *Disparate Access: Head Start and CCDBG Data by Race and Ethnicity*, Center for Law and Social Policy, February 2016,

www.clasp.org; see also Steve Barnett, Megan Carolan, and David Johns, "Equity and Excellence: African-American Children's Access to Quality Preschool," National Institute for Early Education Research, November 2013, https://nieer.org.

86 Erica Greenberg and Tomas Monarrez, "Segregated from the Start: Comparing Segregation in Early Childhood and K–12 Education," Urban Institute, October 1, 2019, www.urban.org.

87 Travis S. Wright, "Countering the Politics of Class, Race, Gender, and Geography in Early Childhood Education," *Educational Policy* 25, no. 1 (January 2011): 240–261; Lev S. Vygotsky, *Mind in Society: The Development of Higher Psychological Processes* (Cambridge, MA: Harvard University Press, 1978).

88 United States Department of Education Office for Civil Rights, "Data Snapshot: School Discipline," Issue Brief No. 1 (March 2014), https://ocrdata.ed.gov; Andrew Bacher-Hicks, Stephen B. Billings, and David J. Deming, "Proving the School-to-Prison Pipeline," *Education Next* 21, no. 4 (2021): www.educationnext.org; Russell J. Skiba, Mariella I. Arredondo, and Natasha T. Williams, "More than a Metaphor: The Contribution of Exclusionary Discipline to a School-to-Prison Pipeline," *Equity & Excellence in Education* 47, no. 4 (November 2014): 546–564.

89 Carmen Dalli, E. Jayne White, Jean Rockel, and Iris Duhn (with Emma Buchanan, Susan Davidson, Sarah Ganly, Larissa Kus, and Bo Wang), *Quality Early Childhood Education for Under-Two-Year-Olds: What Should It Look Like? A Literature Review* (Ministry of Education of New Zealand, 2011), https://thehub.swa.govt.nz.

90 NASEM, *Vibrant and Healthy Kids*.

91 Megan R. Gunnar and Bonny Donzella, "Social Regulation of the Cortisol Levels in Early Human Development," *Psychoneuroendocrinology* 27 (2002): 199–220.

92 NASEM, *Vibrant and Healthy Kids*; UNICEF, "State of the World's Children."

93 Dalli et al., *Quality Early Childhood Education for Under-Two-Year-Olds*.

94 Shantel Meek, Iheoma U. Iruka, Rosemarie Allen, Dawn A. Yazzie, Veronica Fernandez, Evandra Catherine, Kent McIntosh, Lisa Gordon, Walter Gilliam, Mary Louise Hemmeter, Darielle Blevins, and Tunette Powell, *Start with Equity: Fourteen Priorities to Dismantle Systemic Racism in Early Care and Education* (Children's Equity Project, Arizona State University, December 2020), https://childandfamilysuccess.asu.edu.

95 Iheoma U. Iruka, Tonia R. Durden, Kerry-Ann Escayg, and Stephanie M. Curenton, *We Are the Change We Seek: Advancing Racial Justice in Early Care and Education* (New York: Teachers College Press, 2023).

2

Children's Rights Law in Early Childhood

MEREDITH JOHNSON HARBACH

I. Introduction

Childhood is a period of dynamic and continuous (though not always linear) growth and development. In each stage of childhood, important developmental changes occur in children's physical, emotional, and social well-being; expectations and norms about children evolve across the liminal space of childhood, as well.[1]

Early childhood—the years from birth until age eight—is a critical stage in the child's life.[2] Developmental research has established that early childhood is an enormously consequential stage of development, affecting children's cognitive, emotional, social, and physical outcomes (see chapter 1). It is during this stage that children grow and change most rapidly. Young children are also especially vulnerable to the effects of poverty, disease, poor nutrition, social exclusion, and a range of other deprivations. And yet, young children are resilient and capable of extraordinary growth. Prevention and intervention strategies in early childhood can improve young children's current well-being as well as positively impact their futures. These early years are foundational with regard to children's physical and mental health, emotional security, identity, and developing capacities and competencies.

As compared to the literature discussing older children, research and guidance on implementing the Convention on the Rights of the Child (CRC) for the youngest children has been relatively narrow in scope. Even though more than thirty years have passed since the CRC's adoption, early childhood advocates have concluded that "huge challenges remain" and "far too little attention has been afforded to the rights of young children."[3] In particular, child rights advocates have observed that, in the context of early childhood, attention has often been focused on children's need for protection, overshadowing other critical rights in early childhood. Young children are widely regarded as "objects of care and protection"—by their parents, families, and communities.[4] Consequently, scholarship and commentary on child rights in early childhood have often focused predominantly on the issues of child mortality, birth registration, and health care. It has been less common, however, for young children also to be understood as rights holders with their own views and preferences.

While the youngest of children are entirely dependent on others for their development and survival, they are nevertheless more than the passive recipients of care and protection. Instead, they have agency from birth: they are "social actors from the beginning of life, with particular interests, capacities, and vulnerabilities," who require not only protection but also guidance and support in exercising their rights.[5] Thus, young children, just as much as their older counterparts, are entitled to full enjoyment of the rights set forth in the CRC. As observed by the Committee on the Rights of the Child (Committee), "The young child is not merely a fit object of benevolence, but, rather, . . . the young child is a rights-holder as is the older child and, indeed, every human being."[6] Critique of the CRC's implementation of rights in early childhood, consequently, has sought to highlight what has too often been overlooked: the obligation of states parties to develop law and policy programming to ensure that *all* rights articulated in the CRC are recognized and implemented for young children.

States are the ultimate guarantors of children's rights. They have three obligations under the CRC: to respect children's freedoms and entitlements, to protect them, and to fulfill them through provision or facilitation.[7] Article 4 of the CRC obligates states to "undertake all appropriate legislative, administrative, and other measures for the implementation of . . . [all] rights recognized" in the CRC.[8] States parties also play a central role in the development and coordination of early childhood programming. "It is the government's role to create an environment (legal, policy, social) that will permit and encourage the healthy development of young children and their families."[9]

This chapter considers and discusses particular characteristics of early childhood that affect the actualization of young children's rights. After setting out some orienting principles and themes, the chapter surveys children's rights in early childhood across a range of more specific rights guarantees: the right to participation, the best interests of the child, the right to health, the right to education, and the right to protection. The chapter concludes with observations about the need for holistic and comprehensive early childhood development programming, as well as the significance of ensuring rights implementation for the most vulnerable and disadvantaged children.

II. Young Children's Rights in Context

Before exploring specific ways in which child rights are implicated for young children, it is helpful to offer a few orienting principles and themes of particular relevance to early childhood. Here I explore the child's right to life, survival, and development; the significance of "parental guidance" in early childhood; and the CRC's focus on the "evolving capacities of the child."

First, all children have a right to life, survival, and development.[10] Securing these rights is a necessary precondition to implementing the more specific rights articulated in the CRC. The child's right to life, survival, and development is especially significant in early childhood because of the level of dependency and precarity children experience during this stage. It is during these early years that children are most vulnerable physically, emotionally, psychologically. Young children do not have the capacity to secure their own basic needs or to protect themselves from physical, emotional, or psychological harm. In other words, they cannot secure for themselves the necessary goods and supports to safeguard their rights to life, survival, and development. Instead, early childhood is the stage during which children are most dependent (sometimes entirely dependent) on others to exercise and implement these rights. Realizing children's rights in early childhood is thus contingent on the resources and well-being of those who care for them.

Second, especially in early childhood, realizing children's rights requires engagement with the domains and environments in which they are embedded: families, schools, communities, institutions, and religious and cultural systems. Parents are the primary means of realizing rights in early childhood. Because of young children's particular vulnerabilities and needs, the role of parents and caregivers in children's survival and development is especially consequential in early childhood. It is during early childhood that parents' responsibilities are most extensive, relating to all aspects of child safety and well-being. Early childhood is also one of the most demanding phases of parenthood—with regard to time, attention, and material resources. In the preprimary stages of early childhood, some children will have relatively fewer contacts with adults outside of their families. They are more likely to be embedded in private frameworks of care, whether through parental care, relative care, or third-party care within the home.[11] Other young children, particularly those with parents working outside the home, will receive early care and education within private, public, or faith-based settings. As children reach primary-school age, the settings in which they are embedded expand significantly to include formal schooling as well as other institutions and their broader communities.

In many contexts, parents and other caregivers will be the "major conduit through which young children are able to realize their rights."[12] The parental role is to provide "appropriate direction and guidance in the exercise by the child of the rights" in the CRC.[13] Given the important role of parents in early childhood, states parties should take all necessary action to ensure that parents are able to exercise primary responsibility for their children.[14] They are "urged to promote and uphold the responsibilities, rights and duties of parents or legal guardians to provide appropriate direction and guidance to young children in the exercise of their rights."[15] More than that, the CRC requires states parties to "render appropriate assistance to parents and legal guardians in the performance of their child-rearing responsibilities and . . . ensure the development of institutions, facilities and services for the care of children."[16] In regard to children of working parents, the CRC requires states parties to "take all appropriate measures to ensure that [these] children . . . have the right to benefit from child-care services and facilities for which they are eligible."[17]

Finally, the CRC recognizes the "evolving capacities of the child" as relevant to parental responsibilities and rights as well as children's rights.[18] Because of the rapid transformations children undergo in early childhood, respecting children's evolving capacities is especially important.[19] The CRC thus recognizes that child development is dynamic, not static, and children's cognitive, physical, social, and moral capacities evolve and mature over the arc of childhood. These evolving capacities affect children's ability to form views, communicate, make decisions, exercise judgment, process information, and engage in autonomous actions and decision-making. As young children grow and develop, they are increasingly able to think, learn, and do independently, rather than simply relying on adults to do these things for them.

Consequently, young children do not remain entirely dependent on the adults in their lives to vindicate their rights. The framework of evolving capacities recognizes that, over time, children develop the agency to make decisions and to promote and protect their own rights.[20] Parents have a responsibility to adapt the levels of support and guidance they provide. "These adjustments take account of a child's interests and wishes as well as the child's capacities for autonomous decision-making."[21] Thus, children's evolving capacities act as a limit or counterbalance to "parental guidance" under the CRC. As children evolve, the rights of parental guidance diminish, and parental obligations expand to include an obligation to extend to children themselves the ability to exercise increasing control over the exercise of their rights.[22] Failure to recognize and respect evolving capacities in early childhood results in a cramped, paternalistic implementation of rights that ignores children's capacity for agency and autonomy, which is inconsistent with the CRC.

Having foregrounded the right to survival and development in early childhood, the centrality of "parental guidance" in early childhood, and the special relevance of evolving capacities in early childhood, the chapter now turns to consider young children's rights in particular contexts.

A. Participation

Children's participation rights are one of the CRC's guiding principles and are central to the full array of rights guaranteed to children by the CRC.[23] Indeed, young children's participation rights are essential to the implementation of all rights discussed in this chapter. Article 12 obligates states to "assure to the child who is capable of forming his or her own views the right to express those views freely in all matters affecting the child, the views of the child being given due weight in accordance with the age and maturity of the child."[24] This right is commonly interpreted as a child's right to participation—"ongoing processes, which include information-sharing and dialogue between children and adults based on mutual respect, and in which children can learn how their views and those of adults are taken into account and shape the outcome of such processes."[25] As envisioned by the CRC, the right to participation is not one anchored only in specific instances and contexts but instead is a system of extended exchange between children and adults across all relevant contexts in children's lives.

Young children face particular barriers in realizing their participation rights.[26] The Committee recommends that states parties ensure that the notion of young children as rights holders with a right to express their views be implemented as early as possible, consistent with the child's capacity, best interests, and well-being.[27] As articulated by the Committee, "The right to express views and feelings should be anchored in the child's daily life at home . . . and in his or her community; within the full range of early childhood health, care and education facilities, as well as in legal proceedings; and in the development of policies and services, including through research and consultation."[28] Implementing participation rights for young children presents a number of particular challenges. In many cultures, young children are considered undeveloped and lacking the ability to understand, communicate, and make decisions. These assumptions about young children leave them "powerless within their families, and often voiceless and invisible within society."[29] Yet participation is key to respecting young children as full persons entitled to all rights in the CRC. In the context of early childhood, the Committee characterizes this right, broadly speaking, as recognizing "young children as full actors in their own development."[30]

Children have a right not only to have their views heard but also to have them respected, valued, and considered.[31] The Lundy Model of child participation emphasizes the two key elements of Article 12: the right to express a view and the right to have that view given due weight.[32] To fully implement these rights, decision-makers must consider the implications of space, voice, audience, and influence, as articulated in the Lundy Model. In order to implement children's right to express a view, they must be given an opportunity to express the view (space), and their views must be elicited (voice). To implement children's right to have their views given due weight, the view must be considered (audience) and should be acted upon, as appropriate (influence).[33] Each of these factors—space, voice, audience, and influence—has particular implications for young children's participation rights.

A preliminary challenge involves discerning the views of young children. Indeed, Article 12 might be assumed to be limited in application to older children "capable of forming [their] own views."[34] To the contrary, there is no minimum age specified for the applicability of Article 12, and the Committee has made clear that the right to participate "applies both to younger and to older children."[35] Nor is it necessary for children to have comprehensive knowledge of an issue; instead, it is sufficient if they have an understanding that is adequate to render them capable of forming views on the matter.[36]

Given the persistence of limiting beliefs concerning children's ability to participate during early childhood, the notion of children's "evolving capacities" is central to the realization of their participation rights. Rather than acting as a limitation, however, this qualification requires states to ascertain the child's ability to form an autonomous opinion to the maximum extent, with a presumption that a child has the capacity to form views and the right to express them. Likewise, capacity and maturity cannot be systematically linked to biological age, and the right to be heard cannot be implemented in a blanket fashion applying to all children across all contexts. Instead, "research has shown that information, experience, environment, social and cultural expectations, and levels of support all contribute to the development of a children's capacities to form a view."[37] Even the youngest children are capable of forming views in many contexts. As recognized by the Committee, "Young children are acutely sensitive to their surroundings and very rapidly acquire understanding of the people, places and routines in their lives, along with awareness of their own unique identity. They make choices and communicate their feelings, ideas and wishes in numerous ways, long before they are able to communicate through the conventions of spoken or written language."[38]

While young children are capable of forming views in many everyday contexts in their lives, other circumstances, such as legal proceedings or engagement with research, will require additional measures. In more specialized contexts, young children will need support from others to enable them to form and express their views. Thus, when necessary, ensuring "space" for young children's participation rights requires that they receive information to provide context and assist them in forming views. This obligation to assist young children in forming views implicates their Article 13 rights to "receive . . . information and ideas of all kinds."[39] The Committee emphasizes this obligation: "the child has a right to direction and guidance, which have to compensate for the lack of knowledge, experience, and understanding of the child and are restricted by his or her evolving capacities."[40] Adults must meet young children where they are, developmentally, and provide content and information in an accessible way that enables the children to form views. For young children who cannot yet read and/or have limited numeracy skills, visual and kinesthetic approaches are helpful in stimulating discussion and thinking.[41]

A second challenge for young children's participation rights involves their "voice"—the manner in which they express their views. Unlike older children, young children at the earliest stages of development are not able to communicate verbally. Yet research has established that children are able to communicate in nonverbal ways beginning at birth.[42] The Committee explains, "The child is able to form views from the youngest age, even when she or he may be unable to express them verbally. Consequently, full implementation of article 12 requires recognition of, and respect for, non-verbal forms of communication including play, body language, facial expressions, and drawing and painting, through which very young children demonstrate understanding, choices, and preferences."[43]

The young child's right to be heard, then, includes nonverbal forms of communication in which children can express their preferences. The "audience" for young children's expression rights, therefore, must use developmentally appropriate "listening" tools, which will necessarily implicate multiple levels of interpretation beyond simple auditory engagement. To fully implement young children's participation rights, adults must "adopt a child-centered attitude, listening to young children and respecting their dignity and their individual points of view. It also requires adults to show patience and creativity by adapting their expectations to a young child's interests, levels of understanding and preferred ways of communicating."[44]

Special challenges also arise concerning the degree of "influence" young children's views should have on matters affecting them, because under the evolving capacities principle, the weight accorded to those views is determined by the "age and maturity of the child."[45] Young children are "neither incompetent nor fully competent in many situations."[46] They will not always have adequate comprehension and practical knowledge to have their views influence *all* matters affecting them.[47] Young children's participation rights require that young children's views be given appropriate weight but not in a way that might "undermine their other rights (i.e., to education, health, care)."[48] A limiting interpretation of Article 12's requirements, therefore, would be to accord young children's views due weight "wherever their perspective can enhance the quality of solutions."[49]

Young children's participation rights are implicated most prominently in the contexts and settings of their daily lives: parents and families, early care and education, primary education, and their communities. The ability to be heard by parents and the ability to participate in family settings are central to young children's participation rights. To enhance parents' understanding and competence in respecting young children's participation, the Committee recommends that states parties develop parent education programs that support child participation in family life, to include the relationship of mutual respect between parents and children; the involvement of children in decision-making; the implication of giving due weight to the views of every family member; the understanding, promotion, and respect for children's evolving capacities; and ways of addressing conflicting views within the family.[50]

More broadly, states should facilitate the "active involvement of . . . schools and communities at large in the promotion and creation of opportunities for young children to actively and progressively" participate in everyday activities.[51] "Special attention must be given to the freedom of expression, thought, conscience and religion and the right to privacy of the youngest children, according to their evolving capacity."[52] Child participation is a critical element of high-quality early childhood education and care (ECEC). Best practices in the ECEC setting require that teachers value children's perspectives and encourage children to make decisions and exercise agency. Teachers should "listen to children, facilitate children to express their ideas, follow children's initiatives and expand on them to foster new skills."[53] Young children also can exercise their right to participation through play that is child directed.[54] "Play is perhaps the most authentic child-led activity, away from adult-control, instrumented and conducted entirely by the child her/himself."[55] The ability to play empowers children to "create their own forms of engagement and participation on their own terms."[56]

Young children should also have a voice in the institutional design of systems and institutions created to promote their rights and well-being. This includes their active participation in the promotion, protection, and monitoring of their rights under the CRC. "The State, as the ultimate duty-bearer, has obligations to create an enabling environment that allows the views of children . . . to be heard on practices and policies that directly or indirectly concern them."[57] For example, states parties can create specific mechanisms for effectuating child participation in the design of policies, programs, and services via advisory boards and children's forums, in order to provide them structured opportunities to influence policy and program development and implementation.[58] Young children can be involved in brainstorming processes around service development through techniques like playacting, drawing, storytelling, and using digital media.[59] And young children, themselves, can participate in research designed to enhance opportunities for their participation in school and neighborhood settings, as well as executing their own research with adult support.[60]

Instances in which young children have been engaged directly in research design, interpretation, and dissemination have been relatively rare.[61] Yet engaging young children as co-creators of research is possible; they are capable of assisting in the development of research questions, interpreting data, and helping to disseminate research results (see chapter 10).[62] They can also contribute their expertise and lived experiences when interpreting research on young children. Engaging young children as co-researchers can present a number of unique challenges. However, scholars have shown that thoughtfully crafted interventions designed to engage young children with the general context of research, as well as in the development of research questions, can overcome these challenges. Effective engagement of young children in children's rights research requires that adult researchers interact with respect, transparency, and dialogue. Adults must meet young children where they are, developmentally, and—when appropriate—provide content and information in an accessible way that enables the children to form views. Soliciting young children's views and taking them seriously in this context requires asking careful questions, listening closely, and adapting based on feedback from the children. Engaging them in these ways can ultimately lead to higher-quality research data.[63]

Because of the interrelated and interdependent nature of children's rights, young children's participation rights intersect and engage with other rights discussed in this chapter. As is discussed in more detail shortly, child participation is key to accurately assessing a child's best interests. This is necessary, for instance, whenever the custody or support of a child is disputed. Participation is also an integral component of the child's right to education, also discussed later. Indeed, there has been a growing focus on young children's right to participate in early care and education settings, highlighting the importance of participation rights in early childhood.[64] Child participation is also central to implementing young children's protection rights. Not only must children be able to communicate and report the risk or actuality of maltreatment, but they must also be involved in all other aspects of the child protection process, particularly removal, alternative placements, termination of parental rights, and adoption or institutional care.

Taking child participation seriously means recognizing that children's own preferences, interests, and opinions must be given appropriate weight within their families, communities, and society. The Committee warns against "tokenistic approaches" that limit viewpoint expression, fail to consider those views, or manipulate them. Thus, all processes involving child participation must be transparent and informative, voluntary, respectful, relevant, child friendly, inclusive, supported by training, safe, and accountable. At the same time, children's participation rights must be tempered by an understanding that inappropriate implementation or inartful solicitation of children's views can harm children, especially young children. Implementation of children's participation rights must be achieved while also ensuring the child's right to protection.[65]

Young children's participation rights "harness the wisdom, authenticity and currency of children's lived experience in order to effect change."[66] Ultimately, as the Committee explains, "achieving meaningful opportunities for the implementation of article 12 will necessitate dismantling the legal, political, economic, social and cultural barriers that currently impede children's opportunity to be heard and their access to participation in all matters that affect them. It requires a preparedness to challenge assumptions about children's capacities, and to encourage the development of environments in which children can build and demonstrate capacities."[67]

B. Best Interests of the Child

The "best interests of the child," set out in Article 3, is another fundamental principle of the CRC and is among the first concepts articulated in the treaty.[68] The CRC provides that "in all actions concerning children, whether undertaken by public or private social welfare institutions, courts of law, administrative authorities or legislative bodies, the best interests of the child shall be a primary consideration."[69] This duty to consider children's best interests is comprehensive. As the Committee affirms, "The principle of best interests applies to all actions concerning children and requires active measures to protect their rights and promote their survival, growth, and well-being."[70] This "requires a consciousness about the place that children's interests must occupy in all actions and a willingness to give priority to those interests in all circumstances, but especially when an action has an undeniable impact on the children concerned."[71] The ultimate purpose of the best interests assessment is "to ensure the full and effective enjoyment of the rights recognized in the CRC and the holistic development of the child."[72]

The best interests assessment should be tailored to each individual child in light of their interests and the context in which it is being assessed. Although the particular elements or factors relevant to this assessment will vary according to culture and context, the Committee has articulated the following factors to be considered in assessing best interests: the child's views; the child's identity; preservation of the family environment; the care, protection, and safety of the child; situations of vulnerability; the child's right to health; and the child's right to education.[73] These factors will overlap and sometimes be in conflict.

By definition, the right to have one's best interests assessed by others in a variety of contexts is a right that children cannot exercise themselves. Instead, this right must be respected and carried out by adults: parents, guardians, private and public institutions, courts, administrative and legislative bodies. The adult role is especially significant in the context of early childhood. Because of young children's relative developmental immaturity and associated challenges in soliciting their expressed views, parents and other adults across various contexts play a primary role in making assessments of the child(ren)'s best interests.[74] Critiques of the operation of the best interests principle highlight the ways in which it invites paternalism, overlooking the views and wishes of children. The best interests inquiry is intentionally flexible and open-ended, ensuring that the determination can be responsive to the unique experiences and needs of individual children. Yet that flexibility also permits assumptions that children—especially young children—do not really know what they want or what is best for them, thus obscuring their views and according undue weight to adult assessments of best interests. The younger a child is, the more likely it is that an adult's views will dominate.

Ensuring that all children's rights are respected—especially their participation rights—during a best interests analysis helps to limit this paternalism. Despite the centrality of adults in assessing a child's best interests, their views alone are not dispositive of a child's best interests. The Committee has emphasized that "an adult's judgment of a child's best interests cannot override the obligation to respect all the child's rights under the Convention."[75] Children's "right to have their views given due weight cannot be abandoned on the basis that the adults . . . know what is best for them."[76] Thus, "any decision that does not take into account the child's views or does not give their views due weight according to their age and maturity, does not respect the possibility for the child or children to influence the determination of their best interests."[77]

Instead, as part of the best interests assessment, decision-makers must consider the child's views on the matter.[78] "Every attempt to find out the best interests of the child must be confirmed by paying attention so as to capture the views and feelings the child expresses in verbal and non-verbal ways."[79] Consequently, assessments of the child's best interests are intimately tied to the child's participation rights, and the two rights play complementary roles.[80] Therefore, making a best interests assessment necessarily involves the child's participation rights under Article 12. Article 3 cannot be applied correctly unless the child's participation rights are fully respected in all best interests determinations.[81] Those who are weighing children's best interests must therefore respect and honor children's right to participate in all matters affecting them and to have their views considered in making any determination of their best interests. Indeed, states parties are required to "ensure appropriate arrangements, including representation, when appropriate," for the purpose of assessment of children's best interests.[82]

Soliciting and weighing the views of young children can be especially challenging. Consequently, in many contexts in which the best interests of young children are assessed, adults may neglect to solicit children's views and/or fail to give those views the consideration required by the CRC. Yet the fact that children are very young does not negate their right to be heard in all best interest determinations.[83] "Babies and very young children have the same rights as all children to have their best interests assessed, even if they cannot express their views or represent themselves in the same way as older children."[84] For young children, fully eliciting their views may require special measures to ensure their role, particularly if they are preverbal and lack context or understanding of the nature of the matter requiring a best interests determination. Consequently, assessments of young children's best interests must attend to their views and feelings, expressed verbally or nonverbally.[85]

Best interests determinations frequently arise in the context of legal proceedings concerning matters such as child custody, child removal, alternative care, termination of parental rights, adoption, and youth justice. Article 12 makes clear that "the child shall in particular be provided the opportunity to be heard in any judicial and administrative proceedings affecting the child, either directly, or through a representative or an appropriate body, in a manner consistent with the procedural rules of national law."[86] Across legal contexts, there is no consensus whether children have a right to have their views considered in all best interests determinations, particularly when they are very young. Despite Article 12's mandate, which makes no exceptions for very young children, in practice, young children are seldom given an opportunity to express their views and preferences. A standard approach is to permit children's views to be considered in specific circumstances, but only if children are deemed sufficiently "mature." For example, statutes might require courts to consider the views of children of a certain age in some contexts, but below that age, courts might retain discretion to hear from children who are capable of articulating a viewpoint.[87]

The Committee advises that children involved in administrative or legal proceedings should have appropriate legal representation.[88] In some legal contexts in which children's best interests are assessed, children are afforded a right to have a representative, but the representative is not always obliged to articulate the child's expressed wishes. Generally, a "'best interests advocate' does not function as the child's lawyer and is not bound by the child's expressed wishes in determining what to advocate, although the best interests advocate should consider those wishes."[89] Yet, consistent with the CRC, every child has a right to "a voice in any abuse, neglect, dependency, or termination of parental rights proceeding, regardless of developmental level."[90]

To fully implement children's participation in best interests determinations, best practices would provide a representative to articulate and advocate for the young child's expressed wishes. For example, in the *Model Act Governing the Representation of Children in Abuse, Neglect, and Dependency Proceedings*, the American Bar Association (ABA) proposes that all children in abuse, neglect, and dependency proceedings shall have a court-appointed lawyer to advocate for the child's expressed wishes.[91] Consistent with the requirements of the Model Act, the ABA "recognizes the right of every child to have quality legal representation and a voice . . . regardless of developmental level."[92] The ABA recognizes, in the case of younger children, that they may have a diminished capacity to participate. In that event, however, the ABA urges that the child's lawyer should "make a good faith effort to determine the child's needs and wishes."[93] In the event the child lacks capacity to maintain a normal advisory relationship, the ABA directs the attorney to make a substituted judgment determination—"determining what the child would decide if he or she were capable of making an adequately considered decision, and representing the child in accordance with that determination."[94] That is, rather than substituting the representative's *own* views for that of the child, the representative should determine what the *child*'s views would be.[95]

In addition to the best interests principle's applicability in administrative and legal proceedings, it plays a central role in parental relationships with children. The CRC recognizes that the best interests of the child will be parents' "basic concern."[96] For young children, much of their time will be spent in a family setting within the private sphere, as opposed to later, when they enter primary school. This means that parents' own understanding of their children's best interests, and their ability to act in furtherance of those interests, are central to child well-being in early childhood. Given the significance of the parental role in early childhood, the best interests principle requires states to "render appropriate assistance to parents and legal guardians in the performance of their child-rearing responsibilities . . . and ensure the development of institutions, facilities and services for the care of children."[97]

The principle of evolving capacities is especially significant in implementing the best interests principle in early childhood. As young children mature, their views should have increasing weight in best interests determinations. "The more the child knows, has experienced and understands, the more the parent, legal guardian or other persons legally responsible for him or her have to transform direction and guidance into reminders and advice, and later to an exchange on an equal footing."[98] The best interests principle is dynamic, applying to children and contexts that are constantly evolving. It is necessarily flexible, applied on an individual basis according to the situation and needs of the particular child or children. This flexibility of the principle allows it to respond to the individual needs and contexts of children, as well as to accommodate their evolving capacities.

States parties have multiple obligations with respect to the best interests principle. First, they must ensure that children's best interests are considered appropriately and consistently in public actions affecting children. Second, they must ensure that all decisions, legislation, and policies affecting children demonstrate that the child's best interests have been a primary consideration. Finally, states parties must also ensure that all private decisions and actions concerning children have included the best interests of the child as a primary consideration. Implementation measures include incorporating the child's best interests in the allocation of resources for programs and policies to implement children's rights and providing information and training on best interests to all individuals who make decisions that directly or indirectly impact children, including professionals working with or for children. For young children, state implementation measures in this regard should focus particularly on parents and extended family members, as well as on all providers of early care and education.

The best interests principle overlaps with other rights surveyed in this chapter. Intersections with the right to participation have been explored earlier. The child's right to health is also an essential component of the child's best interests. Likewise, the best interests assessment implicates children's right to education, because "it is in the best interests of the child to have access to quality education, including early childhood education, non-formal or informal education and related activities, free of charge."[99] Finally, the state's obligation to protect the child should be considered in every best interests assessment and should be considered in the broadest sense: the "comprehensive ideal of ensuring the child's 'well-being' and development."[100]

C. Right to Health

The child's right to health and nutrition is essential for the full realization of all other rights in the CRC. Article 24 recognizes the "right of the child to the enjoyment of the highest attainable standard of health and to facilities for the treatment of illness and rehabilitation of health" and the obligations of states parties to ensure that "no child is deprived of [the] right of access to such health care services."[101] The "highest attainable standard of health" is assessed through the child's biological, social, cultural, and economic circumstances, as well as the state's available resources.[102]

The Committee has emphasized a focus on the determinants of children's health in relation to individual factors; the environments in which they are embedded, especially the risk of violence; and structural determinants of health, including state policies, regulatory systems, and sociocultural values and norms.[103] Early childhood illness and death are high in part because for those who are most in need, their families and caregivers lack information, financial resources, and/or access to health care to address preventable and treatable diseases.[104] Differential realization of the right to health is also affected by intersectional factors such as poverty, inequality, and discrimination.[105] Article 24 also expressly notes the "dangers and risks of environmental pollution."[106] In addition, the Committee more recently has drawn attention to the broader relevance of the environment to children's health, particularly climate change.[107]

Children's earliest years provide the foundation for their physical and emotional health.[108] In early childhood, states parties must ensure that young children have access to "the highest attainable standard of health care and nutrition in order to . . . enable children to enjoy a healthy start to life."[109] Article 24 requires states parties to take appropriate measures to reduce infant and child mortality.[110] The Committee has singled out neonatal mortality as a particular concern, recommending a range of interventions prenatally and postnatally to address it.[111] The Committee also urges states parties to provide universal access to primary health services for all children.

Adequate nutrition is especially important in early childhood because brain development can be significantly jeopardized prenatally and in the first years of life.[112] Early brain health is critical to healthy child development and future potential (see chapter 1).[113] In early childhood, the right to health also includes appropriate nutritional support for both mothers and children, as well as the provision of micronutrients to support child health and prevent illness and disease.[114] In addition, the Committee emphasizes access to clean drinking water, proper sanitation, appropriate immunizations, and good medical services in early childhood.[115]

Of special significance in early childhood, the right to health recognizes and depends on connections between maternal health and the child's health. Article 24 requires states parties to "ensure appropriate pre-natal and post-natal health care for mothers."[116] In doing so, although the drafters of the CRC did not address the beginning of life in the treaty's definition of the child (Article 1)—leaving that highly contested issue to individual states to determine for themselves—to enable broad-based ratification, the CRC does call on states to provide support to mothers, with a view to ensuring children a healthy start to life.[117] Poor maternal health before, during, and after pregnancy, along with suboptimal breastfeeding, is associated with a significant number of neonatal deaths.[118] Ensuring pregnant mothers' right to health and supporting the role of parents and caregivers are important determinants of children's health, nutrition, and development.[119] Risks that occur before, during, and after birth implicate children's short- and long-term health and well-being. Thus, the care received by those who are pregnant has significant consequences for child health and development. Fulfilling this obligation requires "universal access to a comprehensive package of sexual and reproductive health interventions . . . based on the concept of a continuum of care from pre-pregnancy, through pregnancy, childbirth and throughout the post-partum period."[120]

Gender-based discrimination against girl children is pervasive and impacts the right to health in early childhood.[121] Discrimination in early childhood can manifest itself through selective abortion, genital mutilation, neglect, and infanticide. Girl children may also experience inadequate feeding during infancy.[122] Thus, the right to health must be interpreted within the larger context of Article 2's nondiscrimination principle: "States Parties shall respect and ensure the rights [in the CRC] without discrimination of any kind, irrespective of the child's . . . sex."[123]

Implementing the right to health is a necessary condition for the child's right to survival and development. Using a child rights approach to implement the child's right to health means that this right should be read in tandem with the right to survival and development in Article 6. In the context of the right to health, this means "that all children have the right to opportunities to survive, grow and develop, within the context of physical, emotional and social well-being, to each child's full potential."[124] The Committee understands this right in comprehensive terms, extending beyond prevention, promotion, and treatment of health to, more broadly, children's "right to grow and develop to their full potential and live in conditions that enable them to attain the highest standard of health through the implementation of programmes that address the underlying determinants of health."[125]

As with the rights previously discussed, the child's right to health is closely linked to the child's parents. Parents are responsible for honoring the child's right to health, consistent with their focus on the best interests of the child.[126] "Parents are the most important source of early diagnosis and primary care for small children," and they also "play a central role in promoting healthy child development, protecting children from harm due to accidents, injuries and violence and mitigating the negative effects of risk behaviors."[127] To support these vital relationships for young children, states parties are responsible for encouraging education in child health and development, including an emphasis on issues pertinent to early childhood, such as breastfeeding, nutrition, hygiene, and sanitation.[128] The Committee also urges states to adopt "evidence-based interventions to support good parenting, including parenting skills education, support groups and family counseling, in particular for families experiencing children's health and other social challenges."[129]

Children's participation rights are also significant to the realization of their right to health.[130] Yet often the health-care system is ill prepared to facilitate these rights, ignoring children in the consultation process, failing to prepare them for procedures, and consequently marginalizing them.[131] A focus on the legal capacity of children to provide informed consent for medical treatment, which young children are unlikely to have, obscures the broader set of participation rights to which they are entitled.[132] Even when young children lack legal capacity to consent, they nevertheless often will have capacity to express an informed view, which, under Article 12, should be given due weight.[133] They have a right to receive relevant information and to participate in decisions by sharing views; they may grant or withhold assent; and their privacy, dignity, and confidentiality should be respected.[134] Children's evolving capacities impact the weight to be given to their views, as well as their capacity to engage in independent decision-making on health issues.[135]

Fully implementing young children's participation rights as part of their right to health requires specialized strategies designed to meet young children where they are so as to maximize their participation. First, young children often seek, and have a right to, information about their health care. Providers should give them age-appropriate explanations and information to enable their understanding.[136] In studies, children, even young ones, emphasize the importance of direct communication from health-care providers and seek to have providers communicate directly to them, rather than exclusively to their parents.[137] Communication with young children should use a range of age-appropriate methods, including play, art, and the use of art and other props.[138] Second, verbal children should be able to ask questions and have them answered in accessible ways. Third, providers working with children should be trained in communicating with children and building relationships and have an understanding of children's rights.[139] Finally, respecting young children's participation rights in health care requires careful listening, in the broadest sense of the word, especially in the case of preverbal children. Listening to young children gives them the voice that Article 12 requires. Eliciting young children's views, considering them, and giving them due weight both enhances their participation and has the potential to improve the quality of health care.[140] In one study involving young children receiving palliative care, for example, researchers suggested that engaging children in advance care planning is one mechanism to guarantee child participation in health care.[141] Thus, respecting young children's right to participate in health care "requires adults to understand what children think and feel, to perform honest and . . . respectful communication, and to comprehend their wishes."[142]

The right to health also implicates the best interests principle. States must incorporate the best interests of the child standard in all health-related decisions, as well as in the allocation of resources and the development and implementation of policies affecting the underlying determinants of health, including poverty and inequality.[143] An analysis of the best interests of individual children vis-à-vis their health should include physical, emotional, social, and education needs; age; sex and gender identity; relationship to parents/caregivers; and family and social background.[144]

The state's core obligations with regard to children's right to health include reviewing and reforming law and policy related to children's health, ensuring universal coverage of quality primary health care, responding to underlying determinants of child health, and developing and funding policies that pursue a child rights–based approach to fulfilling children's right to health.[145] Particular to early childhood, the right to health obligates states parties to provide access to the highest standard of health care and nutrition during their early years, to prevent infant mortality and "enable children to enjoy a healthy start in life."[146] The Committee has emphasized state responsibilities to ensure access to clean drinking water, adequate sanitation, appropriate immunization, good nutrition, and medical services, because they are essential to young children's health.[147] Even if states do not provide all services directly to children and their families, they are nevertheless ultimately responsible for ensuring the child's right to health.[148] Finally, the state must "devote attention to the structural factors affecting children's health including laws, policies and budgets."[149]

D. Right to Education

The overall goal of education is to "maximize the child's ability and opportunity to participate fully and responsibly in a free society."[150] The right to education—guaranteed for all children from birth—includes child-specific education that enables each child to reach their full potential.[151] Within the context of early childhood, the CRC specifically requires states parties to "make primary education compulsory and available free to all."[152] Significantly, however, the CRC is silent with regard to early childhood education and care.

Promoting the right to education beginning at birth supports the overarching requirement to ensure the child's right to maximum development.[153] Children have a right to individualized education that develops their own "personality, talents and mental and physical abilities to their fullest potential."[154] The CRC also specifically requires education to develop respect for human rights and freedoms; respect for parents, communities, and cultures within which the child is situated and those of other societies; and respect for the natural environment. The goal is to "empower the child by developing his or her skills, learning and other capacities, human dignity, self-esteem and self-confidence."[155] The Committee thus calls for young children to "receive education in the broadest sense, . . . which acknowledges a key role for parents, wider family and community, as well as the contribution of organized programmes of early childhood education provided by the State, the community or civil institutions."[156]

Human rights education is a central component within the right to education, and states parties are obligated to "make the principles and provisions of the [CRC] widely known . . . to adults and children alike."[157] The Committee recommends ensuring this right in early childhood by including human rights education in pre- and primary school.[158] The Committee endorses incorporation of human rights education in early education to be active and empower children to exercise their rights in practical ways appropriate to their age, development, and environment. Human rights education should be "anchored in everyday issues at home, in childcare centres, in early education programmes and other community settings with which young children can identify."[159] Although young children typically have less exposure to formal classroom settings, unique opportunities exist to provide human rights education. Creative expression through the arts can provide a rich and accessible medium through which young children can learn about their rights, explore their meaning, and learn to be self-advocates.[160] For example, children's literature can be a vehicle for teaching children about their rights and is accessible to even young children.[161]

The right to education is intimately connected to the role of parents in young children's lives. Early learning begins at birth, with a premium on high-quality adult-child interaction, and carries on through early childhood both between children and with family members. During early childhood, the state adopts a supportive role, with the primary obligations for teaching residing with parents and families. Children's first teachers are their parents or guardians, and realizing the right to education in early childhood necessarily implicates attachment relationships with parents and other caregivers. Early interactions with parents and caregivers are crucial to children's development and their earliest education, and states must support parents and families, particularly those with limited resources, to ensure parents have time to bond with and care for their children. Through these relationships, young children begin to develop their identity and learn important skills, knowledge, and behaviors.

In addition to providing early education and care that are of high quality, states should also provide programming to educate, support, and empower parents in their primary child-rearing role.[162] States parties have a responsibility to partner with caregivers together to realize the full development of each child through education, provided by both the family and other public and private institutions. Community-based programs, coordinated with families at the local level, should be designed with parental education and empowerment as key priorities in helping parents fulfill their educational role. Grounding these programs in local communities ensures that they reflect the values and experiences of particular children and families, as opposed to a cookie-cutter model of community-based education programs.

Secondary to early attachments to primary caregivers, ECEC—provided either individually or in groups, in homes, or by institutions—is a primary source of education in early childhood. Thus, children's right to education in early childhood includes not only high-quality care from parents and caregivers but also high-quality ECEC. ECEC is perhaps the most significant component of a broader set of programming on early childhood development—a holistic approach to ensure that young children get the best possible start in life, are ready for primary school, and can develop and grow as young learners. High-quality early childhood programming, therefore, has benefits in the here and now as well as serving as a protective and preventive function into later childhood and even into adulthood. Access to early childhood education and care is determined by socioeconomic status, and globally, many children lack access.[163] Consistent with children's right to be free from discrimination of all kinds, all children—particularly the most vulnerable—should enjoy equal access to ECEC.[164]

Quality is crucial. High-quality ECEC programs promote children's school readiness and enhance their educational progress and their long-term social development. The CRC requires states parties to "ensure that the institutions, services and facilities responsible for the care or protection of children shall conform with the standards established by competent authorities, particularly in the areas of safety, health, in the number and suitability of their staff, as well as competent supervision."[165] In particular, the services and institutions should satisfy professionally developed quality standards, and such quality ECEC should be provided to all children, regardless of background and family resources.

Despite the significance of early care and education for early childhood development and realization of young children's rights, the CRC makes no provision for preprimary education. However, ECEC is receiving increasing attention from the international human rights community, and momentum is building around a right to universal quality preprimary education. For example, in 2015, the United Nations adopted the Sustainable Development Goals (SDGs).[166] Among the SDGs adopted by all UN members is to ensure that all children have access to early childhood care and preprimary education by 2030.[167] More recently, the United Nations Educational, Scientific, and Cultural Organization (UNESCO) convened the World Conference on Early Childhood Care and Education, at which roughly 150 countries adopted UNESCO's *Tashkent Declaration and Commitments to Action for Transforming Early Childhood Care and Education*. The Declaration acknowledges the "relative neglect" of early childhood care and education in national and international policy agendas and adopts a number of ambitious principles and strategies for the "urgent transformation" of ECEC.[168]

The right to education intersects with other rights discussed in this chapter. First, the right to education is essential to vindicating children's participation rights. The rights to education and participation are reciprocal. ECEC settings are a "fundamental microsystem" for children's participation rights, in which ECEC professionals act as gatekeepers in facilitating young children's participation.[169] They provide an environment in which children can "learn the basics of democracy: how to express their desires, how to make plans and carry them through and how to make simple decisions."[170] At the same time, ensuring child participation in ECEC is an important feature of ECEC quality.[171] In early childhood, participation takes place within relationships with ECEC professionals, in which everyday engagement and communication influence young children's participation.[172] Play is one of the most influential contexts in which young children can realize their participation rights.[173] In early-year settings, recognizing young children's participation rights "require[s] the introduction of a culture rooted in a presumption that children are entitled to be involved, are competent to make a valid and valuable contribution, and can provide a unique contribution based on their own experience and operate as active agents influencing the world around them."[174] An example of an ECEC model in which children's participation is central is the Montessori method, in which children are empowered to construct and participate in their own learning as autonomous decision-makers.[175]

Second, the right to education implicates children's best interests, because "it is in the best interests of the child to have access to quality education, including early childhood education, non-formal or informal education and related activities, free of charge."[176] Finally, securing children's rights to education has important intersections with their right to protection. For example, education about children's rights to protection can empower young children to report maltreatment and be active agents in their own protection. Additionally, early care and education professionals are often on the front line of observing and reporting child maltreatment. Moreover, secure relationships with early care providers and teachers can act as mediating influences for children who have been subject to parental maltreatment.

States have broad responsibilities to implement children's right to education. First, they must ensure that primary education is compulsory and available without cost for all children.[177] The CRC also specifically recognizes states parties' obligations to ensure that children receive appropriate child-care services.[178] Even when early education and care are provided in the private sector, states parties bear ultimate responsibility for ensuring the provision of quality early education for all children.[179]

E. Protection from Harm

Children's protection rights under the CRC derive from their vulnerability to violence and harm and directly implicate their right to survival and development as articulated in Article 6. Article 3 provides, broadly, that states shall commit to ensuring "such protection and care as is necessary" for child well-being.[180] Article 19 further obligates states parties to "take all appropriate . . . measures to protect the child from all forms of physical or mental violence, injury or abuse, neglect or negligent treatment, maltreatment or exploitation, including sexual abuse," while in the care of parents, guardians, or other caregivers.[181] The "protective measures" include social programs to support children and those who care for them and other forms of prevention. Traditional views on protecting children have considered them to have little agency and viewed children primarily as "victims" of neglect, abuse, and other forms of violence. By contrast, interpreting the child's right to protection through a child rights lens requires a shift in how we understand children's role. The child rights perspective recognizes the child experiencing violence as a rights-bearing person with rights to physical and psychological integrity.

A primary component of the right to protection centers on what is commonly understood as the child protection or child welfare system—protecting children from abuse or neglect from parents and other caregivers.[182] In this context, the CRC obligates states to establish frameworks for "identification, reporting, referral, investigation, treatment and follow-up" in individual cases of maltreatment.[183] Article 19 and *General Comment No. 13* go into great detail about the various aspects of the child protection system—from prevention, reporting, investigation, and prosecution to treatment, alternative care, and follow-up.

The right to protection is critical during early childhood because of young children's particular risks and vulnerabilities. The Committee has underscored a number of concerns that are especially relevant in early childhood: abuse and neglect, substance abuse, sexual abuse and exploitation, and trafficking.[184] Certain populations of young children are especially vulnerable: those without families, refugees, children with disabilities, and children engaged in harmful work.[185] One of the individual risk factors for child maltreatment is age: being younger than four years old increases the likelihood of experiencing abuse or neglect.[186] Young children are at increased risk for child maltreatment and violence because they depend on others for care and protection and are relatively powerless to protect themselves.[187] Violent discipline is used with children as young as one year old, and UNICEF estimates that six out of ten children ages twelve to twenty-three months experience violent discipline methods.[188] The World Health Organization reports that almost three out of four children ages two to four suffer physical discipline and/or psychological abuse by parents and caregivers.[189] In some countries, younger children (two to four) are more likely than older ones (five to fourteen) to receive physical punishment.[190] Young girl children are especially vulnerable to early sexual abuse and exploitation inside and outside families.[191] Additionally, one in four children under age five worldwide live with a mother who has experienced intimate-partner violence.[192]

In addition to an increased likelihood of harm in early childhood, the harms experienced during early childhood are especially consequential, as discussed by Iruka in chapter 1.[193] A comprehensive understanding of protection from harm must recognize the significance of the family environment in early childhood. As in all contexts discussed in this chapter, the role of parents in children's right to protection has particular significance in early childhood. Most of the risk factors, as well as protective factors, for child maltreatment relate to the conditions, resources, and relationships parents have with their children—and indicate an important role for the state in supporting parents and families to mitigate such risk factors.[194] Early childhood is the stage during which children are most dependent on their parents; yet, in some circumstances, parents may represent the greatest threat to them. Violence against infants and young children often takes place at the hands of parents and caregivers while at home. Protection issues in early childhood often go undetected because most abuse takes place in the private family home.[195] If young children are not seen outside the home, they may remain invisible to state child protection services.[196]

Parental abuse and neglect can create tension with children's rights to know and be cared for by their parents.[197] Even in situations in which parents maltreat their children, separation from parents often represents a significant harm for children.[198] This is especially true in infancy and early childhood, when the development of secure attachments between children and their caregivers first begins. These early attachment relationships are critical for children's emotional and social development (see chapter 1).[199] The harms of separating children from their primary caregivers are exacerbated when out-of-home placements are themselves suboptimal and lacking in attachment figures for the child. Accordingly, Article 9 protects children from unnecessary separation from their parents, and the content of Article 19 complements this protection. Thus, when considering possible interventions in a child welfare investigation, priority must be given to the least intrusive intervention.

Despite the risk of maltreatment within the home, families also are central to the protection of children and the prevention of violence against them. Supportive parents and caregivers are a powerful shield against adversity and toxic stress, and they can empower children to protect themselves.[200] A common research finding in early childhood development is that, even in the face of adversity, children with at least one stable, responsive relationship with a parent, caregiver, or other adult can do well. "These relationships provide the support, scaffolding, and protection that both buffer children from developmental disruptions and help build key capabilities . . . to respond to adversity and thrive."[201]

Given the centrality of parents and other caregivers to young children's lives, a key element in implementing the right to protection for young children is to strengthen family life, support families, and partner with them at every stage of child protection, particularly prevention (through establishing good child caregiving) and in early intervention.[202] "Regardless of whether violence takes place, States Parties have a positive and active obligation to support and assist parents and other caregivers to secure . . . the living conditions necessary for the child's optimal development."[203]

Violence against children impedes the full implementation and realization of all other children's rights. Moreover, children's protection rights implicate and are interdependent on other rights and principles discussed in this chapter. First, the child's right to protection implicates and overlaps with children's participation rights. There is a reciprocal relationship between child protection and child participation: child participation promotes prevention and protection, and child protection enhances child participation. The right to be heard is especially significant for young children who are at a particular risk of violence, because it enables them to signal or report maltreatment or the risk of maltreatment to others. Children have the right to be heard and to have their views considered throughout the child protection process, and child participation is also integral to child caregiving and prevention strategies. Although the best interests principle is the guiding determination in child protection interventions, adults' own sense of what is best for the child cannot override obligations to respect all rights of the child, including the child's right to be heard and to have their views taken into account. Additionally, child participation can help mitigate the inherently disempowering effects of violence against children, and children should be encouraged to participate in interventions, recovery, and rehabilitation.[204]

Second, the best interests principle must permeate the child protection system process, from prevention to reporting, investigation, potential removal, and also the repair and reunification of families. Indeed, the underlying metric the state must use at every juncture in the child welfare system is whether the action or decision advances the best interests of the child.[205] Third, children's right to protection implicates their right to the enjoyment of the highest attainable standard of health.

The child's right to protection is frequently implemented in urgent situations often in a post hoc way, in which states and institutions intervene after serious harm or threatened harm to children has occurred. These interventions, while necessary, come only after harm has come to a child. Responding to harm after the fact has only a limited impact on eliminating and preventing harm. Recognizing these limitations, the Committee has critiqued "reactive efforts focusing on symptoms and consequences rather than causes, and by strategies which are fragmented rather than integrated."[206] The Committee has therefore sought to move beyond a reactive, post hoc approach to child protection, in favor of a "holistic approach to implementing article 19 based on the CRC's overall perspective on securing children's rights to survival, dignity, well-being, health, development, and non-discrimination."[207] In other words, *prevention* is a foundational element of the right to protection. Particularly in early childhood, proactive measures by states to support children and their families are important, because prevention and intervention during early childhood can impact the child's current well-being as well as future development and prospects.[208]

Parent-focused prevention efforts require states to support parents and caregivers in their knowledge and understanding of positive caregiving and creating a safe and enriching family environment in which children can flourish. Especially relevant for early childhood, these prevention measures should include the provision of services that support children and their families and caregivers to enhance the quality of child rearing and care children receive across multiple domains. Particular to young children, this should include prenatal and postnatal services, home visitation programming, and quality early childhood development programming. Beyond individual families, prevention efforts should include community-based programming to assist parents experiencing economic and psychosocial challenges and public assistance programs to strengthen standards of living.[209] Prevention in early childhood also includes caregiver education, in particular education on positive parenting, as well as information on the risks of harm to children and training on how to listen to children (including the youngest children) and respect their views.

Child development science has established that severe neglect appears at least as great a threat to child well-being as physical abuse, and perhaps even greater (see chapter 1).[210] At a societal level, state prevention efforts should be focused on social policies to reduce the root causes of child maltreatment, particularly neglect: inequality, lack of adequate housing and services, poverty and unemployment, substance use disorders, inadequate child protection policies, and other social policies (or the lack of policies) that contribute to poor standards of living, socioeconomic inequality, or instability. Rather than simply guaranteeing protection, Article 3 embodies a broader principle of ensuring the child's well-being and development. Because Article 3 obliges states to provide children with protection and *care*, the right to protection also implicates the right to provision.[211] For example, Article 27 of the CRC recognizes "the right of every child to a standard of living adequate for the child's physical, mental, spiritual, moral and social development."[212] In this broader sense, children's well-being includes their "basic material, physical, educational, and emotional needs, as well as needs for affection and safety."[213]

III. Conclusion

As discussed throughout this chapter, rights in early childhood are interrelated and interdependent, as are children's relationships with the adults and communities in which they live. Successful early childhood development policy must be holistic, recognizing the vulnerabilities, capacities, and views of children, while also supporting the social contexts and institutions with which children most frequently interact in early childhood: parents and families, child care and early education, schools, health-care settings, and state institutions tasked with protecting children. Recognizing this indivisibility, the Committee urges states to create "rights-based, multidimensional and multisectoral strategies that promote a systematic and integrated approach to law and policy development."[214] Given the dynamism and complexity of early childhood, the most effective way to realize children's rights in early childhood is to develop a comprehensive program of complementary laws and policies on early childhood development.

Early childhood development has gained increasing attention and urgency in the children's rights space. Of particular significance, among the SDGs is to ensure that by 2030, all children have access to quality early childhood development programming.[215] Full implementation of children's rights in this stage requires intensive resource investments. As the Committee has observed, "it is important that there are sufficient allocations of public investment in services, infrastructure and overall resources allocated to the field of early childhood development."[216] While not essential to a rights-based analysis of early childhood development programming, abundant research demonstrates that the earliest investments in children yield substantial dividends in human capital over the arc of children's lives, as well as cost savings for society.[217]

A final note: Comprehensive early childhood development services cannot fulfill children's rights if they do not reach the children who most need them. As the Committee has observed, equal access to quality services is important for young children, particularly when important services like health, education, child care, and welfare programming are not universally available.[218] This is especially true for children living in poverty and experiencing other sorts of adversity; it is they who would most benefit from high-quality services. But they are least likely to receive high-quality services in a system in which essential services are provided through a combination of state, private market, and charitable programing.[219] The Committee has observed that "large numbers of young children grow up in difficult circumstances that are frequently in violation of their rights . . . and are especially vulnerable to the harm caused by unreliable, inconsistent relationships with parents and caregivers, or growing up in extreme poverty and deprivation, or being surrounded by conflict and violence or displaced from their homes as refugees, or any number of other adversities prejudicial to their well-being."[220] The Committee, therefore, has urged states to "ensure that all young children [and their primary caregivers] are guaranteed access to appropriate and effective services, including programs of health, care and education specifically designed to promote their well-being."[221]

Thirty years after the CRC's adoption, recent commentary on young children's rights has characterized the field of children's rights in early childhood as a "messy, complex reality" with "flaws, disparities, strengths and weaknesses."[222] And yet, as recognized throughout this chapter, significant progress is being made both in research about young children's rights and in effective implementation of those rights in the lives of young children.

A rights-based approach to early childhood recognizes both children's vulnerability and potential. Effectuating children's rights in early childhood requires programming that is aimed at developing children's strengths—physically, intellectually, socially, and emotionally.[223] This approach emphasizes supporting the strengths and resources of children themselves, as well as the larger domains and contexts in which they live: family, school, community, institutions, and religious and cultural systems.[224] Ultimately, a child rights approach to early childhood requires a "shift away from traditional beliefs that regard early childhood mainly as a period for the socialization of the immature human being towards mature adult status."[225] With the recognition that young children require physical and emotional care and guidance in order to exercise their rights, children must be respected as persons in their own right and recognized as active members in society whose rights must be fully implemented and honored.[226]

NOTES

1 Likewise, expectations and norms about children vary across cultures. Fran Barone, "A Cross-Cultural Perspective on Childhood," Human Relations Area Files, Yale University, February 12, 2015, https://hraf.yale.edu.

2 UN Committee on the Rights of the Child, *General Comment No. 7: Implementing Child Rights in Early Education*, para. 4, CRC/C/GC/7 (November 1, 2005).

3 Jane Murray, Beth Blue Swadener, and Kylie Smith, foreword to *The Routledge International Handbook of Young Children's Rights*, ed. Jane Murray, Beth Blue Swadener, and Kylie Smith (New York: Routledge, 2020), xxiv.

4 Jacob Egbert Doek, Lothar Friedrich Krappmann, and Yanghee Lee, "Introduction to the General Comment," in *A Guide to General Comment 7: "Implementing Child Rights in Early Childhood,"* ed. United Nations Committee on the Rights of the Child, United Nations Children's Fund (UNICEF), and Bernard van Leer Foundation (The Hague: Bernard van Leer Foundation, 2006), 31.

5 UN Committee on the Rights of the Child, *General Comment No. 7*, para. 2(c).

6 Doek, Krappmann, and Lee, "Introduction to the General Comment," 32.

7 Office of the High Commissioner for Human Rights (OHCHR), "International Human Rights Law," December 2, 2022, www.ohchr.org.

8 UN Convention on the Rights of the Child, art. 1, November 20, 1989, 1577 U.N.T.S. 3 (hereafter CRC).

9 Peter Laugharn, "Our Children Are the Future," in UN Committee on the Rights of the Child, UNICEF, and Bernard van Leer Foundation, *Guide to General Comment 7*, 24.

10 CRC, art. 6.

11 Emma Samman and Joa Lombardi, *Childcare and Working Families: New Opportunity or Missing Link?* (New York: UNICEF, July 2019), www.unicef.org.

12 UN Committee on the Rights of the Child, *General Comment No. 7*, para. 16.

13 CRC, art. 5.

14 UN Committee on the Rights of the Child, *General Comment No. 7*, para. 18.

15 Laugharn, "Our Children Are the Future," 25.

16 CRC, art. 18(2).

17 CRC, art. 18(3).

18 CRC, arts. 5, 14(2).
19 UN Committee on the Rights of the Child, *General Comment No. 7*, para. 17.
20 Sheila Varadon, "The Principle of Evolving Capacities under the UN Convention on the Rights of the Child," *International Journal of Children's Rights* 27 (2019): 306–338.
21 UN Committee on the Rights of the Child, *General Comment No. 7*, para. 17.
22 Varadon, "Principle of Evolving Capacities," 318.
23 UN Committee on the Rights of the Child, *General Comment No. 12: The Right of the Child to Be Heard*, para. 5, CRC/C/GC/12 (July 20, 2009).
24 CRC, art. 12(1).
25 UN Committee on the Rights of the Child, *General Comment No. 12*, para. 3.
26 Ibid., para. 4.
27 UN Committee on the Rights of the Child, *General Comment No. 7*, para. 14(a).
28 Ibid., para. 14(b).
29 Ibid., para. 14.
30 National Children's Trust, Costa Rica, "Inputs to the Working Groups of the Committee on the Rights of the Child," in UN Committee on the Rights of the Child, UNICEF, and Bernard van Leer Foundation, *Guide to General Comment 7*, 122.
31 UN Committee on the Rights of the Child, *General Comment No. 12*, para. 28.
32 Laura Lundy, "'Voice Is Not Enough': Conceptualizing Article 12 of the United Nations Convention on the Rights of the Child," *British Educational Research Journal* 33, no. 6 (December 2007): 927–942.
33 Ibid., 931–933.
34 CRC, art. 12(1).
35 UN Committee on the Rights of the Child, *General Comment No. 7*, para. 14.
36 UN Committee on the Rights of the Child, *General Comment No. 12*, para. 21.
37 Ibid., para. 29.
38 UN Committee on the Rights of the Child, *General Comment No. 7*, para. 14.
39 CRC, art. 13.
40 UN Committee on the Rights of the Child, *General Comment No. 12*, para. 84.
41 Laura Lundy, Lesley McEvoy, and Bronagh Byrne, "Working with Young Children as Co-researchers: An Approach Informed by the United Nations Convention on the Rights of the Child," *Early Education and Development* 22, no. 5 (October 2011): 719, 721.
42 Priscilla Alderson and Tamaki Yoshida, "Babies' Rights, When Human Rights Begin," in Murray, Swadener, and Smith, *Routledge International Handbook of Young Children's Rights*, 36.
43 UN Committee on the Rights of the Child, *General Comment No. 12*, para. 21.
44 UN Committee on the Rights of the Child, *General Comment No. 7*, para. 14(c).
45 CRC, art. 12.
46 Lundy, McEvoy, and Byrne, "Working with Young Children as Co-researchers," 732.

47 Ibid., 731–734.
48 Ibid., 733.
49 UN Committee on the Rights of the Child, *General Comment No. 12*, para. 27.
50 Ibid., paras. 93–94.
51 UN Committee on the Rights of the Child, "Recommendations," in UN Committee on the Rights of the Child, UNICEF, and Bernard van Leer Foundation, *Guide to General Comment 7*, 27.
52 Ibid.
53 Thomas Moswer, Paul Leseman, Edward Melhuish, Martine Broekhuizen, and Pauline Slot, *D6.3: European Framework of Quality and Wellbeing Indicators* (Curriculum and Quality Analysis and Impact Review of European Early Childhood Education and Care, February 20, 2017), 34, https://ecec-care.org.
54 Anna Housley Juster and Morgan Leichter-Saxby, "Citizens at Play: Children's Participation through Community-Based Opportunities for Child-Directed Play," *Global Studies of Childhood* 4, no. 2 (2014): 77.
55 Ina Lekkai, "Children's Right to Participate in Early Childhood Education," *Journal of Humanities and Social Sciences (IOSR-JHSS)* 21, no. 12 (2016): 18.
56 Juster and Leichter-Saxby, "Citizens at Play," 86.
57 UNICEF, *Guidance on Child and Adolescent Participation* (New York: UNICEF, December 2021), 4, www.unicef.org.
58 Ibid., 13–14.
59 Ibid., 21.
60 Nigel Thomas, "Children and Young People's Participation in Research," in *International Perspectives and Empirical Findings on Child Participation: From Social Exclusion to Child-Inclusive Policies*, ed. Tali Gal and Benedetta Duramy (New York: Oxford Academic, 2015), 92.
61 Lundy, McEvoy, and Byrne, "Working with Young Children as Co-researchers," 714–736.
62 Ibid., 723–730.
63 Ibid., 734.
64 Nadine Correia, Cláudia Camilo, Cecília Aguiar, and Fausto Amaro, "Children's Right to Participate in Early Childhood Education Settings: A Systematic Review," *Children and Youth Services Review* 100 (2019): 76–88.
65 UN Committee on the Rights of the Child, *General Comment No. 12*, para. 132.
66 Lundy, "Voice Is Not Enough," 940.
67 UN Committee on the Rights of the Child, *General Comment No. 12*, para. 135.
68 Ibid., para. 2.
69 CRC, art. 3(1).
70 UN Committee on the Rights of the Child, *General Comment No. 7*, para. 13.
71 UN Committee on the Rights of the Child, *General Comment No. 14: The Right of the Child to Have His or Her Best Interests Taken as a Primary Consideration*, para. 40, CRC/C/GC/14 (May 29, 2013).
72 Ibid., para. 51.

73 Ibid., para. 52–79.
74 UN Committee on the Rights of the Child, *General Comment No. 7*, para. 13.
75 UN Committee on the Rights of the Child, *General Comment No. 13: The Right of the Child to Freedom from All Forms of Violence*, para. 61, CRC/C/GC/13 (April 18, 2011).
76 Lundy, "Voice Is Not Enough," 938.
77 UN Committee on the Rights of the Child, *General Comment No. 14*, para. 53.
78 Ibid., para. 53.
79 Doek, Krappmann, and Lee, "Introduction to the General Comment," 33.
80 UN Committee on the Rights of the Child, *General Comment No. 14*, para. 43.
81 UN Committee on the Rights of the Child, *General Comment No. 12*, para. 74.
82 UN Committee on the Rights of the Child, *General Comment No. 14*, para. 44.
83 Ibid., para. 54.
84 Ibid., para. 44.
85 UN Committee on the Rights of the Child, *General Comment No. 12*, para. 21.
86 CRC, art. 12(2).
87 Douglas E. Abrams, Naomi R. Cahn, Catherine J. Ross, and Linda McClain, *Contemporary Family Law*, 5th ed. (St. Paul, MN: West Academic, 2019), 862–863.
88 UN Committee on the Rights of the Child, *General Comment No. 14*, para. 96.
89 American Bar Association (ABA), *Model Act Governing the Representation of Children in Abuse, Neglect, and Dependency Proceedings* (2011), § 1, *Commentary*.
90 Ibid., § 3, *Commentary*.
91 Ibid., § 3(a)–(b).
92 Ibid., § 3, *Commentary*.
93 Ibid., § 7(d).
94 Ibid., § 7(d).
95 Ibid., § 7(d), *Commentary*.
96 CRC, art. 18(1).
97 CRC, art. 18(2).
98 UN Committee on the Rights of the Child, *General Comment No. 14*, para. 44.
99 Ibid., para. 79.
100 Ibid., para. 71.
101 CRC, art. 24.
102 UN Committee on the Rights of the Child, *General Comment No. 15: The Right of the Child to the Enjoyment of the Highest Standard of Health*, para. 23, CRC/C/GC/15 (April 17, 2003).
103 Ibid., para. 17.
104 Venkatraman Chandra-Mouli, "A Classroom's Worth of Children under 5 Is Dying Every Minute," in UN Committee on the Rights of the Child, UNICEF, and Bernard van Leer Foundation, *Guide to General Comment 7*, 17–18.
105 Ibid., 18.
106 CRC, art. 24(2)(c).
107 UN Committee on the Rights of the Child, *General Comment No. 15*, para. 50.

108 UN Committee on the Rights of the Child, *General Comment No. 7*, para. 6(e).
109 Ibid., para. 27.
110 CRC, art. 24(2)(a).
111 UN Committee on the Rights of the Child, *General Comment No. 15*, paras. 33–34.
112 Laugharn, "Our Children Are the Future," 20.
113 Centers for Disease Control and Prevention (CDC), "Early Brain Development and Health," accessed August 10, 2023, www.cdc.gov; National Institutes of Health (NIH), "HEALthy Brain and Child Development Study (HBCD)," last modified February 21, 2023, https://heal.nih.gov; Center on the Developing Child, "In Brief: Early Childhood Mental Health," 2013, https://developingchild.harvard.edu.
114 Patrice L. Engle, "Health and Nutrition," in UN Committee on the Rights of the Child, UNICEF, and Bernard van Leer Foundation, *Guide to General Comment 7*, 15.
115 UN Committee on the Rights of the Child, *General Comment No. 7*, para. 27(a).
116 CRC, art. 24(2)(d).
117 Jonathan Todres and Louise Howe, "What the Convention on the Rights of the Child Says (and Doesn't Say) about Abortion and Family Planning," in *The United Nations Convention on the Rights of the Child: An Analysis of Treaty Provisions and Implications of U.S. Ratification*, ed. Jonathan Todres, Mark E. Wojcik, and Cris Revaz (New York: Brill Academic, 2006), 163–175.
118 UN Committee on the Rights of the Child, *General Comment No. 15*, para. 18.
119 I note that women and girls are not the only individuals who can become pregnant, birth a child, and breastfeed. Transgender men and nonbinary individuals can also be gestational parents. For the purposes of this chapter, I use the terminology adopted by the Convention and the Committee on the Rights of the Child.
120 UN Committee on the Rights of the Child, *General Comment No. 15*, para. 53. For specifically recommended interventions, see ibid., para. 54.
121 Ibid., para. 9.
122 UN Committee on the Rights of the Child, "General Comment No. 7: 'Implementing Child Rights in Early Childhood,'" in UN Committee on the Rights of the Child, UNICEF, and Bernard van Leer Foundation, *Guide to General Comment 7*, 39.
123 CRC, art. 2(1).
124 UN Committee on the Rights of the Child, *General Comment No. 15*, para. 1.
125 Ibid., para. 2.
126 Ibid., para. 78.
127 Ibid., para. 67.
128 UN Committee on the Rights of the Child, "General Comment No. 7: 'Implementing Child Rights in Early Childhood,'" 46.
129 UN Committee on the Rights of the Child, *General Comment No. 15*, para. 67.
130 Ibid., para. 19.
131 Mary Donnelly and Ursula Kilkelly, "Participation in Healthcare: The Views and Experiences of Children and Young People," *International Journal of Children's Rights* 19, no. 1 (2011): 107–125.

132 Ibid., 108.

133 UN Committee on the Rights of the Child, *General Comment No. 12*, para. 102.

134 Mary Donnelly and Ursula Kilkelly, "Child-Friendly Healthcare: Delivering on the Right to Be Heard," *Medical Law Review* 19, no. 1 (2011): 27–54.

135 UN Committee on the Rights of the Child, *General Comment No. 15*, para. 21.

136 Donnelly and Kilkelly, "Child-Friendly Healthcare," 53.

137 Donnelly and Kilkelly, "Participation in Healthcare," 115.

138 Ibid., 110.

139 Ibid., 118–120.

140 Luigina Mortari, Ludovica De Panfilis, and Luca Ghirotto, "Listening and Deciding: Children's Rights in Pediatric Palliative Care," in Murray, Swadener, and Smith, *Routledge International Handbook of Young Children's Rights*, 293.

141 Ibid., 300.

142 Ibid., 301.

143 UN Committee on the Rights of the Child, *General Comment No. 15*, para. 13.

144 Ibid., para. 12.

145 Ibid., para. 73.

146 UN Committee on the Rights of the Child, *General Comment No. 7*, para. 27.

147 Ibid., 27(a).

148 UN Committee on the Rights of the Child, *General Comment No. 15*, para. 75.

149 Ibid., 92.

150 UN Committee on the Rights of the Child, *General Comment No. 1: The Aims of Education*, para. 12, CRC/GC/2001/1 (April 17, 2001).

151 CRC, art. 29(1).

152 CRC, art. 28(1)(a).

153 UN Committee on the Rights of the Child, *General Comment No. 7.*, para. 28.

154 CRC, art. 29(1)(a).

155 UN Committee on the Rights of the Child, *General Comment No. 1*, para. 2.

156 UN Committee on the Rights of the Child, *General Comment No. 7*, para. 30.

157 CRC, art. 42.

158 UN Committee on the Rights of the Child, "Recommendations," 28.

159 UN Committee on the Rights of the Child, *General Comment No. 7*, para. 33.

160 Jonathan Todres and Ursula Kilkelly, "Advancing Children's Rights through the Arts," *Human Rights Quarterly* 44, no. 1 (February 2022): 38–55.

161 Jonathan Todres and Sarah Higinbotham, *Human Rights in Children's Literature: Imagination and the Narrative of Law* (New York: Oxford University Press, 2016).

162 UN Committee on the Rights of the Child, "Recommendations," 27.

163 United Nations Educational, Scientific, and Cultural Organization (UNESCO), "Monitoring SDG 4: Early Childhood Care and Education," Global Education Monitoring Report, accessed June 8, 2023, www.unesco.org; Kylie Smith, "Introduction: Young Children's Provision Rights," in Murray, Swadener, and Smith, *Routledge International Handbook of Young Children's Rights*, 228.

164 CRC, art. 2.

165 CRC, art. 3(3).
166 United Nations General Assembly, *Transforming Our World: The 2030 Agenda for Sustainable Development* (2015), Res. 71/1.
167 Ibid., goal 4.2, 17.
168 UNESCO, *Tashkent Declaration and Commitments to Action for Transforming Early Childhood Care and Education* (November 16, 2022), paras. 4, 10.
169 Nadine Correia, Cecília Aguiar, and the PARTICIPA Consortium, "Children's Rights to Participate: The Lundy Model Applied to Early Childhood Education and Care," *International Journal of Children's Rights* 30, no. 2 (2022): 376–403.
170 Patrice L. Engle, "Comprehensive Policy Implications of Child Rights," in UN Committee on the Rights of the Child, UNICEF, and Bernard van Leer Foundation, *Guide to General Comment 7*, 17.
171 Nadine Correia, Cláudia Camilo, Cecília Aguiar, and Fausto Amaro, "Children's Right to Participate in Early Childhood Education Settings: A Systematic Review," *Children and Youth Services Review* 100 (2019): 76–88.
172 Berit Bae, "Children's Right to Participate—Challenges in Everyday Interactions," *European Early Childhood Education Research Journal* 17, no. 3 (September 2009): 391–406.
173 Ibid., 396, 401.
174 Gerison Lansdown, "Can You Hear Me? The Right of Young Children to Participate in Decisions Affecting Them" (Working Papers in Early Child Development 36, Bernard van Leer Foundation, The Hague, 2005), 19.
175 Jane Gibbs and Linda Cooper, "Challenges to Participatory Approaches in Early Years Practice," in *Children's Rights 0–8: Promoting Participation in Education and Care*, ed. Mallika Kanyal (Abingdon, UK: Routledge, 2014), 101, 104.
176 UN Committee on the Rights of the Child, *General Comment No. 14*, para. 79.
177 CRC, art. 28(1)(a).
178 CRC, art. 18(3).
179 UN Committee on the Rights of the Child, *General Comment No. 7*, para. 32.
180 CRC, art. 3(2).
181 CRC, art. 19(1).
182 Critics of the child welfare system in the United States frequently refer to it as the "family regulation system," in recognition that as currently implemented, in practice, the system serves to surveil and police families rather than to promote child well-being.
183 CRC, art. 19(2).
184 UN Committee on the Rights of the Child, *General Comment No. 7*, para. 36.
185 Ibid., 36.
186 CDC, "Risk and Protective Factors," accessed May 1, 2023, www.cdc.gov.
187 UN Committee on the Rights of the Child, *General Comment No. 7*, para. 36.
188 UNICEF, *A Familiar Face: Violence in the Lives of Children and Adolescents* (New York: UNICEF, 2017), 19, 27.

189 World Health Organization, "Child Maltreatment," September 19, 2022, www.who.int.

190 UNICEF, *Familiar Face*, 26.

191 UN Committee on the Rights of the Child, "General Comment No. 7: 'Implementing Child Rights in Early Childhood,'" 51.

192 UNICEF, *Familiar Face*, 19.

193 Center on the Developing Child, *From Best Practices to Breakthrough Impacts: A Science-Based Approach to Building a More Promising Future for Young Children and Families* (Cambridge, MA: Center on the Developing Child, Harvard University, 2016), 4.

194 UN Committee on the Rights of the Child, *General Comment No. 13*, para. 72(e)–(f).

195 Eunice Lumsden, "The (In)Visibility of Infants and Young Children in Child Protection," in Murray, Swadener, and Smith, *Routledge International Handbook of Young Children's Rights*, 110.

196 Ibid.

197 CRC, art. 7(1).

198 Fiona Donson and Aisling Parkes, eds., *Parental Imprisonment and Children's Rights* (Abingdon, UK: Routledge, 2022).

199 John Oates, ed., *Attachment Relationships: Quality of Care for Young Children*, Early Childhood in Focus 1 (Milton Keynes, UK: Open University, 2007).

200 Center on the Developing Child, *From Best Practices to Breakthrough Impacts*, 11.

201 Ibid., 14.

202 UN Committee on the Rights of the Child, *General Comment No. 13*, para. 72(d).

203 Ibid., para. 5.

204 Paulo Sérgio Pinheiro, *World Report on Violence against Children* (Geneva: United Nations, 2006), 20; UN Committee on the Rights of the Child, *General Comment No. 13*, para. 63.

205 UN Committee on the Rights of the Child, *General Comment No. 13*, para. 3(f).

206 Ibid., para. 12.

207 Ibid., para. 11.

208 UN Committee on the Rights of the Child, *General Comment No. 7*, para. 8.

209 CRC, art. 27.

210 Center on the Developing Child, *From Best Practices to Breakthrough Impacts*, 15.

211 Kirsten Sandberg, "Children's Right to Protection under the CRC," in *Human Rights in Child Protection: Implications for Professional Practice and Policy*, ed. Asgeir Falch-Eriksen and Elisabeth Backe-Hansen (Cham, Switzerland: Palgrave Macmillan, 2018), 15–16.

212 CRC, art. 27(1).

213 UN Committee on the Rights of the Child, *General Comment No. 14*, para. 71.

214 UN Committee on the Rights of the Child, "Recommendations," 25.

215 UN General Assembly, *Transforming Our World*, 17.

216 UN Committee on the Rights of the Child, "Recommendations," 26.

217 UNICEF, *A World Ready to Learn: Prioritizing Quality Early Childhood Education* (New York: UNICEF, April 2019), 20.

218 UN Committee on the Rights of the Child, *General Comment No. 7*, para. 12.

219 Ibid., para. 12.

220 Ibid., para. 36.

221 Ibid., para. 24.

222 Murray, Swadener, and Smith, "Introduction," 10.

223 Laugharn, "Our Children Are the Future," 22–23.

224 UN Committee on the Rights of the Child, *General Comment No. 13*, para. 59; Laugharn, "Our Children Are the Future," 20. See also Barbara Bennett Woodhouse, *The Ecology of Childhood: How Our Changing World Threatens Children's Rights* (New York: New York University Press, 2020).

225 UN Committee on the Rights of the Child, *General Comment No. 7*, para. 5. At the same time, the Committee accepts the variety of ways in which early childhood is envisioned across different cultures and urges states to draw on "beliefs and knowledge about early childhood in ways that are appropriate to local circumstances and changing practices, and respect traditional values," as long as these local practices and values are not discriminatory, do not negatively affect children's health and well-being, or are not contrary to children's best interests. Ibid., 8.

226 Ibid., 5.

3

Contemporary Children's Rights Issues in Early Childhood

CARALYN BLAISDELL AND E. KAY M. TISDALL

I. Introduction

The very first article of the United Nations Convention on the Rights of the Child (CRC) sets out the definition of the child, for the Convention, and defines it by age: a child is every human being below the age of eighteen years (Article 1).[1] The diversity of children within this definition is immense, from the intersections of ethnicity, religion, gender, culture, socioeconomic status—and of age. With such diversity, there can be lacunae in the children's rights field, with some issues and some groups of children receiving more attention than others.[2] One such gap is young children: as suggested by Harbach (chapter 2), all too often, children's rights advocacy and academia generally have concentrated on older children and young people. The very active areas in early childhood studies have often not been tapped into by "mainstream" children's rights. Early childhood development, as laid out in chapter 1, has an extensive history of research and attention to young children, including infants and the prenatal stage. But its current research and knowledge has often been ignored by the children's rights field, in part because of concerns that child development has not fully respected children's rights in its assumptions and methods.[3] It is timely to learn from early childhood studies to inform the more general discussions of childhood and children's rights.

As is argued in the next section, the social constructions of childhood differ across disciplines, across time, and across policy domains. Such constructions not only are of academic interest but have pervasive implications for policies and practices that frame young children's lives. Particular constructions of childhood have become predominant in early childhood, as touched on by Harbach (chapter 2): from child development's focus on age, stages, and "evolving capacity" to more recent international attention to investing in early childhood for long-term individual and societal benefits. Such constructions both help and hinder children's human rights in the three "testing" issues explored in this chapter. These three issues have been selected as being of contemporary interest and concern and as raising both conceptual and substantive issues. First, the chapter explores young children's participation rights and how they can be restricted or enhanced by intergenerational relations and power. Second, the chapter considers the pervasiveness of young children's construction as "vulnerable" and dependent, which has led to policy and practice investment in early years but has not always focused attention on how young children are made situationally vulnerable. Third, the chapter discusses the challenges posed by decolonial and antiracist thought in early childhood studies. All three issues are framed by how we, as adults, construct childhood and particularly early childhood.

II. Constructions of Childhood, Children's Rights, and Young Children

Young children have not always been constructed as rights holders. Recognizing young children as such is a particular social construction of childhood. If they are understood as being rights holders, this extends to young children the benefits of rights frameworks: as beings who have human dignity that requires respect and who have entitlements, can make claims, and can expect remedies if required. This is a contrast to "traditional" constructions of childhood, at least in the Global North, which have tended to depict children and childhood (and especially young children and early childhood) as vulnerable, dependent, incompetent, and innocent.[4] Children's rights thus are part of reconstructing childhood.

A fundamental concept within childhood studies is that childhood is socially constructed. This is effectively expressed by Alan Prout and Allison James in their seminal chapter in 1990: "a child's immaturity is a biological fact, but how this immaturity is understood and how it is made meaningful is a fact of culture."[5] Their form of social construction argues that children and childhood are thought of in particular ways, with certain aspects considered important—for example, immaturity—which create certain understandings of children and childhood. With this concept, they go on to suggest a paradigm for the "new sociology of childhood," with a number of principles salient for this chapter:

- Childhood is a variable of social analysis.
- Children's social relationships and cultures are worthy of study in their own right.
- Children are and must be seen as active in the construction and determination of their own social lives, of the lives of the people around them, and of the society in which they live.
- Proclaiming a new paradigm of childhood is also part of reconstructing childhood in society.[6]

These principles underline that it is important to consider childhood as a category in research, as a particular life stage. Poverty statistics, for example, radically change when the analysis is done on numbers of children living in poverty rather than family households: the statistics show far more children living in poverty than family households living in poverty.[7] Many population surveys by governments are done only with adults, leaving lacunae in knowledge about children's experiences, from crime to racism. Recognizing children as social actors has supported the children's rights arguments for participation rights: that children should have their views considered in all matters that affect them, as expressed in Article 12(1) of the CRC. Respecting children's relationships and cultures has inspired research that involves children not only as the objects of research but also as research participants.[8] Thus, while children's rights studies can be differentiated from childhood studies, their mutual respect for children and childhood can reinforce one another in their reconstructions of childhood.[9]

The literature documents a host of constructions of childhood, which are particularly applied to young children. The iconic depictions of vulnerability, innocence, dependence, and incompetence are associated with young children (whereas, for example, teenagers—who are children under the CRC until the age of eighteen—can be treated as "dangerous" and "problematic," should they be considered antisocial or involved in crime). Jens Qvortrup and colleagues introduced the idea that children tend to be seen as "human becomings" rather than "human beings," influenced by child development's highly influential research on children's staged cognitive development.[10] The power of child development over the past century fed into the increased schooling of children and parental investment in their own children's development, so that the focus on "age" became naturalized and was presumed to be universal.[11] Qvortrup reflects on the results: "Adulthood is regarded as the goal and end-point of individual development or perhaps even the very meaning of a person's childhood. [Such a view is] however revealing for the maybe unintended message, which seems to indicate that children are not members or at least not integrated members of society. This attitude, while perceiving childhood as a moratorium and a preparatory phase, thus confirms postulates about children as 'naturally' incompetent and incapable."[12]

Thus, focusing on children as human becomings can risk their not being recognized as social actors in their own societies or not being viewed and valued as fully fledged citizens, until they become adults. This focus on children as human becomings is particularly strong in early childhood, with the emphasis in the Global North on young children meeting their developmental "milestones" and parents urged to recognize the importance of their child's earliest years to their future outcomes.[13]

More recently, commentators such as Anne Trine Kjørholt note the social construction of childhood as an "investment."[14] Exemplified by the economic case put forward for investing in early childhood, referred to in the conclusion of Harbach's chapter (chapter 2), this construction values childhood but primarily in relation to what benefits children will bring society in the longer term.[15] There is often a specific monetary logic to human capital arguments. For example, Jorge Luis García and colleagues claim that high-quality, birth-to-five-year-old early childhood programs for disadvantaged children have a financial return on investment of 13.7 percent.[16] Thus, young children are valued, but primarily in relation to the human capital they will accumulate through schooling and will then contribute to society and the economy once they become adults. Peter Moss, for example, is highly critical of this approach, in crowding out other values such as democracy, experimentation, and potentiality for young children and for society.[17] Young children are the containers for the investment, with pressures on parents and early care providers to ensure that the foundations of literacy and other skills are present and that children are well prepared for formal primary schooling.[18]

The CRC is itself not immune from particular constructions of childhood. For example, it is largely age based, identifying all children under the age of eighteen (unless legal majority is obtained earlier) for the purposes of the CRC (Article 1). It has rights for children that are not found in other international human rights treaties for adults: ranging from children's rights to have their best interests as a primary consideration (Article 3(1)) to specifying children's rights to play and recreation as well as rest and leisure (Article 31(1)).[19] The CRC's preamble stresses that children need "special safeguards and care," because of their "physical and mental immaturity" (referring back to the Declaration of the Rights of the Child), which harks back to Prout and James's quotation earlier: this immaturity is understood as a reason that children need particular and additional rights to adults, because they need special protections. The CRC thus embodies constructions of childhood, within its text, that have both emancipatory and controlling elements, which are discussed in the following section.

III. Constructions of Early Childhood: Exploring Three Contemporary Issues

A. Young Children's Participation Rights and Agency: Relational Understandings

Young children's lives are intertwined with social life, and they are affected by, and have influence on, contemporary social and political issues. A rights-based perspective offers radical potential to take young children seriously, particularly through fulfillment of their participation rights. The right to be heard (Article 12(1)) is a general principle of the CRC, and thus this article should be considered "in the interpretation and implementation of all other rights."[20] Other participation rights enshrined in the CRC include the right to freedom of expression (Article 13), the right to freedom of thought, conscience, and religion (Article 14), the right to freedom of association and peaceful assembly (Article 15), and the right to access, receive, and give information (Article 17).

As Michael Freeman argues, the inclusion of participation rights in the CRC challenges notions of the child as a "concern or object of intervention" and encourages constructions of the child as a subject in their own right.[21]

The implementation of children's participation rights has not been straightforward, however, with one particular area of consideration being child-adult relations. For example, the UN Committee on the Rights of the Child has defined children's participation as "ongoing processes, which include information-sharing and dialogue between children and adults based on mutual respect, and in which children can learn how their views and those of adults are taken into account and shape the outcome of such processes."[22]

Therefore, the ways that both childhood and adulthood are understood, and how those social categories relate to one another, directly shape how children's participation rights are implemented. The interplay, messiness, and blurred boundaries between understandings of childhood and adulthood are particularly relevant.[23] This resonates with broader calls in the childhood studies and children's rights fields to examine how children's participation rights are "lived" and experienced in the context of children's many relationships, rather than by an individuated participating child separated from their life context.[24]

As reviewed in Harbach's chapter 2, early childhood throws up particular considerations for children's participation rights, which are both challenging and generative with regard to children's rights more broadly. There is no lower age limit on participation rights. For example, although Article 12(1) establishes that due weight should be given to the child's views in accordance with the age and maturity of the child, this is not an invitation to create age-based exclusions of young children from their Article 12 entitlement.[25] The UN Committee on the Rights of the Child acknowledged in its *General Comment on Implementing Child Rights in Early Childhood* that young children's agency as participants in social life is often "overlooked, or rejected as inappropriate on the grounds of age and immaturity."[26] Priscilla Alderson suggests that one reason young children's participation rights are overlooked is that participation is often conceptualized very narrowly, as children "talking, thinking and deciding" at the invitation of adults.[27] Under such a narrow model, many young children will be excluded because they do not communicate primarily through speech. Alderson also argues that constructions of (early) childhood play a key role in how participation is understood. If adults believe that they know best and that young children are fundamentally unreliable, they are unlikely to seek young children's views. Alderson argues for the generative potential of young children's participation rights, in which adults trust in young children's ability to think creatively, find enjoyment and excitement in working cooperatively with young children, and have confidence that participation is vital and rewarding.

Perhaps reacting to limited understandings of participation rights as "talking, thinking and deciding," early childhood research has tended to diverge from the language of rights and instead focus on the language of "listening." For example, Moss and colleagues explain their preference for "listening," arguing that rights-based approaches can become too prescriptive, individualized, and tightly bound to notions of autonomy.[28] In their view, "listening" offers more space for a relational understanding of communication and dialogue. However, "listening to children" can just as easily become tokenistic when it is seen as an end in itself or is done for appearances, rather than with meaningful weight being given to children's views.[29] Again, relational understandings of children's rights offer a way through this unhelpful division. Stuart Aitken theorizes children's rights as universal in spirit but without the "annihilation of difference" that universality implies. For Aitken, CRC rights retain their radical potential only if reframed into fluid, relational processes in which difference is at their center. A monadic "universal individual" of children's rights cannot capture the emotionality, specificity, or heterogeneity of young people's lives or their embeddedness in relationships (with other people, with place, with nonhuman actors, with state relations).[30] Looking to early childhood, Aitken's argument points away from a narrow conception of participation rights as "talking, thinking, deciding" and toward close attention to young children's multimodal ways of "being and doing."[31]

A relational understanding of participation rights also helps illuminate young children's agency. Again, theorizations of children's agency have moved toward the relational, with agency understood as exercised within webs of relationships, at multiple scales.[32] If agency is understood as something that is exercised, it can then incorporate relations between self and other that are not necessarily about individuated choice-making.[33] It underlines the importance of scaffolding young children's participation, through information and support. Further, it illuminates the potential for young children to participate in different domains (e.g., in their households, their local communities, early years provisions) and the potential for everyday, localized participation to feed into collective decision-making at larger scales. However, power relations remain key to understanding how young children's agency and participation rights are received and understood. In some formulations, power is framed as a commodity: adults are presumed to possess power, and children to lack power. This theorization of power can be seen in the early childhood literature. Marek Tesar, for example, describes the "ruthless" power that structures an early childhood setting, governing children into compliance.[34] Here, power is somewhat depersonalized and abstract; it exists as a system of control. Michael Gallagher, in contrast, analyzes power as being enacted, through diverse techniques and in diverse circumstances by both adults and children.[35] Despite the ambiguity of power relations between adults and children, there does seem to remain an enduring imbalance between adulthood and childhood as social groups, particularly with regard to resource distribution and control over institutions.[36] In relation to young children's participation rights, this imbalance makes the sensitive and transparent interpretation of children's communication all the more important, requiring that adults show patience and creativity, tuning into young children's interests and preferred ways of communicating. The state, as ultimately accountable for implementing the CRC, has a responsibility in supporting adults to do so, through, for example, training and resourcing the early years workforce; enabling parents, caregivers, and other important adults in children's lives to have the time, values, and skills to listen to young children; and influencing social norms so that young children have opportunities to express their views in daily life as well as within the full range of community, educational, and legal services they encounter.[37]

B. Young Children's Vulnerability

If constructions of childhood as vulnerable, dependent, and innocent can restrict young children's participation rights, such constructions make it easy to claim their rights to protection, prevention, and provision. This is evident in the history of the CRC; the original Geneva Declaration on the Rights of the Child (1924) was adopted by the League of Nations with an emphasis on meeting children's fundamental needs. For example, the Geneva Declaration's introductory paragraph states "that mankind owes to the Child the best that it has to give," while the five subsequent points are oriented toward children's development and protection. The 1959 UN Declaration on the Rights of the Child introduces the wording of children needing "special safeguards and care" in its preamble (repeated in the CRC, as discussed earlier). The expanded list of rights includes more specificity toward protection and provision (e.g., in relation to education and social security) but also some recognition of children as civil rights holders (e.g., that children are entitled to a name and nationality from birth). The 1989 CRC goes even further, with a much-expanded list of rights but still retaining a strong thread of protection and the current articulation of the best interests principle. The origins of international statements on children's human rights, then, start from the protection of vulnerable children, and this remains a key component in their most recent articulations.

The dependency of young children on parents and the family is reified by the CRC in several ways. Article 5, for example, requires states parties to "respect the responsibilities, rights and duties of parents . . . to provide . . . appropriate direction and guidance in the exercise by the child of the rights recognized in the present Convention." Parents must do so "in a manner consistent with the evolving capacities of the child." Notions of child development are thus incorporated into Article 5, with younger children presumably having more limited capacity and thus parents having a greater role in providing direction and guidance. While children have the right to an adequate standard of living, it is the parents who have the primary responsibility to secure this, and states parties have the responsibility to assist parents as required (Article 27). Parents are mentioned thirty-three times in the CRC: as Freeman writes, the CRC is as much a parents' charter as it is a statement of children's rights.[38] As stated in Harbach's chapter 2 and specified in the UN Committee on the Rights of the Child's *General Comment on Early Childhood*, states parties' duties to support parents in realizing their children's rights have particular resonances for young children.[39]

Such international statements demonstrate the increasing recognition of childhood as an important stage, which requires attention, investment, and protection. As traced by historians such as Hugh Cunningham and Harry Hendrick, the rise of child development as a research field in the twentieth century supported and encouraged an emphasis on children's schooling and an interest in children's development.[40] With the addition of neuroscience and attention by economists, this policy interest has expanded to young children in recent decades, with growing investments in early childhood education as a critical stage in children's development that is perceived as having long-term positive effects for children and for society more generally.[41] Over the past century, increased attention has been given to children from the very youngest of ages: infant mortality has become a key indicator, with worldwide programs and surveillance from UNICEF and the World Health Organization to lower the rates in every country. Young children are often the iconic pictures for disaster philanthropy, shown in the media to encourage the public to give money to address crises in different parts of the world.[42] Another example is the international focus on Adverse Childhood Experiences, in which specific childhood experiences are claimed to act as traumatic stressors, having lifelong effects on health and behavior, including disrupting early brain development.[43] (For further discussion, see chapter 1.) In turn, these claims rest on contested arguments that the first three years of life are uniquely vulnerable.[44] These trends demonstrate how the early years of childhood have gained more and more notice and investment, to protect vulnerable children at these critical stages in their development.

Typically, children are considered one of the most vulnerable groups in times of disaster.[45] It was thus unusual that children were not the most at risk from COVID-19 with regard to their survival and health. Evidence quickly settled that older populations were much more vulnerable to severe illness than were younger populations; children's deaths from COVID-19 were greatly outweighed by those of much-older age groups.[46] But young children were very much impacted by the policy responses to COVID-19, which showed the precarity of children's rights.[47] Most countries instituted forms of "lockdown," where people were restricted to their households, with limited to no access to community spaces, and the closing down of schools and early childhood learning centers. Such policy responses sought to protect rights to survival and development, particularly for the more at-risk older groups of people, but they put at risk other rights of young children to protection, play and leisure, education, and more. An analysis in Scotland, for example, shows how families and households were not always safe places for children, in contexts of domestic and child abuse more generally.[48] This was recognized from the start in the Scottish government's responses, but emergency professional responses tended to focus on how adults could access information and help, rather than children's own access. Children who were in unsafe situations at home articulated this, and notably, the nongovernmental sector stepped in to coproduce resources for children to access help. The closing down of learning spaces physically underlined their importance not only for children's learning and access to help but also for children's access to very basic services: for example, young children lost access to food and health services in the Global North and South, to detrimental effect.[49] Evidence from Brazil shows the interdependencies of young children's basic survival rights, their parents' (and particularly their mothers') opportunities, and the situations of more impoverished communities.[50] Many of the mothers lost their income, as they were involved in more informal parts of the economy and lacked access to child care, and thus poverty for their children became even more problematic and prevalent. Violence in both households and in the communities increased, so that young children were even more restricted in their households. Young children thus might not have been particularly vulnerable to the COVID-19 virus with regard to their immediate survival, but the policy responses to the pandemic made them particularly vulnerable with regard to their safety and to barriers to their rights to provision and protection.

Reflecting on the experiences of the COVID-19 pandemic showcases the universality of vulnerability: that we are all potentially vulnerable and dependent, as an inevitable condition of being human and embodied.[51] Vulnerability need not, then, be seen as inevitably negative: it can also inspire creativity, nurture trust, and develop or deepen relationships.[52] Jonathan Herring particularly develops these ideas with a childhood and children's rights focus.[53] He points out that law has constructed children as being inherently vulnerable, with too little attention to how relationally, situationally, and structurally they are made particularly vulnerable. Such ideas provide a foundational challenge to the pervasive construction of early childhood as vulnerable. It questions the special accommodations given to middle-aged, able-bodied adults. The commonalities between young children and adults are recognized. The state would have a role in social provision, addressing people's vulnerability. Young children's "vulnerability" would no longer be a quintessential, defining characteristic based on their age and stage, providing space potentially for more emancipatory constructions of childhood that better recognize children's agency and better address structural disadvantages.[54]

Vulnerability as a particular characteristic of young children and their childhoods has historical roots within children's rights and child development. This has led to particular claims for protection and provision. The experience of COVID-19 shows that such claims were not necessarily strong enough to protect these claims during responses to COVID-19, with children's lack of access to public spaces and public services making them situationally more vulnerable in many contexts. While the recognition of universal vulnerability would need first to be embraced by those who are more powerful, it provides the opportunity to rethink assumptions about children and adults and ensuing policy and practice.

C. Decolonial and Antiracist Perspectives in Early Childhood

Children's right to nondiscrimination (Article 2) is identified as a general principle of the CRC.[55] Article 2 of the CRC puts an obligation on states parties to ensure the rights in the Convention to each child in their jurisdiction without discrimination of any kind. In contemporary times, this obligation is particularly salient, due to a surge in attention to antiracist movements and interlinked attention to the legacies of European colonial projects.[56] Indeed, substantial work in early childhood studies attends to such legacies of colonialism, and early childhood has long been seen as a time to disrupt and challenge racism, often folded into wider discussions of antibias education.[57]

Young children's daily lives are affected by these concerns. To give one example, since 2018, in Denmark, young children living in designated "ghetto" areas are required to attend mandatory preschool for twenty-five hours per week, whereas other Danish families are allowed to choose whether their child attends a preschool. Noncompliance could result in the stoppage of welfare payments for the family.[58] The mandatory preschool focuses on instruction in "Danish values," including the Danish language and Christian traditions, and has been connected to anti-Muslim discrimination in Denmark, as "ghetto" areas are designated, in part, based on the percentage of residents who are immigrants or descendants from so-called non-Western countries.[59] There are clear links in this policy to children's right to nondiscrimination (Article 2), as the policy attaches stigma to individuals of certain backgrounds. "Ghetto" families now carry an extra duty in order to access social welfare rights.[60] However, as Kathrin Houmøller and colleagues suggest, this state intervention is framed as a welfare and integration policy for potentially vulnerable children.[61] In the process, the children from ethnic-minority backgrounds are categorized as inherently "other," with early childhood practitioners using the phrase "these children" and "the kinds of children that we have here" to delineate them as fundamentally different from their white Danish peers.[62] Burcu Yigit Turan argues that these differentiations of ghettos and ghetto children in Danish social policy perpetuate colonial bordering dynamics, in which the state draws lines around spaces, creating racialized, hierarchical classes of people.[63] In the Danish policy, several constructions of children appear to coalesce: the child as inherently vulnerable, the child as an opportunity for early intervention, and the (racialized) child as a threat to society. As this example illustrates, young children do not live outside society or politics; early childhood is not a neutral time of life. Instead, young children's lives are intertwined with political contexts, such as the one in Denmark.

One key area of analysis in early childhood studies has been the international flow of knowledge about young children's development. The knowledge that is privileged tends to be created in Global North contexts and exported internationally—often by large, for-profit companies but also by NGOs and supranational bodies such as the Organisation for Economic Co-operation and Development (OECD).[64] For example, Radhika Viruru describes how the Qatari government, as part of educational reform, hired the RAND Corporation of the United States to provide "proven" techniques for teaching early literacy, despite objections that the techniques were based on Global North approaches and devalued local practices and beliefs.[65] Similarly, Mathangi Subramanian, writing from India, argues that Western theorizations of play see it as a vehicle for individual child development, failing to recognize how play contributes to the collective good.[66] As both examples illustrate, when knowledge about early childhood development is exported, there is a tendency toward "whole world views" on what is best for children, particularly when it comes to education and social welfare.[67] Crucially, this global view of a good early childhood privileges Global North, individualized ways of being and learning, rarely acknowledging other ways of knowing and doing in early childhood.[68] In contrast, decolonial and antiracist scholars have made these global flows of power and knowledge visible and have contested them. For example, Veronica Pacini-Ketchabaw attempts to create friction between different ways of knowing in early years, in the context of a forest visited by young children on traditional Indigenous Songhees (or Lekwungen) land. She brings together the Songhees' names for the places in the forest, the "universal" internationally recognized Latin names given to the plants in the forest, and children's own names for the forest. She particularly notes the ongoing erasure of Indigenous place-names. By holding all three naming practices together, Pacini-Ketchabaw argues, educators make the ethics and politics of the forest space more visible and engage with a construction of childhood as intertwined into historical relations with both human and nonhuman actors.[69]

In critiquing dominant forms of knowledge, therefore, decolonial thought offers space to confront and resist historical and ongoing Eurocentrism.[70] Indeed, early childhood studies offers a hopeful foundation for decolonial, antiracist fulfillment of rights that can be useful in the wider field of childhood studies and children's rights. Michelle Salazar Pérez, for example, argues that Black feminist thought offers radical potential in early years theory, to support early years practitioners to understand power hierarchies, to value the situated experiences of individuals outside of dominant identities, and to inspire social activism among early years practitioners and children.[71] Although the CRC is not specifically named by Pérez, there are clear connections between Pérez's work and young children's rights, particularly in regard to their civil and political rights. For example, her call for social activism relates to young children's right to nondiscrimination (Article 2) and their right to be heard (Article 12), as well as their right to freedom of expression (Article 13) and freedom of thought, conscience, and religion (Article 14). Similarly, Ranita Cheruvu proposes that early childhood educators foster "culturally sustaining pedagogies," in which children's multilingual and multicultural practices are honored.[72] She gives the example of a kindergarten classroom in which children and families were invited to tell the stories of their child's name and to contribute to a class book about names in their own languages and English.[73] Indeed, when approached through a culturally sustaining lens, children's literature offers great potential for fulfillment of children's rights; for example, the Centre for Literacy in Primary Education in London has demonstrated the power of diverse representation in children's texts, when those characters are authentically depicted, thoughtfully developed, and multidimensional.[74] As discussed in Harbach (chapter 2), these concerns relate directly to children's right to an education that realizes the full development of each child, including their cultural identity (Article 29).

Akiea Gross, an early childhood educator, provides concrete examples of what antiracist social activism with young children could look like, creating visual prompts for critical conversations with young children, exploring concepts like police abolition and Indigenous land rights.[75] Rather than envision a particular outcome for these conversations, Gross makes space for young children to engage in a practice of wondering and imagination about how social life could be different.[76] Gross is a pro-Black, abolitionist educator who seeks to disrupt white-centered discourses that ignore the knowledge of Black, Indigenous, and other communities of color.[77] Again, although children's rights are not specifically named by Gross, the work of abolitionist early childhood educators such as Gross links with the underpinning construction of young children as rights holders. In particular, Gross sees young children as co-creators of more liberated futures; like Pérez, the work of abolitionist early childhood educators connects to young children's rights to be heard, freedom of expression, and freedom of thought.[78] Connecting to ideas of vulnerability, Gross's work demonstrates an acknowledgment of sociopolitical concerns that impact directly (and disproportionately) on the vulnerability of particular groups of children to oppression and discrimination, while also emphasizing the agency of young children to engage in social activism in dialogue with adults.

IV. Conclusion

This chapter selected three issues as particular tests for the children's rights field generally, with lessons to learn from considering young children and early childhood studies literature. Across the three issues, relationality is a key theme. Human rights are arguably always dependent on others, as such rights require relationships between the rights holder and the duty bearer and systems for accountability to ensure that rights are respected, fulfilled, and supported. Children's participation rights are particularly circumscribed in the CRC: Article 12(1) is in fact a very modest participation right, with children having the right to have their views be given due weight in decision-making but not necessarily to make the decision.[79] The dependence of young children on adults truly "listening," for much of decision-making, highlights the potential and reality of relationality for children's rights. Aitken's encouragement of us to consider aspects of emotionality and the nonhuman, in spaces and places for participation, and the recognition of multimodal ways of "being and doing" not only apply to young children and their rights but to all people and all human rights. As discussed earlier, the CRC is filled with state parties' obligations to parents and care givers, so they in turn can ensure that young children's human rights are respected, fulfilled, and supported. There are thus interconnections between the child as a rights holder and other rights holders (like parents), and the fulfillment of one person's rights can affect the other person's rights, in positive, neutral, or negative ways. Relationality recognizes these intersections of obligations and rights, between all people's human rights, and how the recognition of one person's rights can shape another's.

Recognizing the importance of relationships is not new in the rights field. From feminist and disability studies to communitarianism and now to vulnerability philosophy, the liberal concept of the rational autonomous individual has been robustly critiqued as fictional and problematic: the argument is that as humans, we are social and inherently dependent on each other and relational.[80] But to maintain the advantages of rights "talk" while developing relational and intergenerational theorizations can be difficult. Human rights are fundamentally about respecting each person's human dignity, including children's human dignity. It is about recognizing children—including very young children—as social actors. It gives recognition to them as rights holders in their own right, within their families, and not only subsumed in their families and households. This is amply exemplified by the potential power relations in young children realizing their participation rights, as the identification of their views is highly dependent on adult interpretation. Thus, articulations of relational rights need to maintain a careful consideration of power and a vigilance to ensure that everyone's human dignity is respected.

Vulnerability is a persistent theme for young children and the social constructions of their childhood, at least in the Global North. This is evident from the early history of the CRC to current worldwide agendas to lessen infant mortality and address Adverse Childhood Experiences (ACEs) and to the experience of developing effective policy responses to the COVID-19 pandemic. All of these examples show the benefits of the construction—children are recognized as important and deserving of special provision and protection—but also the disadvantages: vulnerability is not a position of power, and it can impose other people's (adults') values and views of children's best interests. Legal philosophy's consideration of the universality of vulnerability unsettles this assumption of children as being a quintessentially vulnerable group, to instead consider how children are made situationally, relationally, and systematically vulnerable. It provides challenges to how we (i.e., adults) organize ourselves socially and legally, questioning the assumptions of middle-class, middle-aged (and Global North) individuality and autonomy baked into much of our legislation and children's rights frameworks.

Such unsettling is taken to even more places if we consider the lessons from decolonial and antiracist thought in early childhood studies. By identifying, naming, and resisting Global North knowledge production, researchers and activists make visible the political contexts with which children's lives are intertwined. Research with young children shows the limitations of only considering the human social world, being a forerunner with regard to recognizing the intertwining with materiality and affordances. This has only been furthered by the challenges of decolonization and learning from Indigenous peoples to create a more holistic perspective that no longer distinguishes between "nature" and the "environment" and people and their rights. Research with young children shows the potential of the collective and the relational and the importance of realizing rights in context. In notable examples in the early years and child-care developments in different parts of the world, abolitionist educators draw on liberatory social movements to imagine (young) children as co-creators of more just futures.

The insights of considering how childhood is constructed, across time, geographies, and policies, continue to question assumptions and show new opportunities. They particularly ask us to query knowledge production, that of other disciplines as well as our own, and to be open to the flexibility and dynamic nature of the complexities of young children's lives, the challenges they face, and the responses that are needed.[81] In unsettling times, it may be a protective instinct to deflect or dismiss what is troubling. However, as this chapter has argued, examining constructions of childhood, informed by early childhood studies, offers an opportunity to stay with that trouble and recognize the ways that being unsettled creates space for new understandings and actions.[82]

NOTES

1 UN Convention on the Rights of the Child, art. 1, November 20, 1989, 1577 U.N.T.S. 3 (hereafter CRC) ("Article 1: For the purposes of the present Convention, a child means every human being below the age of eighteen years unless under the law applicable to the child, majority is obtained earlier.").

2 See, for example, Christina McMellon and E. Kay M. Tisdall, "Children and Young People's Participation Rights: Looking Backwards and Forwards," *International Journal of Children's Rights* 28, no. 1 (2020): 158.

3 E. Kay M. Tisdall, John M. Davis, Deborah Fry, Kristina Konstantoni, Marlies Kustatscher, M. Catherine Maternowska, and Laura Weiner, *Critical Childhood Studies: Global Perspectives* (London: Bloomsbury, 2023).

4 In this chapter, the terms "Global North" and "Global South" are used to refer to groups of countries that previously might have been referred to as "developed" and "developing" nations. We recognize the problems of this binary, as countries can differ substantially within these categories. We recognize that the "Majority World"—in relation to population, poverty, land mass, and lifestyles—rests in the Global South, while the Global North is the "Minority World." Samantha Punch and E. Kay M. Tisdall, "Exploring Children and Young People's Relationships across Majority and Minority Worlds," *Children's Geographies* 10, no. 3 (2012): 241–248.

5 Alan Prout, and Allison James, "A New Paradigm for the Sociology of Childhood? Provenance, Promise and Problems," in *Constructing and Reconstructing Childhood: Contemporary Issues in the Sociological Study of Childhood*, ed. Allison James and Alan Prout (London: Falmer, 1990), 7.

6 Paraphrased from ibid., 8.

7 Michael Wyness, *Childhood and Society: An Introduction to the Sociology of Childhood*, 2nd ed. (Basingstoke, UK: Palgrave Macmillan, 2012).

8 E. Kay M. Tisdall, "Applying Human Rights to Children's Participation in Research," in *Seen and Heard: An Interdisciplinary Exploration of Researching Children's Participation, Engagement and Voice*, ed. Miriam Twomey and Clare Carroll (Oxford, UK: Peter Lang, 2018), 17–38.

9 Berry Mayall, "The Sociology of Childhood in Relation to Children's Rights," *International Journal of Children's Rights* 8, no. 3 (2000): 243–259.

10 Jens Qvortrup, Marjatta Bardy, Giovanni Sgritta, and Helmut Wintersberger, eds., *Childhood Matters: Social Theory, Practice and Politics* (Aldershot, UK: Avebury, 1994).

11 Hugh Cunningham, *Children and Childhood in Western Society since 1500* (London: Routledge, 1995); Harry Hendrick, *Children, Childhood and English Society, 1880–1990* (Cambridge: Cambridge University Press, 1997).

12 Jens Qvortrup, "Childhood Matters: An Introduction," in Qvortrup et al., *Childhood Matters*, 2.

13 Cara Dosman and Debbi Andrews, "Anticipatory Guidance for Cognitive and Social-Emotional Development: Birth to 5 Years," *Paediatrics Child Health* 17, no. 2 (2012): 75–80. See, for example, National Academies of Sciences, Engineering, and Medicine, *Parenting Matters: Supporting Parents of Children Ages 0–8* (Washington, DC: National Academies Press, 2016).

14 Anne Trine Kjørholt, "Childhood as Social Investment, Rights and the Valuing of Education," *Children & Society* 27, no. 4 (2013): 245–257.

15 For example, see James Heckman, Rodrigo Pinto, and Peter Savelyev, "Understanding the Mechanisms through Which an Influential Early Childhood Program Boosted Adult Outcomes," *American Economic Review* 103, no. 6 (2013): 2052–2086.

16 Jorge Luis García, James J. Heckman, Duncan Ermini Leaf, María José Prados, "The Life-Cycle Benefits of an Influential Early Childhood Program" (CESR-Schaeffer Working Paper No. 2016-18, 2016), https://papers.ssrn.com.

17 Peter Moss, "Beyond the Investment Narrative," *Contemporary Issues in Early Childhood* 14, no. 4 (2013): 370–372.

18 Organisation for Economic Co-operation and Development (OECD), *Starting Strong: Early Childhood Education and Care* (Paris: OECD, 2001), www.oecd.org.

19 "Rest and leisure" are referred to in other international human rights texts. Article 24 of the Universal Declaration of Human Rights states, "Everyone has the right to rest and leisure, including reasonable limitation and periodic holidays with pay." Universal Declaration of Human Rights (UDHR), art. 24, G.A. Res. 217 (III) A (December 10, 1948). Article 7(d) of the International Covenant on Economic, Social and Cultural Rights states the right of everyone to "rest, leisure and reasonable limitation of working hours and period holidays with pay, as well as remuneration for public holidays." International Covenant on Economic, Social and Cultural Rights, art. 7(d), 993 U.N.T.S. 3 (December 16, 1966).

20 UN Committee on the Rights of the Child, *General Comment No. 12: The Right of the Child to Be Heard*, para. 2, CRC/C/GC/12 (2009).

21 Michael Freeman, "Children's Rights as Human Rights," in *The Palgrave Handbook of Childhood Studies*, ed. Jens Qvortrup, William A. Corsaro, and Michel-Sebastian Honig (Basingstoke, UK: Palgrave Macmillan, 2011), 383.

22 UN Committee on the Rights of the Child, *General Comment No. 12*, para. 3.

23 Madeleine Leonard, *The Sociology of Children, Childhood and Generation* (London: SAGE, 2016).

24 Mehmoona Moosa-Mitha, "A Difference-Centred Alternative to Theorization of Children's Citizenship Rights," *Citizenship Studies* 9, no. 4 (2005): 369–388; Manfred Liebel, Karl Hanson, Iven Saadi, and Wouter Vandenhole, *Children's Rights from Below: Cross-Cultural Perspectives* (Basingstoke, UK: Palgrave Macmillan, 2012).

25 Lothar Krappmann, "The Weight of the Child's View (Article 12 of the Convention on the Rights of the Child)," *International Journal of Children's Rights* 18, no. 4 (2010): 501–513.

26 UN Committee on the Rights of the Child, *General Comment No. 7: Implementing Child Rights in Early Childhood*, para. 14, CRC/C/GC/7 (2005).

27 Priscilla Alderson, *Young Children's Rights: Exploring Beliefs, Principles and Practice*, 2nd ed. (London: Jessica Kingsley, 2008), 79. See also Harbach's chapter 2, for a similar argument.

28 Peter Moss, Alison Clark, and Anne Trine Kjorholt, introduction to *Beyond Listening: Children's Perspectives on Early Childhood Services*, ed. Alison Clark, Anne Trine Kjorholt, and Peter Moss (Bristol, UK: Policy, 2005), 1–16.

29 UN Committee on the Rights of the Child, *General Comment No. 5: General Measures of Implementation of the Convention on the Rights of the Child*, para. 12, CRC/GC/2003/527 (November 2023).

30 Stuart C. Aitken, *Young People, Rights and Place: Erasure, Neoliberal Politics and Postchild Ethics* (London: Routledge, 2018), 11.

31 See Alderson, *Young Children's Rights*, 80.

32 Spyros Spyrou, Rachel Rosen, and Daniel Thomas Cook, eds., *Reimagining Childhood Studies* (London: Bloomsbury Academic, 2019).

33 Sarada Balagopalan, "Childhood, Culture, History: Redeploying 'Multiple Childhoods,'" in Spyrou, Rosen, and Cook, *Reimagining Childhood Studies*, 23–40.

34 Marek Tesar, "Reconceptualising the Child: Power and Resistance within Early Childhood Settings," *Contemporary Issues in Early Childhood* 15, no. 4 (2014): 360–367.

35 Michael Gallagher, "'Power Is Not an Evil': Rethinking Power in Participatory Methods," *Children's Geographies* 6, no. 2 (2008): 137–150.

36 Lesley Gallacher, "Theorising Young Children's Spaces," in *The SAGE Handbook of Early Childhood Research*, ed. Ann Farrell, Sharon L. Kagan, and E. Kay M. Tisdall (London: SAGE, 2016), 118–132; Leonard, *Sociology of Children, Childhood and Generation*.

37 UN Committee on the Rights of the Child, *General Comment No. 7*.

38 E.g., Michael Freeman, "Introduction: Children's Rights Past, Present and Future," in *The Future of Children's Rights*, ed. Michael Freeman (Leiden: Brill Nijhoff, 2014), 3–15.

39 UN Committee on the Rights of the Child, *General Comment No. 7*.

40 Cunningham, *Children and Childhood in Western Society*; Hendrick, *Children, Childhood and English Society*.

41 M. Suzanne Zeedyk, "Wired for Communication: How the Neuroscience of Infancy Helps in Understanding the Effectiveness of Intensive Interaction," in *Intensive Interaction: Theoretical Perspectives*, ed. Dave Hewett (London: SAGE, 2012), 55–71. E.g., Heckman, Pinto, and Savelyev, "Understanding the Mechanisms through Which an Influential Early Childhood Program Boosted Adult Outcomes," 2052–2086; OECD, *Starting Strong 2017: Key OECD Indicators on Early Childhood Education and Care* (Paris: OECD, 2017).

42 Karen Wells, *Childhood in a Global Perspective*, 3rd ed. (Cambridge, UK: Polity, 2021). While such visibility may raise charitable giving, notably children risk being overlooked in disaster responses and reconstruction efforts, or if their particular needs are recognized, the emphasis can be solely on children's physical survival needs, and sometime protection, but not their full range of rights. Amer Jabry, ed., *After the Cameras Have Gone: Children in Disasters*, 2nd ed. (Woking, UK: Plan UK, 2005), www.streetchildren.org; Claire O'Kane, "Children in Conflict Situations: Applying Childhood Research with a Focus on the Early Years," in Farrell, Kagan, and Tisdall, *SAGE Handbook of Early Childhood Research*, 327–344; Jonathan Todres, "Mainstreaming Children's Rights in Post-disaster Settings," *Emory International Law Review* 25, no. 3 (2011): 1233–1261.

43 World Health Organization, "Adverse Childhood Experiences International Questionnaire (ACE-IQ)," January 28, 2020, www.who.int.

44 David Wastell and Sue White, "Blinded by Neuroscience: Social Policy, the Family and the Infant Brain," *Families, Relationships and Societies* 1, no. 3 (2012): 397–414.

45 Montserrat Marin-Ferrer, Karmen Poljanšek, and Luca Vernaccini, *INFORM—Index for Risk Management: Concept and Methodology, Version 2017* (European Commission, Joint Research Centre, 2017); Jabry, *After the Cameras Have Gone*.

46 See, for example, COVID-19 Ined, "An Unprecedented Context of Health Crisis," accessed June 24, 2022, https://dc-covid.site.ined.fr. Although the death or serious illness of any child or older person is a significant loss.

47 Katie Reid, E. Kay M. Tisdall, and Fiona Morrison, "Children's Rights Impact Assessments in Times of Crisis: Learning from COVID-19," *International Journal of Human Rights* 27, nos. 9–10 (2022): 1319–1325.

48 E. Kay M. Tisdall and Fiona Morrison, "Children's Human Rights under COVID-19: Learning from Children's Rights Impact Assessments," *International Journal of Children's Rights* 27, nos. 9–10 (2022): 1475–1491.

49 For example, see Lynn McNair, John Ravenscroft, Irene Rizzini, E. Kay M. Tisdall, Linda Biersteker, Fortunate Shabalala, S'lungile K. Thwala, Clement N.

Dlamini, Malcolm Bush, Malibongwe Gwele, and Lizette Berry, "The Impact of the Covid-19 Global Health Pandemic in Early Childhood Education within Four Countries," *Social Inclusion* 10, no. 2 (2022): 160–171; Niyati Parekh, Shahmir H. Ali, Joyce O'Connor, Yessim Tozan, Abbey M. Jones, Ariadna Capasso, Joshua Foreman, and Ralph J. DiClemente, "Food Insecurity among Households with Children during the COVID-19 Pandemic: Results from a Study among Social Media Users across the United States," *Nutrition Journal* 20, no. 73 (2021): 20–73.

50 McNair et al., "Impact of the Covid-19 Global Health Pandemic."

51 Martha Albertson Fineman, "The Vulnerable Subject: Anchoring Equality in the Human Condition," *Yale Journal of Law and Feminism* 20, no. 1 (2008): 1–18.

52 Danielle Petherbridge, "What's Critical about Vulnerability? Rethinking Interdependence, Recognition, and Power," *Hypatia* 31, no. 4 (2016): 589–604.

53 Jonathan Herring, "Vulnerability, Children and the Law," in *Law and Childhood Studies*, ed. Michael Freeman (Oxford: Oxford University Press, 2012), 243–263; Jonathan Herring, *Vulnerability, Childhood and the Law* (Cham, Switzerland: Springer, 2018).

54 An example would be applying Caroline Criado Perez's searing analysis of priorities in snow clearing to children. In her 2019 book, her first chapter discusses that when a Swedish town prioritized snow clearing sidewalks—which women were more likely to use in taking their children to school and other unpaid care activities—rather than roads, hospital admissions for injuries went down. This underlined how the policies were not gender neutral; nor, we would add, were they age/generation neutral. Caroline Criado Perez, *Invisible Women: Exposing Data Bias in a World Designed for Men* (London: Chatto and Windus, 2019).

55 UN Committee on the Rights of the Child, *General Comment No. 5*.

56 UN General Assembly, *Elimination of Racism, Racial Discrimination, Xenophobia and Related Intolerance: Comprehensive Implementation of and Follow-Up to the Durban Declaration and Programme of Action*, Resolution, A/RES/75/237 (2020).

57 Gaile S. Cannella and Radhika Viruru, *Childhood and Postcolonization: Power, Education, and Contemporary Practice* (London: Routledge, 2004); Radhika Viruru, "The Impact of Postcolonial Theory on Early Childhood Education," *Journal of Education* 35, no. 1 (January 2005): 7–30; Amita Gupta, *Early Childhood Education, Postcolonial Theory, and Teaching Practices in India: Balancing Vygotsky and the Veda* (New York: Palgrave Macmillan, 2006); Amita Gupta, "Tracing Global-Local Transitions within Early Childhood Curriculum and Practice in India," *Research in Comparative and International Education* 3, no. 3 (September 2008): 266–280; Joseph Tobin, Yeh Hsueh, and Mayumi Karasawa, *Preschool in Three Cultures Revisited: China, Japan, and the United States* (Chicago: University of Chicago Press, 2009). Zeenat Janmohamed, "Chapter Eight: Rethinking Anti-Bias Approaches in Early Childhood Education: A Shift toward Anti-Racism Education," *Counterpoints* 252 (2005): 163–182; Louise Derman-Sparks and Patricia G. Ramsey, *What If All the Kids Are White: Anti-Bias Multicultural Education with Young Children and Families*, 2nd ed. (New York: Teachers College Press, 2011);

Frances E. Aboud, Colin Redoux, Linda R. Tropp, Christia Spears Brown, Ulrike Niens, Noraini M. Noor, and the Una Global Evaluation Group, "Interventions to Reduce Prejudice and Enhance Inclusion and Respect for Ethnic Differences in Early Childhood: A Systematic Review," *Developmental Review* 32, no. 4 (2012): 307–336.

58 Ellen Barry and Martin Selsoe Sorensen, "In Denmark, Harsh New Laws for Immigrant 'Ghettos,'" *New York Times*, July 1, 2018, www.nytimes.com.

59 Sara Salem, "Denmark's Quest to Socialize the 'Ghettos': The Dark History of Forced Assimilation in Europe," *Discover Society* (blog), July 3, 2018, https://archive.discoversociety.org; Liz Fekete, "Islamophobia in Denmark: From Parallel Societies to the 'Ghetto List,'" Institute of Race Relations, July 18, 2018, https://irr.org.uk; Anika Seemann, "The Danish 'Ghetto Initiatives' and the Changing Nature of Social Citizenship, 2004–2018," *Critical Social Policy* 41 no. 4 (2021): 586–605.

60 Seemann, "Danish 'Ghetto Initiatives.'"

61 Kathrin Houmøller, Susanne Bregnbæk, and Nanna Jordt Jørgensen, *Mending the Holes in the Map of Denmark? Day Care Institutions in the Borderlands between Inclusion and Exclusion in Social Housing Areas* (Berlin: European Education Research Association, 2018), https://eera-ecer.de.

62 Kathrin Houmøller, "Making the Invisible Visible? Everyday Lived Experiences of 'Seeing' and Categorizing Children's Well-Being within a Danish Kindergarten," *Childhood* 25, no. 4 (2018): 488–500.

63 Burcu Yigit Turan, "Superkilen: Coloniality, Citizenship, and Border Politics," in *Landscape Citizenships*, ed. Tim Waterman, Jane Wolff, and Ed Wall (London: Routledge, 2021), 56–78.

64 Helge Wasmuth and Elena Nitecki, "Global Early Childhood Policies: The Impact of the Global Education Reform Movement and Possibilities for Reconceptualization," *Global Education Review* 4, no. 2 (2017): 1–17.

65 Radhika Viruru, "Postcolonial Perspectives on Early Childhood Literacy," in *The SAGE Handbook of Early Childhood Literacy*, 2nd ed., ed. Joanne Larson and Jackie Marsh (London: Sage, 2013). The RAND Corporation is an American think tank and research institute.

66 Mathangi Subramanian, "Rethinking Play: A Postcolonial Feminist Critique of International Early Childhood Education Policy," *International Journal of Educational Development* 45 (2015): 161–168.

67 Verity Campbell-Barr and Katarina Bogatić, "Global to Local Perspectives of Early Childhood Education and Care," *Early Child Development and Care* 187, no. 10 (2017): 1461–1470.

68 Hasina Ebrahim, "Tensions in Incorporating Global Childhood with Early Childhood Programs: The Case of South Africa," *Australasian Journal of Early Childhood* 37, no. 3 (2012): 80–86; Junehui Ahn, "Finding a Child's Self: Globalization and the Hybridized Landscape of Korean Early Childhood Education," *Anthropology & Education Quarterly* 46, no. 3 (2015): 224–243.

69 Veronica Pacini-Ketchabaw, "Frictions in Forest Pedagogies: Common Worlds in Settler Colonial Spaces," *Global Studies of Childhood* 3, no. 4 (2013): 355–365.
70 Lydia Ayame Hiraide, "Postcolonial, Decolonial, Anti-colonial: Does It Matter?," *New Voices in Postcolonial Studies* 6 (2021): 10–15.
71 Michelle Salazar Pérez, "Black Feminist Thought in Early Childhood Studies: (Re) Centering Marginalized Feminist Perspectives," in *Feminism(s) in Early Childhood: Using Feminist Theories in Research and Practice*, ed. Kylie Smith, Kate Alexander, and Sheralyn Campbell (Singapore: Springer Nature Singapore, 2017), 49–62.
72 Ranita Cheruvu, "Disrupting Standardised Early Education through Culturally Sustaining Pedagogies with Young Children," in *Disrupting and Countering Deficits in Early Childhood Education*, ed. Fikile Nxumalo and Christopher P. Brown (New York: Routledge, 2020), 103–118.
73 Mariana Souto-Manning and Jessica Martell, *Reading, Writing, and Talk: Inclusive Teaching Strategies for Diverse Learners* (New York: Teachers College Press, 2016).
74 Centre for Literacy in Primary Education, *Reflecting Realities—Survey of Ethnic Representation within UK Children's Literature 2019* (London: Centre for Literacy in Primary Education, 2020).
75 Akiea Gross, Woke Kindergarten, home page, accessed August 9, 2023, www.wokekindergarten.org.
76 Akiea Gross, "Woke Wonderings: Unconventional Questions Rooted in Liberatory Thought," Woke Kindergarten, accessed August 9, 2023, www.wokekindergarten.org.
77 For other examples of abolitionist perspectives, see Mariana Souto-Manning, "Critical Race Self-Study: An Abolitionist Methodology," *Asia-Pacific Journal of Teacher Education* 50, no. 3 (2022): 249–265; Fikile Nxumalo and Veronica Pacini-Ketchabaw, "Centering Black Life in Canadian Early Childhood Education," *Gender & Education* 35, no. 2 (2023): 186–198.
78 Gross, "Woke Wonderings"; Pérez, "Black Feminist Thought in Early Childhood Studies."
79 For analysis, see Aoife Daly, *Children, Autonomy and the Courts: Beyond the Right to Be Heard* (Leiden: Brill Nijhoff, 2017).
80 For example, Barbara Arneil, "Becoming versus Being: A Critical Analysis of the Child in Liberal Theory," in *The Moral and Political Status of Children*, ed. David Archard and Colin M. Macleod (Oxford: Oxford University Press, 2002), 70–96; Michael J. Sandel, *Liberalism and the Limits of Justice*, 2nd ed. (Cambridge: Cambridge University Press, 1998).
81 See, for example, Spyros Spyrou, *Disclosing Childhoods: Research and Knowledge Production for a Critical Childhood Studies* (Basingstoke, UK: Palgrave Macmillan, 2018).
82 Donna J. Haraway, *Staying with the Trouble: Making Kin in the Chthulucene* (Durham, NC: Duke University Press, 2016).

PART II

Middle Childhood

4

Middle Childhood Development

JOSEPHINE GRANT

I. Introduction

Compared to the obvious dramas of early childhood and adolescence, middle childhood seems sedate. Freud described the years between six and twelve as *sexual latency*, when drives are submerged, thereby defining the period by what is *not* happening rather than what is. But middle childhood is not a mere way station. Beneath the relative calm of the period runs a hormonal current—*adrenarche*—that powers global shifts in how children think and relate to others.[1] Middle childhood is a years-long apprenticeship in the skills and customs of whatever culture children happen to be born into. The pace may be slow, but the stakes are high.

The aim of this chapter is to bring this slow-motion, consequential period out of the shadows of babyhood and adolescence and into our imaginations. Like the other developmental authors in this volume, I recognize that any attempt to describe "what children are like" at a given stage quickly runs into their individuality and their widely varying contexts. That said, there is a truism in our field. Development is a continual interaction between self and other. In middle childhood, the *quality* of this continual interaction fundamentally transforms. Specific changes in how children think combine with place-based demands to fuel the long business of figuring out how to belong.

II. What Is Middle Childhood For?

The primary purpose of middle childhood is to learn the skills we need to join adult life. Developmentalists may use different terminology, but they reliably converge on this cardinal point. Lev Vygotsky claimed that middle childhood is when we "internalize cultural patterns of thought and speech" and develop "instrumental competencies."[2] Erik Erikson famously characterized middle childhood as a dynamic tension between developing *a sense of industry* and *a sense of inferiority*. Middle childhood, he claimed, is "a most decisive stage" because industry is "the lasting basis for cooperative participation in productive adult life."[3] Children meet this developmental mandate with new cognitive powers, as demonstrated by Jean Piaget in his novel interviews with children.[4] The advances are social as well as cognitive. They include personal regulation and collaboration, developed through play and the right-level frustrations of learning.

Findings from evolutionary developmental psychology and comparative animal studies point to middle childhood years as a uniquely human stage. Evolutionary scholarship begins with something we tend to take for granted: human childhood lasts a long time. Even among highly social mammals, our juvenility is unique. Our bodies, brains, teeth, and sexual systems take longer to develop.[5] Unlike apes, once our brain volume approaches adult size at about age seven, we experience a pause in somatic growth. By elongating childhood, the thinking goes, our species diverts energy away from gaining size. Apes march on to puberty, while we bulk up on cultural know-how. The mechanisms behind this pause are drawn in broad strokes, including the interaction of coevolving realities of bigger brains; larger, more complex social groups; and the adaptive pressures of intense social learning.[6]

Postponing reproduction presents risks to individual survival, so the pause must have a payoff. Evolutionary scholars hypothesize that the extended incubation period is an adaptation necessary for learning the skills and norms required to thrive and successfully reproduce as a cultural species.[7] Our unique attunement to learning rituals and following norms in middle childhood is evident in research comparing children and apes.[8] In a vivid demonstration of children's expectation to be taught, researchers presented apes and children in middle childhood with a black, mechanical box containing a treat.[9] Both the children and the apes successfully imitated a sequence of actions necessary to get the treat from the box. Next, the apes and the children were presented with a transparent version of the same box. The new box reveals the truth:

you can get the treat by simply opening a small door. Apes drop the irrelevant moves and go straight for the treat. The children, however, continue to perform the moves, even though they know the sequence is pointless. The children's "inefficiency" signals a commitment to learning shared behavior, even at the expense of task completion.[10]

The box experiment is a proxy for cultural learning. Scenes like this repeat over and over in middle childhood. We start to accrue *embodied capital*—the skills valued by society that take time to master.[11] The years of schooling we associate with middle childhood come with the implicit understanding that embodying capital is a time-consuming, resource-demanding, community-wide endeavor. Embodied capital is not just individual skills, like foraging, counting, or reading. It is manifest in shared cultural goods like language and myth, carried in the body politic, accumulated over generations. For the community, middle childhood is an investment in cultural continuity and technological advancement. For the individual child, embodied capital feels like a sense of industry.

Another useful way to think about the purpose of middle childhood is through a *cultural microsystem* lens.[12] In contrast to earlier ecological models of development that depict culture as a distal, homogenizing force, the cultural microsystem model highlights how the child's everyday, "micro" experiences are infused with cultural intent.[13] Culture is not just laws, media, and policies handed down by others; it is "the routines we engage in."[14] Peer interactions, caregiving, what is approved, what is upbraided, what is taught, and even what is remembered all direct the child to shared values and practices. This is a life-span experience, but it gains new traction in middle childhood, when the child brings new powers to learning.[15]

III. Markers of Middle Childhood

Psychologists typically define middle childhood as the ages six to twelve.[16] In the past forty years, the boundaries have blurred on both ends. The lower bound has blurred because of the increasing number of children who experience out-of-home care in early childhood. The upper bound has blurred because of the rising rates of earlier puberty, especially for girls.[17] Even so, biological, psychological, and sociocultural evidence supports middle childhood as a universally shared phase between total dependence on caregivers and sexual maturity. A quick tour of the changes that occur around age six will bring the period into focus.

A. Changing Bodies

The onset of middle childhood is not obvious. Physical changes appear in a syncopated pattern. Youngsters lose their baby teeth and gain the adult teeth their faces will slowly grow into. Physical growth tends to be gradual. Body mass index rebounds to catch up to the earlier gains in height, but then it slows substantially, holding puberty at bay. Slower growth leads to improvements in fine and gross motor skills, allowing children to begin to mimic adult maneuvers in labor and play. Gait becomes more adultlike. Sex differences in body composition emerge, with increased muscularity in males and adiposity in females. Under the surface, brain growth slows as volume reaches its adult size, with continued development devoted to efficiency through myelination and synaptic pruning.[18]

Current research points to a hormonal surge, *adrenarche*, as the driver of children's subtly changing bodies, synaptic connectivity, and emerging capacities.[19] Adrenarche is the slow secretion of androgen by the adrenal glands. Adrenal production of the steroids DHEA and DHEAS protects brain matter for the synaptic growth and intensifying axonal connections of middle childhood. Called a "plasticity regulator," adrenarche ushers in a suite of physical, cognitive, and behavioral changes that direct us toward cultural know-how.[20] This slow hormonal wash slicks and shapes neuronal connections and opens the child to the years-long process of learning the skills esteemed by whatever culture they happen to have been born into.

B. Changing Social Expectations

In middle childhood, adults start expecting children to perform and conform. Anthropological reports from hunter-gatherer groups offer striking evidence of the shift in social standing. Children younger than five or six years old may be viewed as lacking sense or unique personhood. In Paraguay, Ayoreo children younger than five are not considered fully human because they lack *aiuketaoitguei*, which translates to "personality" or "understanding." Among Javanese rice farmers, children under five or six years old are *durung ngerti*, or "without understanding." The Sisala-Ghanian child lacks *wijima*, or "knowing things." In some societies, it is considered a waste of time to instruct or reprimand young children because they lack both the status and ability to take personal responsibility.[21]

Then, children "get noticed."[22] Beginning at age five, and certainly by age eight, children merge into a lane of increasing expectations and responsibilities. In literate societies, children enter kindergarten at five or six years old. In Judaism, the obligation to do right (*mitzvot*) begins between six and nine years old. Certain Christian denominations do not permit communion until age seven, while others delay baptism until age eight, based on the assumption that younger children are not capable of true agency, implying that by seven or eight, they are. While definitions of readiness—and, therefore, culpability—vary, the movement toward personal responsibility is the same.

Middle childhood is often synonymous with "school age." Even children who do not experience formal education get schooled in skills and behavior. The curriculum varies, but the focus on developing *industry* in the Eriksonian sense does not. Street children in India bring the same capacities to the same developmental mandate.[23] Children from Martu, the inland desert in Australia, do not attend formal school. Yupa Nakananga, a Martu woman, describes a typical day when she was about nine years old: "Mothers and fathers gone out hunting and leave us kids in camp. When we got hungry, we go hunting for little lizards, get him and cook it, and eat him up. Me a little bit big now, I go hunting myself, tracking goanna and kill him. . . . Take him home before mother and father get back, cook and eat it."[24] Yupa, "a little bit big now," makes concrete contributions by hunting and cooking, and probably child tending, while her parents are out. In sum, industry in middle childhood takes many different forms, but accountability is widely shared across cultures.[25]

C. Reasoning

1. OVERVIEW

Children's slowly changing bodies contrast with big changes in their thinking. Ancients and moderns alike deem seven the age of reason and responsibility.[26] The cognitive achievement of middle childhood described by Jean Piaget—concrete operational thinking—signals a turning point in the development of human cognition. Piaget demonstrated that, at about seven years old, children start reasoning more clearly about the material world.[27] They "pass" Piaget's famous conservation test with glasses of liquid. They can manipulate and reverse simple mathematical operations (3 + 5 = 8, so 8 − 5 = 3). Categorizing, sorting, and collecting all bring the child's nascent logic to bear on the world in front of them. Piaget's focus on logic has been criticized as Western-centric, but around the world, there is a precipitous drop in errors of conservation and classification from early childhood. There is a universal turn away from the charming inaccuracies of early childhood toward more systematic, rational thought.[28]

The rationality that emerges in middle childhood is preceded by the flowering fantasies of our early years. A four-year-old who rides a broom or talks on a banana is a powerfully symbolic thinker—she can use one thing as a stand-in for another. She acts on the world through pretense. To develop a sense of industry, however, she must act on the real world through craft. While children in middle childhood still engage in and enjoy the rich pretend play of their earlier years, they now can separate fantasy from reality. They "get sober."[29] True industry requires bridling one's imagination so that it comports to reality.

Paradoxically, the cognitive advances of middle childhood bring liabilities to children's self-concept, or what they understand about themselves.[30] While their repertoire of social, athletic, and artistic skills grows, they develop a more informed self-concept relative to others. Unlike younger children, who tend to have fanciful ideas about their competence, children now have the insight and interpersonal experiences to make more realistic comparisons.[31]

2. PSYCHOLOGICAL REASONING

Around the world, at about age five, children start to think about other people as psychological beings. They grasp human subjectivity. This socio-cognitive milestone rests on the pedestrian but profound insight that other people have beliefs and desires that differ from one's own.[32] In developmental psychology, we say they have developed a *theory of mind.* Having a theory of mind allows us to take another person's unique perspective into account. We can make predictions and offer psychological explanations for other people's behavior. A six-year-old on the phone will not "show" a toy to the person they are talking to, whereas a four-year-old without a theory of mind will. The six-year-old understands that the other person cannot see it, but the four-year-old does not. This kind of mental-state reasoning is critical for our species's mighty capacity for cooperation and learning, Research has yet to uncover any behavior that reliably shows our close primate kin demonstrating a theory of mind.[33] It avails children of social powers that were unimaginable in the mind meld of their early years.

But having a theory of mind is not "one and done." Just as a child's gait changes dramatically from their taking first steps to running at full speed, children's theory of mind likewise becomes more agile during middle childhood.[34] Children's ability to reason about other people's thinking shifts to a higher gear between eight and ten, creating a second threshold of social cognition in development.[35] They become capable of recursive mental reasoning, or the ability to layer up different individuals' beliefs: *She thinks that he thinks I am hiding something.* A more robust theory of mind is also evident in their ability to break out of parallel play and genuinely collaborate.[36]

The qualitative leaps in reasoning and mentalizing that appear in middle childhood have limitations. Thought experiments that violate reality may be rebuffed as nonsense, illustrating the distance they have yet to travel to the hypothetical, abstract thinking that emerges in adolescence. The clunky problem-solving strategies that first appear in middle childhood get more efficient by age ten.[37] For example, older children understand that effort and strategies may be required to remember something, while their younger siblings are more laissez-faire.[38]

D. Relationships

1. WITH PARENTS

The impact of parent-child attachment reverberates across the life span.[39] In middle childhood, attachment style correlates to the child's sense of belonging in school, emotional regulation, and use of other people as a secure base.[40] It is worth noting the wide variation around the world in parental investment in their children, in the amount of speech directed toward them, and in expectations for how children in middle childhood spend their time (on schoolwork or chores or tending younger siblings).

Developmental psychology has long had a problem of overreliance on participants from Western, educated, industrialized, rich, and democratic cultures.[41] The parenting practices of marginalized groups that live in wealthy societies are often explicitly or implicitly compared to the practices of more privileged families. For much of human history, the child-centric standard of parenting that is now common among well-to-do families has been rare.[42] The focus on optimal parenting styles obscures the value of strategies that are at odds with the recent enrichment practices and safety-ism of well-to-do parents in industrialized economies.[43] Harsh parenting can be seen as deficient or harmful for children, but authoritarian discipline, directive speech, and handing down harsh consequences may in fact be adaptive to dangerous environments.[44] If we neglect the different risks that families face, we risk framing parenting strategies that are downstream of external threats as problematic rather than responsive. This is not to suggest that there is a "natural" style of parenting or a "natural" path thorough middle childhood. What is natural is variability, which facilitates humans' adaptation to innumerable ecologies. The question is whether the warmth and structure that parents provide supports the industry-and-belonging mandate of the stage. Ideally, parents maintain a productive tension between autonomy and protection and do not avoid the tension in favor of too much or too little independence.

2. WITH PEERS

Children's growth in middle childhood depends on play. In contrast to the side-by-side parallel play of earlier years, their play is now more interactive and collaborative. Pretend play, which tends to be viewed as the domain of the very young, carries well into middle childhood, with greater elaboration. Rules for play may be set down in advance (as they are with games), or they may be negotiated on the spot (as in role play), or they may be combined on the fly. Children become more selective about their playmates, and sex-segregated play appears across cultures.

Children will challenge each other in play in ways that adults do not. The fired-up negotiations that emerge in play test children's emotional regulation and contribute to their conversational competence. Didactic interactions cannot match peer play for "cheater detection." Cheater detection is refined in middle childhood and may have served hunter-gathers who depended on reciprocity to share spoils.[45] In play, children learn that cheaters take a hit to their reputations. Research scenarios that compare children's moral behavior when they do and do not have an audience illustrate the role of reputation monitoring. For example, six- and nine-year-olds concealed their own selfish bargaining when the other children did not realize the deal was raw. But when all the children had the same information and stakes were known, they behaved more equitably.[46]

E. Morality

Moral behavior emerges from ordinary human "hypersociality."[47] Infants prefer faces to other stimuli and respond to crying with crying.[48] Toddlers show a preference for helpers over hinderers and will spontaneously help someone struggling to complete a simple task.[49] In early childhood, there is a default to truth-telling thanks to an inability to manage deception.[50] It is a stretch to call these behaviors "moral" in the sense of arising from considered values. They simply track youngsters' innate sociality and cognitive range. In middle childhood, however, that range expands. From six to twelve, shifts in thinking and in social motivation open up worlds of moral decision-making unimagined by the four-year-old. In middle childhood, we can imagine other people's thoughts, including what they think about us. Not surprisingly, the period brings about more lying.[51]

Perhaps more than through parental instruction, children in middle childhood learn moral decision-making in play with peers.[52] The energetic, unscripted, affect-laden exchanges that happen between children—hashing out fairness, policing transgressions, and handing down sanctions—require constant regulation. Games have rules that get enforced, bent, or made up on the spot, providing grist for moral decision-making and reputation-making.

Any discussion of morality in middle childhood leans into experience-dependent learning and variability. Cooperation is innate, but moral codes are learned.[53] In some communities, individual rights take precedence; in others, social harmony does.[54] Stage models of development are less useful. Our moral thinking and behavior vary by culture and our own shifting assessments of what circumstances require.[55] For parents and teachers, the child's ability to imagine another person's point of view is an opportunity to practice empathy. Recent research with children aged six to ten demonstrated that asking children to reflect on how they will feel after sharing or not sharing increased their prosocial behavior.[56]

In becoming more systematic thinkers, children in middle childhood can also be rigid rule followers. They are famous tattlers, policing others when they see them violating rules of right and wrong. They will tattle whether they themselves are the victim or not.[57] Tattling is a way of finding the edges of transgressive behavior, a tool for learning the contours of norms and the consequences of stepping outside of them. Children also, however, start to appreciate the difference between social codes (like dress) and moral codes. After six years of age, they start to differentiate between types of transgressions. Violating a social norm, like not removing one's shoes when entering a home, is different from disobeying a moral norm, like hitting or stealing. Children become active enforcers of normative behavior but reserve their most agitated responses for moral transgressions.[58]

F. Fairness

Understanding human rights probably builds on children's personal experiences with fairness or unfairness, and children energetically attend to fairness in middle childhood.[59] Distribution of goods and favors feature prominently in play. Early in middle childhood, fairness tends to focus on one dimension: equal distribution. This changes at about age ten, when children start to take merit and relative need into account when deciding what is fair.

In middle childhood, children's moral viewfinder widens. For some, a dawning awareness of social inequality begins to influence their moral calculations. In a cross-sectional US study, children of different races (White, Black, multiethnic, Asian) were given tokens to distribute to fictional children who were White or non-White, rich or poor, male, or female.[60] Findings clustered around age-related changes, rather than race or gender. Three- and four-year-old children tended to award tokens equally. Surprisingly, six- and seven-year-old children awarded more tokens to peers they perceived to be well-off (White and wealthy), perhaps to gain favor, to create an alliance, to simply display an understanding that status and wealth go together, or as a signal of their own tacit agreement with the idea that rich people are rich because they are also good. Said one, "He is better because he has a bigger house."[61] By age eleven, however, children actively engaged in redistribution, rationalizing their choice as a redress for broader inequalities or in terms of personal dislike for the well-off child. ("I know that rich people think they are better, so I wanted to not give more stickers to the rich person to show that she is not better.")[62] In another US sample, eleven-year-olds rationalized unequal distribution of favors by citing a desire to address group disadvantage (Blacks and people in poverty), but six-year-olds did not.[63] While the findings were unique to a US sample, they demonstrate the trend toward a dawning awareness of inequality, sensitivity to power, and moral imperatives. To this busy mix of interactions, they bring improved reasoning and perspective-taking.[64]

At this stage, however, children do not engage in the kind of moral reasoning that adolescents do. For example, they do not appear motivated to wrestle with how laws may run afoul of personal morality. The pleasure that children experience in middle childhood after prosocial behavior may be fundamental to the creation of a moral self-concept.[65] Approval, empathy, and glowing self-esteem can charge the moment. The pleasure may provide an on-ramp for abstract concepts like the rights and dignity of other persons.

G. Gender Socialization in Middle Childhood

Gender is an inescapable social category and is one of the earliest social categories to develop.[66] Nine-month-old infants can distinguish between male and female faces.[67] Two-year-olds will sort people according to gender schemas (e.g., hair, clothing, toy preferences).[68] At about age six, children spontaneously describe biological sex as a stable trait, coinciding with Piaget's descriptions of conservation and constancy.[69] Gender stereotyping peaks at this time. During middle childhood, most children conform to some version of their gender schema. Their ideas about gender get more nuanced with time (someone can be both a man and a nurse), but the range has its limits.

As the socialization curriculum kicks into high gear during middle childhood, gender becomes an increasingly salient part of self-concept.[70] Children become "gender detectives," policing each other to comply with expectations.[71] Children who see themselves as within a gender-typical range, and express contentedness with their gender, tend to have higher self-esteem than those who do not. These findings are probably mediated by peer acceptance.[72] Those who behave in nonconforming ways, especially boys, tend to have less social capital.[73] Boys tend to punish nonconforming behavior harshly, a finding that appears cross-culturally, while cross-gender behavior in girls can enhance their social standing.[74]

While children are refining their ideas about gender, they are also attuning to gender-based prejudice. They can be quick to point out and reject gender discrimination by adults, demonstrating their growing ability to distinguish between social norms (performing gender) and moral norms (being fair).[75] Gender norms may be conflated with moral codes in countries where females are routinely sequestered and discriminated against. As Daly and Walsh point out in chapter 5, this raises questions about how gender influences the way children in those countries reason about rights and protection for boys and girls.

IV. Threats to a Sense of Industry in Middle Childhood

A. Bias

As children start navigating institutions on their own, they become increasingly aware of where they might fit in a world stratified by gender, race, and money.[76] Most are spending their days in school, the "quintessential agencies of acculturation."[77] For some, school may be their first direct experience with prejudice. By age eight, ethnic-minority immigrant children in the US voice awareness of ethnic stigma and report more academic anxiety than their ethnic-majority peers do. In the same study, children's sense of belonging to their school varied by locale and positively correlated to motivation, a finding that reiterates the importance of proximal relationships in middle childhood toward maintaining engagement.[78] Aboriginal children who reported racist encounters were more likely to be involved in peer aggression.[79] Black and Hispanic children in the US who reported discriminatory treatment at school were more likely to be identified as having conduct problems, attention deficit disorder, or depressive symptoms than were peers who did not self-report racist interactions or their White peers.[80] The correlation between conduct problems, depression, and anxiety and self-reported racial victimization in middle childhood is well documented.[81]

Studies on the impact of segregated environments on child well-being have yielded some counterintuitive findings. Minority children who attend integrated schools may have access to greater resources, but evidence suggests that they may be at risk for lower self-esteem and may even reject school success as a capitulation to a system that may see them as inferior.[82] Segregated schools and neighborhoods, while often lacking resources, may buffer children from prejudice they encounter in discordant environments.[83] The findings are not an argument for segregation. They point out how inhibiting environments may also be protective. For example, Cambodian, Portuguese, and Dominican children between six and twelve in the US who lived in segregated neighborhoods reported strong ethnic pride and seemed protected from negative mental health outcomes despite experiencing bias in school.[84]

For Black boys in the US, persistent bias has put a squeeze on middle childhood. As of about age ten, Black boys seem to lose the privilege of childhood innocence that White same-age children continue to enjoy.[85] According to the social psychologist Phillip Goff and colleagues, Black boys "enjoy fewer of the basic human protections afforded to their peers because the category 'children' is seen to be a less essential category."[86] Parents, wanting to protect their sons, contribute to the adultification of Black boys, as well.[87] While adultification is pathologized in clinical contexts, it can be seen as adaptive to hostile circumstances.

B. Poverty and Extreme Inequality

A sure indication of a hostile environment is an abbreviated middle childhood. Extreme poverty squeezes out middle childhood.[88] Cross-cultural studies show that "where poverty flourishes, middle childhood as a distinct, culturally constructed period, has almost ceased to exist."[89] In developing countries, children are often expected to contribute to the family economy as soon as they are useful, so their schooling may be brief. In Brazil, for example, with rampant poverty and reified inequality, middle childhood is a privilege of the rich.[90]

Interventions focused on economic mixing have had mixed results on children's self-concept.[91] In middle childhood, children have increased awareness of rank and may see themselves as socially demoted within a community when their circumstances are thrown in unhappy relief. Health outcomes are also worse for poor children in highly unequal settings. While causality is not clear from the data, one hypothesis is that intensified social hierarchies create an additional layer of psychological stress to the stresses already present in poverty.[92]

C. Early Puberty in Girls

Middle childhood typically occurs against the quiescent backdrop of sexual latency. But early puberty in girls has been rising worldwide, creating a mismatch between developmental expectation and biology.[93] Obesity, environmental toxins, marital conflict, and poverty are related to early adrenarche and early puberty, defined as age eight to nine years old for girls.[94] Being an outlier among one's peers in pubertal development often creates psychological and interpersonal stress, elevates the risk of sexual harassment for girls, and has been associated with adult assumptions of promiscuity and deviance.[95] For girls, consequences of early puberty include increased risk for depression, earlier sexual activity, and school avoidance.[96]

D. Pandemic School Closures, Remote Learning

School closures during the COVID-19 pandemic offer an object lesson in how to hijack the social learning agenda of middle childhood. Schools closed in 180 countries, delivering an "unprecedented global shock" to the education of children worldwide.[97] By 2022, an estimated 70 percent of ten-year-olds were unable to read simple text, up from 50 percent pre-pandemic, an already high rate.[98] The three most concerning outcomes for children in middle childhood are (1) learning loss (inability to read simple text), (2) social regulation issues (more disciplinary issues reported in schools), and (3) more children experiencing mental health crises (depression, anxiety, and suicidality).[99] Even in the Netherlands, where the lockdown was relatively short, school funding is equitable, and internet access is widely available, children age eight to eleven years old made little to no progress academically.[100] The learning loss was more pronounced in children from families with low income—a "poor getting poorer" result found repeatedly around the world (e.g., Greece, Pakistan, US, Mexico).[101]

Researchers will be investigating the effects of school closures for decades to come. Previous disruptions to schooling do not provide a comforting outlook for the COVID cohort. Based on US studies of the Great Depression and the recession of 2008, it appears that, as a cohort, children under age seven were able to bounce back from ill effects of economic slowdown and school disruptions. But children in middle childhood were less resilient by psychological and economic measures.[102] It stands to reason that children in middle childhood were uniquely impacted by school disruptions, affecting academic and social learning. In Sierra Leone, after the Ebola outbreak, child labor rates in Sierra Leone increased by almost 20 percent due to school closures.[103] A recent meta-analysis of evidence for COVID's impact on learning two and a half years after the start of the pandemic implies that children have lost, on average, more than one-third of a year of learning.[104] This estimate is probably low, and averages are less meaningful when there are wide discrepancies within a data set. These data vary from country to country, with students in poorer countries faring worse. Math achievement was more negatively impacted, probably because of the importance of instruction and repeated practice to gain mastery. The data do not explain why children in middle childhood fared worse than younger children did. But we can hypothesize that when events dismantle schools—the social structures that support a sense of industry—children may miss the developmental milestones on which later success depends.

V. What Do Children Need?

All children need warm family relationships and safe, stable environments.[105] The following are critical for healthy development in middle childhood:

- Lots of peer interaction to play, to compete, to collaborate, and to experience joy.[106] Recess is a necessity—not a luxury or a reward—for school-age children.
- Schooling in culturally valued skills, in the context of caring relationships, to experience mastery and positive self-worth.[107]
- Parenting that provides children with right-sized opportunities to explore, to contribute to the family, and to develop personal responsibility.[108]

Children's expanded capacities in middle childhood also make them vulnerable to exploitation. They need protection from the following:

- Forced labor that replaces play and school. This is a risk that emerges in impoverished contexts as children in middle childhood are more physically capable.
- Social isolation that interferes with play and learning.
- Online spaces that monetize children's attention, abuse their still-maturing analytical skills, amplify social comparison, and/or reward obsessive use.
- Exposure to violence and threats of violence. As children move into more public arenas in middle childhood, they may become targets for harm and harassment.[109]

The cultural microsystem model reminds us that specific needs of children will look different in different contexts. Middle childhood itself is about fine-tuning to context. Given that children who live outside the Global North have been less studied, humility is warranted when experts evaluate how well or poorly children's needs are being met.[110] Our guiding questions for this age group should be, *What are they learning, from whom, and how well does it serve them?*

VI. Conclusion

In middle childhood, we trade toddler cuteness for fluency in "games, slang, style or behavior."[111] The intuitive, magical thinking of the early years dissipates, and we enter the land of common sense. We are held more accountable for our behavior, but there is no expectation for a coherent narrative of personal identity. We are friend focused but spared the constant peer monitoring that takes hold in adolescence. Ideally, we experience warmth and teaching at home, whether in the suburbs or in the Sahara.

Human flourishing depends on our lengthy childhoods. Unlike other primates, we have an amazing ability to learn and to adapt to wildly diverse landscapes and social structures. Plasticity is our superpower. This superpower depends on slowing development down, not speeding it up.[112] Perhaps middle childhood is neglected because it moves slowly. But its pace is a source of its power.

NOTES

1 Marco Del Giudice, Romina Angeleri, and Valeria Manera, "The Juvenile Transition: A Developmental Switch Point in Human Life History," *Developmental Review* 29, no. 1 (2009): 1–31.

2 Lev Semenovich Vygotsky, *Mind in Society: Development of Higher Psychological Processes* (Cambridge, MA: Harvard University Press, 1978); "instrumental competencies": Cynthia Garcia Coll and Laura A. Szalacha, "The Multiple Contexts of Middle Childhood," *Children of Immigrant Families* 14, no. 2 (2004): 81–97.

3 Erik H. Erikson, *Identity: Youth and Crisis* (New York: Norton, 1968), 126.

4 Jean Piaget and Bärbel Inhelder, *The Psychology of the Child* (New York: Basic Books, 1972).

5 David F. Bjorklund, *How Children Invented Humanity: The Role of Development in Human Evolution* (New York: Oxford University Press, 2020).

6 Ibid.

7 Michael Tomasello, Ann Cale Kruger, and Hilary Horn Ratner, "Cultural Learning," *Behavioral and Brain Sciences* 16, no. 3 (1993): 495–511.

8 Michael Tomasello, *The Cultural Origins of Human Cognition* (Cambridge, MA: Harvard University Press, 2009).

9 Victoria Horner, Andrew Whiten, Emma Flynn, and Frans B. M. De Waal, "Faithful Replication of Foraging Techniques along Cultural Transmission Chains by Chimpanzees and Children," *Proceedings of the National Academy of Sciences* 103, no. 37 (2006): 13878–13883.

10 Jane Leighton, Geoffrey Bird, and Cecilia Heyes, "'Goals' Are Not an Integral Component of Imitation," *Cognition* 114, no. 3 (2010): 423–435.

11 Pierre Bourdieu, "The Forms of Capital," in *The Sociology of Economic Life*, ed. Mark Granovetter and Richard Swedberg (New York: Routledge, 2018), 78–92; Hillard Kaplan, Kim Hill, A. Magdalena Hurtado, and Jane Lancaster, "The Embodied Capital Theory of Human Evolution," *Reproductive Ecology and Human Evolution*, ed. Peter T. Ellison (New York: Aldine de Gruyter, 2001), 293–317.

12 Nicole M. Vélez-Agosto, José. G. Soto-Crespo, Mónica Vizcarrondo-Oppenheimer, Stephanie Vega-Molina, and Cynthia García Coll, "Bronfenbrenner's Bioecological Theory Revision: Moving Culture from the Macro into the Micro," *Perspectives on Psychological Science* 12, no. 5 (2017): 900–910.

13 Urie Bronfenbrenner, "Toward an Experimental Ecology of Human Development," *American Psychologist* 32, no. 7 (1977): 513–531.

14 Vélez-Agosto et al., "Bronfenbrenner's Bioecological Theory Revision," 904.

15 The cultural microsystem model may also provide a theoretical structure for legal scholars investigating how the concept of rights—a cultural tenet—manifests itself differently in different contexts.

16 Benjamin C. Campbell, "An Introduction to the Special Issue on Middle Childhood," *Human Nature* 22, no. 3 (2011): 247–248; National Research Council (US) Panel to Review the Status of Basic Research on School-Age Children, *Development during Middle Childhood: The Years from Six to Twelve*, ed. W. Andrew Collins (Washington, DC: National Academies Press, 1984); David R. Shaffer and Katherine Kipp, *Developmental Psychology: Childhood and Adolescence* (Boston: Cengage Learning, 2013).

17 Nicholas R. Buttrick and Shigehiro Oishi, "The Psychological Consequences of Income Inequality," *Social and Personality Psychology Compass* 11, no. 3 (2017): e12304.

18 Del Giudice, Angeleri, and Manera, "Juvenile Transition"; Bjorklund, *How Children Invented Humanity*.

19 Richard J. Auchus and William E. Rainey, "Adrenarche—Physiology, Biochemistry and Human Disease," *Clinical Endocrinology* 60, no. 3 (2004): 288–296; Campbell, "Introduction to the Special Issue on Middle Childhood," 247–248; Benjamin C. Campbell, "Adrenarche and Middle Childhood," *Human Nature* 22, no. 3 (2011): 327–349.

20 Marco Del Giudice, "Middle Childhood: An Evolutionary-Developmental Synthesis," *Child Development Perspectives* 8, no. 4 (2014): 193–200.

21 David F. Lancy and M. Annette Grove, "Getting Noticed: Middle Childhood in Cross-Cultural Perspective," *Human Nature* 22 (2011): 281–302.

22 Ibid.

23 Bjorklund, *How Children Invented Humanity.*
24 R. Bliege Bird and Douglas W. Bird, "Human Hunting Seasonality," in *Seasonality in Primates: Studies of Living and Extinct Human and Non-human Primates*, ed. Diane K. Brockman and Carel P. van Schaik (Cambridge: Cambridge University Press, 2005), quoted in Melvin Konner, *The Evolution of Childhood: Relationships, Emotions, Mind* (Cambridge, MA; Harvard University Press, 2010), 644–645.
25 Barbara Rogoff, Martha Julia Sellers, Sergio Pirrotta, Nathan Fox, and Sheldon H. White, "Age of Assignment of Roles and Responsibilities in Children: A Cross-Cultural Survey," *Human Development* 18 (1975): 353–369.
26 Theodore Shapiro and Richard Perry, "Latency Revisited," *Psychoanalytic Study of the Child* 31, no. 1 (1976): 79–105; Rogoff et al., "Age of Assignment of Roles and Responsibilities in Children."
27 Bärbel Inhelder and Jean Piaget, *The Early Growth of Logic in the Child: Classification and Seriation* (New York: Routledge, 2013).
28 Michael Shayer, Andreas Demetriou, and Muhammad Pervez, "The Structure and Scaling of Concrete Operational Thought: Three Studies in Four Countries," *Genetic, Social, and General Psychology Monographs* 114, no. 3 (1988): 307–375.
29 Ann Cale Kruger, developmental psychologist, personal communication, August 15, 2023, on file with author.
30 Susan Harter, "The Development of Self-Esteem," in *Self-Esteem Issues and Answers: A Sourcebook of Current Perspectives*, ed. Michael H. Kernis (New York: Psychology, 2006), 144–150.
31 Hazel J. Markus and Paula S. Nurius, "Self-Understanding and Self-Regulation in Middle Childhood," in Collins, *Development during Middle Childhood*, 147–183; Hazel R. Markus and Shinobu Kitayama, "Culture and the Self: Implications for Cognition, Emotion, and Motivation," *Psychological Review* 98, no. 2 (1991): 224–253.
32 Tara Callaghan, Philippe Rochat, Angeline Lillard, Mary Louise Claux, Hal Odden, Shoji Itakura, Sombat Tapanya, and Saraswati Singh, "Synchrony in the Onset of Mental-State Reasoning: Evidence from Five Cultures," *Psychological Science* 16, no. 5 (2005): 378–384; Alison Gopnik and Henry M. Wellman, "Why the Child's Theory of Mind Really Is a Theory," *Mind and Language* 7, nos. 1–2 (1992): 145–171.
33 Michael Tomasello, *Becoming Human: A Theory of Ontogeny* (Cambridge, MA: Harvard University Press, 2021).
34 Amy A. Weimer, Katherine Rice Warnell, Idean Ettekal, Kelly B. Cartwright, Nicole R. Guajardo, and Jeffrey Liew, "Correlates and Antecedents of Theory of Mind Development during Middle Childhood and Adolescence: An Integrated Model," *Developmental Review* 59, no. 4 (2021): 100945.
35 Briana D. Cassetta, Penny M. Pexman, and Vina M. Goghari, "Cognitive and Affective Theory of Mind and Relations with Executive Functioning in Middle Childhood," *Merrill-Palmer Quarterly* 64, no. 4 (2018): 514–538; Christopher Osterhaus and Susanne Koerber, "The Development of Advanced Theory of Mind in

Middle Childhood: A Longitudinal Study from Age 5 to 10 Years," *Child Development* 92, no. 5 (2021): 1872–1888.

36 Rory T. Devine and Ian A. Apperly, "Willing and Able? Theory of Mind, Social Motivation, and Social Competence in Middle Childhood and Early Adolescence," *Developmental Science* 25, no. 1 (2022): e13137.

37 Diana Selmeczy and Simona Ghetti, "Metacognition," in *The Encyclopedia of Child and Adolescent Development*, ed. Jeremy D. Jewell and Stephen Hupp (Hoboken, NJ: Wiley, 2019), https://onlinelibrary.wiley.com.

38 Janet Metcalfe and Bridgid Finn, "Metacognition and Control of Study Choice in Children," *Metacognition and Learning* 8 (2013): 19–46.

39 Julie C. Rothbard and Phillip R. Shaver, "Continuity of Attachment across the Life Span," in *Attachment in Adults: Clinical and Developmental Perspectives*, ed. Michael B. Sperling and William H. Berman (New York: Guilford, 1994), 31–71.

40 David Granot and Ofra Mayseless, "Attachment Security and Adjustment to School in Middle Childhood," *International Journal of Behavioral Development* 25, no. 6 (2001): 530–541; Laura E. Brumariu, "Parent-Child Attachment and Emotion Regulation," *New Directions for Child and Adolescent Development* 2015, no. 148 (2015): 31–45; Ashley C. Seibert and Kathryn A. Kerns, "Attachment Figures in Middle Childhood," *International Journal of Behavioral Development* 33, no. 4 (2009): 347–355.

41 Dorsa Amir and Katherine McAuliffe, "Cross-Cultural, Developmental Psychology: Integrating Approaches and Key Insights," *Evolution and Human Behavior* 41, no. 5 (2020): 430–444.

42 Willem E. Frankenhuis and Dorsa Amir, "What Is the Expected Human Childhood? Insights from Evolutionary Anthropology," *Development and Psychopathology* 34, no. 2 (2022): 473–497.

43 Ruth K. Chao, "Beyond Parental Control and Authoritarian Parenting Style: Understanding Chinese Parenting through the Cultural Notion of Training," *Child Development* 65, no. 4 (1994): 1111–1119; Purificación Checa and Alicia Abundis-Gutierrez, "Parenting Styles, Academic Achievement and the Influence of Culture," *Psychology and Psychotherapy: Research Study* 1, no. 4 (2018): 1–3.

44 Kathryn L. Humphreys and Virginia C. Salo, "Expectable Environments in Early Life," *Current Opinion in Behavioral Sciences* 36 (2020): 115–119.

45 Leda Cosmides and John Tooby, "Evolutionary Psychology and the Emotions," in *Handbook of Emotions*, 2nd ed., ed. Michael Lewis and Jeannette M. Haviland-Jones (New York: Guilford, 2000), 91–115.

46 Gorana Gonzales, Richard E. Ahl, Sara Cordes, and Katherine McAuliffe, "Children Strategically Conceal Selfishness," *Child Development* 93, no. 1 (2022): e71–e86.

47 Tomasello, *Cultural Origins of Human Cognition.*

48 Jamil Zaki and Jason P. Mitchell, "Intuitive Prosociality," *Current Directions in Psychological Science* 22, no. 6 (2013): 466–470.

49 J. Kiley Hamlin, Karen Wynn, Paul Bloom, and Neha Mahajan, "How Infants and Toddlers React to Antisocial Others," *Proceedings of the National Academy of Sciences* 108, no. 50 (2011): 19931–19936; Felix Warneken and Michael Tomasello, "Helping and Cooperation at 14 Months of Age," *Infancy* 11, no. 3 (2007): 271–294.

50 Liyang Sai, Siyuan Shang, Changzhi Zhao, Xinchen Liu, Yuanyuan Jiang, Brian J. Compton, Genyue Fu, and Gail D. Heyman, "The Developmental Origins of a Default Moral Response: A Shift from Honesty to Dishonesty," *Child Development* 93, no. 4 (2022): 1154–1161; Zaki and Mitchell, "Intuitive Prosociality."

51 Sai et al., "Developmental Origins of a Default Moral Response."

52 Konner, *Evolution of Childhood.*

53 P. R. Blake, K. McAuliffe, J. Corbit, T. C. Callaghan, O. Barry, A. Bowie, L. Kleutsch, et al., "The Ontogeny of Fairness in Seven Societies," *Nature* 528, no. 7581 (2015): 258–261.

54 Barbara Rogoff, *The Cultural Nature of Human Development* (Oxford: Oxford University Press, 2003), 222.

55 Anne Colby, Lawrence Kohlberg, John Gibbs, Marcus Lieberman, Kurt Fischer, and Herbert D. Saltzstein, "A Longitudinal Study of Moral Judgment," *Monographs of the Society for Research in Child Development* 48 (1983): 1–124; Jesse Graham, Brian A. Nosek, Jonathan Haidt, Ravi Iyer, Spassena Koleva, and Peter H. Ditto, "Mapping the Moral Domain," *Journal of Personality and Social Psychology* 101, no. 2 (2011): 366–385; Martin D. Ruck, Rona Abramovitch, and Daniel P. Keating, "Children's and Adolescents' Understanding of Rights: Balancing Nurturance and Self-Determination," *Child Development* 69, no. 2 (1998): 404–417.

56 Natalie Christner, Carolina Pletti, and Markus Paulus, "Emotion Understanding and the Moral Self-Concept as Motivators of Prosocial Behavior in Middle Childhood," *Cognitive Development* 55 (2020): 100893.

57 Bailey R. House, Joseph Henrich, Sarah F. Brosnan, and Joan B. Silk. "The Ontogeny of Human Prosociality: Behavioral Experiments with Children Aged 3 to 8," *Evolution and Human Behavior* 33, no. 4 (2012): 291–308.

58 Susanne Hardecker, Marco FH Schmidt, Meike Roden, and Michael Tomasello, "Young Children's Behavioral and Emotional Responses to Different Social Norm Violations," *Journal of Experimental Child Psychology* 150 (2016): 364–379.

59 Hanita Kosher and Asher Ben-Arieh, "What Children Think about Their Rights and Their Well-Being: A Cross-National Comparison," *American Journal of Orthopsychiatry* 87, no. 3 (2017): 256–273.

60 Laura Elenbaas, Katherine Luken Raz, Amanda Ackerman, and Ellen Kneeskern, "'This Kid Looks like He Has Everything': 3-to 11-Year-Old Children's Concerns for Fairness and Social Preferences When Peers Differ in Social Class and Race," *Child Development* 93, no. 5 (2022): 1527–1539.

61 Ibid., 1533.

62 Ibid.

63 Laura Elenbaas and Melanie Killen, "Children Rectify Inequalities for Disadvantaged Groups," *Developmental Psychology* 52, no. 8 (2016): 1318–1329.

64 Ibid.

65 Tehila Kogut, "Knowing What I Should, Doing What I Want: From Selfishness to Inequity Aversion in Young Children's Sharing Behavior," *Journal of Economic Psychology* 33, no. 1 (2012): 226–236.

66 Michael Lewis and Jeanne Brooks-Gunn, *Social Cognition and the Acquisition of Self* (New York: Plenum, 1979).

67 Mary D. Leinbach and Beverly I. Fagot, "Categorical Habituation to Male and Female Faces: Gender Schematic Processing in Infancy" *Infant Behavior and Development* 16, no. 3 (1993): 317–332.

68 Michelle Z. Wang, Vivian Ng, and Tracy R. Gleason, "Toy Stories: Children's Use of Gender Stereotypes in Making Social Judgments," *Acta Psychologica* 235 (2023): 103879; Campbell Leaper, "Gender, Dispositions, Peer Relations, and Identity," in *Gender, Sex, and Sexualities: Psychological Perspectives*, ed. Nancy K. Dess, Jeanne Marecek, and Leslie C. Bell (Oxford: Oxford University Press, 2018), 219–245.

69 Diane N. Ruble, Lisa J. Taylor, Lisa Cyphers, Faith K. Greulich, Leah E. Lurye, and Patrick E. Shrout, "The Role of Gender Constancy in Early Gender Development," *Child Development* 78, no. 4 (2007): 1121–1136; Bärbel Inhelder and Jean Piaget, *The Growth of Logical Thinking from Childhood to Adolescence: An Essay on the Construction of Formal Operational Structures* (London: Routledge, 1958).

70 Eleanor E. Maccoby, *The Two Sexes: Growing Up Apart, Coming Together* (Cambridge, MA: Harvard University Press, 1998); Leaper, "Gender, Dispositions, Peer Relations, and Identity."

71 May Ling Halim and Diane Ruble, "Gender Identity and Stereotyping in Early and Middle Childhood," in *Handbook of Gender Research in Psychology*, vol. 1, *Gender Research in General and Experimental Psychology*, ed. Donald R. McCreary and Joan C. Chrisler (New York: Springer, 2010), 495–525.

72 Leaper, "Gender, Dispositions, Peer Relations, and Identity."

73 Lewis and Brooks-Gunn, *Social Cognition and the Acquisition of Self*; Halim and Ruble, "Gender Identity and Stereotyping in Early and Middle Childhood."

74 Wang, Ng, and Gleason, "Toy Stories."

75 Christia Spears Brown, Sharla D. Biefeld, and Michelle J. Tam, *Gender in Childhood* (Cambridge: Cambridge University Press, 2020).

76 Erikson, *Identity*, 227.

77 Coll and Szalacha, "Multiple Contexts of Middle Childhood," 85.

78 Alejandro Portes and Min Zhou, "The New Second Generation: Segmented Assimilation and Its Variants," *Annals of the American Academy of Political and Social Science* 530, no. 1 (1993): 74–96; Cari Gillen-O'Neel, Diane N. Ruble, and Andrew J. Fuligni, "Ethnic Stigma, Academic Anxiety, and Intrinsic Motivation in Middle Childhood," *Child Development* 82, no. 5 (2011): 1470–1485; Kelly-Ann Allen, Kate C. Fortune, and Gökmen Arslan, "Testing the Social-Ecological Factors of School Belonging in Native-Born, First-Generation, and Second-Generation Australian Students: A Comparison Study," *Social Psychology of Education* 24, no. 3 (2021): 835–856.

79 Naomi Priest, Yin Paradies, Brigid Trenerry, Mandy Truong, Saffron Karlsen, and Yvonne Kelly, "A Systematic Review of Studies Examining the Relationship between Reported Racism and Health and Wellbeing for Children and Young People" *Social Science & Medicine* 95 (2013): 115–127.
80 Tumaini R. Coker, Marc N. Elliott, David E. Kanouse, Jo Anne Grunbaum, David C. Schwebel, M. Janice Gilliland, Susan R. Tortolero, Melissa F. Peskin, and Mark A. Schuster, "Perceived Racial/Ethnic Discrimination among Fifth-Grade Students and Its Association with Mental Health," *American Journal of Public Health* 99, no. 5 (2009): 878–884.
81 Ibid.
82 Coll and Szalacha, "Multiple Contexts of Middle Childhood."
83 Ibid.
84 Amy Kerivan Marks, Laura A. Szalacha, Meaghan Lamarre, Michelle J. Boyd, and Cynthia García Coll, "Emerging Ethnic Identity and Interethnic Group Social Preferences in Middle Childhood: Findings from the Children of Immigrants Development in Context (CIDC) Study," *International Journal of Behavioral Development* 31, no. 5 (2007): 501–513.
85 Phillip Atiba Goff, Matthew Christian Jackson, Brooke Allison Lewis Di Leone, Carmen Marie Culotta, and Natalie Ann DiTomasso "The Essence of Innocence: Consequences of Dehumanizing Black Children," *Journal of Personality and Social Psychology* 106, no. 4 (2014): 526–545; Michael J. Dumas and Joseph Derrick Nelson, "(Re) Imagining Black Boyhood: Toward a Critical Framework for Educational Research," *Harvard Educational Review* 86, no. 1 (2016): 27–47.
86 Goff et al., "Essence of Innocence," 528.
87 Roderick L. Carey, "Making Black Boys and Young Men Matter: Radical Relationships, Future Oriented Imaginaries and Other Evolving Insights for Educational Research and Practice," *International Journal of Qualitative Studies in Education* 33, no. 7 (2020): 729–744.
88 J. Christopher Kovats-Bernat, *Sleeping Rough in Port-au-Prince: An Ethnography of Street Children and Violence in Haiti* (Gainesville: University Press of Florida, 2006).
89 Lancy and Grove, "Getting Noticed," 295.
90 Ibid.
91 Buttrick and Oishi, "Psychological Consequences of Income Inequality."
92 Candice L. Odgers and Nancy E. Adler, "Challenges for Low-Income Children in an Era of Increasing Income Inequality," *Child Development Perspectives* 12, no. 2 (2018): 128–133.
93 Therése Skoog, Sevgi Bayram Özdemir, and Håkan Stattin, "Understanding the Link between Pubertal Timing in Girls and the Development of Depressive Symptoms: The Role of Sexual Harassment," *Journal of Youth and Adolescence* 45 (2016): 316–327; Paula J. Adams Hilliard, "Early Puberty in Girls—What Do We Know in 2022?," *Journal of Pediatric and Adolescent Gynecology* 35, no. 5 (2022): 521–522.

94 Tuck Seng Cheng, Ken K. Ong, and Frank M. Biro, "Trends towards Earlier Puberty Timing in Girls and Its Likely Mechanisms," *Journal of Pediatric and Adolescent Gynecology* 35, no. 5 (2022): 527–531.

95 Skoog, Özdemir, and Stattin, "Understanding the Link"; Priscilla A. Ocen, "(E)racing Childhood: Examining the Racialized Construction of Childhood and Innocence in the Treatment of Sexually Exploited Minors," *UCLA Law Review* 62 (2015): 1586–1640.

96 William E. Copeland, Carol Worthman, Lilly Shanahan, E. Jane Costello, and Adrian Angold, "Early Pubertal Timing and Testosterone Associated with Higher Levels of Adolescent Depression in Girls," *Journal of the American Academy of Child & Adolescent Psychiatry* 58, no. 12 (2019): 1197–1206; Julianna Deardorff, Kristine Marceau, Megan Johnson, Jonathan W. Reeves, Frank M. Biro, Ai Kubo, Louise C. Greenspan, et al., "Girls' Pubertal Timing and Tempo and Mental Health: A Longitudinal Examination in an Ethnically Diverse Sample," *Journal of Adolescent Health* 68, no. 6 (2021): 1197–1203; Skoog, Özdemir, and Stattin, "Understanding the Link."

97 World Bank, *The COVID-19 Pandemic: Shocks to Education and Policy Responses* (Washington, DC: World Bank, 2020).

98 Ibid.

99 Maria Elizabeth Loades, Eleanor Chatburn, Nina Higson-Sweeney, Shirley Reynolds, Roz Shafran, Amberly Brigden, Catherine Linney, Megan Niamh McManus, Catherine Borwick, and Esther Crawley, "Rapid Systematic Review: The Impact of Social Isolation and Loneliness on the Mental Health of Children and Adolescents in the Context of COVID-19," *Journal of the American Academy of Child & Adolescent Psychiatry* 59, no. 11 (2020): 1218–1239.

100 Per Engzell, Arun Frey, and Mark D. Verhagen, "Learning Loss Due to School Closures during the COVID-19 Pandemic," *Proceedings of the National Academy of Sciences* 118, no. 17 (2021): e2022376118.

101 Ibid.

102 Kenneth Shores and Matthew Steinberg, "The Impact of the Great Recession on Student Achievement: Evidence from Population Data," August 28, 2017, available at SSRN, https://ssrn.com; Rashmita S. Mistry, Aprile D. Benner, and Anna M. Kimura, "Covid-19 and Children's Social Development: Insights from the Life-Course Perspective," in *The Wiley-Blackwell Handbook of Childhood Social Development*, ed. Peter K. Smith and Craig H. Hart (Hoboken, NJ: Wiley, 2022), 224–238.

103 World Bank, *COVID-19 Pandemic.*

104 Bastian A. Betthäuser, Anders M. Bach-Mortensen, and Per Engzell, "A Systematic Review and Meta-analysis of the Evidence on Learning during the COVID-19 Pandemic," *Nature Human Behaviour* 7, no. 3 (2023): 375–385.

105 W. Andrew Collins, Eleanor E. Maccoby, Laurence Steinberg, E. Mavis Hetherington, and Marc H. Bornstein, "Contemporary Research on Parenting: The Case for Nature and Nurture," *American Psychologist* 55, no. 2 (2000): 218–232; Kathryn A.

Kerns, Jeffery E. Aspelmeier, Amy L. Gentzler, and Chandra M. Grabill, "Parent-Child Attachment and Monitoring in Middle Childhood," *Journal of Family Psychology* 15, no. 1 (2001): 69–81.

106 Duane Buhrmester and Wyndol Duane Furman, "The Changing Functions of Friends in Childhood: A Neo-Sullivanian Perspective," in *Friendship and Social Interaction*, ed. Valerian J. Derlega and Barbara A. Winstead (New York: Springer, 1986), 41–62; Rachel Maunder and Claire P. Monks, "Friendships in Middle Childhood: Links to Peer and School Identification, and General Self-Worth," *British Journal of Developmental Psychology* 37, no. 2 (2019): 211–229.

107 Erik Erikson, *Childhood and Society* (New York: Norton, 1950).

108 Kerns et al., "Parent-Child Attachment and Monitoring."

109 Angie C. Kennedy, Deborah Bybee, Cris M. Sullivan, and Megan Greeson, "The Effects of Community and Family Violence Exposure on Anxiety Trajectories during Middle Childhood: The Role of Family Social Support as a Moderator," *Journal of Clinical Child & Adolescent Psychology* 38, no. 3 (2009): 365–379.

110 Sabine Doebel and Michael C. Frank, "Broadening Convenience Samples to Advance Theoretical Progress and Avoid Bias in Developmental Science," *Journal of Cognition and Development*, November 12, 2023; Frankenhuis and Amir, "What Is the Expected Human Childhood?"

111 Natalie Angier, "Now We Are Six: The Hormone Surge of Middle Childhood," *New York Times*, December 27, 2011, D1.

112 Del Giudice, Angeleri, and Manera, "Juvenile Transition,"; Bjorklund, *How Children Invented Humanity.*

5

Children's Rights Law in Middle Childhood

AOIFE DALY AND AMY WALSH

I. Introduction

Middle childhood, understood as spanning roughly age six to twelve years, is a crucial phase of human development involving enormous transitions in social behavior, cognition, and motivations.[1] During this phase of development, as explained in chapter 4, children's capacity for problem-solving, abstract thought, and the maintenance of close relationships increases significantly. In middle childhood, children's social lives become more complex as they participate in compulsory formal education and enjoy greater freedom to play with friends. This developmental phase brings transition toward greater responsibility such as "chores" or domestic responsibilities, and for some children, it may mean entering the world of formal work.[2] Yet, despite its distinctive features and its importance as a phase of child development, middle childhood is overlooked in international human rights law, where it is frequently amalgamated with early childhood or adolescence. It is notable, for instance, that the UN Committee on the Rights of the Child (Committee) has produced General Comments on the rights of children in early childhood and in adolescence but none on the rights of the child in middle childhood.[3]

The lack of attention to children's rights in middle childhood is quite striking when one considers that this phase is a vital part of the human experience and a crucial step in our developmental journey. Indeed, Marco Del Giudice opines that we cannot fully understand human development without analyzing middle childhood and the paradoxes that it appears to involve.[4] This emerging view of middle childhood as complex and multifaceted, Del Giudice argues, can help us to appreciate the centrality of the stage of middle childhood in the human life history. Relating this to children's rights is important to ensure a fuller understanding of the rights of the child.

Recognizing middle childhood as an important life stage, therefore, this chapter considers the range of children's rights issues relevant to this distinctive developmental stage. Building on the development research set out in chapter 4, it argues that greater attention should be given to children's rights during middle childhood so that the needs, circumstances, and particular experiences of children during this stage of childhood are taken into account. In order to advance this goal, the chapter examines a selected group of core rights to illustrate how rights operate in, and are relevant to, middle childhood. Although the analysis draws primarily on, and thus may be more applicable to, the Global North, as this is where the authors reside, this chapter also seeks to take account of the views, lives, and experiences of children from the Global South.[5]

The chapter considers children's rights in middle childhood from the perspective of key principles of the CRC. It begins with the right of children to participate—in proceedings and more broadly—before discussing the principle of the best interest of the child as well as the right to protection from harm in middle childhood. The child's health and education rights in middle childhood are then elaborated. Finally, the chapter concludes with some observations that might be taken into account were the Committee to develop a General Comment on children's rights during this important developmental stage.

II. Middle Childhood and the UN Convention on the Rights of the Child

It is well known that Article 1 of the UN Convention on the Rights of the Child (CRC) defines a child as "every human below the age of 18 years unless under the law applicable to the child, majority is attained earlier." Neither in Article 1 nor in any other provision of the CRC are the stages of childhood expressly recognized or defined, leading to the assumption that every right in the CRC must be considered applicable to children at every development stage. The absence from the CRC of any specific ages permits states parties maximum discretion in the application of age limits, leaving the boundaries of stages of development open to interpretation. The Committee acknowledges varying definitions between the age ranges used for development stages, noting, for instance, that the definition of early childhood varies between "different countries and regions, according to local traditions and the organization of primary school systems."[6] Only Article 40(3)(b) requires states parties to establish a minimum age below which children shall be presumed not to have the capacity to infringe the criminal law. Interestingly, in recommending that this age should be set at a minimum of fourteen years, the Committee has relied on the fact that "developmental and neuroscience evidence indicates that adolescent brains continue to mature even beyond the teenage years, affecting certain kinds of decision-making."[7] The relevance of child development to children's exercise of their rights is discussed relatively rarely, however.

Article 5 of the CRC, which recognizes the duty of parents to provide direction and guidance to the child in the exercise of their rights in line with their evolving capacities, highlights that children's autonomy to exercise their rights is not the same at all stages.[8] Questions of capacity dominate analyses of children's rights at all stages—as is illustrated by the consideration elsewhere in this book of children's rights during early childhood (part 1) and adolescence (part 3). While the application of children's rights in each developmental phase offers its own complexity and unique character, in many respects, Article 5 can be said to be most directly relevant to the exercise of children's rights in middle childhood. Found between early years (when the child's capacities are relatively limited and the parental duty to provide guidance is strong) and adolescence (when the child's capacities are advanced and the responsibility of parents is beginning to fade), it is arguably during middle childhood that the real challenges arise as to how best to balance these sometimes-competing considerations.

As Grant illustrates in chapter 4, middle childhood is defined by a sense of slowly evolving reasoning, changing relationships, and self-awareness and a period of apprenticeship as the child hones the skills, customs, and sense of responsibility necessary to thrive in their environment. While the CRC's relative silence on all stages of child development might excuse its failure to take account of the very particular characteristics of middle childhood, the absence of attention from the Committee on these issues is less easy to understand. At the same time, the Committee's somewhat confused position on middle childhood—an analysis of its General Comments suggests that it sees childhood as falling into either early years or adolescence—arguably presents an important opportunity to look afresh at the application of the CRC to this stage of childhood.

The scope of this chapter requires that we select a limited number of CRC provisions for analysis. In line with the approach taken in the other parts of this book, we focus here on child participation (Article 12), the best interests of the child (Article 3), the right to protection from harm (Article 19), and the right to health (Article 24) and education (Articles 28 and 29).

A. Child Participation

The CRC requires in Article 12 that states "shall assure" to children the right to be heard and have their views given due weight in accordance with their age and maturity. In particular, children should be "provided the opportunity" to express their views in all matters affecting them.[9] The right recognized in Article 12 is thus limited not by age but by the child's capability to form a view; as such, it has no specific start or cutoff point. There is little doubt that children in middle childhood are capable of forming a view within the terms of Article 12; the question that then arises is what weight should be attached to that view in line with the remaining terms of Article 12.

1. CHILDREN IN MIDDLE CHILDHOOD AND RIGHTS OF PARTICIPATION

As children branch out during middle childhood, exploring new relationships in their community, in social groups, and in public life, the right to have their views taken into account in matters that affect them, in line with Article 12, takes on increasing importance. The increasing reach of children's lives at this stage of development also brings children's broader participation rights—the right to information (Article 17) and the right to freedom of expression (Article 15), for instance—into view. Nothing in the CRC, with the exception of the requirement for parental guidance and direction in Article 5, suggests that these rights are not to be exercised by children with the capacity to do so, and yet, middle childhood may be considered by adults to be too early for children to enjoy these freedoms, not least given concerns that their exercise of these rights risks bringing them into conflict with others in online and political matters.[10] This highlights one of the key challenges of children's rights during this development phase: that children's capacity to exercise such rights is likely to be contested by those who have responsibility for them.

The CRC correctly, from a development perspective, highlights the importance of family life and relationships. As Grant explains in chapter 4, these are important for children in middle childhood too. Of increasing importance during this stage, however, are children's wider circles of friends and peers that emerge through this phase, as children's social lives move from family into school and sometimes work environments. These relationships and the ideas that children generate through these interactions, however, enjoy far less protection in the CRC, which makes no reference at all to children's friends and peers or the wider community. References to school are limited to the formal process of education (Articles 28 and 29; see later in this chapter), and references to work are confined to limiting children's economic exploitation (Article 32). In these very precise ways, the CRC limits its relevance to the lives of children during middle childhood. By contrast, the Committee has strongly articulated the opportunities that adolescence presents for children, pointing to "growing opportunities, capacities, aspirations, energy and creativity" and identifying children during this phase as "agents of change and a key asset and resource with the potential to contribute positively to their families, communities and countries."[11] Children in middle childhood can also, it is submitted, contribute to a whole range of issues, including "health and education campaigns, family support, peer education, community development initiatives, participatory budgeting and creative arts."[12] They also, including in middle childhood, are uniquely placed to engage very proactively in matters that affect them, such as the environment.[13] In this respect, underestimating the capacity of children to participate during middle childhood not only risks undermining their rights under the CRC but also underplays the impact that their contribution—including in the wider societal context—can have.

The Committee emphasizes that Article 12 of the CRC requires states to introduce measures to ensure that children's views inform "the development, implementation and monitoring of all relevant legislation, policies, services and programmes affecting their lives, at school and at the community, local, national and international levels."[14] The Committee also highlights the online environment as providing crucial opportunities for strengthening and expanding the engagement of adolescents in the world around them (see also Peleg and Varadan, chapter 6). One could envisage, for example, that supporting the exercise of children's rights in the online world would involve providing children in middle childhood with age-appropriate training, through schools and other venues, in online safety and how to navigate and participate in the online world. Interestingly, Finland ranks near the top of international indices for press freedom and education, and it provides education in primary schools to children in middle childhood on how to recognize misinformation ("fake news") online and elsewhere.[15] This is a good example of how to harness the rights of children during middle childhood in a way that supports their continuing development.

One cause for optimism in the Committee's own practice in this regard is its engagement with children from middle childhood in its consultation processes, most recently in the development of its General Comment No. 26 on the right of children to a healthy environment.[16] In the formation of the General Comment, the Committee consulted a dedicated child/youth advisory group, which included a number of children in middle childhood, many of whom began their environmental activism in early childhood, for example, Francisco Javier Vera Manzanares (age fourteen at the time of writing) from Colombia.[17] Children's engagement in environmental activism, including in climate consultations and cases, makes a similar point as to the relevance of participation rights to children during middle childhood.

The capacity of children in middle childhood to contribute to such initiatives in relation to themselves and the world around them must therefore receive greater emphasis in law and policy if children's rights in middle childhood are to be appropriately protected. The CRC requires the participation of children in decision-making in middle childhood; experience demonstrates that this *can* be done. Take, for example, the Irish youth assembly on biodiversity, which involved gathering the views of children to inform the Irish government on the topic.[18] Here, a minimum age of seven years was set for children's participation, and the program was designed to provide for the needs of children in middle childhood through tailored activities and child protection training.

These examples highlight the fact that participation in communities and political initiatives is not only possible and desirable for children in middle childhood but also important for the fulfillment of their rights under the CRC. Relevant here is the Committee's view that a children's rights-based approach, which exists regardless of a child's stage of development "requires a paradigm shift away from child protection approaches in which children are perceived and treated as 'objects' in need of assistance rather than as rights holders entitled to non-negotiable rights to protection. A child rights approach is one which furthers the realization of the rights of all children as set out in the CRC by developing the capacity of duty-bearers to meet their obligations to respect, protect and fulfil rights (art. 4) and the capacity of rights holders to claim their rights."[19]

The Committee went on to outline that children must be seen as rights holders and not simply objects of the "benevolent activities of adults."[20] This requires respecting children as rights holders and engaging in consultation with them when it comes to designing, implementing, monitoring, and evaluating policies and other measures that affect them, in line with their age and evolving capacities.[21] This is a key consideration for children in middle childhood given that the particular characteristics and experiences of children at this stage are so frequently ignored.

2. CHILDREN IN MIDDLE CHILDHOOD AND PARTICIPATION IN PERSONAL AND HOME MATTERS

Children in middle childhood can hold very strong views and preferences about personal matters concerning their upbringing, such as where they will live on family breakdown and where they will attend school.[22] Yet research suggests that these views can be left unheard in relation to personal matters and ignored in family and court settings.[23] Although UK research indicates that children feel most heard in their families, when it comes to court proceedings, such as family law and child protection proceedings, it is quite common in states around the world for judges to arbitrarily pronounce that the views and wishes of children under the age of eleven or twelve years should not be given much weight, because of their developmental stage.[24] The lack of regard for the views of children in middle childhood can lead to seemingly illogical approaches in family law proceedings, as adults attempt to square the right to be heard with their assumptions about children in middle childhood. For instance, as Daly remarks, "In the Scottish case of *M. v M.* an educational psychologist gave evidence that an average 10 year old could be persuaded by arguments, be influenced by the way something was presented, and find it difficult to weigh up all factors in a decision. The Sheriff in his judgment note[d] that the inability of a 10 year old to weigh all factors is 'obvious' which begs the question as to why the court would go to the trouble of having a psychologist give evidence to point out the obvious."[25] It is also common for courts to refrain from even seeking children's views in middle childhood, contrary to the first requirement of Article 12 of the CRC, which requires children who can form a view to be afforded the right to express that view in matters that affect them. For example, children under ten years old are generally not heard in family law proceedings in France, as well as many other jurisdictions, suggesting a misunderstanding of the terms of the CRC in this regard.[26] In this respect, it is arguable that children in middle childhood—who are very likely to be capable of forming a view yet least likely to have that view heard—are among Article 12's greatest victims. It is for children at this developmental stage that much work remains to be done in the implementation of children's participation rights.

To assure to the child in middle childhood their right to be heard, they must first be informed that they are in possession of this right.[27] In this regard, adults must "show patience and creativity by adapting their expectations to a young child's interests, level of understanding and preferred ways of communicating."[28] Even though the Committee was referring to "young" children here, the overlapping definition between early childhood and middle childhood indicates that these points will be crucial for children in the stage of middle childhood as well. Children who do not have capacity to provide views in traditional conversation, the Committee continues, can potentially provide views through communication such as play or art.[29] Therefore, their right to be heard should not be discounted on this basis.

Enjoying the right to be heard is one element of Article 12. Having due weight placed on one's views and wishes is another. The Committee emphasizes that "simply listening to the child is insufficient": the views of a child have to be *seriously considered*.[30] The right to be heard is closely connected to Article 5 of the CRC, which states that parents and other responsible adults are to provide guidance to children in the exercise of their rights "in a manner consistent with the evolving capacities of the child."[31] The "evolving capacities of the child" is not defined in the CRC; however, the Committee on the Rights of the Child opines that it refers to "processes of maturation and learning whereby children progressively acquire knowledge, competencies and understanding, including acquiring understanding about their rights and about how they can best be realized."[32] Evolving capacities are perhaps nowhere more relevant than in middle childhood. As Grant discusses in chapter 4, Piaget identified a "concrete operational" stage beginning at age seven.

Questions sometimes arise that require professionals to formally assess the capacity of children, in order to establish whether, for example, they can consent to medical treatment.[33] It is crucial to acknowledge that autonomy—the ideal that we should decide our own destiny to the extent possible—is arguably the most valued characteristic in a liberal democracy.[34] Evidence indicates that it is inherently good for well-being. Enjoying autonomy has been found to be positively correlated with a number of outcomes for children and even more so when they have experience of making decisions together with adults.[35] Relational autonomy—where children's independence will be operating through the prism of their relationships with others—is key in middle childhood, given, as Grant illustrates in chapter 4, its significance as a developmental stage in which children are typically more dependent on their caregivers than are older children.[36]

The Committee emphasizes that the child is a rights holder, rather than a mere beneficiary of benevolent activities of adults.[37] Article 5 of the CRC therefore is not simply about adults caring for children but about acknowledging that the greater a child's capacity, the more they should enjoy autonomy. For children in middle childhood, taking a children's rights approach to their capacity is particularly crucial. Case law indicates a high level of acceptance among adults that adolescents can increasingly make decisions for themselves. Below this age, however, the same level of acceptance does not always exist. In some contexts, children in middle childhood gain greater independence, such as by taking on greater responsibilities in their families and communities. However, there are areas such as family law where it is evident that there is a tendency *against* seeing children in middle childhood as having the potential to be autonomous (note the Scottish case of *M. v M.* cited earlier), despite the fact that the Committee states that "age alone cannot determine the significance of a child's views" and that other factors such as experience will also be important.[38]

Considering capacity, then, will be particularly important in middle childhood, as it appears that children at this stage are frequently underestimated in relation to their capacities. The exception in this regard appears to relate to criminal capacity, where many states have set the minimum age limit for criminal responsibility of children as low as ten years.[39] This appears in significant contrast to many states' approaches to capacity in areas of civil decision-making, including the level of autonomy children enjoy, for example, in medical and educational decision-making.[40] The incoherence of these approaches appears illogical.[41] Regardless, there are no shortcuts to determining whether a child has capacity or not, and there is evidence that an approach that aims to support children to understand their situation should be the main focus when a child's capacities are in question. Daly opines that, in order to take a rights-based approach to assessing or understanding the capacity of a child, the following concepts should be considered in light of various CRC articles:

1. Autonomy (Article 12): Children have autonomy rights, and to deny them their wishes should be considered a matter of seriousness.
2. Evidence (Article 2): Decision-makers should have basic knowledge about childhood, including psychology and other relevant schools of thought (so that decisions are not based on personal or societal assumptions or biases about children).
3. Support (Article 5): Capacity can be increased through appropriate support, guidance, and information.
4. Protection (Article 3): Children are a group that is in a unique position of relative vulnerability, and adults are obliged to offer them protection from harm.[42]

Because of the existence of adult assumptions that the views and wishes of children in middle childhood should not be given much weight, it is particularly important that a rights-based approach is taken with respect to the capacity of children at this stage, informed by development science. It is vital that professionals are aware of evidence available on children's decision-making capacities in middle childhood. It may be surprising to many people to learn, for example, that evidence points to very strong decision-making abilities among children in middle childhood, with the research of Irma Hein et al., for instance, suggesting that capacity to consent to medical treatment develops on average at age nine.[43]

It is likely that for much of middle childhood, children will be somewhere between having capacity (where formal, legal measurements are applied) and lacking capacity.[44] In reality, where matters such as those concerning medical treatment arise in which formal measurements are necessary, decisions will inevitably either be shared with parents or legal guardians or made exclusively by the child's caregiver. It is likely that applying a rights-based process, such as that outlined earlier (highlighting support and information), will be more important than actually measuring capacity itself. It should be understood that developmental psychology is not always considered to be completely objective and neutral and that it involves theories, rather than inescapable facts.[45] It is also of great importance that both parents and professionals understand that support and information can greatly increase the capacity of children in particular matters. Children should not simply be "assessed," therefore, but rather they should be supported to participate and to understand matters on which they have a right to be heard.[46]

B. Best Interests of the Child

Article 3 of the CRC enshrines the principle of the best interests of the child, which requires states parties to ensure that children's best interests are regarded as "a primary" consideration in all actions affecting them. It also requires protection of children's welfare and safety. As Emma Cave and Zenon Stavrinides point out, "Article 3 places great responsibility on parents and public officials to protect the health and welfare interests of children."[47] The relevance of the principle to children in middle childhood—as in all developmental stages—is obvious. What is less clear is how Article 3 can apply in a way that enhances the interests of children during this distinctive developmental stage of a child's life.

The Committee on the Rights of the Child has emphasized that the best interests of the child must be a primary consideration in all decisions of public policy, and the specificities of middle childhood mean that this requirement has particularly important application in this context, given the effects of such decisions on children during this developmental stage.[48] Children's rights impact assessments could be a useful tool to support this process, ensuring that decisions that affect children take account of the developmental context of middle childhood and children's emergence into the public sphere (e.g., starting schooling) during this stage. Impact assessments involve "predicting the impact of any proposed law, policy or budgetary allocation which affects children and the enjoyment of their rights."[49] In order to ensure such impact is accurately assessed, it needs to take account of the particular experiences and characteristics of children during middle childhood: each unique development stage should thus be built into such instruments. Given the weak understanding of the importance of middle childhood as a stage of development, adapting such instruments to the developmental stage is one way to enable even greater attention to be given to middle childhood in assessment impacts on the rights and best interests of the child.

C. Protection from Harm

The extent of CRC provisions aimed to protect children from harm highlights the range of risks children face with regard to violence, harm from substance use, and harm from labor and sexual exploitation. These provisions include Article 19, the right of children to be free from violence; Article 33, the duty on states to prevent harm to children from "the illicit use of narcotic drugs"; and Article 32, the duty on states to prevent the economic exploitation of children.[50] As with other CRC provisions, these apply generally to all children, and to date, there has been no explicit consideration of the elements of rights protection that might be unique or even particularly important to children in middle childhood, regardless of the specific risks that children face during this developmental phase.

The Committee notes that in early childhood, young children are particularly at risk of violence because of their relative powerlessness.[51] Of course, the same applies to children in middle childhood, who are generally lacking in power and dependent on their adult caregivers. This may be more pronounced when children in middle childhood look older than their age and receive more harsh treatment as a result (see chapter 4). For instance, research indicates that when children hit puberty early, it changes how others relate to them and can lead to mental health problems.[52]

Regarding economic exploitation, developmental science indicates that children in middle childhood have begun to take on greater levels of responsibility relating to chores and other types of work, undoubtedly heightening the risks they face in this regard.[53] In the context of greater responsibilities, child labor may occur in middle childhood—globally, one in ten children aged five and over were involved in child labor in 2020, an estimated 160 million children.[54] The high-profile case of the Pakistani child laborer and anti-child-labor activist Iqbal Masih, murdered at the age of twelve, highlights that children in middle childhood can be trapped in exploitative conditions, suffering significant adverse effects on their education, their health, and indeed their lives. Iqbal's growth, before his murder, had been permanently stunted by the exploitative labor to which he was subjected.[55]

As noted earlier, however, the rights issues specific to children in middle childhood have been insufficiently elaborated. While it is welcome that protection from harm is now a subject of increasing attention at the government level, it is crucial that this process takes explicit account of the particular risks that children face in middle childhood—from forms of maltreatment in the home, which may vary depending on their development, to exploitation and harm experienced outside the home, a setting they increasingly experience as they continue to develop. The Committee on the Rights of the Child states, "Collection of sufficient and reliable data on children, disaggregated to enable identification of discrimination and/or disparities in the realization of rights, is an essential part of implementation."[56] On issues such as child protection, child labor, and similar issues, states should examine the extent to which children in middle childhood are suffering harm, why, and how it can be prevented.

To ensure that children's rights are fully realized in middle childhood, it is crucial that states adopt plans for middle childhood within a rights-based framework. The Committee outlines this obligation on states in the context of early childhood development, in particular emphasizing the importance of early childhood experiences for the long-term prospects of children and youth. This will also be vital context of protection from harm for children in middle childhood and will, as the Committee emphasizes in the case of early childhood, require "an increase in human and financial resource allocations for early childhood services and programmes."[57] This will require resourcing policies, services, and professional training from the explicit standpoint of supporting and protecting children in middle childhood.

The Committee also notes in the context of early childhood that particular groups of young children are at greater risk of harm (possibly rooted in discrimination). The Committee highlights the risk of "harsh treatment and unreasonable expectations, which may be exploitative or abusive."[58] In the case of girls, the Committee notes, for example, that they "may be expected to undertake excessive family responsibilities and deprived of opportunities to participate in early childhood and primary education."[59] There are, of course, other potentially disadvantaged groups that will require particular protection from harm in middle childhood as they do in other stages, such as children with disabilities. The development science, as illustrated in chapter 4, highlights the importance of ensuring that these considerations are built into efforts to protect children from harm in middle childhood.

D. Health Rights

The right to health of children in middle childhood also has particular meaning given the physical and biological changes children experience at this stage. As Grant explains in chapter 4, the onset of the adrenal developments means that children at this stage will experience a number of biological and psychological developments, including the fact that they may have mood swings.[60] Society is relatively familiar with the expectation that this occurs in adolescence and that it is due to changes in hormones. However, many adults are much less familiar with the fact that this is also to be expected in middle childhood. Education about children's development and relationships is increasingly recognized as a right. Age-appropriate material on developments in middle childhood is important to assist children of this age understand their own bodies and measures appropriate to protect their integrity. This is necessary for the enjoyment by children in middle childhood of the right to the highest attainable standard of health under CRC Article 24.

In order to uphold the right to health for children at this stage of middle childhood, it is crucial that parents, professionals, and policy makers also have an adequate understanding of the developmental aspects of middle childhood and that they impart this information with respect and sensitivity in the various settings important to children in middle childhood, including in school. The fact that knowledge about middle childhood is necessary for a children's rights–based approach to children at this stage is highlighted by the Committee, which states that professionals working with children should have the relevant training, including on children's capacities.[61]

The Committee has also been forthright about how adolescents can be seen by governments and policy makers in a negative light: public health issues such as teen pregnancies can be focused on and potential for contributions to communities overlooked. The Committee "regrets the widespread negative characterization of adolescence," which among other things results in a narrow approach to adolescence, focusing on problems and interventions.[62] It is important, therefore, as with adolescence, that states commit to focus on the creation of environments that uphold the rights of children in middle childhood and, as with adolescents, "support the development of their physical, psychological, spiritual, social, emotional, cognitive, cultural and economic capacities."[63] The attention provided to health and well-being at this stage will set the scene for children's health (both physical and mental) into adolescence and adulthood.

E. Education Rights

Education, while important for all children, is especially crucial in middle childhood, given that for most children, formal education begins at this stage. Article 29 of the CRC outlines that states parties shall direct the education of the child to "the development of the child's personality, talents and mental and physical abilities to their fullest potential." It is important to emphasize this right as children move to informal and, in some contexts, formal work, which may deprive them of their right to education. Also, Article 6 of the CRC refers to the child's right to life and the obligation on states to ensure, to the maximum extent possible, the survival and development of children. States are not simply obliged to refrain from harming the life of a child, but rather, they must take all possible measures to create conditions that promote the well-being of children. In the Committee's General Comment on rights in early childhood, it emphasizes that states parties are obliged under Article 6 to uphold and protect rights relating to all aspects of development.[64]

As noted earlier, the transition to formal education is a key feature of middle childhood, at least in the industrialized world. Children's right to access education that is suited to the development of their fullest potential is key during this stage, and children in difficult socioeconomic circumstances risk their right to education when they enter the world of work. In other contexts, the emphasis on educational attainment can also risk placing undue pressure on children. Many do not fit well in the mold of formal schooling, which may require long periods sitting at a desk. This raises the crucial issue that greater attention is required to the right of children to rest, leisure, and play under Article 31 of the CRC. The Committee notes that insufficient attention has been given by states parties and others to implementing Article 31, which guarantees to all children the right to "rest and leisure, to engage in play and recreational activities appropriate to the age of the child and to participate freely in cultural life and the arts." Greater attention and increased resources (both human and financial) must be dedicated by states to the implementation of the right to rest, leisure, and play, specifically tuning into its developmental significance during middle childhood.[65] Professionals must also understand that rest, leisure, and play for children is not a discretionary pastime but a right. As Grant outlines in chapter 4, "Recess is a necessity—not a luxury or a reward—for school-age children." The treatment of children in school is a key issue for those in middle childhood. Frequently, punishment for perceived poor behavior can involve increased workload or exclusion from break times. This should be seen as a rights issue and should not be permitted in schools or other settings. As there is a greater emphasis on formal education for children in middle childhood as opposed to those in early years, arguably this issue is particularly pertinent to middle childhood.

III. A General Comment on Middle Childhood

Despite the particular elements of child development relevant to middle childhood, there has to date been a distinct lack of attention given to children's rights in this context by the Committee, as well as in children's rights scholarship. Although the generality of the CRC has not helped in this regard, the Committee's linear understanding of childhood as a journey, with adulthood as the destination, is also problematic in this respect. This is evident, for example, throughout the General Comment on rights in adolescence: "in order to ensure the optimum development of every child throughout childhood, it is necessary to recognize the impact that each period of life has on subsequent stages."[66] The Committee's reference to "each period of life" appears limited to two stages, early childhood and adolescence; references to middle childhood are rare. And yet, as Grant illustrates in chapter 4, the unique and distinct nature of middle childhood warrants much more careful and deliberate consideration of children's rights during this phase of development. Although this chapter goes some way to identifying the key elements of such an approach, it is vital, specifically to raise the profile of children's rights during middle childhood, that consideration be given by the Committee to adopting a General Comment on this theme.

General Comments are an important avenue through which the Committee can further develop international standards on particular children's rights issues and elaborate on the meaning of those rights. They help to raise the profile of particular issues, while also providing the opportunity to engage in a contemporary analysis of relevant research on the subject. In addition, the adoption of concluding observations on states parties' reports also provides important opportunities for the Committee to develop its jurisprudence on children's rights in middle childhood under the CRC. The reporting process facilitates the

Committee to identify issues of concern at a national level, to highlight those issues, and to provide recommendations to states as to how best to improve their implementation of children's rights under the CRC. As it is doing this, the Committee has the opportunity to further progress understandings of the parameters of international standards on a particular children's rights issue. So far, however, the lack of attention to middle childhood under the CRC is matched by the absence of consideration given to the matter in the Committee's concluding observations and other recommendations.

For the purpose of this chapter, an examination was conducted of the concluding observations and recommendations of the Committee in the February–March 2020 session. This is a small sample of documents selected for the purpose of providing a snapshot of concluding observations to identify any patterns that may exist in relation to the Committee's treatment of rights in middle childhood. It constitutes all nine concluding observations and recommendations produced by the Committee in 2020 (on Micronesia, the Cook Islands, Tuvalu, the state of Palestine, Austria, Costa Rica, Hungary, Belarus, and Rwanda). Although it is a small number of concluding observations, it is offered as illustrative of the lack of attention to middle childhood in concluding observations.

Our review of these Committee concluding observations found a number of references to early childhood and to adolescents/adolescence but no references to middle childhood. References to early childhood ranged from one mention (e.g., in relation to Belarus) to five mentions (in the case of the state of Palestine). References to adolescence/adolescents ranged from two (Austria) to thirty-one mentions (Costa Rica); and references on average tended to be in the teens. References to early childhood rights in the Committee's concluding observations were in the context of education, while the references to adolescents' rights were in the context of health. It is not clear why the Committee made no references to middle childhood in any of these concluding observations, but it further highlights the attention gap to this important life stage.

The absence of attention by the Committee to the category of middle childhood points to the need for initiatives on this front. The first and most obvious step would be to draft a General Comment on the rights of children in middle childhood. The value of such an exercise is seen in the objectives that the Committee cites in the General Comment on the rights of children in early childhood, which could equally be applied to children in middle childhood. The Committee emphasizes that one objective is to strengthen the rights of young children and to draw the attention of states to their obligations toward young children.[67] Another purpose of that General Comment is to elaborate on the particular features of that stage of childhood and what this means for children's rights. The General Comment also seeks to position young children as "social actors from the beginning of life" and to emphasize the particular interests of this group as well as the capacities and vulnerabilities of children of this age.[68] The Committee also indicates the diversity of interests and experiences of children in this group, pointing to different cultural experiences. The Committee also aims to highlight states' obligations to introduce "comprehensive policies, laws, programmes, practices, professional training and research specifically focused on rights in early childhood."[69] All these rationales apply equally to middle childhood.

There are numerous points that should be considered in such a General Comment. As noted earlier, the features of middle childhood include those relating to increased capacity, and therefore increased responsibilities, and children's emergence into the public sphere at this stage. Many rights issues arise in relation to these developments: there is an increased ability of children to form views and therefore enjoy greater participation rights. Children may be exposed to risks of being economically exploited, and therefore laws and policies must address these risks. In many countries, middle childhood comes with potential criminal responsibility. The need to address this issue is reflected in the fact that many countries have minimum ages of criminal responsibility in middle childhood, which is contrary both to children's rights law and to what we know about hot and cold cognition and child development more generally.

That middle childhood may be accompanied by the beginning of formal schooling in many contexts means a lack of sufficient opportunities for play. Gender roles may become pronounced, and there may be sex segregation, for example, in schools. These moves may be accompanied by lesser attention to the education of girls, affecting their right to education, right to freedom from discrimination, and other rights. Although middle childhood is accompanied by hormonal changes (see Grant, chapter 4), this is not widely known, and its implications on issues relating to the right to education and the right to health have not been adequately accounted for.

A General Comment on middle childhood would permit the Committee to elaborate from a children's rights perspective the features of childhood in this period and to highlight crucial developmental psychology research in the area.[70] Another crucial point is that it may encourage the Committee itself to focus on this vital life period and to consider it explicitly in its concluding observations on states parties' reports.[71] It would also encourage more broadly a perception of children in middle childhood as active actors. It would urge states to enact policies, laws, practices, professional training, and other activities geared at better acknowledging and understanding middle childhood. The drafting processes of recent General Comments on children and street situations and the right of children to a healthy environment, respectively, have engaged civil society, children from all over the world, and other stakeholders in exercises that gave much-needed attention to these crucial issues. Doing this for the theme of middle childhood could go a long way toward unifying the children's rights community in pursuit of a better understanding of rights issues at this important life stage, spurring children's rights researchers and other professionals to examine and better elucidate the implementation of children's rights in middle childhood.

To support this process, it is useful to bring together a number of points considered in relation to protecting children's rights in middle childhood to highlight the obligations of states to children at this stage (see table 5.1). It should be noted that the list of rights in table 5.1 is not an exhaustive list, and as all rights are interdependent and indivisible, there is some overlap. These points are presented bearing in mind some of the key characteristics of middle childhood, including hormonal changes (adrenarche), greater capacity than early childhood, greater independence from the family unit, greater responsibilities (which may include formal work), formal schooling, and gender segregation in school and play.

TABLE 5.1. Children's Rights in Middle Childhood: States' Obligations

Article 3: the principle of the best interest of the child	Articles 24 and 28/29: the rights to health and to education
The rights and best interests of children in middle childhood should be explicitly considered in policy making relevant to their rights and interests. Areas of law/policy particularly relevant to this developmental stage are those related to age of entry to work, facets of education, and the age of criminal responsibility. States must give due attention to whether and how play/leisure (as opposed to formal education) is in the interests of children in middle childhood.	States should ensure awareness of middle childhood as a distinct developmental phase among individuals working with children, parents, and others. Such awareness raising should include teaching children themselves about the physical and mental development associated with middle childhood. States should produce laws and policies to ensure that, while children in middle childhood can have responsibilities and duties, their labor cannot be exploited.
Article 3 and Article 19: protection from harm	**Article 12: child participation**
States should ensure that laws and policies relating to children's online activities are appropriate to their best interests and fulfill their rights in middle childhood, including training in schools to enable capacity building. States should consider the particular needs of children in middle childhood in relation to various types of harm that children need protection from. This includes protection from violence, substance use, and economic exploitation. States should ensure that particular groups of children in middle childhood, such as girls and those with disabilities, do not face particular harm.	States should ensure that children are involved in the creation of law and policy relating to middle childhood. States should ensure that courts consider the views/wishes of children in middle childhood. States should ensure that the views of children in middle childhood are not simply listened to but rather *seriously considered.* States should increase opportunities of children in middle childhood for political participation, including training and awareness raising for adults on the abilities of children in middle childhood.

IV. Conclusion

Middle childhood is a crucial phase of human development. Children at this stage undergo enormous transitions in social behavior, cognition, and motivations.[72] This chapter has demonstrated some of the many children's rights issues and considerations that arise in the context of middle childhood and analyzed them through the lens of the CRC.

To date, middle childhood, however, has been almost completely overlooked as a developmental phase for explicit consideration in international human rights law and is instead amalgamated with the analysis of rights in early childhood or adolescence stages. This is perhaps most pointedly demonstrated by the fact that the Committee has produced General Comments on the rights of children in these two stages but as yet has produced none on rights in middle childhood. Taking a sample of the concluding observations of the Committee (from the year 2020) also indicates a sense of confusion or ignorance as to the boundaries and the significance of middle childhood.

The broad definitions proposed by the Committee of both early childhood and adolescence mean that middle childhood can, for the most part, be encompassed in these other stages. Yet we can see obvious children's rights obstacles in the failure to focus explicitly on middle childhood. An explicit focus would provide much-needed understanding of the clear evidence of the existence of middle childhood as a developmental phase and the distinct changes that it brings for children, including cognitive, hormonal, and social changes. This would in turn highlight that states have particular obligations toward children at this stage, in the same way that, for example, the General Comment on rights in early childhood does for children at that stage.[73] States would be reminded that they are required to explicitly collect data about the experiences of children in middle childhood, as well as across other age ranges. It would bring attention to the fact that it is not just adolescents but also children in middle childhood who have the potential to be powerful social actors. Children in middle childhood can contribute to their communities and even globally, as demonstrated by environmental activists at this age.[74]

A General Comment on middle childhood would also have the effect of drawing explicit attention to the vulnerabilities of children of this age. As children in middle childhood become more capable of engaging in work and other activities, they are at risk of being exploited by adults who do not have their best interests at heart. Explicit focus on rights in middle childhood would highlight states' obligations to introduce laws, policies, programs, practices, professional training, and research focused specifically on the rights of children at this stage.[75] Ultimately, ensuring that the rights of children in middle childhood are properly appreciated and understood will help to implement the CRC and children's rights as a whole.

NOTES

1 Marco Del Giudice, "Middle Childhood: An Evolutionary-Developmental Synthesis," in *Handbook of Life Course Health Development*, ed. Neal Halfon, Christopher B. Forrest, Richard M. Lerner, and Elaine M. Faustman (Cham, Switzerland: Springer, 2018), 95–107.

2 Barbara Rogoff, Martha Julia Sellers, Sergio Pirrotta, Nathan Fox, and Sheldon H. White, "Age of Assignment of Roles and Responsibilities to Children: A Cross-Cultural Survey," *Human Development* 18 (1975): 353–369.

3 UN Committee on the Rights of the Child, *General Comment No. 7: Implementing Child Rights in Early Childhood*, para. 3, CRC/C/GC/7/Rev.1 (2006); UN Committee on the Rights of the Child, *General Comment No. 20: On the Implementation of the Rights of the Child during Adolescence*, para. 1, CRC/C/GC/20 (2016).

4 Del Giudice, "Middle Childhood."

5 For example, Benedetta Faedi Duramy and Tali Gal, "Understanding and Implementing Child Participation: Lessons from the Global South," *Children and Youth Services Review* 119 (2020): 105645; Louie Talitha Claasen and Gloudina Maria Spies, "The Voice of the Child: Experiences of Children, in Middle Childhood, Regarding Children's Court Procedure," *Social Work* 53, no. 1 (2017): 74–95; David Lancy and Annette Grove, "Getting Noticed: Middle Childhood in Cross-Cultural Perspective," *Human Nature* 22, no. 3 (2011): 281–302.

6 UN Committee on the Rights of the Child, *General Comment No. 7*, para. 4.

7 UN Committee on the Rights of the Child, *General Comment No. 24 on Children's Rights in Child Justice Systems*, para. 22, CRC/C/GC/24 (2019).

8 Sheila Varadan, "The Principle of Evolving Capacities under the U.N. Convention on the Rights of the Child," *International Journal of Children's Rights* 27 (2019): 306–338.

9 UN Committee on the Rights of the Child, *General Comment No. 12: The Right of the Child to Be Heard*, para. 86, CRC/C/GC/12 (2009).

10 Aoife Daly, *Article 15: The Right to Freedom of Association and to Freedom of Peaceful Assembly* (Leiden: Brill, 2016).

11 UN Committee on the Rights of the Child, *General Comment No. 20*, para. 2.

12 Ibid., para. 208.

13 Aoife Daly, "Climate Competence: Youth Climate Activism and Its Impact on International Human Rights Law," *Human Rights Law Review* 22, no. 2 (2022): ngac011.

14 UN Committee on the Rights of the Child, *General Comment No. 20*, para. 23.

15 Jon Henley, "How Finland Starts Its Fight against Fake News in Primary Schools," *The Guardian*, January 29, 2020, www.theguardian.com.

16 UN Committee on the Rights of the Child, *General Comment No. 26: On Children's Rights and the Environment with a Special Focus on Climate Change*, CRC/C/GC/26 (2023).

17 See Child Rights Environment, "Meet Our Advisors," accessed November 17, 2023, https://childrightsenvironment.org.

18 Children and Young People's Assembly on Biodiversity Loss, home page, accessed November 17, 2023, https://cyp-biodiversity.ie.

19 UN Committee on the Rights of the Child, *General Comment No. 13: The Right of the Child to Freedom from All Forms of Violence*, para. 59, CRC/C/GC/26 (2011).

20 Ibid., para. 72.

21 Ibid., para. 72(a).

22 Aoife Daly, *Children, Autonomy and the Courts: Beyond the Right to Be Heard* (Leiden: Brill Nijhoff, 2018).

23 Ibid.

24 Ibid.

25 Ibid., 299, citing *M. v M.*, Fam L.R. 90 (2008), paras. 53, 54.

26 See Luc Briand, "L'audition du mineur devant le JAF: Examen des arrêts d'appel," *AJ Famille*, January 2014, 22–24.

27 UN Committee on the Rights of the Child, *General Comment No. 12*, para. 20.

28 UN Committee on the Rights of the Child, *General Comment No. 5: General Measures of Implementation of the Convention on the Rights of the Child*, para. 11(c), CRC/C/GC/26 (2011).

29 See UN Committee on the Rights of the Child, *General Comment No. 12*, para. 21; Daly, *Children, Autonomy and the Courts*, 49.

30 UN Committee on the Rights of the Child, *General Comment No. 12*, para. 28.

31 UN Convention on the Rights of the Child, art. 5, November 20, 1989, 1577 U.N.T.S. 3 (hereafter CRC); see also Varadan, "Principle of Evolving Capacities."

32 UN Committee on the Rights of the Child, *General Comment No. 7*, para. 17.

33 Aoife Daly, "Assessing Children's Capacity: Reconceptualising Our Understanding through the UN Convention on the Rights of the Child," *International Journal of Children's Rights* 28, no. 3 (2020): 471–499.

34 Daly, *Children, Autonomy and the Courts.*

35 Samantha W. Bindman, Eva M. Pomerantz, and Glenn I. Roisman, "Do Children's Executive Functions Account for Associations between Early Autonomy-Supportive Parenting and Achievement through High School?," *Journal of Educational Psychology* 107, no. 3 (2015): 775.

36 John Christman, "Relational Autonomy, Liberal Individualism, and the Social Constitution of Selves," *Philosophical Studies* 117, nos. 1–2 (2004): 147.

37 UN Committee on the Rights of the Child, *General Comment No. 13*, para. 72(a).

38 UN Committee on the Rights of the Child, *General Comment No. 12*, para. 29.

39 Aaron Brown and Anthony Charles, "The Minimum Age of Criminal Responsibility: The Need for a Holistic Approach," *Youth Justice* 21, no. 2 (2021): 153–171.

40 Daly, "Assessing Children's Capacity."

41 Barry Goldson, "'Unsafe, Unjust and Harmful to Wider Society': Grounds for Raising the Minimum Age of Criminal Responsibility in England and Wales," *Youth Justice* 13, no. 2 (2013): 111–130.

42 Daly, "Assessing Children's Capacity."

43 Irma M. Hein, Pieter W. Troost, Robert Lindeboom, Imke Christiaans, Thomas Grisso, Johannes B. van Goudoever, and Ramón J. L. Lindauer, "Feasibility of an Assessment Tool for Children's Competence to Consent to Predictive Genetic Testing: a Pilot Study," *Journal of Genetics Counselling* 24, no. 6 (2015): 971–977.

44 See, e.g., Daly, "Assessing Children's Capacity."

45 Ibid.; Matias Cordero Arce, "Maturing Children's Rights Theory: From Children, with Children, of Children," *International Journal of Children's Rights* 23, no. 2 (2015): 283.

46 Daly, "Assessing Children's Capacity."

47 Emma Cave and Zenon Stavrinides, *Medical Practitioners, Adolescents and Informed Consent: Final Report* (Leeds, UK: University of Leeds, 2013), 13.

48 UN Committee on the Rights of the Child, *General Comment No. 14: On the Right of the Child to Have His or Her Best Interests Taken as a Primary Consideration*, CRC/C/GC/14 (2013).

49 European Union Agency for Fundamental Rights, "Child Rights Impact Assessment," accessed November 17, 2023, https://fra.europa.eu.

50 See also CRC, arts. 34 (sexual abuse and exploitation), 35 (abduction, sale, and trafficking), and 36 (other forms of exploitation).

51 UN Committee on the Rights of the Child, *General Comment No. 7*, para. 11.

52 American Psychological Association, "The Risks of Earlier Puberty," March 2016, www.apa.org.

53 See, e.g., Del Giudice, "Middle Childhood"; Rogoff et al., "Age of Assignment of Roles and Responsibilities"; Lancy and Grove, "Getting Noticed."

54 United Nations, "World Day against Child Labour," accessed November 17, 2023, www.un.org; UN Committee on the Rights of the Child, *General Comment No. 14*, para. 6.

55 World Children's Prize, "Iqbal Masih," accessed November 17, 2023, https://worldschildrensprize.org.

56 UN Committee on the Rights of the Child, *General Comment No. 5*.

57 UN Committee on the Rights of the Child, *General Comment No. 7*, para. 38.

58 Ibid.

59 Ibid., para. 11.

60 UN Committee on the Rights of the Child, *General Comment No. 7*, para. 34. Lawrence N. Parker, "Adrenarche," *Endocrinology and Metabolism Clinics of North America* 20, no. 1 (1991): 71–83.

61 UN Committee on the Rights of the Child, *General Comment No. 20*, para. 37(e).

62 Ibid., para. 15.

63 Ibid.

64 UN Committee on the Rights of the Child, *General Comment No. 7*, para. 10.

65 Ibid., para. 34.

66 UN Committee on the Rights of the Child, *General Comment No. 20*, para. 11.

67 UN Committee on the Rights of the Child, *General Comment No. 7*, para. 2.

68 Ibid.

69 Ibid.

70 UN Committee on the Rights of the Child, *General Comment No. 7*, paras. 6, 8.

71 It should be noted, however, that research indicates that General Comments by the Committee do not necessarily influence future Committee pronouncements. See Charlotte Alexander and Jonathan Todres, "Evaluating the Implementation of

Human Rights Law: A Data Analytics Research Agenda," *University of Pennsylvania Journal of International Law* 43 (2021): 1–77.

72 Del Giudice, "Middle Childhood."

73 UN Committee on the Rights of the Child, *General Comment No. 7*, para. 2.

74 Daly, "Climate Competence."

75 This is equivalent to states' obligations in relation to early childhood, as pointed out in the UN Committee on the Rights of the Child's *General Comment No. 7*.

6

Contemporary Children's Rights Issues in Middle Childhood

NOAM PELEG AND SHEILA VARADAN

I. Introduction

Middle childhood has been called a "decisive stage" marked by a child's emerging capacities or growing sense of industry within and outside the family.[1] It is a period of intense social learning as children begin to take notice of context and culture and the various overlapping and intersecting social positions they occupy in their lives.[2] As children merge into "a lane of increasing expectations and responsibilities," they start to engage with their broader social environment.[3] This social learning takes place both inside and outside the home, among and within a community of peers.[4] Through this process, children cultivate a unique ecological system, distinguishing themselves from parents and family and increasingly taking steps toward forging an identity.[5] How a child navigates this period of intense social learning will depend, in some measure, on how they are empowered as active agents in their own development and importantly how their evolving capacities are enabled and supported by parents and other adults exercising influence over their everyday lives.[6]

With the advent of the internet and the increasing accessibility of mobile devices, the location of social interactions has begun to shift from physical spaces to online platforms. For a child in middle childhood, online platforms have provided new and different avenues for play and social interaction; and in combining the real world and the virtual one (with the help of augmented reality apps), children are now able to exercise greater agency in seeking out peers and obtaining direct, unmitigated, and unfiltered access to the outside world. At the same time, children's rights in this space and time are being diluted, truncated, and substituted, overtaken by protectionist approaches, stemming from a heightened anxiety among parents and adults more generally over child development, safety, and well-being.[7] Social media has become a particular concern for adults, as more children between the ages of eight and twelve years are turning to social media platforms, and increasingly it is cast as a dangerous and damaging space for children's mental health and well-being.[8]

This new way of being a child in middle childhood, however, gives rise to a different set of questions, which relate to agency; privacy, including information sharing and surveillance; and rights. A child entering the age bracket of six to twelve years will probably begin to share information individually online, knowingly or unknowingly, with or without parental knowledge or consent, which may affect their privacy now and in the future. Once information is shared, a child may lose control over it and may not be able to remove it from the public domain in the future. Similarly, parents may share photographs or other details about their children's lives over the internet or via messaging apps, a phenomenon known as "sharenting," with or without their child's awareness, let alone consent.[9] Again, this information, once shared and uploaded onto a third-party server (whether it is made "public" or kept "private"), can be used to surveil or exploit the child or their family, raising questions regarding a child's privacy, best interests, and right to development. It also raises the question of whether the "right to be forgotten"—often defined as the right to have private information about a person removed from internet searches—will extend to children in the age bracket of six to twelve years, particularly, as mentioned before, when information is shared unknowingly by the child or by parents and other adults around the child.[10]

In this chapter, we consider the utility of the UN Convention on the Rights of the Child (CRC) as a framework to support children as they navigate emerging concepts of self and social belonging during middle childhood. Building on Grant's developmental analysis in chapter 4 and Daly and Walsh's children's rights framework in chapter 5, we examine how rights are manifested, protected, fulfilled, or derailed by adult-dominated narratives of children's experiences in middle childhood. Some of the key CRC provisions explored are the right to development (Article 6(2)), the best interests of the child principle (Article 3(1)), the right to participation

(Article 12), and the role of parents and other caregivers in supporting the evolving capacities of the child (Article 5). Other rights that come into play include the right to information (Article 17), the right to freedom of expression (Article 13), and the right to privacy (Article 16). Ultimately, we ask whether the CRC is relevant for the middle childhood period, particularly in how children "do" childhood today.[11]

The rapid digitization of children's lives has radically changed their experience of childhood, eroding boundaries between public and private spaces and transforming the geography of childhood itself.[12] We consider the heterogeneity of children's online use and the diversity of opportunities and risks that have emerged in this new terrain. We then consider the adult-led "safety agenda" that has worked to exclude children from the discourse on their own protection and, in the process, narrowed their access to online spaces—a critical avenue for self-exploration and social positioning in the world. We note from the outset that access to and engagement with the online world is not a universal experience for children but rather one that is reserved for a particular cohort, marking a clear division between and among children in how they experience middle childhood. This discrepancy in childhood experiences shapes and influences children in the later stages of their lives, similar to other formative experiences. But when it comes to digital literacy skills, the middle childhood experience can also affect educational pathways and "readiness" for the modern, post-COVID, global work world. In other words, opportunities (or lack thereof) to engage with the digital world, as we discuss in this chapter, can introduce differences that not only influence how children experience childhood but also impact their developmental future. This can also lead to de facto exclusion from educational or vocational opportunities, with socioeconomic and political consequences. In children's rights terms, this structural opportunity (or lack thereof) directly affects how children are able to enjoy and realize their rights, notably their right to development.

In the second part of this chapter, we discuss the utility and relevance of the CRC in capturing the new and different ways of being a child in the digitized world. With children increasingly turning to digital platforms (and social media) for social learning and peer-to-peer connection, the scope and breadth of children's rights is being tested, with regard to both how rights are conceived and how they are practiced.

These practical and normative challenges may be mitigated to an extent, by how we listen to children, care for their right to development, and respect their evolving capacity to exercise their rights. We suggest that the children's rights discourse may enrich the discussion, offering a vital layer of insight and perspective to guide parents and adults more generally in understanding what it means to be a child and experience middle childhood in the online world during these critical years.

II. Navigating a New Frontier for Middle Childhood: Children's Online Lives

A. Digital by Default

The advent of the internet and rapid uptake of home computing in the latter decades of the twentieth century gave way to a new generation of children whose lives are now being cast as "digital-by-default."[13] The internet opened new and dynamic opportunities for immersive and interactive social learning, enhancing peer-to-peer interaction in parallel with more traditional forms of play.[14] It offered alternatives to in-person dialogue where social contact was restricted or limited due to health, distance, or other reasons.[15] With mobile technologies now increasingly affordable and accessible, more children are spending time online, essentially living out their everyday lives in "anywhere, anytime" connectivity.[16] For a child in the age bracket of six to twelve years, this has meant access to the online world, whereas in earlier generations, internet access was reserved for adults or was accessible only through a stationary desktop computer. As Donell Holloway and colleagues observed more than a decade ago (in 2013), internet usage patterns are sharply increasing among younger children, with children between nine and twelve years exhibiting usage patterns similar to those of adolescents.[17]

As children move organically between physical and virtual spaces in everyday social interactions, these two worlds are now intersecting and merging in their lives earlier on and in more complex ways, blurring the boundaries between the digital and "offline" realms.[18] This shift from the stability of the physical world to the ephemerality of the digital realm has allowed children to become the architects of their own social spaces, affording them greater agency and autonomy in shaping their world.

These spaces also introduce a new and different dimension to imaginary worlds that children have long inhabited in childhood play. An imaginary world, unlike a virtual one, is invisible, intangible, and inaccessible to the outside world. A child can share an imaginary world through words or pretend play, but its realm ultimately remains inside the head of a child. The virtual world, while also intangible, can be made accessible to peers, parents, and strangers, who are able not only to enter this realm but also to interact and engage with the child in real time. However, this also presents a concern, as virtual worlds can be accessed by private companies, which may be able to control, manipulate, and monetize these spaces along with the child's personal information. So, while the virtual world opens new avenues to enhance children's imagination, it also invites opportunities for children's human rights to be abused, penetrated, manipulated, or monetized, with or without the child's (or their parents') knowledge, awareness, or consent. The positionality of the child in middle childhood and their particular age-based, capacity-related vulnerabilities bear mentioning here. Children begin to cultivate digital citizenship skills in middle childhood, and their resilience, as chapter 4 highlights, depends on personal hardiness and an ecosystem of social supports. These are required for the development of their digital citizenship. This, in turn, can enable children to identify, and cope with, attempts to abuse their online presence.

During the COVID-19 pandemic, many children (or at least those who had the structural and material means to do so) turned to digital platforms as a "lifeline" for social interaction, creating new avenues for peer-to-peer connection and "togetherness" where in-person play was not possible.[19] Digital platforms offer opportunities for creativity and play, which might not be as easy or practicable in the physical world. For instance, they allow parents or grandparents to engage in interactive play with their young grandchildren, introducing new forms of intergenerational play. Digital platforms also enhance and extend common forms of play from the physical world. For example, world-building and sandboxing games, such as Minecraft, specifically compelling for children during middle childhood, allow children to construct things that would never be possible in real life.[20] Specific features of digital platforms, such as visual chat or whiteboard functions, can prompt new forms of creativity and learning and extend common games from early childhood into the middle childhood years.[21]

More children are engaging with social media, with the biggest jump in use occurring between ten and eleven years, when children start looking to platforms such as TikTok, Snapchat, and other sites to seek out peer-to-peer interaction away from parents.[22] These engagements invariably happen on "adult" (or general) websites, as the intake and popularity of "kids dedicated sites" such as YouTube Kids remain limited.[23] Virtual spaces introduce new opportunities and avenues for youth activism, something that was rarely available for children in this age bracket in the past.[24] A flurry of youth activism has emerged in recent years, aided in some measure by social media and digital platforms. Notable youth activists such as Greta Thunberg have relied on digital platforms to galvanize and connect with other young people around the world, and this activism has been translated into the physical world, for example, through Fridays for Future and other protests around the world led by children and young adults. Other youth social movements, such as March for Our Lives and the Sunrise Movement, leverage social media networks not only to mobilize but also to influence political discourse in the United States.[25]

While much of this activism has been led by adolescents, for a child in middle childhood, it has provided a front-row seat to learn from other children and, when given the space and opportunity, a chance to participate themselves. For example, twelve-year-old Mariana Agostinho is among the six complainants who filed a complaint in the European Court of Human Rights against thirty-two governments for their failure to take action over climate change.[26] As Nicole Rogers points out, "for a growing number of children and young people, the climate crisis has become a source of empowerment rather than despair"; and with the help of older peers, children in middle childhood are increasingly being given a platform to test out, express, and engage with critical social issues.[27] The internet thus offers not only access to the outside world but also valuable peer-to-peer interaction and social learning on different social drivers (bias, privilege, social stratification) that shape the child's unique ecological system.[28] This online activism, as we discuss in this chapter, is a new avenue for children to realize their rights to freedom of expression and freedom of assembly as well as exercise their citizenship in ways that were formerly not available to them.

These various new ways of "doing" middle childhood online are not a universal experience, nor do they preclude offline living. Socioeconomic status continues to play a key role, privileging those children with the physical infrastructure to access online spaces: a reliable internet connection, a consistent electricity grid. It also presumes that children will have the financial means to acquire the latest technology and the space and (leisure) time to access and cultivate an online life. At the same time, the "digital divide" does not fall neatly across class lines, and the heterogeneity of children's online experiences will not be explained by socioeconomic status alone.[29] As Ana Nunes de Almeida and colleagues point out, parental oversight and parental digital literacy will also play an important role in shaping children's access and use of online spaces.[30] This, in turn, will affect how and to what extent children are exposed to risk and the skills they cultivate to protect themselves in their online lives.[31] How children access and use online spaces will thus be influenced by a range of factors, including but not limited to socioeconomic status; the role that parents (and other caregivers) play in supporting, mediating, or restricting children's access to online spaces; and the overall attitude to their rights.[32] For children in middle childhood, these factors are inherently related and intertwined with parental attitudes toward safety, protection, and control of children's lives more broadly. This, in turn, impacts how and to what extent children are afforded space to engage online.

These structural inequalities affecting how and whether children can access the internet mean that two children of similar ages could experience childhood in completely different ways, with one engaging in the online world while the other is excluded. This difference affects a child's enjoyment and exercise of their rights; however, it also affects their future development and who they grow up to be. In other words, structural inequalities are a division marker not only in the present for children but also for their futures. For a child in middle childhood, the ability to access and enjoy the benefits and opportunities of the digital realm, and the exponential future opportunities it provides in life, is thus evident.

B. Navigating Children's Online Lives during Middle Childhood: Taming the Moral Panic

As children enter middle childhood and begin exercising greater agency over their everyday lives, they may be more likely to also share information online, such as their name, date of birth, address, personal pictures (of themselves, family members, friends, their home, their room, or their neighborhood), and stories about their family. They may also share details for payment methods like their parents' credit card information or, in a click or two, payments via platforms like Apple Pay or Paypal. These activities can then be monitored by the apps and websites that a child visits and, through the cookies installed, allow companies to commodify and monetize information without the child's knowledge. Over time, algorithms can identify an individual child's interests and, with technical know-how, serve to increase user engagement and time spent on specific platforms (whether gaming apps or social media sites). Companies can then push more extreme content onto children's devices, which in turn can influence a child's knowledge and perceptions of the outside world. This can directly impact a child's development, including, for example, their sense of self, body image, and political opinion.[33]

Some websites have introduced age restrictions, whereby users are asked to provide a date of birth as part of the log-in registration process. In other cases, a potential user may be asked to declare that they are below a certain age (not necessarily the age of eighteen), and parental consent might be needed. Some websites require children to be above the age of thirteen to access a platform, while other gaming sites, like the very popular site Roblox, have no age restrictions, instead offering parental control features.[34] These age-based restrictions can be managed in a number of ways (e.g., sending a verification email to parents); however, none can guarantee that consent or approval will indeed be provided by a parent, nor can they ensure that children will not gain access to the content on these platforms in other ways. From a child rights perspective, these mechanisms trigger questions regarding children's agency, protection, and evolving capacities, including the principal question of whether relying on age as a regulatory benchmark is appropriate and the micro-level question of whether setting a specific age that (arbitrarily) differentiates between children is at all effective or enforceable. In other words, while the efficacy of these mechanisms is somewhat speculative, the principal question about their compliance with children's rights remains.

Social media platforms have been shown to prioritize profits over children's mental health, and popular gaming platforms operate such that children are able to wander into spaces with violence and other disturbing content.[35] This means that children entering middle childhood, assuming they have the relevant technology, may be able to access these sites without parental consent or knowledge. While parents, and adults more generally, may be less troubled by the prospect of adolescents entering these online spaces, there remains a heightened concern when it comes to children in middle childhood, in part because children at this stage may lack the skills, experience, and maturity needed to consume this content, differentiate between reality and fiction, or process disturbing images or narratives. The challenges of children accessing such information and content are therefore twofold: the absence of parental knowledge, approval, or guidance; and the child's lack of skills and experience to engage with this material.

For society, a term that generally refers to adults, the digital age raises alarm bells for children's moral, physical, spiritual, and social development. Some adults believe that online spaces challenge traditional constructs of childhood, which have focused on protecting and sheltering children from the "dangers" of the public domain, the outside world, and unscreened, age-inappropriate content.[36] However, the nature of these risks and the extent to which children are able to cope or manage risk have tended to vary.[37] With media focusing on tragic stories of child self-harming or suicide, "risky" antisocial behavior, or gaming and gambling addictions, the distinction between risk and harm has tended to be blurred.[38] Uwe Hasebrink and colleagues have introduced a framework to categorize online risk that reflects both the child's role and the nature of prospective harm.[39] With respect to the child's role, they identify three modes of risk: content risk (where the child receives an unwelcome or inappropriate mass communication); contact risk (where the child participates in risky peer-to-peer communications); and conduct risk (where the child engages in conduct that contributes to risk to themselves or others).[40] With respect to the nature of the harm, consideration is given to underlying motivation and resultant consequences of an online interaction using four broad categories: commercial (related to financial or commercial interests); aggressive (related to personal safety and well-being); sexual (related to personal contact and/or relationships with strangers, as well as harms related to sexual orientation); and value driven (related to values or ideology).[41] In creating this typology for online risks, Hasebrink and colleagues are able to delineate between risk and harm, suggesting that while a large proportion of children may be exposed to risk online, not all children will experience harm in a similar way.[42] Moreover, in spending more time online, children may be able to cultivate a wider range of tools to avoid and manage risks, which, in turn, builds their resilience against harm.[43] In other words, older children, such as adolescents, may be more capable of discerning risk and exercising caution online compared to younger children, such as children in the middle childhood, who may still be developing the capacity to manage and avoid risk.[44]

Inversely, children with limited access to online spaces may have had little opportunity to develop the tools or skills to identify risks or take measures to protect themselves from harm.[45] An example illustrating this point goes to the potential harm that children might experience when encountering strangers in online platforms. These strangers could be fellow gamers who just want to have fun, or they could be predators seeking to groom children. With the benefit of experience and guidance, a child can acquire the tools and skills to discern different levels and types of risk, taking measures that protect themselves from uninvited or unwanted interactions. Elisabeth Staksrud and Sonia Livingstone stress the importance of supporting children's evolving capacities to allow them to develop the tools needed to cope with online risk.[46] Using their words, "a risk free internet for children and young people is an illusion"; rather, what we need to accept is that "risky encounters are necessary to the development of resilience."[47] The challenge thus lies in balancing the level of risk in a way that enables children to build up resilience as digital citizens.[48] To do this, there needs to be a shift away from protectionist frameworks toward an approach that seeks to manage online risk in a way that supports children's evolving capacities, enabling them to access the benefits of online spaces safely.[49] The experience that parents and teachers have developed over the years in teaching children about the potential danger that strangers can present to them can be useful in developing pedagogical tools to support building children's evolving capacities in the online space. In the physical world, children as young as five or six, and into their primary school years, have been taught about the potential danger that strangers can present to them and how to avoid it. However, some empirical studies have shown that children at the ages of six, eight, and even ten have had some difficulties comprehending the concepts of "danger" and "stranger."[50] It is worth noting that this fear of a stranger, as founded as it might be, can also be seen as a reflection of parents' identities and views about society, racism, xenophobia, and so on.[51] In other words, and as discussed earlier, concerns about online safety can be value driven too.

Adults' sharing of pictures of children online, a phenomenon that is probably more common when the children are in their early childhood but is nonetheless prevalent in their middle childhood years, has been described as having the potential to undermine a whole range of children's rights, including their rights to privacy and development, even when there is no intention to cause any sort of harm.[52] This is primarily due to the unforeseen or unwanted distribution and sharing of images and information online.[53] Such unforeseen consequences can also arise when children use education technologies, as we saw during the COVID-19 pandemic, when schools around the world moved to online learning platforms. Human Rights Watch, investigating dozens of platforms, concluded that data from children were being harvested, without the knowledge or consent of children, parents, or schools and with no accountability regarding how this data was used or stored in the future.[54] For the most part, however, the impact of children's online lives on their cognitive development has remained understudied in middle childhood, particularly when compared to adolescence. As a result, the extent of the risks and harm is not fully known, as there are simply not enough data to assess the effects of online platforms (games and apps) on children's development.[55]

Whereas formerly a child in middle childhood could be restricted from accessing dangerous spaces in the physical world, with key sites of interactions (playgrounds and schools) subject to health and safety regulations, it is far less easy to monitor children's presence on platforms such as Instagram, TikTok, or YouTube. Nor is it possible to effectively regulate the conduct of adult users in these spaces. Parents might therefore feel all the more anxious about the prospect of their children spending time online, given parents' limited ability to guide or protect their children. In that sense, restricting a child from using the online world altogether might be viewed as the best protection from the potential harm that these interactions can create. However, as most parents already realize, this "all or nothing" approach to regulating screen time and digital activity is almost impossible to implement. This means that parents, who often assert control over their children's engagements with the physical world during middle childhood have less control, or ability to guide and mitigate risks, in the online space.

The transition toward greater autonomy and independence in navigating the outside world happens during middle childhood, and it requires an adjustment for parents and children alike. How we support parents in enabling their child's evolving capacities will be pivotal to a child's development during these critical years. Articles 18 and 5 of the CRC may offer guidance in this respect, providing a framework that supports parents and children in adjusting to this new phase of their lives and the new ways of being a child in a digitized world. This subject is discussed in greater detail in the next section.

That parents, policy makers, and other adults should harbor anxieties over online risk, harm, and the loss of childhood needs to be understood against a long history of moral panic and concern over the general decline in our ability to regulate and curate the information to which children are exposed.[56] It should also be situated within the narrative of what adults consider as the loss of innocence, naivete, and other purity conceptions of childhood. Whether it was the introduction of radio or broadcast television, this concern, which Lynn Spigel traces back to the beginning of the twentieth century, has tended to resurface with the introduction of a new technology of mass communication.[57] One notable difference between past eras and the present one, however, is the child's positionality in the online space. Whereas previously children were passive consumers of content curated by adults (magazines, radio, network television, cable television, and the first phases of internet usage), they are now active producers as well as consumers of content created by themselves, or by other children and adults, for collective consumption.

As more children turn to online platforms in middle childhood and take their first strides toward developing a sense of self and an understanding of social positioning within the world, parents too must take measures to support their children's agency in their own developmental journey. The UN Committee on the Rights of the Child (Committee) has described "evolving capacities" as "an enabling principle that addresses the process of maturation and learning through which children progressively acquire competencies, understanding and increasing levels of agency to take responsibility and exercise their rights."[58] The Committee has further said that respecting children's evolving capacities will be "crucial for the realization of their rights" in early childhood and will be critical to ensuring their protection in adolescence.[59] We argue that it holds a similar, if not more profound, importance for middle childhood, particularly in the online world. As children "grow, develop, mature, and expand their social circle beyond their family, they are entitled to an increasing level of responsibility, agency, and autonomy in the exercise of those rights."[60] This is especially crucial during middle childhood, as children negotiate a competing sense of inferiority and industry in their development.[61] As Gerison Lansdown explains, the principle of evolving capacities is as much a developmental concept as it is a protective and participatory framework, providing levers for children to participate and actively contribute in the decisions affecting their everyday lives, while also receiving guidance, support, and direction that accounts for their protection and developmental needs.[62] Respecting children's emerging sense of autonomy and agency during middle childhood will be critical for this period of early identity formation, not only to enable children to be involved in the process of their own development but also to ensure their protection in the realization of their rights in the online world.

C. Children's Rights in Their Online Lives: Privacy, Autonomy, Identity, and Protection

The online space gives rise to a new and different set of questions related to children's rights, notably in the intersection between privacy, autonomy, and identity and the role that parents (and other caregivers) should play in supporting children as they begin to engage with the outside world in middle childhood. The CRC provides protection for various aspects of identity (Articles 7 and 8); however, for the most part, the focus of these articles is on legal and static dimensions of identity, rather than a developmental and evolutive process led by the child. Article 7 recognizes the child's right to identity, requiring name and nationality to be registered immediately after birth and "as far as possible, the right to know and be cared for by his or her parents." These dimensions of identity are no doubt part of one's sense of self, but they are predetermined for the child and form part of what John Tobin and Florence Seow call "historical identity."[63] Article 8 speaks about the right of the child to preserve their identity, but the text does not explicitly mention the child's right to establish or explore their identity (or identities). This omission is crucial to child development, particularly in middle childhood, when children start to take meaningful steps toward developing their own separate sense of self. In other words, the CRC does not directly recognize an autonomous, comprehensive right to formulate an identity. However, it has been suggested that Article 8 could be interpreted to include protection for the right to establish identity in at least two ways. John Tobin and Jonathan Todres, for example, distinguish between the child's heritage, such as culture or religion of origin, and elements of identity that the child participates in forming, which should be supported by their parents in accordance with the child's evolving capacities.[64] They therefore propose that the term "identity" include not only static, historical elements, such as name and nationality, but also dynamic attributes, such as physical ability and gender identity.[65] They further suggest that Article 8 should be read to require that states take measures to enable the child to develop their identity, foster respect for that identity, and actively protect children from unlawful interference with their identity.

Taking this approach one step further, we suggest viewing this social exploration in middle childhood, and indeed the early stages of identity formation, as part of the child's right to development under Article 6(2). Identity, much like development, represents a process and an outcome, and this dualism is inherent to the CRC's protection of the child's right to development and the process of maturation into an adult.[66] Arguably, the right to development protects these dual dimensions of development too, namely, the process of development that occurs during the course of childhood and the outcome(s) of it during childhood and when the child becomes a (legal) adult. Identity, as a category and component of development, is formed during childhood, and its many components and elements begin to take shape during middle childhood.[67] For adults and other duty bearers, this establishes duties to support children rather than suppress them in this journey of self-discovery and growth. Alongside Article 6(2) of the CRC is Article 5, which articulates a framework to support children in their developmental journey by recognizing the duty of parents (or guardians and other caregivers) to provide appropriate guidance and direction that is consistent with and cognizant of their evolving capacities as agents and participants in their own development. As underscored by Daly and Walsh in chapter 5, a child's "evolving capacities are perhaps nowhere more relevant than in middle childhood," and striking the right balance between protection and empowerment will be critical to ensure children are able to engage in the "years-long apprenticeship in the skills and customs" of the world around them. For parents, that will mean maintaining "a productive tension between autonomy and protection" that avoids leaning too far in favor of protection at the cost of independence.[68] Article 5, and indeed the CRC as a whole, provides a framework to instruct this process by placing emphasis on the child's evolving capacities as the guiding principle to navigate this delicate balance.[69] In the context of early childhood, the Committee has said that "evolving capacities should be seen as a positive and enabling process, not an excuse for authoritarian practices that restrict children's autonomy and self-expression."[70] Similarly, in adolescence, the Committee has said that supporting and enabling a child's evolving capacities should not "obviate States' obligations to guarantee protection" and that "consideration should be given to a range of factors . . . including the level of risk involved, the potential for exploitation," and an appreciation that children's development will not be uniform or linear but rather informed by a child's unique experiences, culture, and background.[71]

What we suggest here is that the Committee's observations be applied to middle childhood, with Article 5 providing the basis to navigate the dynamic tension between children's sense of industry and sense of inferiority.[72] In the context of children's online lives, where access to information and privacy will have a direct bearing on how a child is able to freely express and test out thoughts and ideas, it will fall on parents and those adults closest to the child to both enable and safeguard this process in a way that allows children to explore a diverse sense of self and belonging in the broader world.

Reading Article 7 together with Articles 5 and 6(2) will thus require that children receive the necessary support and appropriate guidance to begin developing their own unique, separate sense of self and identity or identities. Parental and societal support should facilitate and enable the child to access, explore, and engage with the world, enabling them to begin making sense of the different social categories forming their own identity, particularly in middle childhood. Moreover, it provides a framework to interpret further rights linked to the work of identity formation that will come later in adolescence, notably in respect of Articles 13 (freedom of expression) and 17 (freedom to receive information). Articles 13 and 17 serve dual roles in this context: these rights are the preconditions for the realization of the right to identity formation and expression, and together, these articles provide the necessary elements for children to take steps toward developing a concept of self and belonging and to position themselves against social expectations and social norms.

Another relevant right is the right to privacy under Article 16 of the CRC. The right to privacy protects the child from unlawful and arbitrary interference with their privacy, family, home, or correspondence and has been said to "fully accommodate the privacy experiences of children."[73] The Committee on the Rights of the Child has yet to issue a General Comment specifically on Article 16, but it has addressed children's privacy across a number of settings, notably in the digital environment, where it stated that "privacy is vital to children's agency, dignity and safety and for the exercise of their rights."[74] The Committee has further acknowledged that "threats to children's privacy . . . may also arise from children's own activities and from the activities of family members," including from "parents sharing photographs online."[75] To this end, the Committee has underscored the importance of the concept of the evolving capacities of the child and its "particular significance" when designing measures that protect children but also facilitate their access to online spaces.[76]

Children's present and future privacy interests can be impacted in multiple ways by their online engagement. One aspect is that children do not necessarily control the information shared online, which can compromise not only their right to privacy but also their right to define and control their future identity (in the sense of how they present themselves to the world). The question, then, is whether children hold a right to be forgotten and, if so, what that might involve. The right to be forgotten is often defined as the right to have private information about a person removed from internet searches, so they can, as Alessandro Mantelero argues, "determine the development of their life in an autonomous way, without being perpetually or periodically stigmatized as a consequence of a specific action performed in the past."[77] This right is not free from contention, and questions about its merit (for example, whether it can be used for censorship or rewriting history) or utility (cross-border enforcement) are beyond the scope of this chapter. However, what is of interest here is whether children in middle childhood have the right to be forgotten too and whether the CRC can be interpreted to include it. Anna Bunn argues that the "right to be forgotten," originally envisaged as a remedy for adults, should extend to children, as the presence of unwanted shared information can undermine children's sense of self and their future development.[78] While this argument can result in limiting the right to freedom of expression of others, giving children a tool to control how they are presented to the world is vital for their mental development, their expressions of identity, and how, for example, future or potential partners or employers see them.

The right to be forgotten has particular significance for children in middle childhood, due to the increased exposure and sharing of their identity online and their lack of full control from parents, or the state, in how and where this private information is being stored. During middle childhood today, the child is growing up in a mostly unregulated digital world with an undisclosed amount of information being uploaded about their lives almost daily, without their or their parents' knowledge or consent. The following example can illustrate this point: In the analogue era, a child's medical records were kept with the child's doctors (if we think about a child growing up in a country where medical services are available and accessible), and that patient's privacy was regulated and protected. But in the digital era, a child's medical records are stored in the cloud and on parents' smartphones. The cloud computing service is usually owned and operated by a for-profit corporation, and like the smartphone, it not only is vulnerable to cyber security hacks but also might be subject to unfavorable terms of service. This means that parents and children have weaker control of their private information, and as children begin to independently engage with the digital world and share information, the question of whether they can then control their information, or retract it from the public domain, becomes relevant.

In children's rights terms, a right to be forgotten can be seen as a remedy for a violation of the child's right to development, right to identity, and when it comes to information shared by others without the child's knowledge or consent, right to privacy.

It is worth mentioning that a similar process, whereby children's past can be concealed, exists in many legal systems as part of the criminal justice system. Convictions, sentences, or even indictments involving children below a certain age are unreported, expunged, and made inaccessible to the public. The reason for this is to ensure that children are able to enjoy a "new start" to adulthood that is unscathed by conduct in their past. However, this process has limited utility for children in middle childhood, given that in many countries, the minimum age of criminal responsibility is above the age range of middle childhood. However, in some countries, such as England and Wales or in the states and territories of Australia, the minimum age for criminal responsibility remains at ten years old, and thus children in the upper age bracket of middle childhood are covered by these policies. In other words, sealing children's past from the public eyes depends, by and large, on laws and policies that sit in the criminal justice domain.[79]

Parents will probably need to be involved in supporting and protecting their children in this context, and as such, Article 5 will play a critical role in informing that process. The UN Special Rapporteur on privacy has warned that "adults' interpretations of children's privacy needs can impede the healthy development of autonomy and independence and restrict children's privacy in the name of protection."[80] In other words, the duties of parents are known, and the rights of their child have not changed, as children spend more time online. But the key factor that requires more attention is the ways in which parents exercise their parental duties and the support envelope that states provide for parents and children. This support should include, first and foremost, digital literacy skills but also dedicated regulatory efforts to better protect children's online privacy. The opportunities that the online world presents and the subsequent outcry are not new and follow similar waves of concerns that we saw with the infiltration of television sets in people's living rooms or the radio a few decades before that.[81]

Many parents feel that the presence of the online world inhibits their ability to protect their children, stemming from an inability, or reduced ability, to regulate or mediate a child's social interaction in the digital space compared with the physical one.[82] The dominant narrative that drives this fear is the unknowing and inherently vulnerable "child internet user" pitted against the expert, predatory "adult internet user."[83]

However, children's online lives also alter the parent-child dynamic, with the child now introducing new technologies to their parents, via smartphones or tablets. This can put parents in an uncomfortable situation, relying or depending on their child to navigate and mediate their experiences in the digital world. This may lead to conflict and potentially fuel resistance and resentment toward children's online lives.[84] Although some parents might feel uncomfortable with this flipped dynamic and with the new "power" or authority that their young, innocent, and immature children may wield, studies have found that parents have adopted positive attitudes toward their children's use of internet-based technology.[85] As one study shows, most parents believe that using technological devices benefits their children in the long run, by preparing them for the workforce.[86] It also diminishes the ability of parents to control, mediate, or translate the information, content, or narratives that their children are exposed to from the outside world. For example, when families used to watch the evening news together, a child could ask questions, with a parent explaining or offering their opinion on current affairs. However, now, when the child consumes news or other information online, it is often done in the confines of their own room or on the bus or walking down the street, and it comes from whatever source is available on the screen. That the parent is completely removed from the situation, with the child exercising greater independence, presents a challenge in children's rights terms, not only for parents seeking to protect their child but also for states seeking to support parents and enable children's evolving capacities pursuant to obligations under Articles 5 and 18 of the CRC.

This shift in the parent-child power dynamic can also be compared to situations in some migrant families in which children as young as six or seven years old act as language brokers, translating for their parents and other family members who are not as proficient in the new local language. This role that children accept or find themselves in by virtue of acquiring the new language much more quickly than their parents has been shown to empower children, giving them more agency in the family dynamic.[87] Research also shows, however, that while some parents accept or welcome this support from their children and recognize their abilities to help navigate a new place and a new culture, others feel vulnerable, expressing a loss of parental authority or concern with the burden that this role has created for their children.[88] Digital brokering, however, as Shane Worrell argues, presents a new type of intergenerational support, for which parents seem to demonstrate less resistance.[89]

Thinking about this situation from a children's rights perspective and in the context of children in middle childhood, the dynamic concerning the protection and realization of several children's rights in the context of children's online lives (the right to information, the right to education, the right to privacy, and the right to development), and the role of parents concerning their child's upbringing and development, changes. Less regulated and controlled environments enable more children in this age group to exercise greater agency, thus providing space for exercising children's autonomy rights.

Article 5, and indeed the whole of the CRC, will be instructive in navigating this new terrain for middle childhood. The CRC affirms the special role played by parents (and family members) in supporting their children; however, it also requires that due attention and acknowledgment be given to the child's evolving agency and autonomy. This is not necessarily or inherently a "good" or a "bad" change but rather a change that should be accounted for when thinking about children's rights, children's images, parental duties, and how parents execute them. As mentioned earlier in this chapter, these opportunities to exercise agency at a younger age might make some parents uncomfortable, but these new dynamics brought about by the digital age are something that parents need to learn to navigate and get help with, where and if needed. It should not be a justification for limiting children's rights.

As the Committee explains, "guidance should support parents in sustaining an appropriate balance between the child's protection and emerging autonomy, based on mutual empathy and respect, over prohibition or control."[90] This will mean maintaining "a balance between parental responsibilities and children's rights," with "the best interests of the child, applied together with consideration of the child's evolving capacities," as "the guiding principles."[91] In practical terms, children in middle childhood will need support that encourages and enables opportunities for social and creative learning, while also maintaining the necessary oversight and protection.

III. Conclusion: Charting a Path for Children's Rights in Middle Childhood in a Digitized World

When the CRC Working Group was discussing and drafting the provisions of the Convention more than thirty years ago, it could not have predicted the transformative implications that a digital world would hold for a child, nor could it have anticipated the new and different ways that children would experience childhood as a result of their online lives.[92] In 2010, Philip Veerman sounded an alarm that the CRC would no longer be relevant to address the realities facing children today.[93] Veerman warned that the rapid uptake of digital technology had changed how children were behaving, with new findings in neuroscience and neuroimaging transforming our understandings of childhood and giving rise to new concerns about children's safety and well-being.[94]

Navigating this new terrain for children, particularly in middle childhood, when children start engaging more independently with the outside world, probably earlier than previous generations, will require some rethinking of how rights are conceptualized and practiced. But rather than questioning the relevance of the whole of the CRC or looking to adults or parents to reformulate the scope of rights, we propose engaging with children themselves, empowering them to lead the narrative on the diversity of their experiences, and relaying back to parents and those adults closest to them the realities and concerns that arise during this critical period of development. By actively listening to children, enabling their evolving capacities, and respecting their right to begin exploring a sense of self, children can be empowered to chart a new pathway for their development in middle childhood—one that recognizes and respects their agency, evolving capacities, and participation rights in their everyday lives.

Actively listening to children and enabling their meaningful participation in the matters of concern in their everyday lives may hold the key to ensuring that the CRC remains relevant and responsive to the challenges and issues facing children today. Article 12(1)—the child's right to be heard—will serve an "instrumentalist" role in this regard, providing an opportunity to make sense of the emerging issues surrounding children's rights, including questions related to children's privacy rights in the future and remedies such as the "right to be forgotten."[95] The Committee on the Rights of the Child has said that child participation should act as "a tool to stimulate the full development of the personality and the evolving capacities of the child consistent with Article 6."[96] In this regard, Article 12(1) may offer a framework to inform the discourse surrounding risks and harm in the online world, which has, to an extent, relied on an old taxonomy, while also helping to decipher what children feel and think as they develop a sense of belonging and an understanding of their social position in the broader world.

Children's online lives require revisiting, with more consideration given not only to children's participation but also key concepts used in children's rights theory and law, to reframe issues such as identity and virtual life, peers and play, and also harm and risk. There is a need to move beyond what Robert Payne has called "a small range of expedient categories that serve adult imperatives," with more focus on children's rights, interests, and well-being.[97] Engaging meaningfully with children in middle childhood will require adults not only to actively support children but also to listen to their perspectives with an open mind, giving due respect to the child's perspectives, while accounting for their developmental stage, their need for protection, and their well-being. In the context of middle childhood, in which parents continue to play a significant role in the everyday care and upbringing of their child, this may pose challenges both in how adults choose to listen to their own children and in how they accord respect to other children who express and perform in ways that do not align with their values or beliefs. Participation rights, as Daly and Walsh remind us in chapter 5, do not constitute decision-making power, nor do they provide children with the authority to override their parents' decisions.

The CRC identifies a set of rights that are both relevant and operational for navigating the complexities of being a child in middle childhood today. New events in children's lives and diverse ways of being a child present some conceptual and practical challenges to how we think about children's rights and how they can, or should, be realized in practice. But the CRC, as we argue, has the potential to help meet these new challenges, offering diverse ways of protecting these new ways of being a child. An inclusive approach to children's rights can make good use of the full potential of the CRC. In this sense, while we acknowledge Veerman's warning, we do not share his concern about the continued relevance of the CRC. Rather, we suggest that the real challenge will lie with us adults, who are tasked with enabling our children as agents in their own lives and accepting that their experience of middle childhood may be different from our own but not necessarily negative, bad, or scary.

NOTES

1 Grant, chapter 4 of this volume.
2 Noam Peleg, *The Child's Right to Development* (Cambridge: Cambridge University Press, 2019), 203.
3 Grant, chapter 4 of this volume.
4 Ibid.
5 Barbara Bennett Woodhouse, *The Ecology of Childhood: How Our Changing World Threatens Children's Rights* (New York: New York University Press, 2020).
6 Peleg, *Child's Right to Development*; John Tobin and Sheila Varadan, "Article 5: The Right to Parental Direction and Guidance Consistent with a Child's Evolving Capacities," in *The UN Convention on the Rights of the Child: A Commentary*, ed. John Tobin (Oxford: Oxford University Press, 2019), 159–185.
7 Laura Lundy, "A Lexicon for Research on International Children's Rights in Troubled Times," *International Journal of Children's Rights* 27, no. 4 (2019): 595–601; Keri Facer, "After the Moral Panic? Reframing the Debate about Child Safety Online," *Discourse: Studies in the Cultural Politics of Education* 33, no. 3 (2012): 397–413.
8 Claire Kathryn Pescott, "'I Wish I Was Wearing a Filter Right Now': An Exploration of Identity Formation and Subjectivity of 10- and 11-Years Olds' Social Media Use," *Social Media + Society* 6, no. 4 (2020): 1–10; United States Department of Health and Human Services, "Social Medial and Youth Mental Health: The U.S. Surgeon General's Advisory 2023," May 2023, www.hhs.gov; Elisabeth Staksrud and Sonia Livingstone, "Children and Online Risk: Powerless Victims or Resourceful Participants?," *Information, Communication & Society* 12, no. 3 (2009): 364–387.
9 Stacy B. Steinberg, "Sharenting: Children's Privacy in the Age of Social Media," *Emory Law Journal* 66, no. 4 (2017): 839–884; Karen Verswijvel, Michel Walrave, Kris Hardies, and Wannes Heirman, "Sharenting, Is It a Good or a Bad Thing?

Understanding How Adolescents Think and Feel about Sharenting on Social Network Sites," *Children and Youth Service Review* 104 (2019): 401–411.

10 The "right to be forgotten" is commonly understood as the right to have one's personal and private information removed from the internet so as to ensure their continued development in an autonomous way and "without being perpetually or periodically stigmatized as a consequence of a specific action performed in the past." Alessandro Mantelero, "The EU Proposal for a General Data Protection Regulation and the Roots of the 'Right to Be Forgotten,'" *Computer Law & Security Review* 29, no. 3 (2013): 229–235.

11 Philip E. Veerman, "The Ageing of the UN Convention on the Rights of the Child," *International Journal of Children's Rights* 18, no. 4 (2010): 585–618.

12 Sonia Livingstone, "Realizing Children's Rights in Relation to the Digital Environment," *European Review* 29, no. 1 (February 2021): 20–33; Facer, "After the Moral Panic?"

13 Marc Prensky, "Digital Natives, Digital Immigrants," *On the Horizon* 9, no. 5 (2001): 1–6; Tom Boonaert and Nicole Vettenburg, "Young People's Internet Use: Divided or Diversified?," *Childhood* 18, no. 1 (2011): 54–66; Ana Nunes de Almeida, Nuno de Almeida Alves, Ana Delicado, and Tiago Carvalho, "Children and Digital Diversity: From 'Unguided Rookies' to 'Self-Reliant Cybernauts,'" *Childhood* 19, no. 2 (2011): 219–234; Livingstone, "Realizing Children's Rights"; Facer, "After the Moral Panic?"; Mariya Stoilova, Sonia Livingstone, and Rishita Nandagiri, "Digital by Default: Children's Capacity to Understand and Manage Online Data and Privacy," *Media and Communication* 8, no. 4 (2020): 197–207.

14 Augmented reality and motion-sensing technology introduce new opportunities for social interaction beyond the screen. These hybrid technologies can be "highly immersive" and "competitive," heightening and enhancing opportunities for peer-to-peer interaction and social learning. See Sonia Livingstone and Kruakae Pothong, "Imaginative Play in Digital Environments: Designing Social and Creative Opportunities for Identity Formation," *Information, Communication & Society* 25, no. 4 (2022): 485–501.

15 See ibid.; Livingstone, "Realizing Children's Rights."

16 David Smahel, Hana Machackova, Giovanna Mascheroni, Lenka Dedkova, Elisabeth Staksrud, Kjartan Ólafsson, Sonia Livingstone, and Uwe Hasebrink, *EU Kids Online 2020: Survey Results from 19 Countries* (London: EU Kids Online, London School of Economics and Political Science, 2020), www.eukidsonline.ch.

17 Donell Hollaway, Lelia Green, and Sonia Livingstone, *Zero to Eight: Young Children and Their Internet Use* (London: London School of Economics and Political Science, 2013).

18 Angela Colvert, "The Kaleidoscope of Play in a Digital World: A Literature Review," Digital Futures Commission, https://digitalfuturescommission.org.uk; see also Hollaway, Green, and Livingstone, *Zero to Eight*; Livingstone and Pothong, "Imaginative Play in Digital Environments," 489–490.

19 Livingstone and Pothong, "Imaginative Play in Digital Environments," 492.

20 Ibid., 493.

21 Ibid., 491–492.

22 Holloway, Green, and Livingstone, *Zero to Eight*, 12–13; see also Pescott, "I Wish I was Wearing a Filter Right Now."

23 Simone van der Hof, Eva Lievens, Ingrida Milkaite, Valerie Verdoodt, Thijs Hannema, and Ton Liefaard, "The Child's Right to Protection against Economic Exploitation in the Digital World," *International Journal of Children's Rights* 28 (2020): 833–859.

24 E. Kay M. Tisdall and Patricio Cuevas-Parra, "Beyond the Familiar Challenges for Children and Young People's Participation Rights: The Potential of Activism," *International Journal of Human Rights* 26, no. 5 (2022): 792–810.

25 Emily Witt, "From Parkland to Sunrise: A Year of Extraordinary Youth Activism," *New Yorker*, February 13, 2019, www.newyorker.com.

26 *Duarte Agostinho and Others v. Portugal and 32 Other States*, European Court of Human Rights, November 13, 2020, https://hudoc.echr.coe.int; Selin Girit, "Climate Change: Six Young People Take 32 Countries to Court," *BBC News*, September 27, 2023, www.bbc.com.

27 Nicole Rogers, "Victim, Litigant, Activist, Messiah: The Child in a Time of Climate Change," *Journal of Human Rights and the Environment* 11, no. 3 (December 2020): 103–121.

28 Ibid.

29 Sonia Livingstone and Alicia Blum-Ross, "Social Inequality," in *Parenting for a Digital Future* (Oxford: Oxford University Press, 2020), 59–87; de Almeida et al., "Children and Digital Diversity."

30 De Almedia et al, "Children and Digital Diversity," 224–225.

31 Uwe Hasebrink, Sonia Livingstone, and Leslie Haddon, *Comparing Children's Online Opportunities and Risks across Europe: Cross-National Comparisons for EU Kids Online* (London: London School of Economics and Political Science, 2009).

32 Livingston and Blum-Ross, "Social Inequality"; de Almeida et al., "Children and Digital Diversity"; Boonaert and Vettenburg, "Young People's Internet Use."

33 Victoria Goodyear, "Narrative Matters: Young People, Social Media and Body Image," *Child and Adolescent Mental Health* 25, no. 1 (February 2020): 48–50; Emma A. Bäck, Hanna Bäck, Annika Fredén, and Nils Gustafsson, "A Social Safety Net? Rejection Sensitivity and Political Opinion Sharing among Young People in Social Media," *New Media & Society* 21, no. 2 (2018): 298–316.

34 Many social media platforms have an age restriction of thirteen years. See Facebook, accessed November 17, 2023, www.facebook.com; TikTok, accessed November 17, 2023, www.tiktok.com; Snapchat, accessed November 17, 2023, www.snapchat.com; Instagram, accessed November 17, 2023, www.instagram.com; Roblox, accessed November 17, 2023, www.roblox.com.

35 Cecilia Kang, "Facebook Grilled by Senators over Its Effect on Children," *New York Times*, September 30, 2021, www.nytimes.com; Jim Waterson and Dan Milmo, "Facebook Whistleblower Frances Haugen Calls for Urgent External Reg-

ulation," *The Guardian*, October 25, 2021, www.theguardian.com; James Clayton and Jasmin Dyer, "Roblox: The Children's Game with a Sex Problem," *BBC News*, February 15, 2022, www.bbc.com; Joe Tidy, "Kardashians Deny Faking Roblox Sex Tape Scene," *BBC News*, April 22, 2022, www.bbc.com.

36 Facer, "After the Moral Panic?," 398; Catherine Page Jeffery, "Too Sexy Too Soon, or Just Another Moral Panic? Sexualization, Children and 'Technopanics' in the Australian Media 2004–2015," *Feminist Media Studies* 18, no. 3 (2018): 366–380.

37 Staksrud and Livingstone, "Children and Online Risk."

38 Dan Milmo, "Molly Russell Coroner Calls for Review of Children's Social Media Access," *The Guardian*, October 14, 2022, www.theguardian.com; Frank W. Paulus, Susanne Ohmann, Alexander von Gontard, and Christian Popow, "Internet Gaming Disorder in Children and Adolescents: A Systematic Review," *Developmental Medicine & Child Neurology* 60, no. 7 (July 2018): 645–659; Facer, "After Moral Panic?"; Jeffery, "Too Sexy Too Soon, or Just Another Moral Panic?"

39 Hasebrink, Livingstone, and Haddon, *Comparing Children's Online Opportunities and Risks across Europe.*

40 Ibid.; Facer, "After the Moral Panic?"

41 Hasebrink, Livingstone, and Haddon, *Comparing Children's Online Opportunities and Risks across Europe.*

42 Staksrud and Livingstone, "Children and Online Risk," 380–382; see also Hasebrink, Livingstone, and Haddon, *Comparing Children's Online Opportunities and Risks across Europe.*

43 Hasebrink, Livingstone, and Haddon, *Comparing Children's Online Opportunities and Risks across Europe*, 33–35.

44 Ibid.

45 Staksrud and Livingstone, "Children and Online Risk"; Hasebrink, Livingstone, and Haddon, *Comparing Children's Online Opportunities and Risks across Europe.*

46 Staksrud and Livingstone, "Children and Online Risk."

47 Ibid., 382–383; see also European Commission, *Safer Internet and Online Technologies for Children* (Brussels: European Commission, 2007), http://ec.europa.eu.

48 Staksrud and Livingstone, "Children and Online Risk"; see also Hasebrink, Livingstone, and Haddon, *Comparing Children's Online Opportunities and Risks across Europe.*

49 Staksrud and Livingston, "Children and Online Risk."

50 Ellen Moran, David Warden, Lindsey Macleod, Gillian Mayes, and John Gillies, "Stranger-Danger: What Do Children Know?," *Child Abuse Review* 6, no. 1 (March 1997): 11–23.

51 See, for example, Jacinta Francis, Karen Martin, Lisa Wood, and Sarah Foster, "'I'll Be Driving You to School for the Rest of Your Life': A Qualitative Study of Parents' Fear of Stranger Danger," *Journal of Environmental Psychology* 53 (2017): 112–120.

52 See, among others, Steinberg, "Sharenting"; Verswijvel et al., "Sharenting, Is It a Good or a Bad Thing?"

53 Anna Bunn, "Unwanted Distribution of Children's Images and the Right to Development," *Modern Law Review* 84, no. 2 (November 2020): 334–270.
54 Hye Jung Han, *"How Dare They Peep into My Private Life?": Children's Rights Violations by Governments That Endorsed Online Learning during the Covid-19 Pandemic* (New York: Human Rights Watch, 2022), www.hrw.org.
55 Fran C. Blumberg, Kirby Deater-Deckard, Sandra L. Calvert, Rachel M. Flynn, C. Shawn Green, David Arnold, and Patricia J. Brooks, "Digital Games as a Context for Children's Cognitive Development: Research Recommendations and Policy Considerations," *Social Policy Report* 32, no. 1 (April 2019): 1–33.
56 Facer, "After the Moral Panic?"; Staksrud and Livingstone, "Children and Online Risk."
57 Lynn Spigel, "Seducing the Innocent: Childhood and Television in Postwar America," in *The Children's Cultural Reader*, ed. Henry Jenkins (New York: New York University Press, 1998), 110–129.
58 UN Committee on the Rights of the Child, *General Comment No. 20: On the Implementation of the Rights of the Child during Adolescence*, para. 18, CRC/C/GC/20 (2016); see also Sheila Varadan, "The Principle of Evolving Capacities under the UN Convention on the Rights of the Child," *International Journal of Children's Rights* 27 (2019): 306–338.
59 UN Committee on the Rights of the Child, *General Comment No. 7: Implementing Child Rights in Early Childhood*, para. 17, CRC/C/GC/7 (2006); UN Committee on the Rights of the Child, *General Comment No. 20*, para. 20.
60 UN Committee on the Rights of the Child, *Statement of the Committee on the Rights of the Child on Article 5 of the Convention on the Rights of the Child*, para. 5 (October 11, 2023).
61 See Grant, chapter 4.
62 Gerison Lansdown, *The Evolving Capacities of the Child* (Florence: UNICEF Innocenti Research Centre, 2005).
63 John Tobin and Florence Seow, "Article 7: The Rights to Birth Registration, a Name, Nationality and to Know and Be Cared For by Parents," in *The UN Convention on the Rights of the Child: A Commentary*, ed. John Tobin (Oxford: Oxford University Press, 2019), 237–280.
64 John Tobin and Jonathan Todres, "Article 8: The Right to Preservation of a Child's Identity," in Tobin, *UN Convention on the Rights of the Child*, 281–306.
65 Ibid., 295.
66 Peleg, *Child's Right to Development*.
67 Tracy L. Cross and Jennifer Riedl Cross, "Maximizing Potential: A School-Based Conception of Psychosocial Development," *High Ability Studies* 28, no. 1 (2017): 43–58.
68 Grant, chapter 4.
69 Tobin and Varadan, "Article 5: The Right to Parental Direction and Guidance"; Varadan, "Principle of Evolving Capacities."
70 UN Committee on the Rights of the Child, *General Comment No. 7*, para. 17.

71 UN Committee on the Rights of the Child, *General Comment No. 20*, para. 20.
72 Grant, chapter 4.
73 UN Special Rapporteur on the Right to Privacy, *Article Intelligence and Privacy, and Children's Privacy*, para. 70, A/HRC/46/37 (January 25, 2021); see also John Tobin and Sarah M. Field, "Article 16: The Right to Protection of Privacy, Family, Home, Correspondence, Honour and Reputation," in Tobin, *UN Convention on the Rights of the Child*, 551–599.
74 UN Committee on the Rights of the Child, *General Comment No. 25: On Children's Rights in Relation to the Digital Environment*, para. 67, CRC/C/GC/25 (March 2, 2021).
75 Ibid.
76 Ibid., para. 19.
77 Mantelero, "EU Proposal for a General Data Protection Regulation," 231.
78 Bunn, "Unwanted Distribution of Children's Images," 336.
79 Claire McDiarmid, "An Age of Complexity: Children and Criminal Responsibility in Law," *Youth Justice* 13, no. 2 (2013): 145–160.
80 UN Special Rapporteur on the Right to Privacy, *Article Intelligence and Privacy, and Children's Privacy*, para. 80.
81 Neil Postman, *The Disappearance of Childhood* (New York: Vintage Books, 1994).
82 Madeleine J. George and Candice L. Odgers, "Seven Fears and the Science of How Mobile Technologies May Be Influencing Adolescents in the Digital Age," *Perspectives on Psychological Science* 10, no. 6 (2015): 832–851; Kathryn L. Modecki, Rachel E. Goldberg, Pamela Wisniewski, and Amy Orben, "What Is Digital Parenting? A Systematic Review of Past Measurement and Blueprint for the Future," *Perspective on Psychological Science* 17, no. 6 (2022): 1673–1691.
83 Facer, "After the Moral Panic?"; Boonaert and Vettenburg, "Young People's Internet Use"; Staksrud and Livingstone, "Children and Online Risk."
84 Sara Nelissen and Jan Van den Bulck, "When Digital Natives Instruct Digital Immigrants: Active Guidance of Parental Media Use by Children and Conflict in the Family," *Information, Communication & Society* 21, no. 3 (2018): 240–256.
85 Peter Nikken and Jeroen Jansz, "Developing Scales to Measure Parental Mediation of Young Children's Internet Use," *Learning, Media and Technology* 39, no. 2 (2014): 250–266.
86 Brigitte Vittrup, Sharla Snider, Katherine K. Rose, and Jacqueline Rippy, "Parental Perceptions of the Role of Media and Technology in Their Young Children's Lives," *Journal of Early Childhood Research* 14, no. 1 (2016): 43–54.
87 Aran Romero-Moreno and Mireia Vargas-Urpí, "The Gift of Language: An Anthropological Approach to Child Language Brokering in Barcelona," *Children & Society* 36, no. 3 (2022): 415–431.
88 Federica Ceccoli, *Migrant Children on Stage: Their Role as Bilingual Brokers* (Bologna: Bologna University Press, 2022); Elaine Bauer, "Practising Kinship Care: Children as Language Brokers in Migrant Families," *Childhood* 23, no. 1 (2016): 22–36; Marjorie Faulstich Orellana and Ann Phoenix, "Re-interpreting: Narra-

tives of Childhood Language Brokering over Time," *Childhood* 24, no. 2 (2017): 183–196.

89 Shane Worrell, "From Language Brokering to Digital Brokering: Refugee Settlement in a Smartphone Age," *Social Media + Society* 7, no. 2 (2021): 1–11.

90 UN Committee on the Rights of the Child, *General Comment No. 25*, para. 86.

91 Ibid.

92 Stoilova, Livingstone, and Nandagiri, "Digital by Default," 198; Prensky, "Digital Natives, Digital Immigrants"; Veerman, "Ageing of the UN Convention on the Rights of the Child," 598.

93 Veerman, "Ageing of the UN Convention on the Rights of the Child," 585, 611, 613.

94 Ibid., 586, 589.

95 Laura Lundy, John Tobin, and Aisling Parkes, "Article 12: The Right to Respect for the Views of the Child," in Tobin, *UN Convention on the Rights of the Child*, 399.

96 UN Committee on the Rights of the Child, *General Comment No. 12: The Right of the Child to Be Heard*, para. 79, CRC/C/GC/12 (2009).

97 Robert Payne, "Virtual Panic: Children Online and the Transmission of Harm," in *Moral Panics over Contemporary Children and Youth*, ed. Charles Krinsky (Aldershot, UK: Ashgate, 2008), 31–46.

PART III

Adolescence

7

Adolescent Development

JOANNA WILLIAMS

I. Introduction

Adolescence is the period bridging childhood and adulthood, roughly spanning from about age ten to the midtwenties.[1] Adolescents make up nearly one-quarter of the world's population (23.8 percent in 2021), although this percentage varies at a country level as a function of national income. In countries categorized by the World Bank as "low income," one-third of the population is between ten and twenty-four years old, while in high-income countries, where life expectancies are much longer, adolescents make up only 17 percent of the population.[2] Adolescence is a dynamic period of remarkable diversity and complexity. One only needs to think about how different a twelve-year-old is from a twenty-two-year-old to get a sense of how much change takes place during this time. The science of adolescence has grown extensively over the past two decades and addresses a wide array of domains in individual (e.g., cognitive, emotional, physical, and psychosocial) and interpersonal development (e.g., peer and youth-adult relationships), as well as development in contexts spanning from micro-level (e.g., families, schools) to macro-level (e.g., juvenile justice, mass media) settings. Technological advances have facilitated a surge in research on neurobiological development, adding more nuance to our understanding of normative developmental processes and outcomes. Collectively, the science points to the adolescent years as a significant period of rapid growth, learning, and potential.[3]

The boundaries distinguishing adolescence from childhood are generally framed in biological terms; however, both sociocultural and sociohistorical factors influence how adolescence is defined. Researchers studying adolescence assert that age ten reflects the lower bound of this period.[4] This is related to pubertal shifts taking place around this time. In particular, changes that activate gonadal growth occur, on average, around age ten. The onset of menstruation in biological females, another common indicator of pubertal shifts, happens a few years later, around ages twelve to thirteen. These kinds of pubertal changes have followed a secular trend, happening at earlier ages in most places around the world now than they did 150 years ago, probably due to changes in nutrition and health.[5] Of course, these averages are just that—puberty remains a process that varies greatly in timing and tempo across place (local and global) and across people. Yet, there exist enough data to suggest that the kinds of biological changes that signal the transition into adolescence take place toward the end of the first decade of life. We might consider ten-year-olds to be "very young adolescents" who are also still children with respect to the resources they need and the roles they have.[6] This recognition is significant with respect to issues of children's rights. Across several topics addressed by Rap (chapter 8) and Lee and Kim (chapter 9), including civic and workforce participation, personal health, and digital technology access, the needs, capabilities, and circumstances of young adolescents are probably different compared to older youth and require more nuanced considerations of the immense changes taking place from ten to eighteen years of age.[7]

Although biological maturation is more often used to define the start of adolescence, physical and neurobiological growth continue through the mid- to late twenties. Indeed, the end of adolescence is harder to define, as it is often culturally and contextually bound. Cognitively, an adolescent's logical reasoning and capacity for abstract thinking are similar to those of an adult by age sixteen; however, continuing neurobiological maturation is associated with marked development of social processing, decision-making, and self-regulation through the midtwenties. Social transitions often marking the "end" of adolescence, for example, marriage, childbirth, and economic independence, have shifted from the early twenties to the late twenties and beyond in many places around the world, although there is great variation across contexts and cultures. Whether a young person is considered an "adult" can also be based on legal definitions (i.e., the age of majority). In many countries, the age at which a person is legally recognized as an adult is eighteen years; however, some countries allow for customary or religious exceptions that bring this boundary lower or higher. The minimum working age for countries that have one is often thirteen to fourteen years old; in contrast, many countries consider children as young as six or seven as being capable of criminal behavior and able to stand trial.[8] Context and culture inform when, where, and how a youth is considered an adult.

This chapter adopts the parameters used by the National Academies of Sciences, Engineering, and Medicine, the Lancet Commission on Adolescent Health and Well-Being, and other scholars and defines adolescence as inclusive of young people between the ages of ten and twenty-five years old.[9] As discussed throughout the chapter, there is a great deal of change that happens during this period, so when possible, we distinguish young adolescents (ages ten to thirteen) from middle adolescents (ages fourteen to eighteen) and older adolescents or "emerging adults" (ages nineteen to twenty-five). It is important to note that developmental research on adolescence is biased toward middle and late adolescence, and some researchers argue that the needs and experiences of young adolescents have been largely overlooked.[10] Blurred lines between middle childhood and early adolescence mean that youth ages ten to thirteen are represented in research on both children and adolescents and, as noted previously, may be treated more like children with respect to issues of personal agency and decision-making.

II. Narratives of Adolescence

Narratives of adolescence are grounded in sociohistorical context. Social constructions of adolescence vary across cultural contexts: in some settings, the transition into adolescence is accompanied by ceremonial recognition; in others, the designation of "adolescent" and processes considered hallmarks of adolescence (e.g., identity development) are less salient.[11] In the United States, the recognition of adolescence as a unique period is often credited to psychologist G. Stanley Hall, who, in his 1904 publication "Adolescence: Its Psychology and Its Relations to Physiology, Anthropology, Sociology, Sex, Crime, Religion and Education," popularized the idea of adolescence as a time of storm and stress.[12] There was pushback to Hall's conceptualization of adolescence, which was grounded in theories of racial supremacy, yet his "storm and stress" frame grew roots that have been difficult to shake.[13] Stereotypes about adolescents often center on raging hormones, risky behavior, apathy, or antisocial peer culture.[14] Even today, cultural models of adolescence center on "dangerous times" or a period of "biological takeover."[15] More positive narratives often remain, at best, mixed, and we continue to "celebrate youthfulness and malign youth simultaneously."[16] Moreover, Western narratives of adolescence tend to be grounded in heteronormativity, masculinity, colonialism, and whiteness.[17] Youth from racially, ethnically, and culturally minoritized groups have been even further maligned by deficit-focused research centering problem behavior.[18] Indigenous and African-centered theoretical frameworks/philosophies of youth remain invisible, especially those centering strengths and positive development.[19]

Fortunately, new cultural narratives of adolescence are emerging that are supported by developmental science. The Center for the Developing Adolescent and the FrameWorks Institute offer this summary of adolescence: "Adolescence is a time of remarkable opportunity. The years between age 10 to about 25 mark a period of rapid growth, development, and learning as we discover and adapt to the world around us. We forge our sense of who we are and who we aspire to be. We learn to make decisions, manage our emotions, and create deeper connections with peers, romantic partners, and others in our communities. We also build resilience, and develop interests, passions, and meaningful goals that shape our adult lives."[20] In addition to (re)framing adolescence as a period of opportunity with important foundations for the life course, recent narratives also acknowledge that the promise of this period is severely curtailed by economic, social, and structural disadvantage.[21] Social systems intended to support adolescents—including education, health, justice, and child welfare—are often poorly suited to meet adolescents' developmental needs. Moreover, worsening inequities disproportionately expose some youth to excess stresses and risks, which, from an epigenetic perspective, can "get under the skin" and adversely impact development.[22]

Even in the face of adversity and toxic stressors, the science of adolescence affirms that this period is marked by flexibility and adaptability.[23] This makes it a critical period for investing in programs and interventions that can alter downward trajectories leading to a poor quality of life and instead support changes that promote thriving.[24]

In addition to secure access to stable housing, nutritious food, and a quality education, core developmental needs of adolescence, as described by the Center for the Developing Adolescent, include the following:

- Safe and satisfying ways to explore the world and take healthy risks to test out new ideas and experiences
- Real-world scenarios in which to build decision-making and emotional regulation skills
- Avenues to develop a sense of meaning and purpose by contributing to peers, families, and communities
- Positive ways to earn respect and social status among peers and adults
- Experiences that help define personal values, goals, and a positive sense of identity
- Warmth and support from parents and other caring adults[25]

The final point aligns with Article 7 of the Convention on the Rights of the Child (CRC), that children have the right to know and be cared for by their parents.[26] Indeed, caring adults remain an important source of support and should be responsive to adolescents' "evolving capacities," a point that the Committee on the Rights of the Child (Committee) elaborated on in its 2016 *General Comment No. 20 on the Implementation of the Rights of the Child during Adolescence.*[27] The Committee notes that adolescents' developing capabilities should be considered in balance with the need to protect them from harm.

So much change happens over the course of adolescence: youth advance physically, cognitively, and psychosocially, while also experiencing changing contexts (e.g., increasingly complex educational institutions, entry to the labor force), responsibilities (e.g., greater autonomy in personal, educational, and work domains), and roles (e.g., student, romantic partner, employee, family caregiver, or young parent). The dynamic changes taking place in adolescence uniquely prepare us to meet the challenges of this period, like building nonfamilial relationships, exploring new and increasingly complex environments, developing an integrated sense of self, and strengthening social, emotional, and cultural competence. The growth and plasticity of this period offer important opportunities for learning and adaptation. Ideally, as adolescents, we develop strengths, assets, and skills to support our future health and well-being and prepare us for adult roles and responsibilities.[28]

III. Adolescents' Developing Bodies and Minds

A. Pubertal Development

Pubertal changes are perhaps one of the most distinctive features of adolescence, although some aspects of puberty (e.g., the release of adrenal hormones) actually begin in middle childhood. It is likely that the physical changes in height, weight, and the emergence of secondary sex characteristics, as well as the transition to reproductive capability, influence the way in which perceptions of puberty and adolescence are intertwined. Importantly, however, emerging science offers evidence of other ways in which puberty contributes to both the activation and (re)organization of neural systems and structures that are unique to the adolescent period.[29] For instance, pubertal stage appears to be related to the volume of the amygdala, a region of the brain associated with emotional reactivity. Pubertal stage and timing are also linked to decreases in outer-layer (cortical gray matter) volume and increases in inner-layer (subcortical white matter) volume, particularly in the frontal lobe region of the brain, as well as in tracts connecting different brain regions.[30] Adolescent-onset mental health disorders are associated with puberty via pathways involving concurrent neurobiological and psychosocial changes (e.g., in self-perception and social relationships).[31] Finally, although the science is still emerging, studies employing functional magnetic resonance imaging (MRI) methods suggest associations between pubertal maturation and emotional and motivational processes in adolescence. While there is evidence supporting longitudinal associations between pubertal processes and brain development, more work is needed to unpack the nature of these processes (e.g., linear or nonlinear) as well as the mechanisms underlying the associations.[32]

There is a great deal of variation across youth in the timing and tempo of puberty, and adolescents who experience atypical pubertal timing (i.e., early or late onset) compared to peers may have a heightened risk for negative mental and behavioral health outcomes.[33] Researchers theorize that early puberty in particular may confer risk due to myriad factors—from psychological to interpersonal to behavioral. Appearing physically more developed than one's peers or being perceived as older when one's cognitive and psychosocial maturation is still developing can create vulnerabilities, especially in early adolescence, when our sensitivity to social comparison and belonging is often heightened.[34] Researchers find that early pubertal maturation, especially in girls, is associated with greater anxiety and negative self-focus, greater social problems and less effective coping skills, more affiliation with deviant peers, and higher levels of interpersonal stress.[35] The effects of early pubertal timing can also be compounded by a youth's racial-group membership. For instance, teachers expect early-maturing girls to have more academic and social problems than their on-time or late-maturing peers do; however, teachers have lower expectations for the academic and social functioning of early-maturing Black girls compared to early-maturing White girls.[36] Importantly, however, there remains a dearth of research on puberty among racially and ethnically minoritized youth and youth from all racial-ethnic groups who are biologically male or a member of a sexual or gender minoritized group.[37]

The physical changes of puberty along with the accompanying psychological and social correlates represent a powerful shift in the life course. All adolescents have the need (and the right) to understand the changes their body and mind are going through, with an accompanying need for bodily autonomy. For youth experiencing atypical pubertal timing, when physical development may be out of step with cognitive and socioemotional development, people in positions of power must recognize the potential mismatch and support youth accordingly. Research documents that pubertal timing is related to environmental factors; environmental toxins, childhood sexual and physical abuse, obesity, and stress are related to quicker pubertal tempo and earlier timing.[38] Pubertal changes impact adolescent sleep cycles, and poor sleep can severely impact decision-making and elevate risk for poor mental, physical, and behavioral health outcomes.[39] Thus, careful consideration must be given to the conditions in which adolescents are experiencing puberty and the interrelated aspects of physical, neurobiological, and psychosocial development discussed in the following sections.

B. Neurobiological Development

The role of pubertal changes notwithstanding, we now know much more about neurobiological development during adolescence than we did thirty years ago. That new knowledge has helped transform our understanding of adolescence as a simple, linear progression from childhood to adulthood, to one characterized by specific changes uniquely suited to the tasks of this period.[40] There remains debate, however, over what neurobiological changes are most meaningful in relation to adolescent behavior.[41] The popular "dual-systems" model suggests that a socioemotional system related to reward sensitivity and sensation seeking matures rapidly in adolescence before declining in early adulthood, while a cognitive control system responsible for impulse control and planful behavior develops more slowly over the full course of adolescence.[42] This model has been critiqued for oversimplifying complex processes and for overstating direct links between brain development and behavior.[43] Some proponents, however, believe that its utility in explaining observed patterns still holds.[44] Other models move away from the orthogonal systems view and focus instead on the development of neural networks within and across inner and outer brain regions. Proponents of the circuit-based "imbalance model" describe strengthening connections first between circuits in inner brain regions in early adolescence, followed by connections between outer and inner regions in mid-adolescence, and then connections within outer brain regions in late adolescence.[45] The fine-tuning of connections within and across brain regions is hypothesized to better reflect the complexities that may correspond to observed changes in adolescent behavior over time and across contexts.[46]

C. Cognitive and Behavioral Changes

Regardless of which model fits best, we know there are complex changes taking place in adolescents' brains and bodies, as well as in their roles, settings, and relationships. Broadly speaking, different cognitive and socioemotional capacities appear to mature at different points across adolescence. Research on decision-making across the period of adolescence suggests an uneven progression from early through late adolescence.[47] Affective decision-making, assessed with tasks that capture impulsive behavior under emotionally arousing situations (i.e., involving risks and rewards), appears to get worse in early adolescence compared to middle childhood, before improving in middle and late adolescence. In contrast to this J-shaped trajectory of affective decision-making, cognitive decision-making skills (e.g., memory and processing speed) improve linearly across adolescence.

On many cognitive tasks relying on short-term memory, peak performance often occurs in mid-adolescence, while older adolescents and emerging adults typically fare best on tasks requiring mental manipulation of multiple pieces of information at one time.[48] Other cognitive skills, like logical reasoning, typically look similar during mid-adolescence to how they look in adulthood, especially in the absence of emotional arousal.[49] In contrast, cognitive tasks that rely on accumulated knowledge (e.g., tests of vocabulary and comprehension) continue to improve well past adolescence into middle adulthood.[50] Importantly, context—particularly emotional arousal—makes a difference. For instance, on cognitive control tasks, adolescents in their midteens perform worse than those in their late teens to early twenties in the context of positive emotional arousal. Similarly, youth in their midteens and those eighteen to twenty-one perform worse than twenty-two- to twenty-five-year-olds in the context of threat arousal.[51]

With regard to psychosocial behaviors, international studies from multiple countries show that antisocial risk behaviors (e.g., fighting, stealing) and scores on lab-based measures of risk propensity peak in mid-adolescence, while health risk behaviors (e.g., drinking, unsafe sexual activity) peak in the mid- to late twenties.[52] Researchers studying adolescents across countries also find that sensation-seeking behaviors peak around age nineteen, while self-regulation skills increase throughout adolescence and peak in the midtwenties.[53] Adolescents are also sensitive to social norms, although they often misperceive the behavior of peers, assuming that it is very similar to their own or overestimating their peers' involvement in risky behavior.[54] In general, the science of adolescence suggests that it is a period of heightened sensitivity to social inputs, rewards, and novel experiences, and adolescents' cognitive and socioemotional development has long had implications for the kinds of rights adolescents are afforded.[55] While, on the one hand, these sensitivities can contribute to health-risk behaviors, it is equally important to acknowledge that the same changes, and, in particular, the high level of cognitive flexibility, offer unique opportunities for learning, discovery, problem-solving, adaptation, and creativity.[56]

Research on adolescent brain development, cognitive capacity, self-regulation, and risk-taking has dominated the discourse around the question of when an adolescent can or should be considered an "adult."[57] In the United States, eighteen is considered the "age of majority" (i.e., adult status); however, in the criminal justice system, youth in their early teens or younger can be prosecuted as adults. In most states, adolescents can vote at age eighteen, but some states have proposed lowering the voting age to sixteen (and some localities have made this change), based on the science demonstrating that most youth are capable of political maturity by this age.[58] In chapter 8 in this volume, Rap notes that other countries have reduced their voting ages with positive benefits, and while the Committee has suggested in a General Comment that adolescents be offered resources (e.g., citizenship education) in states that allow voting before age eighteen, voting rights are not explicitly addressed in the CRC.[59] Generally speaking, by the mid- to late teen years, youth have the capacity to reason and draw conclusions very much similar to the capacity of adults; however, youth appear to be more sensitive to the social and emotional conditions under which decisions are made relative to adults, and individual differences (in experience, emotion regulation, and sensitivity, for example) abound. Moreover, the focus on the narrow age band between sixteen and the early twenties has obscured more detailed, nuanced discussions about the capacity of younger adolescents, with much of the social policy landscape lumping them together with children.

IV. Adolescents' Developing Selves

A. Identity Development

Debates about the age of majority and its implication for laws and policies impacting adolescents' rights have largely been devoid of discussions of adolescent identity development, despite widespread agreement that identity exploration is a hallmark of the adolescent period. While identity development is a lifelong process, growing cognitive and psychosocial abilities along with contextual shifts (e.g., in education and workforce settings and in relationships) in adolescence make it a period of active identity exploration for most young people. An integrated set of answers to the question "Who am I?" provides a foundation that informs our values, behaviors, goals, decisions, sense of purpose and direction, and more.[60] Multiple factors—family, cultural, and societal expectations; peers; and experiences with institutions like school and the media—shape identity development, but young people are also agents in the process. They select the environments and people they want to be around, adjust their beliefs and behaviors on the basis of feedback, and reflect on these elements as they work to figure out who they are.

Identity development and self-construction are quite different for young adolescents compared to older youth.[61] In tandem with ongoing pubertal and neurobiological changes, young adolescents are more attuned to social feedback, particularly from peers, and navigating where they fit into the social landscape informs the identity process.[62] Young adolescents may desire to identify themselves in multiple ways outside of their role in the family and may begin to notice how their behavior differs across social contexts. Developing flexibility in how youth present themselves in different situations takes time and practice and can create stress for some youth. Over time, however, adolescents become better able to weave these different self-presentations into a coherent narrative.[63] Older teens can also imagine their own identity and role in the larger world and often have more opportunity to explore identity alternatives.

Identities develop in sociocultural contexts and are both personal (reflecting the talents and traits that make us unique) and social (reflecting our connections to broader social and cultural groups). Western contexts tend to emphasize individuality, so young people's self-definitions typically include elements that make them distinct. But domains of social identity are also part of the self-narrative, and many youth spend time considering themselves through the lens of race, ethnicity, gender, sexuality, faith, and the like. In their daily experiences, adolescents do not experience their identities in silos: social identity categories intersect in important ways and manifest themselves differently across individuals and contexts, making heterogeneity the norm rather than the exception.[64] In contrast to childhood, adolescents become more purposeful as they build their self-narratives, with their own values, motives, and hopes anchoring the process.[65] While one's identity may increase in stability and coherence, there remain dynamic elements that shape the relationship between identity and behavior; adolescents often select activities that feel identity congruent and may interpret and respond to a given situation on the basis of aspects of identity that are salient at that moment.[66] Adolescents can also be increasingly attuned to bias and discrimination, particularly when an important aspect of their identity is targeted.[67]

B. Gender and Sexuality

Gender and sexuality are dimensions of social identity that become more salient in adolescence, due, in part, to pubertal transitions. Adolescent exploration of gender and sexual identities often occurs as peers begin to regulate norms and boundaries around what a particular category means.[68] The historical and sociopolitical context is important to consider in relation to these identity domains. For instance, in recent years, the identity language and labels that youth use to describe their gender or sexuality have become more dynamic. Notably, a growing number of youth labeled as lesbian, gay, bisexual, transgender, or queer (LGBTQ) say that they have a nonbinary gender identity (i.e., neither male or female) or sexual identity (e.g., pansexual, bisexual, queer).[69] How these identities manifest themselves and the role they play in young people's overall well-being depends a great deal on immediate context. For instance, there is robust evidence that LGBTQ+ youth who attend schools with gay-straight alliances report lower levels of health-compromising behaviors and greater school belonging compared to peers, and for some LGBTQ+ youth, the internet can provide identity-affirming spaces that buffer against the negative effects of hostile family or community contexts.[70] Despite widespread increases in public support for people with LGBTQ+ identities and for LGBTQ+ issues, adolescents from sexual and gender minority groups continue to face higher levels of discrimination and greater risks for adverse mental health challenges compared to their non-LGBTQ+ peers.[71]

C. Race, Ethnicity, and Culture

The context of growing ethnic-racial diversity and globalization provides tremendous opportunity for growth and enrichment for all adolescents, but at the same time, historical patterns of exclusion and marginalization contribute to meaningful variations in experience.[72] Thus, it is paramount to consider how adolescents navigate issues of race, ethnicity, and identity as a normative part of development.[73] While many youth spend time thinking about what it means for them to be a member of a particular racial or ethnic group, ethnic-racial identity may be especially meaningful for youth from racially minoritized groups, who are often viewed by others in "racial" terms, and for immigrant youth as they navigate their heritage and adopted cultures.[74] The context of a racially and ethnically stratified society provides ongoing exposure to messages about the value and expectations of different ethnic and racial groups. Such socialization messages—from family, media, peers, school, and so on—inform young people's racial knowledge and factor into ethnic-racial identity development.[75] Youth can vary in how central their ethnicity, race, or culture is to their self-definition; how they feel about their ethnic, racial, or cultural group; how they think others view their group; and their beliefs about how members of their group should behave.[76] Notably, as youth become more aware of ethnic, racial, and culture stereotypes and for those who encounter discrimination, public regard declines; in other words, throughout adolescence, youth from historically marginalized ethnic, racial, or cultural groups increasingly believe that society holds negative views about their group.

D. Identity in Context

How we view ourselves is connected to our values, motivations, and behaviors, and having an integrated sense of identity that feels consistent across contexts and over time offers an important foundation for thriving. Moving toward that integrated sense of self often involves testing and experimenting, and adolescents need safe opportunities to explore without fear of rejection or punishment. Adolescents' identities also have bearing on decision-making; increasing evidence suggests that identity-based values impact the choices youth make.[77]

Importantly, our identities are rooted in culture, and in some cultural contexts, there are expectations of conformity to group norms and values and less individual agency in constructing one's identity.[78] In other words, "self" definitions are tightly bound to cultural traditions, and the process of identity development (or even the concept of "adolescence" as a distinctive period) may not be salient in all cultural settings.[79] The CRC briefly acknowledges cultural identity with respect to educational rights (Article 29) and children's right to enjoy their own culture (Article 30) but offers little elaboration. Importantly, the UN Committee on the Rights of the Child provides a more expansive view on the role and importance of identity exploration for all adolescents, with specific recognition of the needs of gender-, cultural-, and racial-minority youth.[80]

While cultures vary with respect to an emphasis on individuality and independence versus collectivism and group allegiance, it remains important for adolescents to have the right to express the plurality of their identities and the accompanying cultural practices. Unfortunately, these rights are often compromised in the presence of fear and xenophobia, resulting, for example, in the criminalization and overpunishment of Black youth, hypersurveillance of Muslim and Arab youth, and violence against LGBTQ+ youth.[81] In addition, these normative processes and needs can be manipulated, and research suggests that a youth's likelihood of involvement in extremist groups may increase as they seek personally meaningful in-groups, particularly if they condone a group's beliefs without questioning them.[82]

V. Development in Context

A. Proximal Settings: Peers and Family

All development is culturally situated, and bidirectional, person-context interactions are central drivers of developmental trajectories.[83] Much of developmental science has focused on the more proximal contexts that youth regularly encounter, including peer groups, families, and educational settings. These settings play a critical role in supporting adolescent development, although individual trajectories are influenced by social stratification forces, along with the supports and challenges in a youth's immediate environment.[84]

Although a detailed discussion of the peer and family contexts in adolescence is beyond the scope of this chapter, their importance cannot be understated. During adolescence, the nature of friendships becomes more intense and complex. These changes are intricately related to puberty, autonomy, and cognitive development and set the stage for the emergence of intimacy and mutual responsiveness.[85] Peer groups provide a space for youth to practice social skills, like communication, conflict resolution, and cooperative learning. In step with physical, neurobiological, psychosocial, and contextual shifts (e.g., transition to secondary schools), peer-group "cliques" often become more prevalent in early adolescence. Cliques can meet developmental needs related to identity exploration and belonging, and younger and middle adolescents tend to report greater conformity pressures and lower resistance to peer influence compared to older adolescents.[86] Adolescence is a time when youth have an enhanced desire for respect and social status, and peer groups can meet or thwart these needs.[87] Being around peers also appears to enhance reward-seeking behaviors, which may involve unhealthy risk-taking; these effects are strongest during mid-adolescence.[88]

The family context remains critical for adolescents despite normative increases in autonomy and independent decision-making during this period. Parenting practices are culturally grounded and vary widely, yet international studies of mid-adolescent youth suggest that parental support and behavioral control facilitate positive psychosocial and behavioral outcomes, while high levels of psychological control can be harmful.[89] Strong cultural values and practices like communalism, shared caregiving and kinship networks, and ethnic-racial socialization can help youth thrive in the face of stressors like discrimination and xenophobia.[90] Importantly, the family context is situated in broader settings that have bearing on family and youths' experiences. Family economic, psychological, and social resources are critical factors impacting developing adolescents, and social stratification, inequality, and marginalization can amplify stress on the family system.[91]

While keeping young and middle adolescents with their families reflects a central aspect of youths' rights, a young person's right to safety takes precedence and can lead to child welfare system involvement. In the United States, 30 percent of all youth entering the foster care system each year are adolescents (ages eleven to twenty), and adolescents make up 36 percent of all youth in foster care.[92] Abuse and neglect often precede the involvement of the child welfare system; such maltreatment can have negative impacts on adolescents' social-emotional and neurobiological development.[93] Moreover, older adolescents who "age out" of foster care (i.e., at ages eighteen to twenty-one) often have high rates of homelessness, incarceration, and other negative outcomes.[94] Developmental research suggests that older adolescents, who are still undergoing normative physical, cognitive, and psychosocial maturation, require supports and scaffolds (e.g., supportive networks; education, housing, and employment resources) as they transition into independent self-care.[95] For other adolescents, the family context may require youth to take on a caregiving role for a health-impaired parent, grandparent, or sibling. Data on caregiving youth under age eighteen are not well tracked, but recent estimates suggest that 5.4 million youth in the US hold this role; they are more likely to be female than male, to be an early or middle adolescent rather than a younger child, and to live in a family experiencing financial hardship.[96] On the one hand, by early to middle adolescence, youth have the capacity to contribute to the care of a family member, and the responsibility may support confidence and resilience; but, on the other hand, the caregiving role may be burdensome and create stress for youth, particularly when other supports are minimal.[97] Globally, multiple countries recognize the important role of caregiving youth for families and have implemented laws and policies to support and protect them; this is not the case in the US, however, where caregivers under eighteen do not have access to the resources afforded to those who are eighteen and older.[98]

B. Macro-Level Settings

It is critical to acknowledge the role of macro-level systems as contributors to adolescent development.[99] The role of structural and systemic factors in promoting or curtailing opportunities for thriving can be difficult to pinpoint, but leaving them out allows for narratives about the role of the individual or of a particular group as the central cause of their own success or demise to prevail. Racism, sexism, heteronormativity, classism, and capitalism are all implicated in the differential access to resources and supports and disparate adultification and dehumanization that exist across groups of youth.[100] There is ample evidence demonstrating that economic, social, and structural disadvantages, which manifest themselves as disparities in neighborhood and family resources, institutional biases, and interpersonal discrimination, shape adolescents' life-course trajectories in multiple ways. While adolescence offers an opportunity to rebound from early adversity, exposure to physically or psychologically toxic environments can exacerbate stressors and contribute to suboptimal health and development during and beyond adolescence. In other words, experiences and settings matter a great deal.[101]

VI. Conclusion

The science of adolescent development points clearly to a set of needs and capabilities that accompany this period of life. Adolescents need opportunities to explore, take healthy risks, build decision-making and regulation skills, develop a sense of purpose, earn respect, define and refine personal identities and values, and experience warmth and support from peers, parents, and other caring adults.[102] These needs are matched with developmental changes that optimize adolescents' readiness to try new experiences, take on greater responsibilities, navigate increasingly complex systems, and build more intimate relationships. An ongoing challenge for the field is to delineate how these needs and capabilities manifest themselves and are potentially distinct for young, middle, and older adolescents. Indeed, with respect to rights, complex questions remain regarding blurred lines between middle childhood and early adolescence—for instance, are the changes catalyzed by pubertal and neurobiological shifts (and the reproductive capabilities that accompany them) meaningful enough to warrant different considerations for youth ages eight to nine and youth ages ten to twelve? It is also important to acknowledge that while the age of eighteen may afford youth with legal rights as adults, many young people at that age are still oriented toward sensation seeking and may behave impulsively with peers and in other emotionally arousing situations. They also have a heightened vulnerability to substance use and mental health disorders and may be in need of particular policy supports and programming to ensure a healthy transition into adulthood.[103]

Developmental science is also culturally situated, and there remains a need to interrogate ethnocentric and heteronormative theories, assumed to apply universally to all adolescents. The National Scientific Council on Adolescence wrote recently,

> Within the space of scientific scholarship—including scholarship about adolescent development, a cycle of bias has shaped our collective understanding. . . .
>
> . . . As this pattern continues for many researchers over many years, a biased accumulation of knowledge builds and ultimately shapes what we "know" about particular topics. . . . This bias in science alters our collective knowledge about what constitutes healthy adolescent development, and influences future scientific research, funding, and policy.[104]

Gaps in the research exist with respect to particular populations, and dominant theories and assumptions about adolescence are sorely lacking perspectives from research conducted with "majority world" adolescents (i.e., from Africa, the Caribbean, Asia, and Latin America).[105] Within Western, industrialized countries, adolescents from historically resilient racial-ethnic backgrounds (e.g., African American/Black, Latinx, Indigenous) are overrepresented in research on risk and underrepresented in research on positive development; moreover, comparative approaches have contributed to deficit-oriented framing of their experiences and outcomes. The experiences of new immigrant youth, queer youth, and youth involved in the justice and child welfare systems are also missing from research on normative development.

Adolescents' inclination for exploration and discovery, their deepening understanding of social injustice, and their desire to develop purpose and meaning support their capacity for leadership and contribution. Moreover, their cognitive flexibility and related skills (e.g., ability to process and manipulate new information nimbly and efficiently) mean that older adolescents can offer creative and innovative solutions to complex challenges. Globally, adolescents, particularly those in their midteens and older, are leading social movements to advocate for pressing social issues like climate justice and political freedom.[106] Adolescent participation can inform policies and practices to make them more relevant to young people's lives, empower youth to challenge various forms of oppression, increase the accountability of individuals in positions of power, and support positive youth development.[107] Our understanding of adolescent development and the implications of the science for adolescents' rights will remain incomplete until the voices of young people themselves are more meaningfully integrated.

NOTES

1 Susan M. Sawyer, Peter S. Azzopardi, Dakshitha Wickremarathne, and George C. Patton, "The Age of Adolescence," *Lancet Child & Adolescent Health* 2, no. 3 (March 2018): 223–228.

2 United Nations Population Division, "World Population Prospects 2022," accessed August 16, 2022, https://population.un.org.

3 National Academies of Sciences, Engineering, and Medicine (NASEM), *The Promise of Adolescence: Realizing Opportunity for All Youth* (Washington, DC: National Academies Press, 2019).

4 Sawyer et al., "Age of Adolescence."

5 Grace Wyshak and Rose E. Frisch, "Evidence for a Secular Trend in Age of Menarche," *New England Journal of Medicine* 306, no. 17 (April 29, 1982): 1033–1035.

6 Sawyer et al., "Age of Adolescence."

7 International Labour Organization, *Global Employment Trends for Youth 2022: Investing in Transforming Futures for Young People* (Geneva: ILO, 2022); Jan Eichhorn and Johannes Bergh, "Lowering the Voting Age to 16 in Practice: Processes and Outcomes Compared," *Parliamentary Affairs* 74, no. 3 (July 2021): 507–521; Vanessa Woog and Anna Kågesten, "The Sexual and Reproductive Health Needs of Very Young Adolescents Aged 10–14 in Developing Countries: What Does the Evidence Show?," Guttmacher Institute, May 24, 2017, www.guttmacher.org; World Health Organization (WHO), *The Sexual and Reproductive Health of Young Adolescents in Developing Countries: Reviewing the Evidence, Identifying Research Gaps, and Moving the Agenda: Report of a WHO Technical Consultation, Geneva, 4–5 November 2010* (Geneva: WHO, 2011), https://iris.who.int; Lucia Magis-Weinberg, Ahna Ballonoff Suleiman, and Ronald E. Dahl, "Context, Development, and Digital Media: Implications for Very Young Adolescents in LMICs," *Frontiers in Psychology* 12 (April 2021); Candice Odgers, Nick Allen, Jennifer Pfeifer, Ronald Dahl, Jacqueline Nesi, Stephen Schueller, Joanna Lee Williams, and the National Scientific Council on Adolescence, *Engaging, Safe, and Evidence-Based: What Science Tells Us about How to Promote Positive Development and Decrease Risk in Online Spaces* (Los Angeles: National Scientific Council on Adolescence, 2022); UN Committee on the Rights of the Child, *General Comment No. 20: On the Implementation of the Rights of the Child during Adolescence*, CRC/C/GC/20 (2016).

8 George C. Patton, Susan M. Sawyer, John S. Santelli, David A. Ross, Rima Afifi, Nicholas B. Allen, Monika Arora, et al., "Our Future: A Lancet Commission on

Adolescent Health and Wellbeing," *The Lancet* 387, no. 10036 (June 2016): 2423–2478.

9 NASEM, *Promise of Adolescence*; Patton et al., "Our Future"; Sawyer et al., "Age of Adolescence."

10 Robert W. Blum, Nan Marie Astone, Michele R. Decker, and Venkatraman Chandra Mouli, "A Conceptual Framework for Early Adolescence: A Platform for Research," *International Journal of Adolescent Medicine and Health* 26, no. 3 (2014): 321–331; NASEM, *Promise of Adolescence*; WHO, *Sexual and Reproductive Health of Young Adolescents in Developing Countries.*

11 Mihalyi Csikszentmihalyi, "Adolescence | Definition, Characteristics, & Stages," *Britannica*, accessed August 16, 2022, www.britannica.com; Anne-Marie Tupuola, "Participatory Research, Culture and Youth Identities: An Exploration of Indigenous, Cross-Cultural and Trans-national Methods," *Children, Youth and Environments* 16, no. 2 (2006): 291–316.

12 John Demos and Virginia Demos, "Adolescence in Historical Perspective," *Journal of Marriage and Family* 31, no. 4 (November 1969): 632–638; Joseph F. Kett, "Reflections on the History of Adolescence in America," *History of the Family* 8, no. 3 (2003): 355–373.

13 Katie Johnston-Goodstar, "Decolonizing Youth Development: Re-imagining Youthwork for Indigenous Youth Futures," *AlterNative: An International Journal of Indigenous Peoples* 16, no. 4 (December 2020): 378–386.

14 Daniel Busso, Andrew Volmert, and Nathaniel Kendall-Taylor, *Building Opportunity into Adolescence: Mapping the Gaps between Expert and Public Understandings of Adolescent Development* (Washington, DC: FrameWorks Institute, 2018), www.frameworksinstitute.org; Nancy Lesko, *Act Your Age! A Cultural Construction of Adolescence*, 2nd ed. (New York: Routledge, 2012).

15 Daniel S. Busso, Andrew C. Pool, Nathaniel Kendall-Taylor, and Kenneth R. Ginsburg, "Reframing Adolescent Development: Identifying Communications Challenges and Opportunities," *Journal of Research on Adolescence* 32, no. 4 (2021).

16 Kenneth R. Ginsburg, Andrew C. Pool, and Jennifer Nichols, "Reframing Adolescence: Holding Youth to High Expectations and Refuting Undermining Portrayals," FrameWorks Institute, June 29, 2020, 17, www.frameworksinstitute.org.

17 Johnston-Goodstar, "Decolonizing Youth Development"; Lesko, *Act Your Age!*

18 Cynthia García Coll, Gontran Lamberty, Renee Jenkins, Harriet Pipes McAdoo, Keith Crnic, Barbara Hanna Wasik, and Heidie Vázquez García, "An Integrative Model for the Study of Developmental Competencies in Minority Children," *Child Development* 67, no. 5 (October 1996): 1891; Margaret Beale Spencer, Vinay Harpalani, Elaine Cassidy, Cleopatra Y. Jacobs, Sapana Donde, Tyhesha N. Goss, Michèle Muñoz-Miller, Nicole Charles, and Shaunqula Wilson, "Understanding Vulnerability and Resilience from a Normative Developmental Perspective: Implications for Racially and Ethnically Diverse Youth," in *Developmental Psychopathology*, ed. Dante Cicchetti and Donald J. Cohen (Hoboken, NJ: Wiley, 2015), 627–672.

19 Johnston-Goodstar, "Decolonizing Youth Development"; Husain Lateef and Elizabeth K. Anthony, "Frameworks for African-Centered Youth Development: A Critical Comparison of the Nguzo Saba and the Five Cs," *Journal of Ethnic & Cultural Diversity in Social Work* 29, no. 4 (July 2020): 270–285.

20 UCLA Center for the Developing Adolescent, "The Core Science of Adolescent Development," accessed August 16, 2022, https://developingadolescent.semel.ucla.edu; see also FrameWorks Institute, "The Core Story of Adolescence," accessed August 16, 2022, www.frameworksinstitute.org.

21 NASEM, *Promise of Adolescence.*

22 Ibid.

23 Eveline A. Crone and Ronald E. Dahl, "Understanding Adolescence as a Period of Social-Affective Engagement and Goal Flexibility," *Nature Reviews Neuroscience* 13, no. 9 (September 2012): 636–650; NASEM, *Promise of Adolescence.*

24 Ronald E. Dahl, Nicholas B. Allen, Linda Wilbrecht, and Ahna Ballonoff Suleiman, "Importance of Investing in Adolescence from a Developmental Science Perspective," *Nature* 554, no. 7693 (February 2018): 441–450; NASEM, *Promise of Adolescence*; Patton et al., "Our Future."

25 UCLA Center for the Developing Adolescent, "Core Science of Adolescent Development."

26 UN Convention on the Rights of the Child, art. 7 (November 20, 1989), 1577 U.N.T.S. 3 (hereafter CRC).

27 UN Committee on the Rights of the Child, *General Comment No. 20*, paras. 18–20.

28 NASEM, *Promise of Adolescence*; UCLA Center for the Developing Adolescent, "Core Science of Adolescent Development."

29 Cheryl L. Sisk and Douglas L. Foster, "The Neural Basis of Puberty and Adolescence," *Nature Neuroscience* 7, no. 10 (October 2004): 1040–1047; Nandita Vijayakumar, Zdena Op de Macks, Elizabeth A. Shirtcliff, and Jennifer H. Pfeifer, "Puberty and the Human Brain: Insights into Adolescent Development," *Neuroscience & Biobehavioral Reviews* 92 (September 2018): 417–436.

30 Vijayakumar et al., "Puberty and the Human Brain."

31 George C. Patton, Sheryl A. Hemphill, Jennifer M. Beyers, Lyndal Bond, John W. Toumbourou, Barbara J. McMorris, and Richard F. Catalano, "Pubertal Stage and Deliberate Self-Harm in Adolescents," *Journal of the American Academy of Child & Adolescent Psychiatry* 46, no. 4 (April 2007): 508–514; Julia A. Graber, "Pubertal Timing and the Development of Psychopathology in Adolescence and Beyond," *Hormones and Behavior* 64, no. 2 (July 2013): 262–269; Jennifer H. Pfeifer and Nicholas B. Allen, "Puberty Initiates Cascading Relationships between Neurodevelopmental, Social, and Internalizing Processes across Adolescence," *Biological Psychiatry* 89, no. 2 (January 2021): 99–108.

32 Vijayakumar et al., "Puberty and the Human Brain."

33 Graber, "Pubertal Timing and the Development of Psychopathology"; Pfeifer and Allen, "Puberty Initiates Cascading Relationships"; Karen D. Rudolph, Wendy

Troop-Gordon, Sharon F. Lambert, and Misaki N. Natsuaki, "Long-Term Consequences of Pubertal Timing for Youth Depression: Identifying Personal and Contextual Pathways of Risk," *Development and Psychopathology* 26, no. 4 (November 2014): 1423–1444.

34 Xiaojia Ge and Misaki N. Natsuaki, "In Search of Explanations for Early Pubertal Timing Effects on Developmental Psychopathology," *Current Directions in Psychological Science* 18, no. 6 (December 2009): 327–331; Pfeifer and Allen, "Puberty Initiates Cascading Relationships."

35 Jane Mendle, Eric Turkheimer, and Robert E. Emery, "Detrimental Psychological Outcomes Associated with Early Pubertal Timing in Adolescent Girls," *Developmental Review* 27, no. 2 (2007): 151–171; Sonya Negriff and Elizabeth J. Susman, "Pubertal Timing, Depression, and Externalizing Problems: A Framework, Review, and Examination of Gender Differences," *Journal of Research on Adolescence* 21, no. 3 (2011): 717–746.

36 Rona Carter, Faheemah N. Mustafaa, and Seanna Leath, "Teachers' Expectations of Girls' Classroom Performance and Behavior: Effects of Girls' Race and Pubertal Timing," *Journal of Early Adolescence* 38, no. 7 (August 2018): 885–907.

37 Julianna Deardorff, Lindsay T. Hoyt, Rona Carter, and Elizabeth A. Shirtcliff, "Next Steps in Puberty Research: Broadening the Lens Toward Understudied Populations," *Journal of Research on Adolescence* 29, no. 1 (March 2019): 133–154.

38 NASEM, *Promise of Adolescence.*

39 Leila Tarokh, Jared M. Saletin, and Mary A. Carskadon, "Sleep in Adolescence: Physiology, Cognition and Mental Health," *Neuroscience and Biobehavioral Reviews* 70 (November 2016): 182–188.

40 NASEM, *Promise of Adolescence.*

41 Jennifer H. Pfeifer and Nicholas B. Allen, "Arrested Development? Reconsidering Dual-Systems Models of Brain Function in Adolescence and Disorders," *Trends in Cognitive Sciences* 16, no. 6 (June 2012): 322–329.

42 Elizabeth P. Shulman, Ashley R. Smith, Karol Silva, Grace Icenogle, Natasha Duell, Jason Chein, and Laurence Steinberg, "The Dual Systems Model: Review, Reappraisal, and Reaffirmation," *Developmental Cognitive Neuroscience* 17 (February 2016): 103–117; Laurence Steinberg, Grace Icenogle, Elizabeth P. Shulman, Kaitlyn Breiner, Jason Chein, Dario Bacchini, Lei Chang, et al., "Around the World, Adolescence Is a Time of Heightened Sensation Seeking and Immature Self-Regulation," *Developmental Science* 21, no. 2 (2018): e12532.

43 Pfeifer and Allen, "Arrested Development?"

44 Shulman et al., "Dual Systems Model."

45 B. J. Casey, Adriana Galván, and Leah H. Somerville, "Beyond Simple Models of Adolescence to an Integrated Circuit-Based Account: A Commentary," *Developmental Cognitive Neuroscience* 17 (February 2016): 128–130; B. J. Casey, Aaron S. Heller, Dylan G. Gee, and Alexandra O. Cohen, "Development of the Emotional Brain," *Neuroscience Letters* 693 (February 2019): 29–34.

46 Casey, Galván, and Somerville, "Beyond Simple Models of Adolescence."

47 Dana G. Smith, Lin Xiao, and Antoine Bechara, "Decision Making in Children and Adolescents: Impaired Iowa Gambling Task Performance in Early Adolescence," *Developmental Psychology* 48, no. 4 (2012): 1180–1187.

48 Joshua K. Hartshorne and Laura T. Germine, "When Does Cognitive Functioning Peak? The Asynchronous Rise and Fall of Different Cognitive Abilities across the Life Span," *Psychological Science* 26, no. 4 (April 2015): 433–443.

49 B. J. Casey and Kristina Caudle, "The Teenage Brain: Self Control," *Current Directions in Psychological Science* 22, no. 2 (April 2013): 82–87.

50 Hartshorne and Germine, "When Does Cognitive Functioning Peak?"

51 Kaitlyn Breiner, Anfei Li, Alexandra O. Cohen, Laurence Steinberg, Richard J. Bonnie, Elizabeth S. Scott, Kim Taylor-Thompson, et al., "Combined Effects of Peer Presence, Social Cues, and Rewards on Cognitive Control in Adolescents," *Developmental Psychobiology* 60, no. 3 (2018): 292–302; Jason Chein, Dustin Albert, Lia O'Brien, Kaitlyn Uckert, and Laurence Steinberg, "Peers Increase Adolescent Risk Taking by Enhancing Activity in the Brain's Reward Circuitry," *Developmental Science* 14, no. 2 (2011): F1–F10; Alexandra O. Cohen, Kaitlyn Breiner, Laurence Steinberg, Richard J. Bonnie, Elizabeth S. Scott, Kim Taylor-Thompson, Marc D. Rudolph, et al., "When Is an Adolescent an Adult? Assessing Cognitive Control in Emotional and Nonemotional Contexts," *Psychological Science* 27, no. 4 (2016): 549–562.

52 Natasha Duell, Laurence Steinberg, Grace Icenogle, Jason Chein, Nandita Chaudhary, Laura Di Giunta, Kenneth A. Dodge, et al., "Age Patterns in Risk Taking across the World," *Journal of Youth and Adolescence* 47, no. 5 (May 2018): 1052–1072.

53 Steinberg et al., "Around the World, Adolescence Is a Time of Heightened Sensation Seeking."

54 Eva H. Telzer, Jorien van Hoorn, Christina R. Rogers, and Kathy T. Do, "Social Influence on Positive Youth Development: A Developmental Neuroscience Perspective," in *Advances in Child Development and Behavior*, vol. 54, ed. Janette B. Benson (Cambridge, MA: Elsevier, 2018), 215–258.

55 Alexandra O. Cohen, Richard J. Bonnie, Kim Taylor-Thompson, and B. J. Casey, "When Does a Juvenile Become an Adult: Implications for Law and Policy," *Temple Law Review* 88, no. 4 (2016): 769–788; NASEM, *Promise of Adolescence*; Telzer et al., "Social Influence on Positive Youth Development"; Laurence Steinberg, Elizabeth Cauffman, Jennifer Woolard, Sandra Graham, and Marie Banich, "Are Adolescents Less Mature than Adults? Minors' Access to Abortion, the Juvenile Death Penalty, and the Alleged APA 'Flip-Flop,'" *American Psychologist* 64, no. 7 (2009): 583–594.

56 Crone and Dahl, "Understanding Adolescence"; NASEM, *Promise of Adolescence*.

57 Cohen et al., "When Does a Juvenile Become an Adult"; Cohen et al., "When Is an Adolescent an Adult?"; Steinberg et al., "Are Adolescents Less Mature than Adults?"

58 Benjamin Oosterhoff, Laura Wray-Lake, and Daniel Hart, "Reconsidering the Minimum Voting Age in the United States," *Perspectives on Psychological Science* 17, no. 2 (March 2022): 442–451.

59 UN Committee on the Rights of the Child, *General Comment No. 20*, para. 24; Eichhorn and Bergh, "Lowering the Voting Age to 16 in Practice."

60 Mesmin Destin and Joanna Lee Williams, "The Connection between Student Identities and Outcomes Related to Academic Persistence," *Annual Review of Developmental Psychology* 2, no. 1 (2020): 437–460; Laura Ferrer-Wreder and Jane Kroger, *Identity in Adolescence: The Balance between Self and Other*, 4th ed. (New York: Routledge, 2020); Jennifer H. Pfeifer and Elliot T. Berkman, "The Development of Self and Identity in Adolescence: Neural Evidence and Implications for a Value-Based Choice Perspective on Motivated Behavior," *Child Development Perspectives* 12, no. 3 (September 2018): 158–164.

61 Kenneth R. Ginsburg, Andrew Majek, and Joanna L. Williams, "Understanding and Supporting Healthy Adolescent Development," in *Reaching Teens: Strength-Based, Trauma-Sensitive, Resilience-Building Communication Strategies Rooted in Positive Youth Development*, ed. Kenneth R. Ginsburg and Zachary Brett Ramirez McClain, 2nd ed. (Washington, DC: American Academy of Pediatrics, 2020), 85–101.

62 Sarah-Jayne Blakemore and Kathryn L. Mills, "Is Adolescence a Sensitive Period for Sociocultural Processing?," *Annual Review of Psychology* 65, no. 1 (2014): 187–207; Sarah-Jayne Blakemore, "Avoiding Social Risk in Adolescence," *Current Directions in Psychological Science* 27, no. 2 (April 2018): 116–122; Jennifer L. Kerpelman and Joe F. Pittman, "The Instability of Possible Selves: Identity Processes within Late Adolescents' Close Peer Relationships," *Journal of Adolescence* 24, no. 4 (August 2001): 491–512; Carlos E. Santos, Olga Kornienko, and Deborah Rivas-Drake, "Peer Influence on Ethnic-Racial Identity Development: A Multi-site Investigation," *Child Development* 88, no. 3 (May 2017): 725–742.

63 Susan Harter, *The Construction of the Self: Developmental and Sociocultural Foundations*, 2nd ed. (New York: Guilford, 2015).

64 Gabriel Velez and Margaret Beale Spencer, "Phenomenology and Intersectionality: Using PVEST as a Frame for Adolescent Identity Formation amid Intersecting Ecological Systems of Inequality," *New Directions for Child and Adolescent Development* 2018, no. 161 (2018): 75–90; Carlos E. Santos and Russell B. Toomey, "Integrating an Intersectionality Lens in Theory and Research in Developmental Science," *New Directions for Child and Adolescent Development* 2018, no. 161 (September 2018): 7–15.

65 Dan P. McAdams, "The Psychological Self as Actor, Agent, and Author," *Perspectives on Psychological Science* 8, no. 3 (May 2013): 272–295.

66 Daphna Oyserman, *Pathways to Success through Identity-Based Motivation* (New York: Oxford University Press, 2015); Daphna Oyserman and Mesmin Destin, "Identity-Based Motivation: Implications for Intervention," *Counseling Psychologist* 38, no. 7 (October 2010): 1001–1043.

67 Christina Spears Brown and Rebecca S. Bigler, "Children's Perceptions of Discrimination: A Developmental Model," *Child Development* 76, no. 3 (2005): 533–553.

68 Heather A. Priess, Sara M. Lindberg, and Janet Shibley Hyde, "Adolescent Gender-Role Identity and Mental Health: Gender Intensification Revisited," *Child Development* 80, no. 5 (2009): 1531–1544; Deborah L. Tolman and Sara I. McClelland, "Normative Sexuality Development in Adolescence: A Decade in Review, 2000–2009," *Journal of Research on Adolescence* 21, no. 1 (2011): 242–255.

69 Phillip L. Hammack, Sam D. Hughes, Julianne M. Atwood, Elliot M. Cohen, and Richard C. Clark, "Gender and Sexual Identity in Adolescence: A Mixed-Methods Study of Labeling in Diverse Community Settings," *Journal of Adolescent Research* 37, no. 2 (March 2022): 167–220.

70 NASEM, *Promise of Adolescence*; V. Paul Poteat, Katerina O. Sinclair, Craig D. DiGiovanni, Brian W. Koenig, and Stephen T. Russell, "Gay-Straight Alliances Are Associated with Student Health: A Multischool Comparison of LGBTQ and Heterosexual Youth," *Journal of Research on Adolescence* 23, no. 2 (2013): 319–330.

71 Stephen T. Russell and Jessica N. Fish, "Mental Health in Lesbian, Gay, Bisexual, and Transgender (LGBT) Youth," *Annual Review of Clinical Psychology* 12 (March 2016): 465–487.

72 García Coll et al., "Integrative Model for the Study of Developmental Competencies"; Spencer et al., "Understanding Vulnerability and Resilience."

73 Joanna Lee Williams, Patrick H. Tolan, Myles I. Durkee, Amir G. Francois, and Riana E. Anderson, "Integrating Racial and Ethnic Identity Research Into Developmental Understanding of Adolescents," *Child Development Perspectives* 6, no. 3 (September 2012): 304–311.

74 Andrew J. Fuligni and Kim M. Tsai, "Developmental Flexibility in the Age of Globalization: Autonomy and Identity Development among Immigrant Adolescents," *Annual Review of Psychology* 66, no. 1 (January 2015): 411–431.

75 Diane L. Hughes, Jon Alexander Watford, and Juan Del Toro, "A Transactional/Ecological Perspective on Ethnic-Racial Identity, Socialization, and Discrimination," in *Advances in Child Development and Behavior*, vol. 51 (Cambridge, MA: Elsevier, 2016), 1–41; Beverly D. Tatum, *Why Are All the Black Kids Sitting Together in the Cafeteria? And Other Conversations about Race*, 20th anniversary ed. (New York: Basic Books, 2017).

76 Robert M. Sellers, Mia A. Smith, J. Nicole Shelton, Stephanie A. J. Rowley, and Tabbye M. Chavous, "Multidimensional Model of Racial Identity: A Reconceptualization of African American Racial Identity," *Personality and Social Psychology Review* 2, no. 1 (February 1998): 18–39.

77 Jennifer H. Pfeifer and Elliot T. Berkman, "The Development of Self and Identity in Adolescence: Neural Evidence and Implications for a Value-Based Choice Perspective on Motivated Behavior," *Child Development Perspectives* 12, no. 3 (September 2018): 158–164.

78 Kate C. McLean and Moin Syed, "Personal, Master, and Alternative Narratives: An Integrative Framework for Understanding Identity Development in Context," *Human Development* 58, no. 6 (2015): 318–349.

79 Ibid.; Tupuola, "Participatory Research, Culture and Youth Identities."

80 UN Committee on the Rights of the Child, *General Comment No. 20.*

81 Ann Arnett Ferguson, *Bad Boys: Public Schools in the Making of Black Masculinity* (Ann Arbor: University of Michigan Press, 2020); Monique W. Morris, *Pushout: The Criminalization of Black Girls in Schools* (New York: New Press, 2016); Colleen Boland, "Hybrid Identity and Practices to Negotiate Belonging: Madrid's Muslim Youth of Migrant Origin," *Comparative Migration Studies* 8, no. 26 (August 2020): 1–17; Sunaina Marr Maira, *The 9/11 Generation: Youth, Rights, and Solidarity in the War on Terror* (New York: New York University Press, 2016); Michelle M. Johns, Richard Lowry, Laura T. Haderxhanaj, Catherine N. Rasberry, Leah Robin, Lamont Scales, Deborah Stone, and Nicolas A. Suarez, "Trends in Violence Victimization and Suicide Risk by Sexual Identity among High School Students—Youth Risk Behavior Survey, United States, 2015–2019," *CDC Morbidity and Mortality Weekly Report* 69, no. 1 (August 2020): 19–27.

82 Christopher Dean, "The Role of Identity in Committing Acts of Violent Extremism—and in Desisting from Them," *Criminal Behaviour and Mental Health* 27, no. 4 (2017): 281–285; NASEM, *Promise of Adolescence*; Seth J. Schwartz, Curtis S. Dunkel, and Alan S. Waterman, "Terrorism: An Identity Theory Perspective," *Studies in Conflict & Terrorism* 32, no. 6 (May 2009): 537–559.

83 Urie Bronfenbrenner and Pamela A. Morris, "The Bioecological Model of Human Development," in *Handbook of Child Psychology: Theoretical Models of Human Development*, ed. Richard M. Lerner and William Damon (Hoboken, NJ: Wiley, 2007).

84 García Coll et al., "Integrative Model for the Study of Developmental Competencies"; Spencer et al., "Understanding Vulnerability and Resilience."

85 B. Bradford Brown and James Larson, "Peer Relationships in Adolescence," in *Handbook of Adolescent Psychology: Contextual Influences on Adolescent Development*, ed. Richard M. Lerner and Laurence Steinberg (Hoboken, NJ: Wiley, 2009).

86 Ibid.; Institute of Medicine and National Research Council, *The Science of Adolescent Risk-Taking: Workshop Report* (Washington, DC: National Academies Press, 2011); Laurence Steinberg and Kathryn C. Monahan, "Age Differences in Resistance to Peer Influence," *Developmental Psychology* 43, no. 6 (November 2007): 1531–1543.

87 David S. Yeager, Ronald E. Dahl, and Carol S. Dweck, "Why Interventions to Influence Adolescent Behavior Often Fail but Could Succeed," *Perspectives on Psychological Science* 13, no. 1 (January 2018): 101–122.

88 Jason Chein, Dustin Albert, Lia O'Brien, Kaitlyn Uckert, and Laurence Steinberg, "Peers Increase Adolescent Risk Taking by Enhancing Activity in the Brain's Reward Circuitry," *Developmental Science* 14, no. 2 (2011): F1–F10; Margo Gardner and Laurence Steinberg, "Peer Influence on Risk Taking, Risk Preference, and Risky Decision Making in Adolescence and Adulthood: An Experimental Study," *Developmental Psychology* 41, no. 4 (2005): 625–635; Laurence Steinberg, "A Social Neuroscience Perspective on Adolescent Risk-Taking," in *Biosocial Theories of Crime*, ed. Kevin M. Beaver and Anthony Walsh (New York: Routledge, 2017), 435–463.

89 Brian K. Barber, Heidi E. Stolz, and Joseph A. Olsen, "Parental Support, Psychological Control, and Behavioral Control: Assessing Relevance across Time, Culture, and Method," *Monographs of the Society for Research in Child Development* 70, no. 4 (2005): 1–147; Robert W. Blum, Nan Marie Astone, Michele R Decker, and Venkatraman Chandra Mouli, "A Conceptual Framework for Early Adolescence: A Platform for Research," *International Journal of Adolescent Medicine and Health* 26, no. 3 (2014): 321–331.

90 Enrique W. Neblett Jr., Deborah Rivas-Drake, and Adriana J. Umaña-Taylor, "The Promise of Racial and Ethnic Protective Factors in Promoting Ethnic Minority Youth Development," *Child Development Perspectives* 6, no. 3 (2012): 295–303; Norma J. Perez-Brena, Deborah Rivas-Drake, Russell B. Toomey, and Adriana J. Umaña-Taylor, "Contributions of the Integrative Model for the Study of Developmental Competencies in Minority Children: What Have We Learned about Adaptive Culture?," *American Psychologist* 73, no. 6 (2018): 713–726.

91 García Coll et al., "Integrative Model for the Study of Developmental Competencies"; Spencer et al., "Understanding Vulnerability and Resilience"; NASEM, *Promise of Adolescence.*

92 Kids Count Data Center, "Trusted Well-Being Data on Children and Young People in the United States," accessed October 10, 2023, https://datacenter.kidscount.org.

93 NASEM, *Promise of Adolescence.*

94 Ibid.

95 Ibid.

96 American Association of Retired Persons (AARP) and National Alliance for Caregiving, *Caregiving in the United States 2020* (Washington, DC: AARP, May 2020), www.aarp.org; Emma Armstrong-Carter, Catherine Johnson, Julia Belkowitz, Connie Siskowski, and Elizabeth Olson, "The United States Should Recognize and Support Caregiving Youth," *Social Policy Report* 34, no. 2 (2021): 1–24; Gail Hunt, Carol Levine, and Linda Naiditch, *Young Caregivers in the U.S.: Findings from a National Survey* (Bethesda, MA: National Alliance for Caregiving and United Hospital Fund, 2005).

97 Emma Armstrong-Carter, Elizabeth Olson, and Eva Telzer, "A Unifying Approach for Investigating and Understanding Youth's Help and Care for the Family," *Child Development Perspectives* 13, no. 3 (2019): 186–192; Armstrong-Carter et al., "United States Should Recognize and Support Caregiving Youth."

98 Armstrong-Carter et al., "United States Should Recognize and Support Caregiving Youth"; Stephen Joseph, Claire Kendall, Deirdre Toher, Joe Sempik, Jennifer Holland, and Saul Becker, "Young Carers in England: Findings from the 2018 BBC Survey on the Prevalence and Nature of Caring among Young People," *Child: Care, Health and Development* 45, no. 4 (2019): 606–612; Elizabeth Olson, "Coordinating the Youth Caregiver in the United States," *ACME: An International Journal for Critical Geographies* 18, no. 5 (2019): 1150–1166.

99 Leoandra Onnie Rogers, Erika Y. Niwa, Kara Chung, Tiffany Yip, and David Chae, "M(Ai)Cro: Centering the Macrosystem in Human Development," *Human Development* 65, nos. 5–6 (2021): 270–292.

100 Karlyn R. Adams-Wiggins and Daphne V. Taylor-García, "The Manichean Division in Children's Experience: Developmental Psychology in an Anti-Black World," *Theory & Psychology* 30, no. 4 (August 2020): 485–506; García Coll et al., "Integrative Model for the Study of Developmental Competencies"; Johnston-Goodstar, "Decolonizing Youth Development"; Rogers et al., "M(Ai)Cro."

101 NASEM, *Promise of Adolescence.*

102 FrameWorks Institute, "Core Story of Adolescence"; UCLA Center for the Developing Adolescent, "Core Science of Adolescent Development."

103 Michelle Jackson and Joanna Lee Williams, "COVID-19 Mitigation Policies and Psychological Distress in Young Adults," *SSM-Mental Health* 2 (2022): 100027; Clare Stroud, Leslie R. Walker, Maryann Davis, and Charles E. Irwin Jr., "Investing in the Health and Well-Being of Young Adults," *Journal of Adolescent Health* 56, no. 2 (2015): 127–129; Richard J. Bonnie, Clare Stroud, and Heather Breiner, eds., *Investing in the Health and Well-Being of Young Adults* (Washington, DC: National Academies Press, 2014).

104 National Scientific Council on Adolescence, *The Intersection of Adolescent Development and Anti-Black Racism*, Council Report 1 (Los Angeles: National Scientific Council on Adolescence, 2021), https://developingadolescent.org.

105 Marcela Raffaelli, Vanja Lazarevic, Silvia H. Koller, A. Bame Nsamenang, and Deepali Sharma, "Introduction: Special Issue on Adolescents in the Majority World," *Journal of Research on Adolescence* 23, no. 1 (2013): 1–8.

106 Farnaz Fassihi, "Stymied by Protests, Iran Unleashes Its Wrath on Its Youth," *New York Times*, November 14, 2022; United Nations Children's Fund (UNICEF), "Young Climate Activists Demand Action and Inspire Hope," accessed January 6, 2023, www.unicef.org.

107 Julio Cammarota and Michelle Fine, eds., *Revolutionizing Education: Youth Participatory Action Research in Motion* (New York: Routledge, 2008); UNICEF, *Engaged and Heard! Guidelines on Adolescent Participation and Civic Engagement* (New York: UNICEF, July 2020), www.unicef.org.

8

Children's Rights Law in Adolescence

STEPHANIE RAP

I. Introduction

Adolescence is traditionally considered a transitional phase between childhood and adulthood. As Williams notes in chapter 7, young people develop rapidly during this developmental stage, which has been described in terms of "storm and stress" due to the many physical, emotional, and cognitive developments that occur during this period.[1] Although it is difficult to find consensus in the developmental literature on the age range of adolescence, it is most often considered to start around the ages of ten to twelve and end in the early to midtwenties.[2]

As detailed by Williams in chapter 7, children experience profound changes during adolescence. Physically, children change dramatically, their intellectual abilities develop significantly, and they are able to think in more advanced, abstract, efficient, and effective ways, compared to younger children.[3] During adolescence, children also develop and establish a sense of autonomy or independence.[4] They also develop a greater self-awareness and are increasingly able to have more reciprocal interpersonal relationships with others.[5] Identity development takes place during adolescence, with coherent self-image and identity typically arising at the end of adolescence.

The nature of adolescence means that adolescents experience particular challenges and opportunities from a children's rights perspective. This chapter thus aims to analyze the meaning and application of children's rights in this distinct phase in life. In line with Julia Sloth-Nielsen's view that the implementation of children's rights requires ongoing norm setting and clarification, it is important to continue to elaborate on the meaning of children's rights for adolescents given the emerging research in this area.[6]

This chapter starts with general observations concerning the meaning and role of adolescence in children's rights implementation. It analyzes the General Comments of the Committee on the Rights of the Child (Committee) and explores its views on the implementation of children's rights in adolescence.[7] These international standards are further scrutinized in light of scholarship on the real-world experiences of adolescents. Consistent with other chapters in this volume, the chapter then examines the following four rights areas with a view to detailing their meaning for adolescence: participation, best interests of the child, protection from harm, and health and education. Finally, the chapter addresses youth justice, as a topic of special relevance to adolescents, while also considering the age limits that are likely to affect adolescents' enjoyment of their rights.

II. Application of the CRC to Adolescence

A. Limited Coverage of Adolescence

With the adoption of the Convention on the Rights of the Child (CRC) in 1989, children under eighteen years were acknowledged as having legal status as rights holders, requiring an adapted and specific set of human rights protections.[8] As is noted throughout this volume, however, the CRC makes no distinction in its provisions for different ages and stages of children's development. The definitions of childhood, adolescence, and adulthood in society are influenced by the cultural and normative framework on which society is built, and for this reason, perhaps, Article 1 gives latitude to states parties to set the age of majority below eighteen years.[9] At the same time, most countries have set the legal age of majority at eighteen years, giving persons certain civil rights (e.g., right to vote, right to marriage) at this point, even though this age is rather arbitrary from a child development perspective. Numerous studies on brain development indicate that the human brain, specifically the prefrontal cortex, which is involved in cognitive control, is not fully developed until the midtwenties (see Williams, chapter 7), and accordingly, scientists argue that, based on biological markers, the definition of adolescence should be extended at least to the midtwenties.[10] This has special resonance in the area of youth justice, as is further discussed later in this chapter. While the Committee "recognizes that adolescence is not easily defined," as Daly and Walsh note in chapter 5, it has chosen to focus on the period from age ten to eighteen years.[11] The Committee also highlights that this definition is influenced by biological, contextual, environmental, and cultural factors, which result in the adoption of a variety of age ranges in defining adolescence.[12]

In 2003, fourteen years after the adoption of the CRC, the Committee issued its first General Comment on adolescence: *General Comment No. 4: Adolescent Health and Development in the Context of the Convention on the Rights of the Child*. In doing so, it noted that insufficient attention had been given to the rights and concerns of adolescents in the implementation of the CRC.[13] The Committee acknowledged the distinct developmental phase of adolescence and the associated tasks, capacities, and vulnerabilities of the child at this stage. Interestingly, it took another thirteen years before the Committee issued more general guidance in *General Comment No. 20 on the Implementation of the Rights of the Child during Adolescence*, which was adopted in 2016 after a consultation with one hundred adolescents from thirty-six countries and an online survey with thirteen hundred adolescents.[14] The Committee observed then that states did not recognize or invest in measures that support adolescents to enjoy their rights and that therefore the potential of adolescents was "widely compromised."[15] The Committee explained that "adolescence is a valuable period of childhood in its own right but is also a critical period of transition and opportunity for improving life chances."[16]

Ellen Desmet had already observed, in 2012, the problematic relationship between the CRC and youth, noting that the implementation of adolescents' rights received less attention from states, compared to that of young children.[17] It is material that the scientific understanding of adolescent development has expanded since the CRC was adopted, leaving some observers to comment that in its original form, the CRC is overly focused on child protection and other aspects relevant to younger children and does not fit well with adolescents' current needs and expectations.[18]

With the adoption of its first General Comment on the rights of children in adolescence, the Committee seemed responsive to these critiques. The newer General Comment highlights the agency, empowerment, and active participation of adolescents in their own lives, acknowledging adolescents' increasing influence over and involvement in issues that concern them, in line with the concept of evolving capacities (CRC, art. 5).[19] However, as the following sections detail, this growing recognition of the importance of the rights of adolescents remains insufficient to fully protect them.

B. Evolving Capacities and the Role of Parents

The introduction of the concept of "evolving capacities" in Article 5 of the CRC represented a distinct break from previous conceptions of childhood and children and a radical departure from the traditional parent-child relationship.[20] It provides that parents (or other persons responsible for the child) have the responsibilities, rights, and duties to provide appropriate direction and guidance to the child in the exercise of their rights, in a manner consistent with the child's evolving capacities. The concept of evolving capacities embodies the balance between recognizing children as vulnerable individuals entitled to protection and as active agents entitled to increasing autonomy.[21] Article 5 also balances the rights of the child with those of the family. While reasserting parents' primary responsibility in the child's upbringing, it balances parental authority with children's emerging autonomy and capacity to exercise their rights.[22] Of particular importance to adolescents, the Committee explains that "the more the child knows, has experienced and understands, the more the parent or legal guardian has to transform direction and guidance into reminders and advice, and later to an exchange on an equal footing."[23] This enables the CRC to adapt to children's development, granting adolescents the right to exercise increasing levels of responsibility.

However, the CRC's focus on the parent-child relationship and the omission of recognition of other relationships in a child's life illustrate that the instrument is not sufficiently adapted to adolescents' realities. In its preamble, the CRC recognizes that children should grow up in a family environment for the "full and harmonious development" of their personality. The CRC further recognizes that parents have the primary responsibility for the upbringing and development of their child (CRC, Art. 18). It emphasizes parents' "responsibilities, rights and duties" to guide and direct their child in the exercise of their rights (CRC, Art. 5), including their right to freedom of thought, conscience, and religion (CRC, Art. 14), in a manner consistent with children's evolving capacities. The CRC protects children from separation from their parents against their will, except when necessary for their best interests (CRC, Art. 9), guarantees their right to preserve family relations (CRC, Art. 8), and secures their right to know and be cared for by their parents (CRC, Art. 7).

The relationship between children and their parents remains important during adolescence.[24] Warmth and support from parents is one of the core developmental needs of adolescence, and research has shown that parental support and behavioral control have an impact on adolescents' psychosocial and behavioral outcomes (see Williams, chapter 7).[25] Nonetheless, throughout adolescence, the parent's role becomes less foregrounded as children take on an increasingly active role, exercising more decision-making powers, and their peers take an important role in their lives.[26] The Committee acknowledges the key role of peers in adolescents' lives, stating that they "want and need to spend an increasing amount of time with their peers," such association constituting "a major building block in adolescent development."[27] Unfortunately, however, the CRC does not contain provisions explicitly aimed at protecting peer relationships.

III. Implementing Specific Rights in Adolescence

A. Participation

The right to be heard, as set out in Article 12 of the CRC, holds particular resonance for older children along with the CRC's other participatory rights (e.g., right to freedom of expression, CRC, Art. 13; right to association and peaceful assembly, CRC, Art. 15).[28] The right to be heard requires that children who are capable of forming their own views have the right to express those views freely in all matters affecting them and to have these views taken into account in line with their age and maturity (CRC, Art. 12(1)). This right, read in conjunction with children's evolving capacities (CRC, Art. 5), requires more weight to be attached to the views of more mature children in decisions affecting them. Consistent with this notion, adolescents are less likely than younger children to be cut off from participating in decision-making minimum age rules. However, adolescents still experience barriers to their meaningful participation. The Committee explains that adolescents should, for example, be involved in "decisions relating to their education, health, sexuality, family life and judicial and administrative proceedings."[29] This right does not explicitly grant adolescents decision-making powers on these matters, but rather it mandates that they be given the opportunity to be involved in these decision-making processes and that their views be given due consideration.

A common critique on child participation is that it is a Western construct that is not compatible with non-Western cultural traditions. Martin Ruck and colleagues, however, state that "adolescents across diverse cultural contexts and settings appear to value opportunities for participation."[30] They note that a growing body of empirical evidence shows that young people from diverse cultural backgrounds endorse participatory rights and that a restriction of participatory rights is associated with negative effects on psychological health and adjustment.[31]

The child's age and maturity play an important role in the weight decision-makers give to the views of the child. However, the Committee states that the child's biological age does not define their understanding and capacity to form their views and recommends that states should not impose minimum age requirements for the exercise of the right to be heard.[32] It observes, however, that the concept of maturity, referring "to the ability to understand and assess the implications of a particular matter," is difficult to define.[33] Nonetheless, in practice, adolescents' views are typically given more weight than those of younger children. According to Aoife Daly, research indicates that the wishes of older children are given greater consideration than those of younger children—and this occurs in various countries, including, for example, in Norway, the United States, and England.[34] The framing and working of the right to be heard in the CRC therefore appears to favor adolescents and gives them increased autonomy in the exercise of their rights, as compared to younger children. However, this does not mean that adolescents' participation rights are themselves fully respected. For example, adolescents' views are frequently dismissed by policy makers on issues ranging from school COVID policies to gun violence to climate change.[35]

The digital environment has become an important tool for adolescents' participation. The Committee explains in its General Comment on children's rights in relation to the digital environment that "states parties should take into account the changing position of children and their agency in the modern world, children's competence and understanding, which develop unevenly across areas of skill and activity, and the diverse nature of the risks involved."[36] Opportunities as well as risks emanating from the digital environment change depending on children's age and developmental stage.[37] The online environment provides significant emerging opportunities for strengthening and expanding the participation of adolescents in the development, implementation, and monitoring of relevant legislation, policies, services, and programs affecting their lives at school, in the community, and at the local, national, and international levels.[38]

As adolescents exercise their participation rights with increasing autonomy, states are still required to respect, protect, and fulfill their other CRC rights. When engaging and participating in the digital environment, adolescents are exposed to risks, such as online fraud, violence, hate speech, sexist speech, and grooming, that they must be protected from in accordance with their rights to protection from violence (CRC, Art. 19), economic exploitation (CRC, Art. 32), or sexual abuse and exploitation (CRC, Art. 34).[39] Depression, dietary issues, and psychological problems are also major risks that can arise from adolescents' social media use, implicating health rights (CRC, Art. 24).[40] As such, states must perform a balance between enabling children's participation and protecting them from the risks that may arise from it. States should not restrict adolescents' access to the digital environment, but their safety should be promoted through holistic strategies, such as digital literacy, legislation and law enforcement mechanisms tackling abuse online, and training for parents and professionals working with children.[41] Recent research has found that equipping adolescents with information skills achieves positive results for their experiences online.[42] States must also guarantee that adolescents' right to privacy is respected and protected (CRC, Art. 16). The need for privacy becomes increasingly important to children personally as they become older.[43] While some adolescents may share a lot of information online, Mary Madden and colleagues found that adolescents take steps to manage their identity and protect sensitive information.[44] However, even older children struggle to understand the complexities of data flows and commercialization online.[45] States need to take measures to protect adolescents' privacy online while enabling them to participate in that environment.[46]

The Committee also highlights the importance of participation as a means of political and civil engagement: "States should adopt policies to increase opportunities for political participation, which is instrumental in the development of active citizenship."[47] One way to do so is to lower the voting age below the age of eighteen. Jaap Doek argues that, generally, children have all dimensions of citizenship under the CRC that are applicable to adults, except the right to vote, which represents the "highest form of participation in public discourse and decision-making."[48] In several Latin American (Argentina, Brazil, Cuba, Ecuador, and Nicaragua) and European counties (e.g., Austria, Scotland, Germany, the UK, and Estonia), sixteen- and seventeen-year-olds have the right to vote in national or local elections.[49] Generally, discussions around lowering the voting age revolve around issues such as whether young people are politically mature enough to vote, whether it affects their political engagement, and how it relates to other age limits that are defined in the national law of a country.[50] In this context, there is growing evidence that sixteen- and seventeen-year-olds have the same developmental capacity for voting that adults do.[51] Jan Eichhorn and Johannes Bergh conclude on the basis of empirical research that having the right to vote at sixteen has positive outcomes for political socialization and political behaviors and attitudes of young people.[52] Research from Latin America shows that voters who could vote at age sixteen show more positive democratic attitudes and more trust in national parliaments and parties.[53] However, this right is notably absent from the CRC. While the Committee does not explicitly recommend that states lower their voting age below eighteen, it nonetheless affirms that those that do should invest in measures that support adolescents to understand, recognize, and fulfill their role as active citizens, including through citizenship and human rights education.[54] This highlights the importance of access to information, in line with Articles 13 and 17 of the CRC, in formats appropriate to adolescents' age and capacities.[55] The right to information is a precondition for children and adolescents to make thoughtful and informed decisions.[56]

The participation of young people in decision-making has been shown to have positive effects in other domains. In judicial proceedings, children from around the age of twelve are often allowed to participate in some manner.[57] Several studies show that young people value being heard—directly rather than through a representative—in important judicial decisions that affect their lives.[58] It makes them feel respected as an autonomous person.[59] A lack of (perceived) autonomy, on the other hand, decreases young people's self-esteem and negatively affects the development of their reasoning skills and ability to express views.[60] Research conducted with young people between twelve and fourteen years old showed that they then "learn" not to have a say and, as a consequence, do not develop trust in their ability to make decisions.[61] Studies about young people in child care and protection have shown that repeated exclusion from participation can result in children experiencing feelings of frustration, desperation, and powerlessness and even problem behavior.[62] Adults may see participation as a stressful experience for children.[63] However, stress often seems to relate to a lack of knowledge regarding the procedure and what the child can expect.[64]

B. Best Interests of the Child

The best interests of the child principle, set out in Article 3(1) of the CRC, states that the best interests of the child shall be a primary consideration in all actions concerning children. This applies to actions or decisions that concern the child in both the public and the private spheres.[65] Precisely what is required by the best interests of the child standard is left to states parties' interpretation in implementing these rights in specific contexts, such as in adolescence.[66] Further, applying the best interests of the child principle (CRC, art.3(1)) in the context of adolescence necessarily implicates the child's right to have their views given due weight in accordance with their age and maturity (CRC, art. 12(1)) and their evolving capacities (CRC, art. 5).[67] Appropriate weight should be afforded to adolescents' views consistent with their understanding and maturity.[68] According to the Committee, approaches to the implementation of the rights of adolescents should differ significantly from those employed for younger children.[69] It recommends that states' legislation should recognize the rights of adolescents to take increasing responsibility for decisions affecting their lives.[70]

Balancing these considerations to reflect adolescents' individual development and maturity requires some level of flexibility and discretion on the part of decision-makers. The Committee states, "assessing the child's best interests is a unique activity that should be undertaken in each individual case and in the light of the specific circumstances of each child or group of children, including age, sex, level of maturity, whether the child or children belong to a minority group and the social and cultural context in which the child or children find themselves."[71] The Committee also highlights that assessment of capacities need to be done by professionals specialized in child psychology and child development and ideally by a multidisciplinary team.[72]

In all cases concerning the best interests of the child, professionals should explicitly address children's autonomy and take children more seriously, irrespective of their age.[73] However, Daly argues that courts rely too heavily on biological age to determine competence, while ignoring the context, support, information, and experience surrounding the child.[74] Moreover, the nature and gravity of risks involved for children (e.g., life-threatening medical decisions) often determine the court's acknowledgment of autonomy and inform whether or not the court overrides a child's wishes. Therefore, a more nuanced assessment of the child's best interests, which factors in both the nature of the decision and the greater maturity enjoyed by adolescents, is possible.

Overall, adolescents are more likely than younger children to have greater involvement in the assessment and determination of their best interests, at least in judicial proceedings. While the views of *all* children should be sought and taken seriously in assessing the best interests of the child, adolescents' views should be given increasing weight. Though adolescents have increased responsibility and autonomy, they should still benefit from care and protection under the CRC. Such tensions are particularly evident in decision-making related to health care, as discussed later in this chapter, and they are also relevant to the treatment of children in conflict with the law, where holding the child responsible for infringing the criminal law often trumps regard for their best interests, contrary to the guidance of the Committee.[75]

C. Protection from Harm

When children reach adolescence, they may be exposed to a range of risks, including violence and abuse, sexual or economic exploitation, trafficking, or radicalization or recruitment in gangs or militia, which can be exacerbated by the digital environment.[76] Contact with the justice system, including police contact, and experiencing the deprivation of liberty are also heightened risks during adolescence for a variety of reasons.[77] The CRC contains a number of provisions aimed at protecting children from harm. For example, Article 19 requires states parties to protect children from all forms of physical or mental violence, injury or abuse, neglect, maltreatment, or exploitation including sexual abuse, while in the care of parents or people who have the care of the child. Further, Article 34 protects children from sexual abuse and exploitation. Interestingly, in *General Comment No. 20*, the Committee does not address specific forms of violence that children might suffer during adolescence in its section on violence against children, referring to *General Comment No. 13* on freedom from all forms of violence and *General Comment No. 18* on harmful practices.[78] The obligation to protect children from violence, including domestic violence, also covers violence perpetrated by other children.[79] Adolescents, especially girls, are at higher risk of harm from their romantic partner, also called "teen-dating violence." Leyla-Denisa Obreja frames teen-dating violence as a child rights violation, addressing it in relation to children's right to life, protection from violence, and freedom from discrimination.[80] The World Health Organization has estimated that almost one in four adolescent girls between fifteen and nineteen years old who has had a partner or been married has been subject to intimate-partner violence at least once.[81] The Committee underlines the "crucial" role of the adults responsible for children in preventing and responding to violence among children.[82] It considers that children who perpetrate violence should be treated as "victims of their child-rearing conditions," highlighting the role of parents in adolescents' development.[83] This emphasis on support for families and child development is also considered important in strategies aimed at preventing children from coming into conflict with the law.[84]

Adolescents can also be at risk of trafficking for labor or sexual exploitation.[85] Nesha Dixon has identified that while some younger children are exploited, the most common age range of criminally exploited children reported in the Scottish literature is between fourteen and seventeen years old.[86] Under the CRC, states parties have an obligation to take all appropriate measures to prevent trafficking in children (Art. 35) and to protect children from economic exploitation (Art. 32), sexual abuse and exploitation (Art. 34), and all forms of exploitation prejudicial to the child's welfare (Art. 36). The Committee recommends that states parties collect data on the prevalence of the issue and invest in rehabilitation and reintegration services as well as psychosocial support for child victims, in line with obligations under Article 39 of the CRC.[87] Moreover, it underlines the importance of awareness-raising activities, directed at parents and children, on the dangers of human trafficking.[88] As trafficking of adolescents can be facilitated through the digital environment, states should develop and update antitrafficking legislation to prohibit technology-facilitated recruitment of children by criminal groups.[89] Jonathan Todres argues that adopting a comprehensive child rights–based approach to trafficking in children would facilitate early intervention and ultimately prevention of child trafficking.[90]

To protect adolescents from economic exploitation and the worst forms of child labor, states must establish minimum ages for admission to employment, appropriate regulation of employment hours and conditions, and penalties or other sanctions to ensure the effective enforcement of children's protection from economic exploitation (CRC, Art. 32(2)).[91] However, the Committee does acknowledge the importance of age-appropriate forms of work to equip adolescents with skills and allow them to learn responsibility, and the CRC permits work so long as it does not interfere with the education or healthy development of the child, as further discussed in chapter 9.[92] Adolescents may need to contribute to their families' economic well-being and support their own access to education, so states must achieve a balance between children's right to compulsory education (CRC, Art. 28) and the positive role of work in adolescents' lives (and the lives of their families).[93] In any case, all children under eighteen, including adolescents, should be protected from hazardous work, in line with the International Labor Organization Minimum Age Convention (No. 138) and the Worst Forms of Child Labor Convention (No. 182).[94]

States parties have an obligation to take appropriate measures to protect children from the illicit use of narcotic drugs and psychotropic substances (CRC, Art. 33). Adolescents are at a higher risk of drug-related harm, in particular adolescents in street situations; those excluded from school; those with histories of trauma, family breakdown, or abuse; and those living in families coping with drug dependence.[95] The Committee provides that states parties should put in place "prevention, harm-reduction and dependence treatment services, without discrimination and with sufficient budgetary allocation."[96] It welcomes the use of alternatives to repressive drug-control policies, without obliging states to adopt such policies.[97] Damon Barrett argues that the appropriate measures required under Article 33 of the CRC are unclear. He considers that the Committee has been reticent to challenge drug laws and has not sufficiently elaborated on legal and policy structures surrounding interventions relating to drug use among children.[98]

Adolescents also face greater risks than young children when they come into conflict with the law. The Committee notes that a negative image of adolescents exists in many societies. In particular, it points to negative perceptions of boys with regard to purported increased levels of nuisance, vandalism, and delinquency.[99] On the basis of developmental studies, the Committee acknowledges that risk-taking is developmentally appropriate behavior that contributes to identity development (see chapter 7).[100] It explains, however, that adolescents "are widely perceived as a threat by widespread negative media coverage and representation, and discouraged from using public spaces," which can create a biased and stereotyped image of children, in particular of disadvantaged children or adolescents.[101] This negative narrative about youth may spur states to adopt punitive approaches toward adolescents, and the Committee comments that "zero tolerance" policies are destructive and victimizing for children.[102]

It could thus be argued that adolescents—particularly those in conflict with the law—benefit from less protection from harm than younger children do, a discrepancy that is inconsistent with Article 2 of the CRC. Adolescents are more likely to be arrested, prosecuted, and deprived of liberty than are younger children, and even progressive systems increasingly favor the prosecution of sixteen- and seventeen-year-olds involved in more serious offending.[103] Indeed, children who are tried in adult court may receive treatment that is more punitive than that of their adult counterparts.[104] Racial disparities mean that minoritized children have even higher chances of being arrested and incarcerated.[105]

Failure to take account of children's lived experiences, including their development, can have grave consequences for their protection from harm. For instance, Priscilla Ocen finds that historical constructions of childhood, innocence, and sexuality in the United States have resulted in a failure to protect Black girls from antitrafficking law enforcement practices, resulting in Black girls who are subject to sexual exploitation often being labeled as offenders, rather than victims.[106] The Committee has recommended that states remove so-called status offenses from their laws (i.e., behavior that would not be punishable when committed by an adult, such as truancy), given that they also contribute to criminalizing adolescent behavior, with far-reaching negative consequences.[107]

D. Health Rights

As explained in chapter 7, hormonal, physical, and sexual developments take place during adolescence that mark the transition from childhood to adulthood. In relation to adolescence, the Committee has paid particular attention to the rights of adolescents in relation to their physical and mental health, observing that they are vulnerable to violence, mental ill health, suicide, substance use, sexually transmitted infections (STIs) including HIV/AIDS, and injuries.[108] A UNICEF study estimates that more than 13 percent of adolescents between ten and nineteen years old live with a diagnosed mental disorder, of which 40 percent have anxiety and depression.[109] This study also estimates that 45,800 adolescents die from suicide each year, making it the fifth most prevalent cause of death for adolescents aged ten to nineteen years.[110]

Article 24(1) of the CRC recognizes every child's right to the highest attainable standard of health, to facilities for the treatment of illness and rehabilitation of health, and to access such health-care services. This includes the obligation to provide adequate treatment and rehabilitation for children with mental health issues.[111] Moreover, states parties must ensure the availability of health facilities, goods, and services, including counseling and health services for mental and sexual and reproductive health, of appropriate quality and sensitive to adolescents' concerns.[112]

However, the Committee has observed that health services are generally not adapted to the specific health needs of adolescents.[113] Adolescents also "often experience legal and financial barriers, discrimination, lack of confidentiality and respect, violence and abuse, stigma and judgmental attitudes from health-care personnel."[114] States are encouraged to adopt child-sensitive health approaches throughout different periods of childhood, including adolescent-friendly health services.[115]

Philip Cook finds that adolescent participation in health programs can result in the strengthening of specific protective factors that can reduce health risks.[116] Several factors can contribute to the success of these programs, such as the age of young people (younger adolescents between ten and fourteen years of age are usually more responsive to these strategies), the social context (programs taking place in the community), and the social environment (an enabling environment where young people can engage in critical discourse and social learning).[117]

With regard to medical treatment, the Committee has recommended that the voluntary and informed consent of adolescents should be obtained, whether or not parental consent is required.[118] That is, even when parental consent is required and obtained, medical providers should still seek to obtain the adolescent's consent as well. In addition, recognizing the importance of educating and informing young people about health issues, the Committee suggests that adolescents should have the right to access confidential medical counseling and advice without the consent of a parent or guardian.[119] Evidence shows that involvement and participation of children in health-care decisions may have a positive effect on a treatment's outcome.[120]

The issue becomes more complex when the adolescent and other stakeholders have different views and wishes, including on what is in the adolescent's best interests.[121] When assessing the child's maturity to determine the weight afforded to their view, the Committee affirms that "the impact of the matter on the child" must be taken into consideration.[122] John Tobin advances a threefold model regarding decision-making in medical proceedings involving children, as reflected in *General Comment No. 4*: informed consent by parents in circumstances in which a child lacks competency, assent by the child to the extent of their evolving capacities, and informed consent by the child who is determined to be competent.[123] The World Health Organization developed a four-step process to assess and support adolescents' capacity for autonomous decision-making in health-care settings: (1) joint exploration of the situation and options; (2) common synthesis of the situations; (3) decision point; and (4) follow-up.[124] Conversely, the Committee encourages states parties to introduce fixed age limits at which the right to consent transfers to the child, as further discussed in the fourth section of this chapter.[125] However, the CRC does not impose an obligation on states to guarantee that children past a certain age or level of maturity have decision-making powers, equivalent to adults, on matters regarding their health. Rather, it recognizes that states need to balance children's best interests, right to be heard, evolving capacities, and right to protection.

In some countries, a distinction is made between routine medical treatment and interventions with more significant implications, with regard to the age at which a child can provide consent or have a refusal to treatment overruled (e.g., South Africa). In other countries, no strict age limits apply. For example, in Belgium, France, Finland, and Sweden, doctors make an individual assessment of the child's capacity to consent to treatment on the basis of the child's age and maturity in the given circumstances.[126] Katherine Federle has expanded this discussion to immunizations of children, in particular with respect to COVID-19 vaccinations, showing that giving adolescents the right to consent to vaccinations may circumvent vaccine-hesitant parents in the United States.[127] Some states have lowered the age of consent for medical treatments for adolescents (to fourteen, fifteen, or sixteen years). Others allow adolescents who are capable of understanding the nature and consequences of the proposed medical intervention to consent or provide exceptions in case of special circumstances, such as homelessness, pregnancy, marriage, living independently, or parental unavailability.[128]

Sexual maturation is an important development in adolescence; however, it is also associated with health-related risks, such as STIs, HIV/AIDS, and early pregnancies and related risks.[129] The Committee recommends that states "should ensure that health systems and services are able to meet the specific sexual and reproductive health needs of adolescents."[130] States should consider adolescents "competent to seek and have access to preventive or time-sensitive sexual and reproductive health commodities and services."[131] Girls are disproportionally affected by lack of information, advice, and guidance.[132] For example, Magdalena Mattebo and colleagues found that lack of knowledge about sexual and reproductive health and rights and lack of adolescent-friendly facilities offering such services were among the main reasons why adolescent girls did not seek sexual and reproductive health care in Nepal.[133] The Committee argues that "adolescent girls should have access to information on the harm that early marriage and early pregnancy can cause."[134]

It is important that adolescents have access to adequate information on which they can base their behavior choices, tailored to the age, capacities, and different levels of understandings.[135] Adolescents should have "access to free, confidential, adolescent-responsive and non-discriminatory sexual and reproductive health services, information and education, available both online and in person."[136] Aoife Daly and Catherine O'Sullivan argue that sexuality education is a child's human right, and they contend that there is a strong basis to affirm that there is a right to comprehensive sexuality education under international law. In particular, they highlight that children's right to access information for the promotion of their health (CRC, Art. 17), states parties' obligation to develop preventive health care, education, and services (CRC, Art. 24), and the aims of education under Article 29 of the CRC support this right.[137]

Moreover, preventive programs and policies should acknowledge the realities of the lives and lifestyles of adolescents, in order to effectively reach and sensitize adolescents.[138] In *General Comment No. 25*, the Committee highlights that "digital technologies can facilitate access to health services."[139] The Committee notes that adolescents have indicated a preference for access to mental health and sexual and reproductive health services online.[140] Adolescents may also prefer increased privacy around their health care.[141]

In line with Article 2 of the CRC, states have an obligation to ensure that the health of adolescents is not undermined in a discriminatory manner. At the same time, Ruck and colleagues note that Indigenous youth, immigrant and refugee youth, ethnic-minority youth, LGBTQI+ youth, and homeless and street-involved youth often face health inequities, stigmatization, discrimination, and violence, because of their minority position in society.[142] The Committee highlights that specific strategies should be adopted to reach Indigenous adolescents with sexual and reproductive information and services.[143] Adolescents with disabilities should also receive specific information and guidance that is adapted to their disability and the specific challenges and risks they face with regard to peer relationships and reproductive health.[144]

E. Rights in Education

Article 28 of the CRC ensures the right to education to all children, imposing on states parties the obligation to make primary education free and compulsory. However, only primary education is compulsory under Article 28, while the mandate on states is to make secondary education "available and accessible" to all and to "make higher education accessible to all on the basis of capacity." The CRC thus provides less protection for adolescents' right to education, which given the later life stage, is no longer compulsory under international law. At the same time, secondary education is considered critical to adolescents' empowerment, development, and protection.[145] The Committee recognizes the importance of education for adolescents, stating that "the right to universal, quality and inclusive education and training is the single most important policy investment that States can make to ensure the immediate and long-term development of adolescents."[146] This seems to have been acknowledged by states, with most extending the requirement of compulsory education to include up to five years of mandatory secondary education (though it is often not free).[147]

Adolescents should also have access to vocational training or higher education to support their successful transition to adulthood, as further discussed in chapter 9.[148] This is particularly important for adolescents with disabilities or mental health issues, as well as for girls, specifically adolescent mothers.[149] Gender inequalities become more apparent in adolescence, and adolescent girls are disproportionately left behind when they leave primary education.[150] This disparity may stem from the fact that girls are more often confined to the home and domestic responsibilities. The Committee encourages states to "challenge patriarchal and other harmful gender norms and stereotyping and . . . direct and indirect discrimination against girls."[151] Research has shown how education can be used as a tool to promote adolescent girls' empowerment.[152] Relatedly, under the CRC, states have an obligation to reduce dropout rates and work to keep all children in school. For those who leave school, states must support their transition to work so that they may build a stable and sustainable future.[153]

IV. Age and the Application of Children's Rights in Adolescence

As explained earlier, children are entitled to enjoy their rights in a dynamic way that reflects their increasing maturity under the CRC, including both protection and participation rights. This is often expressed in domestic law through the establishment of different minimum and maximum age laws and regulations, as a way to navigate the inherent tension between children's right to protection and their evolving capacities and autonomy.[154] Although age limits are not uncontroversial—they have little basis in the CRC—in *General Comment No. 20*, the Committee explains that the use of minimum legal age limits should be "consistent with the right to protection, the best interests principle and respect for the evolving capacities of adolescents."[155] Importantly, minimum age restrictions can be used to protect children, including adolescents, from certain types of harm. For example, the Committee provides that states parties should set a minimum age for sexual consent, marriage, and the possibility of medical treatment without parental consent.[156] While the goal of protecting children from harm is laudable, the imposition of age restrictions nonetheless reduces or removes the autonomy that children have to decide on these matters. For this reason, scholars such as Michael Freeman and John Eekelaar advocate that such limitations on autonomy rights should be well substantiated, for example, with reference to the protection of children's unhindered development.[157] Similarly, in the case of child marriage, the Committee affirms that states parties should set eighteen years old as the minimum age limit for marriage, to protect children from what it considers as forced marriage and the many harms that can result for the child, such as violence, sexual abuse and exploitation, and lack of access to education.[158] However, to respect children's evolving capacities and autonomy in decision-making, the Committee considers that marriage may be allowed for children of at least sixteen years old in exceptional circumstances, confirmed by a judge and not based on culture and tradition but on the maturity of the child, indicating again that the capacities of the adolescent play an important role in making the decision to marry.[159] Michelle Lokot and colleagues note that most attention has been focused on the negative consequences of child marriage for girls, such as poor mental health, school dropout, and gender-based violence. For boys, it has been noted that it negatively influences their educational and employment opportunities. Some scholars criticize the ban on child marriage on the basis that it ignores the relevance of adolescents' autonomy, agency, and maturity to decision-making regarding relationships and marriage.[160] Framing child marriage as "forced marriage" and dismissing "tradition" as harmful practice have been identified as a blind spot in the human rights framework.[161] In addition, this narrative focuses on girls' agency to resist marriage, while ignoring their agency and autonomy to engage in a (child-led) marriage.[162] Interestingly, in the case of legal age for sexual consent, the Committee has not defined a specific age but leaves this to states, explaining that protection and evolving capacities should be balanced in defining an acceptable minimum age for sexual consent.[163]

The minimum age of criminal responsibility is another interesting age limit as, while it protects children under the age from being held criminally liable, it neither protects nor empowers the children, usually adolescents, who fall above that age. Article 40(3)(a) of the CRC provides that states parties should establish a minimum age of criminal responsibility, without specifying what this age should be. In *General Comment No. 24*, the Committee recommends that states should not prosecute children below fourteen years of age (an increase from twelve years of age, on the basis of developmental science), because children below that age are considered not sufficiently mature to be held criminally responsible before the law.[164] At the same time, the absence of a precise age from the CRC, and indeed the failure to prohibit the prosecution of children under eighteen years altogether, leaves states with very wide discretion as to the age at which children may be prosecuted and the limitations on their rights when this happens.[165] This position appears at odds with the developmental science set out in chapter 7. Nessa Lynch and Ton Liefaard note that, in fields such as "education, medical decision-making, voice of the child, citizenship and gender identity," children's rights advocates consider that younger children should be capable of exercising agency, whereas in other fields, such as criminal responsibility, there is a call to raise the minimum age.[166] It appears that age limits are set in some circumstances to protect adolescents (e.g., high age for minimum age of criminal responsibility, child marriage, sexual consent) and in others to respect their autonomy (e.g., lower age for sexual consent, right to vote, decision-making in health care). Decisions on how best to balance these apparently competing interests should be informed by developmental science to ensure that the adolescent's rights to protection and autonomy are equally safeguarded. This may require attention to the fact that the nature of the activity (e.g., choosing candidates for office privately in a voting booth versus deciding among a group of peers whether to break the law) may present tasks that require different capacities developmentally, meaning that an adolescent might be considered fully capable of mature judgment for one activity but less so for another (see Williams, chapter 7). In some instances, regard to development science may help to soften the impact of risks associated with adolescent autonomy or the state's preference to hold children responsible, thereby maximizing their right to protection. For instance, developmental science has been used in the justice system to support more proportionate responses to children's decision-making, by creating sentencing practices that take better account of children's development.[167]

The issue of maximum ages, referring to the age after which children and young people no longer benefit from the protections afforded to children under national law, is also relevant to the application of children's rights in adolescence, as older children in certain situations are sometimes "adultified." This is often the case for children in conflict with the law and children in the migration and asylum systems, where the public interest—including national security—is often used to justify a more punitive response. These inequities, which frequently fall disproportionately on older children, have no basis in the CRC; indeed, all children are entitled to enjoy all CRC rights, while such children have additional rights to special care and protection (CRC, Arts. 20, 22, 40). Refugee and migrant children, between the ages of fifteen and eighteen years, are often provided with much lower levels of protection than are younger children, and they can be treated as adults, a status that deprives them of the CRC's protections.[168] For instance, the Refugee Council (UK) found that, out of the 263 young people it helped who had been determined by the Home Office to be "certainly" adults, only fourteen were found to be adults.[169]

Despite evidence on the incomplete cognitive and emotional development of adolescents, young people's susceptibility to peer pressure, risk-taking behavior, and lesser capabilities for self-control and self-regulation, many jurisdictions permit or require children accused of certain crimes to be adjudicated in the adult criminal justice system, an approach that the Committee has condemned.[170] Based on the CRC, the child justice system should apply to all children until the age of eighteen, with no exceptions.[171] In the United States, the findings of neuroscientific studies have heavily influenced several US Supreme Court judgments, resulting in the acknowledgment of the lesser culpability of adolescents, as compared to adults, and enhanced legal protections (e.g., the prohibition of capital punishment for offenses committed by juveniles and the restriction of mandatory life-without-parole sentences).[172] At the same time, adolescents continue to receive lengthy sentences and are frequently detained in the harshest prison conditions, suffering deprivations of their rights.[173]

The Committee acknowledges that developmentally, adulthood is usually not reached at the age of eighteen and that, for example, brain maturation continues well into an individual's twenties.[174] There has been debate about whether young people, especially those in vulnerable situations, should benefit from continued protection from the state after they reach majority (usually at eighteen years old). For example, David Farrington and colleagues argue that the child justice system is better suited to young adults, because it takes greater account of a young person's risks and needs and includes more effective rehabilitation programs.[175] In addition, research in the Netherlands found that applying juvenile justice sanctions to young adults could reduce crime and recidivism.[176] The Committee also commends states that allow the application of the youth justice system to young people of eighteen years and older, in line with evidence from developmental science and neuroscience.[177] These neuroscientific findings have informed legislation in certain states, such as the Netherlands, where legislation was amended in 2014, making it possible for young adults until the age of twenty-three to be given a youth justice sentence in criminal court.[178] These protections have been extended in other contexts too. In a Joint General Comment with the Committee on the Protection of the Rights of All Migrant Workers and Members of Their Families, the Committee on the Rights of the Child encouraged states to take protective and supportive measures beyond the age of eighteen years when engaging with young refugees and migrants.[179] Similarly, children in the care of the state also face risks when aging out of the system, leading in many cases to sudden adulthood and situations of "premature independence."[180] For adolescents who "age out" of care, the period of transition to adulthood and independent living can be a period of increased vulnerability, when the stress they are subjected to is heightened in the absence of any social support system.[181] Angela Palmer and colleagues argue that care leavers' transition into adulthood should be gradual, including through the provision of aftercare support for an extended period after they have left care.[182] The Committee also recommends that follow-up mechanisms for children in alternative care settings as they transition into adulthood should be established, to avoid an abrupt termination of support and services.[183]

V. Discussion and Conclusion

This chapter has analyzed the meaning and application of children's rights during adolescence. Children's rights law and standards and their application have often been criticized for focusing on younger children due to their vulnerable position in society. However, in particular through the concept of evolving capacities enshrined in Article 5, the CRC acknowledges that children are human beings in development and that with their growing maturity, capacities, and autonomy, the role they play in the implementation of their rights changes and increases. As they age and mature, adolescents will have increased autonomy in the exercise of their rights, and parents' role and responsibilities will diminish, signifying adolescents' growing independence from their parents. This is reflected in the increased attention to the participation of adolescents in decision-making in individual cases but also in relation to their real-world challenges related to the digital world and to climate change.[184]

Although, in child development research, adolescence extends into one's midtwenties, in the children's rights framework, childhood ends at eighteen years of age, which coincides with the legal age of adulthood in most countries. The Committee acknowledges that developmentally adulthood is reached at a later age, but it is bound by the legal range that the CRC covers. However, the Committee has addressed the transition to adulthood, highlighting the importance of continued care and attention for care leavers and refugee and migrant children, as well as access to vocational training and (higher) education for those who have turned eighteen. The Committee acknowledges that child and adolescent development takes place at an individual pace and therefore that individual assessments of maturity and needs are necessary in implementing rights and protections for children and adolescents. With respect to selected issues, however, the Committee has given more concrete guidance to states, by defining age limits, in order to provide protections to children. This has occurred in relation to child marriage (eighteen years, with exceptions from sixteen years of age), the minimum age of criminal responsibility (fourteen years), and the age for sexual consent (to be defined by individual states). Age minimums are recommended in these cases to protect children from practices that may harm their physical and mental development, such as early marriage or coming in contact with the justice system. However, these minimum ages are also subject to debate. On the one hand, some scholars and advocates argue that children's rights protections should be applied to all children until they reach the age of eighteen, banning, for example, child marriage. Others argue that this does not do justice to the agency and growing autonomy of adolescents, who should be able to make certain decisions that are aligned with their level of development.

Overall, international children's rights law provides adolescents with increasing opportunities to participate in decisions affecting them and supports their views being given due weight. As such, it can be considered that the CRC is favorable to older children in the exercise of their participation rights, compared to younger children. International children's rights also protect adolescents against risks, in particular through the Committee's focus on adolescents' physical and mental health. The Committee urges states to implement health services that are adapted to the needs of adolescents, given their physical, mental, and sexual maturation. Adolescents' evolving capacities and relationship vis-à-vis parents are acknowledged by advocating for confidential medical counseling and advice and adolescents' consent for medical treatments, irrespective of parents' consent, in appropriate circumstances. Such a position reflects the growing agency and autonomy in adolescents but does not indicate no role for parents (indeed, many adolescents still rely on parents' guidance in decision-making). Adolescents are also particularly susceptible to other types of harm, such as teen dating violence, trafficking, economic exploitation, and drug-related harms. Although the CRC contains general obligations protecting children from these harms, it does not provide sufficient guidance on how they should be addressed in a manner that respects all the rights of adolescents. Coupled with societies' often negative views toward adolescents, particularly minoritized youth, this can result in adolescents being subject to punitive approaches rather than benefiting from the CRC's protective framework. The Committee has condemned punitive and zero-tolerance policies, instead urging adolescent-friendly approaches that take into account the developmental needs of adolescents to socialize and meet with peers and to experiment with behavior. However, the CRC framework lacks concrete guidance on how to implement these adolescent-friendly services. Further, some scholars argue that rights-based approaches may not be adequate to ensure services that are sensitive to the needs of adolescents, because these are too much focused on the needs of younger children and do not sufficiently take into account the needs and wishes of adolescents.[185]

From the analysis of the children's rights framework in this chapter, one can conclude that the Committee acknowledges the special position of adolescents in the implementation of children's rights. However, this special attention to adolescents is rather limited, focusing mostly on health-related issues. It is encouraging to observe, however, that in more recent General Comments, more attention is paid to the situation of adolescents with some cross cutting analysis between General Comments demonstrating a deepening of the Committee's awareness of this distinct developmental phase in the child's life. As Ruck and colleagues rightly observe, a workable balance should be maintained between protection and participation rights for adolescents, "recognizing the important ways in which adolescents are not fully mature is important to maintaining or establishing a number of legal protections."[186]

A comprehensive rights-based approach, across all domains of the child's life during adolescence, remains a work in progress, however. If this is to be achieved, states should be encouraged to develop adolescent-friendly services, in consultation with adolescents, to understand and better reflect their wants and needs. These services should reflect the balance to be struck between adolescents' growing autonomy and participation rights, on the one hand, and their right to protection from harm, on the other, in order to achieve maximum implementation of these rights. Protecting adolescents from harm should not be used as an excuse to deny adolescents their emerging autonomy. Similarly, adolescents' growing capacities to participate—or, indeed, state preference that they should bear such responsibility—does not absolve states from the duty to protect all adolescent rights under the CRC.

NOTES

1 Ivy N. Defoe, Stephanie E. Rap, and Daniel Romer, "Adolescents' Own Views on Their Risk Behaviors, and the Potential Effects of Being Labeled as Risk-Takers," *Frontiers in Psychology, Sec. Developmental Psychology* 13 (2022): 945775.

2 Eveline A. Crone and Ronald E. Dahl, "Understanding Adolescence as a Period of Social-Affective Engagement and Goal Flexibility," *Nature Reviews Neuroscience* 13, no. 9 (2012): 636–650; Ivy N. Defoe, "Towards a Hybrid Criminological and Psychological Model of Risk Behavior: The Developmental Neuro-ecological Risk-Taking Model (DNERM)," *Developmental Review* 62 (2021): 1–12; Jeffrey J. Arnett, "Emerging Adulthood: A Theory of Development from the Late Teens through the Twenties," *American Psychologist* 55, no. 5 (2000): 469–480.

3 Laurence Steinberg and Robert G. Schwartz, "Developmental Psychology Goes to Court," in *Youth on Trial: A Developmental Perspectives on Juvenile Justice*, ed. Thomas Grisso and Robert G. Schwartz (Chicago: University of Chicago Press, 2000), 9–31.

4 Ibid.; Elizabeth Scott and Laurence Steinberg, *Rethinking Juvenile Justice* (Cambridge, MA: Harvard University Press, 2008); Laurence Steinberg and Elizabeth Cauffman, "Maturity of Judgment in Adolescence: Psychosocial Factors in Adolescent Decision Making," *Law and Human Behavior* 20, no. 3 (1996): 249–272.

5 Steinberg and Cauffman, "Maturity of Judgment in Adolescence."

6 Julia Sloth-Nielsen, "Monitoring and Implementation of Children's Rights," in *International Human Rights of Children*, ed. Ursula Kilkelly and Ton Liefaard (Singapore: Springer Nature, 2019), 31–64.

7 To analyze the Committee's approach toward adolescents, all current twenty-five General Comments were systematically searched, using the following search terms: adolescence, adolescent(s), age, maturity, due weight, evolving capacities, and youth. The relevant excerpts from the General Comments have been coded and grouped together to find overarching themes.

8 Eugene Verhellen, "The Convention on the Rights of the Child: Reflections from a Historical, Social Policy and Educational Perspective," in *Routledge International Handbook of Children's Rights Studies*, ed. Wouter Vandenhole, Ellen Desmet,

Didier Reynaert, and Sara Lembrechts (London: Routledge, 2015), 43–59; Bruno Vanobbergen, "Children's Rights and Childhood Studies: From Living Apart Together to a Happy Marriage," ibid., 60–76.

9 Defoe, "Towards a Hybrid Criminological and Psychological Model"; Defoe, Rap, and Romer, "Adolescents' Own Views on Their Risk Behaviors."

10 Crone and Dahl, "Understanding Adolescence"; Ellen Desmet, "Implementing the Convention on the Rights of the Child for 'Youth': Who and How?," *International Journal of Children's Rights* 20 (2012): 3–23.

11 UN Committee on the Rights of the Child, *General Comment No. 20: On the Implementation of the Rights of the Child during Adolescence*, para. 5, CRC/C/GC/20 (2016).

12 Ibid.

13 UN Committee on the Rights of the Child, *General Comment No. 4: Adolescent Health and Development in the Context of the Convention on the Rights of the Child*, para. 3, CRC/GC/4 (2003).

14 UN Committee on the Rights of the Child, *General Comment No. 20*.

15 Ibid., para. 3.

16 Ibid., para. 11.

17 Desmet, "Implementing the Convention on the Rights of the Child for Youth."

18 Martin D. Ruck, Daniel P. Keating, Elizabeth M. Saewyc, Felton Earls, and Asher Ben-Arieh, "The United Nations Convention on the Rights of the Child: Its Relevance for Adolescents," *Journal of Research on Adolescence* 26, no. 1 (2014): 16–29; Desmet, "Implementing the Convention on the Rights of the Child for Youth," 5; Mourad Mahidi, *The Young and the Rightless? The Protection of Youth Rights in Europe* (Brussels: European Youth Forum, 2010), 16, 91.

19 UN Committee on the Rights of the Child, *General Comment No. 20*, para. 4.

20 Sheila Varadan, "The Principle of Evolving Capacities under the UN Convention on the Rights of the Child," *International Journal of Children's Rights* 27, no. 2 (2019): 306–338.

21 Gerison Lansdown, *The Evolving Capacities of the Child* (Florence: UNICEF Innocenti Research Centre, 2005).

22 Noam Peleg, "International Children's Rights Law: General Principles," in Kilkelly and Liefaard, *International Human Rights of Children*, 135–157.

23 UN Committee on the Rights of the Child, *General Comment No. 21 (2017) on Children in Street Situations*, para. 35, CRC/C/GC/21 (2017); UN Committee on the Rights of the Child, *General Comment No. 20*, para. 18.

24 UN Committee on the Rights of the Child, *General Comment No. 20*, para. 50.

25 UCLA Center for the Developing Adolescent, "The Core Science of Adolescent Development," accessed August 16, 2023, https://developingadolescent.semel.ucla.edu; Brian K. Barber, Heidi E. Stolz, Joseph A. Olsen, W. Andrew Collins, and Margaret Burchinal, "Parental Support, Psychological Control, and Behavioral Control: Assessing Relevance across Time, Culture, and Method," *Monographs of the Society for Research in Child Development* 70, no. 4 (2005): 1–147; Robert W.

Blum, Nan Marie Astone, Michele R. Decker, and Venkatraman Chandra Mouli. "A Conceptual Framework for Early Adolescence: A Platform for Research," *International Journal of Adolescent Medicine and Health* 26, no. 3 (2014): 321–331.

26 UN Committee on the Rights of the Child, *General Comment No. 20*, para. 43; B. Bradford Brown and James Larson, "Peer Relationships in Adolescence," in *Handbook of Adolescent Psychology*, ed. Richard M. Lerner and Laurence Steinberg (Hoboken, NJ: Wiley, 2009), 74–103.

27 UN Committee on the Rights of the Child, *General Comment No. 20*, para. 44.

28 Laura Lundy, "'Voice' Is Not Enough: Conceptualising Article 12 of the United Nations Convention on the Rights of the Child," *British Educational Research Journal* 33 (2007): 927–942.

29 UN Committee on the Rights of the Child, *General Comment No. 20*, para. 23.

30 Ruck et al., "United Nations Convention on the Rights of the Child," 24.

31 Ibid.

32 UN Committee on the Rights of the Child, *General Comment No. 12: The Right of the Child to Be Heard*, paras. 29 and 21, CRC/C/GC/12 (2009); see also UN Committee on the Rights of the Child, *General Comment No. 16: On State Obligations Regarding the Impact of the Business Sector on Children's Rights*, para. 69, CRC/C/GC/16 (2013).

33 UN Committee on the Rights of the Child, *General Comment No. 12*, para. 30.

34 Aoife Daly, *Children, Autonomy and the Courts: Beyond the Right to Be Heard* (Leiden: Brill Nijhoff, 2018); Norway: Kirsten Skjørten, "Children's Voices in Norwegian Custody Cases," *International Journal of Law, Policy and the Family* 27, no. 3 (2013): 289–309; United States: Jacqueline Clarke, "Do I Have a Voice? An Empirical Analysis of Children's Voices in Michigan Custody Litigation," *Family Law Quarterly* 47, no. 3 (2013): 457–484; England: Vanessa May and Carol Smart, "Silence in Court? Hearing Children in Residence and Contact Disputes," *Child and Family Law Quarterly* 16, no. 3 (2004): 305–315.

35 Jonathan Todres, Charlene Choi, and Joseph Wright, "A Rights-Based Approach to Youth Participation in the United States," *Temple Law Review* 95, no. 3 (2023): 411–455.

36 UN Committee on the Rights of the Child, *General Comment No. 25 (2021) on Children's Rights in Relation to the Digital Environment*, para. 20, CRC/GC/C/25 (2021).

37 Ibid., para. 19.

38 UN Committee on the Rights of the Child, *General Comment No. 20*, para. 23.

39 Ibid., para. 48.

40 Elena Bozzola, Giulia Spina, Rino Agostiniani, Sarah Barni, Rocco Russo, Elena Scarpato, Antonio Di Mauro, Antonella Vita Di Stefano, Cinthia Caruso, Giovanni Corsello, and Annamaria Staiano, "The Use of Social Media in Children and Adolescents: Scoping Review on the Potential Risks," *International Journal of Environmental Research and Public Health* 19, no. 16 (2022): 9960.

41 UN Committee on the Rights of the Child, *General Comment No. 20*, para. 48.

42 Sonia Livingstone, Giovanna Mascheroni, and Mariya Stoilova "The Outcomes of Gaining Digital Skills for Young People's Lives and Wellbeing: A Systematic Evidence Review," *New Media & Society* 25, no. 5 (2023): 1176–1202.

43 UN General Assembly Human Rights Council, *Artificial Intelligence and Privacy, and Children's Privacy: Report of the Special Rapporteur on the Right to Privacy, Joseph A. Cannataci*, para. 83, A/HRC/46/3 (2021).

44 Mary Madden, Amanda Lenhart, Sandra Cortesi, Urs Gasser, Maeve Duggan, Aaron Smith, and Meredith Beaton, *Teens, Social Media, and Privacy* (Washington, DC: Pew Research Center, May 2013).

45 Sonia Livingstone, Mariya Stoilova, and Rishita Nandagiri, *Children's Data and Privacy Online: Growing Up in a Digital Age, an Evidence Review* (London: London School of Economics and Political Science, 2019), 4.

46 UN Committee on the Rights of the Child, *General Comment No. 25*, Section E.

47 UN Committee on the Rights of the Child, *General Comment No. 20*, para. 24.

48 Jaap E. Doek, foreword to *Children and Citizenship*, ed. Antonella Invernizzi and Jane Williams (Thousand Oaks, CA: Sage, 2008), xii–xvi. But see Todres, Choi, and Wright, "Rights-Based Approach"; Usang Maria Assim, "Civil Rights and Freedoms of the Child," in Kilkelly and Liefaard, *International Human Rights of Children*, 402.

49 Norberto Ribeiro, Carla Malafaia, and Teresa Ferreira, "Lowering the Voting Age to 16: Young People Making a Case for Political Education in Fostering Voting Competencies," *Education, Citizenship and Social Justice* 18 no. 3 (2022): 2.

50 Johannes Bergh and Jan Eichhorn, introduction to *Lowering the Voting Age to 16: Learning from Real Experiences Worldwide*, ed. Jan Eichhorn and Johannes Bergh (Cham, Switzerland: Palgrave Macmillan, 2020), 1–12.

51 See Hiroharu Saito, "Equal Protection for Children: Toward the Childist Legal Studies," *New Mexico Law Review* 50, no. 2 (2020): 262–264.

52 Jan Eichhorn and Johannes Bergh, conclusion to Eichhorn and Bergh, *Lowering the Voting Age to 16*, 231–241.

53 Constanza Sanhueza Petrarca, "Does Voting at a Younger Age Have an Effect on Satisfaction with Democracy and Political Trust? Evidence from Latin America," in Eichhorn and Bergh, *Lowering the Voting Age to 16*, 103–119.

54 UN Committee on the Rights of the Child, *General Comment No. 20*, para. 23.

55 Laura Lundy and Lesley McEvoy, "Children's Rights and Research Processes: Assisting Children to (In)formed Views," *Childhood* 19, no. 1 (2020): 129–144; UN Committee on the Rights of the Child, *General Comment No. 12*, paras. 19–20.

56 UN Committee on the Rights of the Child, *General Comment No. 12*, para. 10.

57 Stephanie E. Rap, Eva P. Schmidt, and Ton Liefaard, "Safeguarding the Dynamic Legal Position of Children: A Matter of Age Limits? Reflections on the Fundamental Principles and Practical Application of Age Limits in Light of International Children's Rights Law," *Erasmus Law Review* 1 (2020): 4–12.

58 Judith Cashmore and Patrick Parkinson, "What Responsibilities Do Courts Have to Hear Children's Voices?," *International Journal of Children's Rights* 15,

no. 1 (2007): 43–60; Karen J. Saywitz, Lorinda B. Camparo, and Anna Romanoff, "Interviewing Children in Custody Cases: Implications of Research and Policy for Practice," *Behavioral Sciences and the Law* 28, no. 4 (2010): 542–562.

59 Judith Cashmore and Patrick Parkinson, "Children's Participation in Family Law Disputes: The Views of Children, Parents, Lawyers and Counsellors," *Family Matters* 82 (2009): 15–21.

60 Paul A. Klaczynski, James P. Byrnes and Janis E. Jacobs, "Introduction to the Special Issue: The Development of Decision Making," *Journal of Applied Developmental Psychology* 22, no. 3 (2001): 225–236.

61 Caroline Leeson, "My Life in Care: Experiences of Non-participation in Decision-Making Processes," *Child & Family Social Work* 12, no. 3 (2007): 268–277.

62 Sharon Bessell, "Participation in Decision-Making in Out-of-Home Care in Australia: What Do Young People Say?," *Children and Youth Services Review* 33, no. 4 (2011): 496–501.

63 Ganna G. van Bijleveld, Christine W. M. Dedding, and Joske G. F. Bunders-Aelen, "Children's and Young People's Participation within Child Welfare and Child Protection Services: A State-of-the-Art Review," *Child and Family Social Work* 20, no. 2 (2015): 129–138.

64 Rebecca Nathanson and Karen J. Saywitz, "Preparing Children for Court: Effects of a Model Court Education Program on Children's Anticipatory Anxiety," *Behavioural Sciences and the Law* 33, no. 4 (2015): 459–475.

65 UN Committee on the Rights of the Child, *General Comment No. 14 (2013) on the Right of the Child to Have His or Her Best Interests Taken as a Primary Consideration (art. 3, para. 1)*, para. 1, CRC/C/GC/14 (2013).

66 Ton Liefaard, *Deprivation of Liberty of Children in Light of International Human Rights Law and Standards* (Antwerp: Intersentia, 2008).

67 Aoife Daly, "No Weight for 'Due Weight'? A Children's Autonomy Principle in Best Interest Proceedings," *International Journal of Children's Rights* 26 (2018): 61–92; Karl Hanson, "Children's Participation and Agency When They Don't 'Do the Right Thing,'" *Childhood* 23 (2016): 471–475; Kay Tisdall, "Children and Young People's Participation: A Critical Consideration of Article 12," in Vandenhole et al., *Routledge International Handbook of Children's Rights Studies*, 185–200.

68 UN Committee on the Rights of the Child, *General Comment No. 20*, para. 22.

69 Ibid., para. 1.

70 Ibid., para. 39.

71 UN Committee on the Rights of the Child, *Joint General Comment No. 3 (2017) of the Committee on the Protection of the Rights of All Migrant Workers and Members of Their Families and No. 22 (2017) of the Committee on the Rights of the Child on the General Principles Regarding the Human Rights of Children in the Context of International Migration*, para. 31, CRC/C/GC/22-CMW/C/GC/3 (2017).

72 UN Committee on the Rights of the Child, *General Comment No. 14*, para. V.B(d).

73 Daly, "No Weight for 'Due Weight'"; David Archard and Marit Skivenes, "Balancing a Child's Best Interests and a Child's Views," *International Journal of Children's*

Rights 17 (2009): 1–21; Pricilla Alderson, "Giving Children's Views 'Due Weight' in Medical Law," *International Journal of Children's Rights* 26 (2018): 16–37.

74 Daly, "No Weight for 'Due Weight.'"

75 UN Committee on the Rights of the Child, *General Comment No. 24 on Children's Rights in the Child Justice System*, para. 76, CRC/C/GC/24 (2019).

76 UN Committee on the Rights of the Child, *General Comment No. 20*, para. 12.

77 Richard J. Bonnie and Elizabeth S. Scott, "The Teenage Brain: Adolescent Brain Research and the Law," *Current Directions in Psychological Science* 22, no. 2 (2013): 158–161.

78 UN Committee on the Rights of the Child, *General Comment No. 13 (2011): The Right of the Child to Freedom from All Forms of Violence*, CRC/C/GC/13 (2011); UN Committee on the Rights of the Child, *General Comment No. 20*, Section IX.

79 UN Committee on the Rights of the Child, *General Comment No. 13*, para. 52.

80 Leyla-Denisa Obreja, "Intimate Partner Violence in Childhood: Human Rights Implications in Multiple Exposure Scenarios," *International Journal of Children's Rights* 27 (2019): 99–121.

81 World Health Organization, *Global and Regional Estimates of Violence against Women: Prevalence and Health Effects of Intimate Partner Violence and Nonpartner Sexual Violence* (Geneva: World Health Organization, 2018), 17.

82 UN Committee on the Rights of the Child, *General Comment No. 13*, para. 27.

83 Ibid., para. 52; Obreja, "Intimate Partner Violence in Childhood."

84 UN Committee on the Rights of the Child, *General Comment No. 24*, para. 9.

85 UN Committee on the Rights of the Child, *General Comment No. 20*, para. 78.

86 Nesha Dixon, *Understanding Child Criminal Exploitation in Scotland: A Scoping Review* (Glasgow: Children and Young People's Centre for Justice, 2023), 21.

87 UN Committee on the Rights of the Child, *General Comment No. 20*, para. 78.

88 Ibid.; UN Committee on the Rights of the Child, *General Comment No. 25*, para. 104.

89 UN Committee on the Rights of the Child, *General Comment No. 25*, para. 115.

90 Jonathan Todres, "A Child Rights Framework for Addressing Trafficking of Children," *Michigan State International Law Review* 22, no. 2 (2014): 557–594.

91 UN Committee on the Rights of the Child, *General Comment No. 20*, para. 84.

92 Ibid., para. 85.

93 Ibid., para. 86.

94 Ibid.

95 Ibid., para. 64.

96 Ibid.

97 Ibid.

98 Damon Barrett, *Child Rights and Drug Control in International Law* (Leiden: Brill Nijhoff, 2020), 172.

99 UN Committee on the Rights of the Child, *General Comment No. 20*, para. 30.

100 UN Committee on the Rights of the Child, *General Comment No. 17 (2013) on the Right of the Child to Rest, Leisure, Play, Recreational Activities, Cultural Life and*

the Arts (Art. 31), para. IV.A(e), CRC/C/GC/17 (2013); see Williams, chapter 7 in this volume.

101 UN Committee on the Rights of the Child, *General Comment No. 17*, para. 37; UN Committee on the Rights of the Child, *General comment No. 13*, para. 30.

102 UN Committee on the Rights of the Child, *General comment No. 13*, paras. 30 and 15.

103 Nessa Lynch and Ton Liefaard, "What Is Left in the 'Too Hard Basket'? Developments and Challenges for the Rights of Children in Conflict with the Law," *International Journal of Children's Rights* 28, no. 1 (2020): 102.

104 Brian D. Johnson and Megan, C. Kurlychek, "Transferred Juveniles in the Era of Sentencing Guidelines: Examining Judicial Departures for Juvenile Offenders in Adult Criminal Court," *Criminology* 50 (2012): 525–564.

105 See Kristin Henning, "Criminalizing Normal Adolescent Behavior in Communities of Color: The Role of Prosecutors in Juvenile Justice Reform," *Cornell Law Review* 98, no. 2 (2013): 383–462.

106 Priscilla A. Ocen, "(E)racing Childhood: Examining the Racialized Construction of Childhood and Innocence in the Treatment of Sexually Exploited Minors," *UCLA Law Review* 62 (2015): 1586–1640.

107 UN Committee on the Rights of the Child, *General Comment No. 24*, para. 12.

108 UN Committee on the Rights of the Child, *General Comment No. 15 (2013) on the Right of the Child to the Enjoyment of the Highest Attainable Standard of Health (art. 24)*, paras. 5, 8, and 38, CRC/C/GC/15 (2013); UN Committee on the Rights of the Child, *General Comment No. 20*, paras. 58, 62, 64, and 65; UN Committee on the Rights of the Child, *General Comment No. 13*, para. 28; UN Committee on the Rights of the Child, *General Comment No. 4 (2003) Adolescent Health and Development in the Context of the Convention on the Rights of the Child*, para. 22, CRC/GC/2003/4 (2003); UN Committee on the Rights of the Child, *General Comment No. 3 (2003) HIV/AIDS and the Rights of the Child*, para. 2, CRC/GC/2003/3 (2003).

109 United Nations Children's Fund (UNICEF), *The State of the World's Children 2021: On My Mind—Promoting, Protecting and Caring for Children's Mental Health* (New York: UNICEF, 2021).

110 Ibid.

111 UN Committee on the Rights of the Child, *General Comment No. 15*, para. 39.

112 UN Committee on the Rights of the Child, *General Comment No. 4*, para. 39(c).

113 UN Committee on the Rights of the Child, *General Comment No. 20*, para. 56; UN Committee on the Rights of the Child, *General Comment No. 3*, para. 20.

114 UN Committee on the Rights of the Child, *General Comment No. 20*, para. 56

115 UN Committee on the Rights of the Child, *General Comment No. 15*, Section III.B.

116 Philip Cook, "Understanding the Effects of Adolescent Participation in Health Programmes," *International Journal of Children's Rights* 16 (2008): 121–139.

117 Ibid.

118 UN Committee on the Rights of the Child, *General Comment No. 20*, para. 39.

119 Ibid.; UN Committee on the Rights of the Child, *General Comment No. 4*, paras. 11 and 33.
120 Mary Donnelly and Ursula Kilkelly, *The Child's Right to Be Heard in the Healthcare Setting: Perspectives of Children, Parents and Health Professionals* (Dublin: Office of the Ministers for Children, 2006).
121 Julian W. März, "What Does the Best Interests Principle of the Convention on the Rights of the Child Mean for Paediatric Healthcare?," *European Journal of Pediatrics* 181 (2022): 3805–3816.
122 UN Committee on the Rights of the Child, *General Comment No. 12*, para. 30.
123 John Tobin, "Children's Right to Health," in *International Human Rights of Children*, 277–298.
124 World Health Organization, *Assessing and Supporting Adolescents' Capacity for Autonomous Decision-Making in Healthcare Settings: A Tool for Health-Care Providers* (Geneva: World Health Organization, 2021).
125 UN Committee on the Rights of the Child, *General Comment No. 12*, para. 102.
126 Thierry Vansweevelt and Nicola Glover-Thomas, "Comparative Conclusions: Towards a Global Vision of Informed Consent?," in *Informed Consent and Health: A Global Analysis*, ed. Thierry Vansweevelt and Nicola Glover-Thomas (Cheltenham, UK: Edward Elgar, 2020), 256–270.
127 Katherine Hunt Federle, "The Child's Right to Be Vaccinated," *International Journal of Children's Rights* 29 (2021): 897–919.
128 Ibid.
129 Ruck et al., "United Nations Convention on the Rights of the Child."
130 UN Committee on the Rights of the Child, *General Comment No. 15*.
131 UN Committee on the Rights of the Child, *General Comment No. 20*, para. 39.
132 Ibid., para. 59.
133 Magdalena Mattebo, Malin Bogren, Nadja Brunner, Alma Dolk, Christina Pedersen, and Kerstin Erlandsson, "Perspectives on Adolescent Girls' Health-Seeking Behaviour in Relation to Sexual and Reproductive Health in Nepal," *Sexual and Reproductive Healthcare* 20 (2019): 7–12.
134 UN Committee on the Rights of the Child, *General Comment No. 4*, para. 31.
135 UN Committee on the Rights of the Child, *General Comment No. 14*, para. 78; UN Committee on the Rights of the Child, *General Comment No. 3*, para. 16.
136 UN Committee on the Rights of the Child, *General Comment No. 20*, para. 59; see also UN Committee on the Rights of the Child, *General Comment No. 4*, para. 28.
137 Aoife Daly and Catherine O'Sullivan, "Sexuality Education and International Standards: Insisting upon Children's Rights," *Human Rights Quarterly* 42, no. 4 (2020): 835–858.
138 UN Committee on the Rights of the Child, *General Comment No. 3*, paras. 11 and 39.
139 UN Committee on the Rights of the Child, *General Comment No. 25*, para. 93.
140 Ibid., para. 94.
141 Ruck et al., "United Nations Convention on the Rights of the Child."

142 Ibid.
143 UN Committee on the Rights of the Child, *General Comment No. 11 (2009): Indigenous Children and Their Rights under the Convention*, para. 54, CRC/C/GC/11 (2009).
144 UN Committee on the Rights of the Child, *General Comment No. 9 (2006): The Rights of Children with Disabilities*, para. 59, CRC/C/GC/9 (2006).
145 UNICEF, *State of the World's Children 2011*.
146 UN Committee on the Rights of the Child, *General Comment No. 20*, para. 69.
147 Laura Lundy and Patricia O'Lynn, "The Education Rights of Children," in Kilkelly and Liefaard, *International Human Rights of Children*, 259–276.
148 UN Committee on the Rights of the Child, *General Comment No. 6 (2005): Treatment of Unaccompanied and Separated Children Outside Their Country of Origin*, para. 42, CRC/GC/2005/6 (2005); UN Committee on the Rights of the Child, *General Comment No. 4*, para. 17.
149 UN Committee on the Rights of the Child, *General Comment No. 9*, para. 65; UN Committee on the Rights of the Child, *General Comment No. 4*, paras. 29 and 9; UN Committee on the Rights of the Child, *General Comment No. 20*, para. 27.
150 UN Committee on the Rights of the Child, *General Comment No. 20*, paras. 27 and 69.
151 Ibid., para. 28.
152 Monisha Bajaj, "'I Have Big Things Planned for My Future': The Limits and Possibilities of Transformative Agency in Zambian Schools," *Compare* 39, no. 4 (2008): 551–568; Mary Ann Maslak, *The Agency and Structure of Women's Education* (Albany: SUNY Press, 2007); Erin Murphy-Graham and Cynthia Lloyd, "Empowering Adolescent Girls in Developing Countries: The Potential Role of Education," *Policy Futures in Education* 14, no. 5 (2016): 556–577.
153 UN Committee on the Rights of the Child, *General Comment No. 20*, para. 73.
154 Rap, Schmidt, and Liefaard, "Safeguarding the Dynamic Legal Position of Children."
155 UN Committee on the Rights of the Child, *General Comment No. 20*, para. 39.
156 UN Committee on the Rights of the Child, *General Comment No. 4*, para. 9.
157 Michael Freeman, "Taking Children's Rights More Seriously," *International Journal of Law and the Family* 6, no. 52 (1992): 68; John Eekelaar, "The Emergence of Children's Rights," *Oxford Journal of Legal Studies* 6, no. 2 (1986): 170–171.
158 UN Committee on the Rights of the Child, *General Comment No. 20*, para. 40; UN Committee on the Rights of the Child, *Joint General Comment No. 18*, para. 20.
159 UN Committee on the Rights of the Child, *Joint General Recommendation No. 31 of the Committee on the Elimination of Discrimination against Women/General Comment No. 18 of the Committee on the Rights of the Child on Harmful Practices*, para. 20, CEDAW/C/GC/31-CRC/C/GC/18 (2014); see also UN Committee on the Rights of the Child, *General Comment No. 4*, para. 20.
160 Michelle Lokot, Holly Baker Shakya, and Beniamino Cislaghi, "The Limits of Child Agency? Dissonances and Contradictions in Conceptualisations of Agency

within Child-Led Marriage in Somalia and Cameroon," *International Journal of Children's Rights* 30 (2022): 173–203.

161 Hoko Horii, "A Blind Spot in International Human Rights Framework: A Space between Tradition and Modernity within the Child Marriage Discourse," *International Journal of Human Rights* 24, no. 8 (2020): 1057–1079.

162 Lokot, Shakya, and Cislaghi, "Limits of Child Agency?"

163 UN Committee on the Rights of the Child, *General Comment No. 20*, para. 40.

164 Ibid., para. 22; see also UN Committee on the Rights of the Child, *General Comment No. 24*, paras. 21–22.

165 Ursula Kilkelly "'Evolving Capacities' and 'Parental Guidance' in the Context of Youth Justice: Testing the Application of Article 5 of the Convention on the Rights of the Child," *International Journal of Children's Rights* 28, no. 3 (2020): 500–520.

166 Lynch and Liefaard, "What Is Left in the 'Too Hard Basket'?"

167 Laurence Steinberg, "The Influence of Neuroscience on US Supreme Court Decisions about Adolescents' Criminal Culpability," *Nature Reviews Neuroscience* 14 (2013): 513–518.

168 UN Committee on the Rights of the Child, *Joint General Comment No. 4 (2017) of the Committee on the Protection of the Rights of All Migrant Workers and Members of Their Families and No. 23 (2017) of the Committee on the Rights of the Child on State Obligations Regarding the Human Rights of Children in the Context of International Migration in Countries of Origin, Transit, Destination and Return*, para. 3, CMW/C/GC/4-CRC/C/GC/23 (2017).

169 Refugee Council, *Identity Crisis: How the Age Dispute Process Puts Refugee Children at Risk* (London: Refugee Council, 2022).

170 Thomas Grisso and Robert G. Schwartz, "Adolescents' Capacities as Trial Defendants," in *Youth on Trial: Developmental Perspectives on Juvenile Justice*, ed. Thomas Grisso and Robert G. Schwartz (Chicago: University of Chicago Press, 2000), 67–71; Defoe, Rap, and Romer, "Adolescents' Own Views on Their Risk Behaviors"; Eva Huls, Stephanie E. Rap, and Yannick N. van den Brink, "Responses to Serious Offending by Children in Northwestern Europe," in *Responding to Children Who Commit Serious Crimes: Global Perspectives on Law, Principle and Practice*, ed. Nessa Lynch, Yannick N. van den Brink, and Louise Forde (Oxon, UK: Routledge, 2022), 174–184; UN Committee on the Rights of the Child, *General Comment No. 24*, para. 30; UN Committee on the Rights of the Child, *General Comment No. 20*, para. 88.

171 UN Committee on the Rights of the Child, *General Comment No. 24*, paras. 29–30.

172 Ruck et al., "United Nations Convention on the Rights of the Child"; Lynch and Liefaard, "What Is Left in the 'Too Hard Basket'?"

173 Ursula Kilkelly and Pat Bergin, *Advancing Children's Rights in Detention: A Model for International Reform* (Bristol, UK: Bristol University Press, 2022).

174 See Williams, chapter 7, in this volume.

175 David P. Farrington, Rolf Loeber, and James C. Howell, "Increasing the Minimum Age for Adult Court," *Criminology and Public Policy* 16, no. 1 (2017): 83–92.

176 André M. van der Laan, Marinus G. C. J. Beerthuizen, and Charlotte S. Barendregt, "Juvenile Sanctions for Young Adults in the Netherlands: A Developmental Perspective," *European Journal of Criminology* 18, no. 4 (2021): 526–546.

177 UN Committee on the Rights of the Child, *General Comment No. 24*, para. 32.

178 Eva P. Schmidt, Stephanie E. Rap, and Ton Liefaard, "Young Adults in the Justice System: The Interplay between Scientific Insights, Legal Reform and Implementation in Practice in the Netherlands," *Youth Justice* 21, no. 2 (2021): 172–191.

179 UN Committee on the Rights of the Child, *Joint General Comment No. 4 and No. 23*, para. 3.

180 Harriet Ward, "Continuities and Discontinuities: Issues Concerning the Establishment of Persistent Sense of Self amongst Care Leavers," *Children and Youth Services Review* 33, no. 1 (2011): 2512–2518; see also Linda Burton, "Childhood Adultification in Economically Disadvantaged Families: A Conceptual Model," *Family Relations* 56, no. 4 (2007): 329–345.

181 Miranda J. Cunningham and Marcelo Diversi, "Aging Out: Youths Perspectives on Foster Care and the Transition to Independence," *Qualitative Social Work* 12, no. 5 (2013): 587–602; Michelle Munson, Victoria Stanhope, Latoya Small, and Kendall Atterbury, "'At Times I Kinda Felt I Was in an Institution': Supportive Housing for Transition Age Youth and Young Adults," *Children and Youth Services Review* 73, no. 2 (2017): 430–436; Wendy Sims-Schouten and Carol Hayden, "Mental Health and Wellbeing of Care Leavers: Making Sense of Their Perspectives," *Child & Family Social Work* 22, no. 4 (2017): 1480–1487; Rosemary J. Avery and Madelyn Freundlich, "You're All Grown Up Now: Termination of Foster Care Support at Age 18," *Journal of Adolescence* 32 (2009): 247–257.

182 Angela Palmer, Michelle Norris, and Joanne Kelleher, "Accelerated Adulthood, Extended Adolescence and the Care Cliff: Supporting Care Leavers' Transition from Care to Independent Living," *Child & Family Social Work* 27, no. 4 (2022): 748–759.

183 UN Committee on the Rights of the Child, *General Comment No. 21*, para. 16.

184 See UN Committee on the Rights of the Child, *General Comment No. 25*; UN Committee on the Rights of the Child, *General Comment No. 26 (2023): Children's Rights and the Environment with a Special Focus on Climate Change*, CRC/C/GC/26 (2023).

185 Kelly Bracewell, Cath Larkins and Nicky Stanley, "'They Class Me as a Child Because I'm 15. But They Don't Want Me at the Kid's Club': Towards Rights Respecting Refuges for Teenagers," *International Journal of Children's Rights* 30 (2022): 297–321.

186 Ruck et al., "United Nations Convention on the Rights of the Child," 18.

9

Contemporary Children's Rights Issues in Adolescence

YANGHEE LEE AND SANGWON KIM

I. Introduction

Adopted unanimously in 1989, the Convention on the Rights of the Child (CRC) marked the beginning of a definite shift in societies' perception of children, from recipients of care and welfare services to subjects of rights.[1] An innovative aspect of the CRC is that it recognizes children's development and their evolving capacities, providing children with greater autonomy as they grow and develop their capacity to exercise their rights (Article 5).[2] Adolescents are often better positioned than younger children to exercise their rights on their own behalf due to their increased levels of understanding and maturity. Yet, while older children and adolescents are getting closer to full maturity, they have not yet reached that level (see Williams, chapter 7). As the age of children increases, states parties should have in place a variety of measures to empower young people, consistent with their evolving capacities, so that they can gradually and voluntarily exercise their rights under the CRC. Therefore, a delicate balance should be carefully considered between affording adolescents sufficient protection and ensuring that they are given the opportunity, and are empowered, to participate.

Adolescents have the same rights as young children, but, ironically, because they are assumed to have greater capacity than younger children, they are often neglected or forgotten by states parties when implementing the CRC.[3] The rights of younger children have often received greater attention, as evidenced, for example, through campaigns focusing on reducing infant and child mortality or promoting breastfeeding.[4] The UN Committee on the Rights of the Child (Committee)—the independent body in charge of monitoring states parties' implementation of the CRC—has emphasized that adolescents' rights are generally compromised because governments may fail to recognize or invest in the necessary measures for their full enjoyment.[5]

During the drafting of the CRC—from 1979 to 1989—there was less scientific understanding of adolescent development; thus, the implementation of the CRC, and children's rights more generally, should be interpreted based on the rapidly evolving understanding of adolescent development.[6] As children go through adolescence, they engage in more diverse spheres as agents of change with the potential to contribute to their families, communities, countries, and the world. Children expand their scope of life by interacting with different people, including in the digital environment, outside the boundaries of their homes. This process increases their opportunities while also potentially putting them in more vulnerable situations. Therefore, approaches to guarantee children's rights in adolescence may differ significantly from approaches to realize those of younger children.

This chapter covers contemporary children's rights issues that children may encounter in adolescence and explores how and the extent to which their rights are realized in these situations. Adolescents, and the adults who care for them and support their development, must navigate the balance between emerging autonomy and vulnerability. This chapter explores this balancing along with, and in the context of, the following key aspects of the lives of adolescents: individual self-determination, political and social participation, the work environment, the digital environment, and mental health. During adolescence, young people are increasingly exploring their emerging unique identities, making self-determination and mental health issues particularly relevant. Similarly, adolescents spend more and more time outside of the family, and therefore their social and political interactions, participation in work settings, and exploration of the digital environment come to the foreground in adolescence. While some of these issues, like children's experience in the digital environment, have emerged only recently, others have been relevant in the lives of adolescents for a long time: child labor exploitation has been an issue for centuries, while identity development has long been the work of adolescence, though perhaps more under the radar until recently. What these five issues share in common is that most adolescents, except perhaps for the small percentage who do not have to work before becoming adults or those who have no or limited access to the digital environment, confront these issues and spaces. Therefore, for nearly all societies, how young people realize their rights in these contexts is critical to ensuring their healthy development and emergence into adulthood. These issues are illustrative rather than exhaustive, and they demonstrate some of the unique ways that rights are implemented and exercised in adolescence.

II. Prominent Issues in Adolescents' Lives

A. Self-Determination

At every moment of children's lives, they live in situations where they must make choices, regardless of their age. As children go through adolescence, their prominent life circles extend beyond the home to schools, communities, and, more recently, the online environment, providing them with more diversified and complex choices. These expansions in the scope of children's activities to emerging locations (e.g., online), as well as the spread of awareness of children as rights holders (e.g., the right to be heard in the course of medical treatment), support why the right to self-determination remains a contemporary issue in adolescence. Due to children's "subordinate" status in society, children can be unable to exercise their own rights, resulting in adults determining or controlling a large part of their right to self-determination.[7] However, compared to premature independence or prolonged subservience, the sequential transfer of decision-making power from parents to children should be positively recognized, requiring a balance between continued protection of children and recognition of their increasing autonomy according to their evolving capacities.[8]

Self-determination rights are characterized by giving the child developmentally appropriate freedom in their own development.[9] Acknowledging the right to self-determination implies a transformation from protecting children to safeguarding and supporting their rights and emerging autonomy. This is particularly important in adolescence, as this period marks a time of active identity exploration for most young people (see Williams, chapter 7). Young people explore and forge their own identities during adolescence, on the basis of a complex interaction with their own families, cultural history, social groups, and experiences of the creation of an emergent sense of self.[10]

These rights have often been explained in connection with nurturance rights.[11] The balance between nurturance and self-determination rights is clear in the CRC, through the concepts of the best interests of the child (Art. 3) and the child's evolving capacities (Art. 5). The relationships and distinctions between nurturance and self-determination rights are connected to children's development.[12] The nurturance orientation views that parents or society are responsible for making decisions that are in children's interests. It allows children's authority figures to determine what is appropriate or desirable for children, to protect them from harm, and to shape their development. If these tendencies continue and intensify during adolescence, they may eventually deprive children of their opportunities for self-determination and infringe on their rights and development. On the other hand, the self-determination orientation emphasizes that children should be empowered to make their own decisions.

The concepts of nurturance and self-determination rights are not necessarily contradictory. It has been argued that children's right to nurturance, or protection, is best achieved by promoting their "individual autonomy and active construction of their own development."[13] Acknowledging children's right to self-determination does not mean simply giving adolescents complete freedom to decide matters independently. The Committee has highlighted that, even though adolescents are at a later development stage, they still need support for their psychological and developmental needs.[14] However, the Committee has not set out in detail how to interpret the right to development and the independent developmental elements that require protection.[15] We argue that children must continuously be empowered to enjoy their right to self-determination fully in a formal system. To do so, governments should first adopt legislation and policies that recognize adolescents' right to take increasing responsibility to make decisions on issues that affect their lives and to exercise their own rights.

The lowering of the voting age to under eighteen years old is one example of providing additional responsibility to children. Though notably absent from the CRC, the right to vote is closely linked to children's right to freedom of association and peaceful assembly (Art. 15), their right to be heard (Art. 12), and their freedom of expression (Art. 13). As discussed in chapter 8, there is growing advocacy to grant this right to children (usually children of sixteen years and older). However, this is not enough: states must slowly increase children's responsibilities and continuously empower them to exercise their rights—including by providing means of participating beyond the right to vote.[16] Where the voting age is lowered to under eighteen years, governments should invest resources in and provide measures to help children understand, recognize, and fulfill their role as active citizens.[17] Governments can create policies to support adolescents' efforts to connect with peers, participate in political processes, and make informed decisions. This support should extend to recognizing that adolescents can establish their own associations, clubs, organizations, parliaments, and forums; form online networks; join political parties; and, if applicable, join their own trade unions.[18] States should invest in the provision of citizenship and human rights education and in identifying and addressing barriers to adolescents' engagement and participation.[19] The question of political participation is further discussed later in this chapter.

To empower adolescents to exercise their autonomy, states should invest in training and awareness-raising targeting caregivers, professionals working with young people, and policy makers, aimed at changing the prevalent view that adolescents can only be engaged citizens after reaching adulthood.[20] Through training and awareness-raising, adults can act as mentors and facilitators, encouraging children to gradually take more responsibility for their own decisions.[21] In this process, and in compliance with Article 12 of the CRC, it is imperative to consider children's views when designing and developing programs, policies, and public-awareness campaigns.[22]

Unfortunately, states tend to prioritize problem-focused interventions or services, focused on protection, rather than creating a supportive environment to develop the physical, psychological, spiritual, cognitive, cultural, and economic capacities that can help children's self-determination.[23] As the Committee recommends, states and nonstate actors should promote environments acknowledging the intrinsic value of adolescence and introduce measures for young people to explore their emerging identities, beliefs, and opportunities; balance risk and safety; build capacity for free, informed, and positive decisions and life choices; and successfully navigate the transition to adulthood.[24] As adolescents acquire these competencies, understanding, and increasing levels of agency, they can gradually exercise their right to self-determination. The Committee has suggested several factors to promote the resilience and healthy development of adolescents:

1. Strong relationships with and support from the key adults in their lives
2. Opportunities for participation and decision-making
3. Problem-solving and coping skills
4. Safe and healthy local environments
5. Respect for individuality
6. Opportunities for building and sustaining friendships[25]

Adolescents' right to self-determination also requires that they receive the appropriate and necessary information, in line with Articles 13 and 17 of the CRC. For adolescents, mobile technology and social media are increasingly becoming their primary means of communication to receive, create, and disseminate information. The online environment can be used to explore one's identity, share information, socialize, or engage in other activities, all of which will serve as resources for children to exercise their right to self-determination. Thus, when establishing the environment to nurture the preceding factors, states need to pay attention to the digital environment.[26] Governments should also consider using the internet to communicate and engage with adolescents.[27]

When taking measures to respect, protect, and fulfill children's right to self-determination, states should ensure that all adolescents, including vulnerable adolescents, are provided with the appropriate protection, support, and environment in line with the right to freedom from discrimination under Article 2 of the CRC. For example, Article 23(1) of the CRC recognizes the right of children with disabilities to "enjoy a full and decent life, in conditions which ensure dignity, promote self-reliance and facilitate the child's active participation in the community." Children with disabilities have a right to special care (CRC, Art. 23(2)). As such, states must provide adolescents with disabilities with opportunities for supported decision-making to facilitate their active participation in all matters affecting them, while ensuring their protection.[28]

B. Social and Political Participation

Children are rights holders, and in accordance with Article 12 of the CRC (right to be heard) and Article 13 (right to freedom of expression), they have a right to participate by speaking out on matters affecting them and contributing to the development of policies and programs that affect their lives. As discussed in chapter 8, children's capacities to understand information and competence to make decisions increase as they grow older, and, as such, adolescents' views should be afforded increasing weight, in both individual and collective decision-making.[29] Children and adolescents, under their right to freedom of expression (CRC, Art. 13), have the right not to be restricted by states in the opinions they hold.[30]

Increasingly, adolescents are coming to the forefront of social movements, around issues such as climate change, immigration, and gun violence.[31] The scope of children's participation has expanded into political and social environments, with children leading change at times.[32] Fridays for Future (the climate justice movement started by Greta Thunberg in 2018), the March for Our Lives movement (organized by the student survivors of the high school shooting in Florida), and #MeToo at school (the movement against sexual abuse, harassment, and rape culture at school) are examples of social participation that brought about change led by adolescents.[33] While adolescents become increasingly active in social and political participation, however, states need to ensure that they still receive protection from harm and violation of their other rights under the CRC.

Participation is not just about guaranteeing opportunities to participate but requires viewing children and adolescents as active agents in their own right.[34] Young people should be considered as legitimate political actors, with a right to participate in public decision-making.[35] To ensure the participation of adolescents, all sectors of society should employ a variety of approaches. More specifically, measures promoting youth participation should be systematized. Youth participation should be voluntary, and their participation should be protected from any potential harm or discrimination through the establishment of effective participation mechanisms.[36] For example, youth climate activism often faces intimidation, harassment, criminalization, stigmatization and violent attacks, and there is evidence that youth climate activists, particularly girls, face extensive online abuse for their activism.[37] States should provide for safe and empowering contexts for activism and take all appropriate measures to ensure that children's lives are not negatively affected as a result of their activism and that their rights are not infringed during or because of it. In addition, reports have found that children who participated in the #MeToo movement suffered wrong accusations, sex segregation, and work-related disadvantage, which also indicates the need for states to establish an environment that provides adolescents with the appropriate social support and legal protection.[38]

As adolescents gain autonomy in their social and political participation, they should be protected from discrimination in accessing forums for participation. Many studies find that adolescents from disadvantaged backgrounds are less likely to have access to education on political engagement and that injustice and exclusion may occur.[39] These inequities may further limit adolescents' opportunities to have their voices and experiences heard and considered in the development of policies, services, and programs affecting them. The Committee encourages the introduction of child-friendly school programs that could offer children interactive, caring, protective, and participatory environments.[40] Activities or programs that promote political and social participation in schools should be guided by adolescents' competencies, skills, and interests. In a study examining the influence of social background on learning political engagement in the school environment for adolescents aged ten to sixteen years old in England, Bryony Hoskins and colleagues found that there was unequal access by social background to learning political engagement through political activities in school and through an open classroom climate for discussion.[41] They suggested that compulsory citizenship education should be provided to children until eighteen years old and that quality citizenship education in vocational education and training should be provided to support young people from disadvantaged backgrounds to gain greater political voice.[42] Furthermore, teachers should be better trained to ensure that adolescents' participation in debates and discussions in schools is not adversely affected by their economic or other status. However, since not all adolescents are enrolled in schools—about 199 million children aged twelve to seventeen years worldwide are out of school—efforts to promote adolescents' political participation must go beyond the school and formal education system.[43] Outreach efforts should, for example, include youth centers, religious centers, sports centers, and neighborhood/community centers.

Norway provides an example of good practice of providing a public platform for adolescents' political participation. In 2017, Save the Children Norway launched Barnas Valg (children's election), providing an online parliamentary voting opportunity for children in grades 5–10 (approximately aged ten to sixteen years old) to vote for a political party. A variety of online educational resources were developed to help children understand the process, including video clips explaining political concepts and political parties. Although this project preceded the official parliamentary election, it offers an example of how states can promote young people's political and social participation.[44] While this project took place online, facilitating access to some youth, it is important to recognize that not all adolescents have online access. Therefore, offline programs should also be implemented to ensure that all adolescents can realize their participation rights in social and political spheres.

C. Work Environment

Adolescence is a period when children reach the minimum legal working age. In accordance with international standards, in particular as set forth in the International Labour Organization (ILO) conventions, by middle adolescence, young people have a right to engage in work under safe and appropriate conditions, which includes respecting their rights to education and rest, leisure, play, recreational activities, cultural life, and the arts.[45] This provides adolescents with greater autonomy, while ensuring that they are adequately protected as children. The ILO Minimum Age Convention states that the minimum age for admission to employment or work shall not be younger than fifteen years old (Art. 2) and twelve years old for states in which the economy and educational facilities are insufficiently developed (Art. 2(4)).[46] On the other hand, it provides that the minimum age for work that is likely to harm children's health or safety or to harm them morally by its nature or circumstances—that is, child labor—should not be under eighteen years old (Art. 3(2)), leaving leeway to states to set that age at sixteen years provided that children are sufficiently protected and have received specific instruction or vocational training (Art. 3(3)). The ILO Convention on the Worst Forms of Child Labor aims to secure the prohibition and elimination of the worst forms of child labor for all children under eighteen years old (Art. 1), acknowledging adolescents under eighteen sometimes have to work but that their work should not cause harm or interfere with their healthy development.[47] The capacity to enter employment, and the type of work that adolescents are permitted to undertake, thus evolves with their age and development.

Despite these international standards, millions of adolescents are still subject to child labor. Out of the 160 million children who were estimated to be in child labor in 2020, 70.6 million were twelve to seventeen years old.[48] Children, including adolescents, have long been forced to work as a source of household income.[49] Child labor was further accelerated during the COVID-19 pandemic.[50] According to the Committee, states parties should take comprehensive measures, including school-to-work transitions, social and economic development, poverty eradication programs, and universal and free access to quality, inclusive primary and secondary education, to tackle child labor in adolescence.[51] Minimum working ages should match the age for compulsory education. Often, this has meant raising the age of compulsory education so that adolescents would not be lured into labor before completing education.

In recent years, issues in the context of domestic work have received growing attention. The ILO estimated in 2012 that 9.77 million children aged twelve to seventeen years are employed to perform domestic work in the home, and about 72.1 percent of all child domestic laborers are girls. Female adolescents have frequently been subjected to domestic labor.[52] Of adolescents engaged in domestic work, 2.7 million work in hazardous conditions.[53] Although children worldwide are still vulnerable in the working environment, a number of states have addressed this issue by enacting or revising relevant laws that increase the minimum legal working age and the age for compulsory education.[54]

However, as stated earlier, the need to protect children from workplace harms does not mean that adolescents should be prohibited from engaging in any form of work. Instead, age-appropriate and decent work conditions should be designed and provided for adolescents above the minimum age of employment. Age-appropriate and decent work conditions can contribute significantly to the development of adolescents, helping them gain skills and learn various responsibilities. In fact, the Committee has recommended that states parties adopt a transitional approach to achieve a balance between the positive role of work in adolescents' lives and ensuring the right to compulsory education without discrimination, underlining that schooling and decent working conditions should be well coordinated.[55] The provision of vocational training is particularly important to adolescents, as acknowledged in Article 6 of the ILO Minimum Age Convention, which states that the Convention does not apply to work done by adolescents of at least fourteen years old in schools for general, vocational, or technical education or in other training institutions, allowing adolescents to learn particular skills through working.[56] The Committee underlines that out-of-school adolescents should be supported in transitioning to decent work, including by making educational and vocational information and guidance available and accessible in line with Article 28(1)(d) of the CRC.[57] In this context, many governments have introduced vocational training schools or career and technical education programs for adolescents to prepare them for work. Moreover, the curriculum should reflect a wide range of knowledge, skills, and abilities that meet the current labor-market demands and also prepare young people for the future in a rapidly changing world.

Internships and apprenticeships must offer a safe environment and can be supported through public–private sector partnerships to ensure that adolescents avoid job-related injuries and harms, including exposure to radiation, hazardous chemicals, violence and harassment, infections, stress, and death.[58] Work conditions and environments should be regularly monitored with clear standards, and states should establish mechanisms to regulate such work and provide remedies in cases in which young people's rights are violated.[59] Social support from management has been emphasized as a protective factor in reducing the likelihood of work-related harms.[60] Further research is needed to explore and identify other protective factors that support adolescents' healthy development and ensure their safe transition into adulthood.

One of the emerging issues related to children in the workplace is how much children's rights are guaranteed in the entertainment field; in this regard, the rights of adolescent "influencers" merit attention. Although it can be considered that working in entertainment is a means for adolescents (and younger children) to realize their creative potential, they are often exposed to various forms of discrimination, violence, and exploitation, which leaves them vulnerable to rights violations, especially in relation to their rights to protection from violence (CRC, Art. 19), to education (CRC, Arts. 28–29), to rest (CRC, Art. 31), to privacy (CRC, Art. 16), and sometimes to self-determination.[61] Since it is difficult to guarantee these rights by relying solely on the entertainment industry's efforts, laws and regulations must be devised to guarantee the rights of child entertainers. As part of these efforts, although not targeting adolescents solely, the International Federation of Actors (FIA) published the *FIA Child Performer Toolkit*, and in some countries, such as Canada and India, government organizations or related associations have published guidelines regulating working conditions (e.g., prohibiting participation in programs that ridicule, embarrass, or distress children and young people), working hours (e.g., requiring breaks and prohibiting overnight filming), and other key issues.[62]

The scope of activities of child entertainers has expanded in recent years to social media platforms, with the rise of child influencers, that is, children who have large followings on social media and who often earn money from posting sponsored content.[63] Child influencers are a growing phenomenon, one that many children and adolescents find appealing.[64] However, it is not clear whether existing guidelines apply to these new platforms. Child and adolescent influencers are at particular risk from economic exploitation, prohibited by Article 32 of the CRC. In most jurisdictions, they have no legal ownership over their earnings, unless allowed by their parents.[65] In addition, they are likely not to be considered as employees of the companies that sponsor them. Thus, they may not be covered under certain employment regulations that offer protection, and they may lack legal protections for their working conditions.[66] Some states have enacted legislation to protect child influencers; France introduced legislation in 2020 to regulate online work hours for adolescents under sixteen years old and their earnings, offering the same protections as those given to child models and actors.[67] Social media companies have created their own guidelines for their platforms, but the efficacy of that self-regulation is unclear. Thus, it is essential that states establish practical guidelines/regulations addressing social media platforms to ensure that the rights of child entertainers are protected. More importantly, child entertainers should participate in creating those guidelines.

D. Digital Environment

As daily life routines in education, communication, business, leisure, and other areas have shifted to an online medium, the digital environment has been enjoyed by both children and adults. It is estimated that one-third of internet users worldwide are children.[68] With the spread of smartphones and various digital devices, the digital environment has gained greater prominence.[69] The digital environment provides significant opportunities for strengthening and expanding adolescents' engagement in their communities—from the local to the global. In line with children's evolving capacities, the risks and opportunities associated with engagement in the digital environment change depending on their age and maturity.[70] Adolescents are likely to engage in online activities independently from supervision by their parents/caregivers.[71] As such, they face specific risks, including fraud, violence, hate speech, sexist remarks, cyberbullying, grooming for sexual exploitation, trafficking, child pornography, oversexualization, and engagement in extremist behavior.[72] Adolescents spent more time online during the COVID-19 pandemic and lockdown, which may have increased their exposure to these risks.[73] Digital experiences contribute to shaping adolescents' identity in both healthy and unhealthy ways, and these events are particularly critical during the transition from childhood into adolescence.[74]

The digital environment may be a platform that facilitates violence against children and sexual exploitation and abuse. During adolescence, such violence can be perpetrated by intimate partners, among others.[75] Adolescents can also be subject to grooming online (the act of approaching, enticing, and cultivating adolescents online to facilitate sexual exploitation, while preventing them from revealing the victimization). The prevalence of online grooming intensified globally during COVID-19 lockdowns.[76] In addition, the practice of sharing self-generated sexual material is not marginal among adolescents, and this practice can present risks such as "sextortion," secondary sexting, or grooming.[77] When the sharing of sexual content is consensual, however, it can be part of exploration and experimentation of adolescents' sexual identity, as well as the identification of valuable sexual information and advice.[78]

Preventing adolescents from accessing the online environment should not be the answer to avoid risks. Instead, holistic strategies should be designed and implemented to ensure young people's safety online. It is crucial that states review, adopt, and update laws and enforcement mechanisms to ensure that CRC rights are respected, protected, and fulfilled in the digital environment. States could start by establishing proactive measures to tackle emerging forms of violence against adolescents, such as hateful or sexual communications online or automated processes based on biased or unfairly obtained data about children. Such measures must include identifying and addressing the emerging risks. For example, defining and regulating sexual violence against adolescents, in advance of its occurrence, and criminalizing it will also be a way to protect adolescents from violence online.

Content moderation and data collection practices by companies, usually big technology companies, are another concern. As a result, adolescents' online experiences are likely to be determined by algorithm content filtering based on their social media posts, search results, time spent online, and other factors. In other words, based on data collected by technology companies (often without the consumer's knowledge), companies can modify the environment that adolescents experience as they iteratively refine the process of tracking their online interactions and distributing and curating content tailored to their preference.[79] Moreover, these companies can anticipate and influence adolescents' actions to encourage them to pursue more extreme content.[80] To respond to this issue, states' cooperation with technology companies and relevant service providers with a firm understanding of children's rights is imperative to prevent technology companies from prioritizing profits over children's rights and well-being. Governments should compel technology companies to develop guidelines enabling adolescents' safe access to their platforms, adhering to the UN Guiding Principles on Business and Human Rights.[81] For example, the Committee recommends that governments should regularly review privacy and data protection legislation to prevent deliberate or accidental violations of children's privacy and stresses the role of the business sector in implementing children's rights.[82] Though companies can be reluctant to cooperate in implementing children's rights, as a result of continuous advocacy, tech companies have imposed some restrictions on ads targeted to adolescents. For example, Meta, the parent company of Facebook and Instagram, has declared that it will no longer target children under eighteen for ads based on gender or the types of posts they have engaged with.[83] Whether and how effectively the company follows through on this commitment remains to be seen. States should require the business sector to undertake due diligence and an effective monitoring system, in particular through publicly disclosed child rights impact assessments.[84]

Despite all the aforementioned risks that adolescents face in the digital environment, this new technology also presents them with positive opportunities. For example, the digital environment can provide significant benefits with regard to education.[85] Moreover, the digital environment and social media have been incremental in increasing adolescents' participation, including in social and political participation, as discussed earlier.[86] Article 17 of the CRC recognizes the importance of the "mass media" in the provision of information to children. Access to information through the digital environment is particularly important to adolescents, including access to online health information, protective support, and sources of advice and counseling on the internet.[87] Adolescents want access to free, confidential, age-appropriate, and nondiscriminatory mental health and sexual and reproductive health services online.[88] States should provide and support the creation of age-appropriate and empowering digital content, including on information about their rights in the digital environment.[89]

In the new digital environment, it is important not only to improve the system but also to develop and strengthen children's competencies. As such, particular attention should be paid to securing access to the digital environment, developing digital literacy, and protecting children's privacy and safety. The Committee recommends that governments ensure that digital literacy is taught in schools.[90] Media literacy has a protective and a participatory function by providing adolescents with the skills and abilities to take steps to manage their online lives.[91] In a small number of countries, such as France, students and teachers are required to meet national standards of critical and functional media literacy in relation to information and communications technologies.[92] Se-Hoon Jeong and colleagues conducted a meta-analytic assessment of the effects of media literacy and found that these interventions were overall effective, in particular on reducing potentially harmful effects of media messages.[93] These efforts should be accompanied by training for parents and professionals to help assist adolescents in realizing their rights while simultaneously ensuring their protection.[94] Throughout the development of digital literacy policies and programs, the active involvement of adolescents, including peer mentoring, is recommended to reflect their needs and actual situations.[95] It is also critical to work to include children with no or limited access to the digital environment so as to avoid further discrimination and prevent a greater digital divide. The Committee's *General Comment No. 25 on Children's Rights in Relation to the Digital Environment* was developed based on workshops with children and young people, aged nine to twenty-two, in more than twenty-five countries. At the end of the workshops, participants, including children, recommended that the following eight aspects be improved for a safe and child-friendly digital environment:

- Affordable, accessible, and reliable access to devices and connectivity
- Age-appropriate content in children's own language
- Action to prevent and remedy discriminatory or aggressive behaviors
- Trusted and truthful information, including less inappropriate content and transparent information from online services themselves
- Greater privacy, in particular less surveillance by commercial entities and parents
- Greater understanding from, and better digital literacy for, parents
- Services that are designed to protect children from predators and abuse
- Access to confidential and trustworthy sources of health information[96]

Although, in some countries, 90 percent of teenagers are exposed to online environments on a daily basis, a 2020 UNICEF report shows that 2.2 billion children and young people aged twenty-five or younger do not have internet access at home.[97] The report added that only 6 percent of the age group in low-income countries has access to the internet, whereas about 87 percent have it in high-income countries.[98] This discrepancy according to countries, regions, and financial status could result in inequality in adolescents' experiences, in clear violation of children's right to protection from discrimination (CRC, Art. 2). In fact, states must ensure that all children have equal and effective access to the digital environment in ways that are meaningful to them.[99] In this context, securing internet access is essential not only to support children's development but also to narrow inequality.

E. Mental Health

Many mental health issues begin in adolescence, and 75 percent of chronic and persistent severe mental health issues are known to occur between the ages of ten and twenty-four, making it a significant issue in adolescence that must be addressed.[100] There are still many unknowns, but according to the World Health Organization, about 14 percent of children aged ten to nineteen are experiencing mental health issues, possibly leading to other forms of violation of children's rights, such as discrimination, stigma, social exclusion, and others. Moreover, in the absence of appropriate interventions, mental health issues can lead to suicide, which is the fourth leading cause of adolescent death (ages fifteen to nineteen).[101] Adolescents need to be protected from mental health issues and subsequent harms. However, states must not only adopt a protectionist approach in this regard. Adolescents should also be included in designing strategies and programs to address mental health issues, so that they are not excluded from participation in certain sectors of society because it might negatively affect their mental health. They should also be empowered and given the necessary information to make informed decisions on their mental health.

The COVID-19 pandemic had a dramatic effect on adolescents' mental health. For example, research covering eighty thousand youth globally found that depressive and anxiety symptoms doubled during the pandemic, with 25 percent of youth experiencing depressive symptoms and 20 percent experiencing anxiety symptoms.[102] In addition, during the pandemic, many other challenges may have affected adolescents' mental health; for example, in the United States, the deaths of Black Americans at the hands of the police, COVID-related violence against people of Asian descent, gun violence, polarization in political dialogue, climate change, and emotionally charged misinformation all contributed to the mental health crisis.[103] The pandemic also posed particular mental health concerns for some vulnerable groups in states with a history of conflict and forced displacement.[104]

Adding to the challenges facing adolescents, when they seek help, they often face legal and financial barriers, discrimination, lack of confidentiality, violence, stigma, and judgmental or patronizing attitudes from health-care providers.[105] Adolescents suffering from poor mental health are too often ignored or misunderstood, leading to hesitation or delay in seeking assistance and further treatment.[106] Children tend to use more mental health services when they are consulted; provided with a wide range of clear, affordable, supportive, and consistent information; and listened to for their needs, preferring confidential and nonjudgmental processes.[107]

Policies, programs, and services have been generally designed for adults. Much more attention should be given to the best interests of the child principle when designing services for adolescents.[108] Dialogue and engagement with adolescents are imperative in designing and building public health policies, programs, and services. Such dialogue can both improve services and provide youth with opportunities to explore their identities, beliefs, and emotions to help balance between risk and safety and support them to make informed decisions on relevant matters.[109]

Digital technologies are also becoming an important part of mental health and psychosocial support.[110] Adolescents value being able to search online for mental, sexual, and reproductive health information and supports (ensuring their privacy when they do is critical).[111] Data processing should be done only to the extent necessary for mental health service and by trained professionals with regulated oversight mechanisms. Governments should introduce or update legislation requiring child rights–based health technologies and services, compatible with ones in the offline environment.

Moreover, by utilizing digital technologies, mental and physical health services can be made more accessible.[112] Although school curricula and mass media offer means of communicating with young people, informal media should also be considered to ensure access to children in vulnerable or exceptional situations. Occasionally, some governments fail to fulfill their obligations to ensure children's health, stating a lack of financial, technical, and human resources. In this regard, Article 24(5) of the CRC stipulates the essential role of international cooperation in relation to the right to health.

The Committee recommends that governments adopt approaches emphasizing public health and psychosocial care instead of overmedicalizing and institutionalizing. Adolescent mental health requires a comprehensive multisectoral response, including parents, peers, the wider family and schools, and trained personnel to support and assist young people.[113] Children's mental health information should not be disclosed to a third party without the children's consent. When children participate in clinical trials, these must be sufficiently tested, and consent procedures should be developmentally appropriate, taking into consideration their evolving capacities.[114]

Moreover, states must not only protect adolescents against poor mental health but must also promote adolescents' healthy development. This is intertwined with a more comprehensive range of issues, including strong relationships with, and support from, family and other significant individuals in their lives, an adequate standard of living, access to secondary education, protection from violence and discrimination, opportunities for decision-making, mental health awareness, problem-solving and coping skills, and safe and healthy local environments.[115] Poor mental health makes vulnerable adolescents more vulnerable. Among the factors promoting healthy development, it is noteworthy that the support from significant others has greater impact on more vulnerable groups of youth.[116]

III. Conclusion

Adolescents' rights have long been compromised because governments have failed to recognize or invest in measures necessary to promote the enjoyment of these rights.[117] Children during adolescence have been placed in limbo: on the one hand, they are considered more capable of exercising their rights than younger children and have thus received less attention, but, on the other hand, they are better equipped to exercise their rights on their own behalf, in line with their evolving capacities, and deserve opportunities to do so. While they are still entitled to the protection rights enshrined in the CRC, they are also taking a leading role in the exercise of their "participation" or "freedom" rights.

Adolescence is a period in children's development in which there can be a strong tension between protecting and empowering them to exercise their own rights, take decisions, and make choices that will have an impact on their lives and the lives of others, in line with their evolving capacities. For adolescents to realize their potential in adulthood and function well as constructive members of society, governments must provide appropriate support and guidance consistent with young people's age and maturity throughout childhood and adolescence.

This chapter has identified selected issues including self-determination, political and social participation, work environment, digital environment, and mental health as prominent topics during adolescence. Governments should develop capacities to fulfill their obligations to respect, protect, and fulfill children's rights by taking appropriate legislative, administrative, and other measures for the realization of children's rights in these and other areas. Also, governments should empower adolescents to build their capacity to claim their rights. This can be achieved by securing adolescents' access to information on related matters and opportunities to make decisions. This process cannot be done without close and systematic cooperation and coordination and full participation of all relevant government agencies and other stakeholders, including children, their families, and their communities. Furthermore, international cooperation can play a crucial role in providing financial, technical, and human resources so that governments can guarantee the rights of all adolescents. Building this support for adolescents is challenging, but it is vital to ensuring that they can realize their rights and develop to their full potential.

NOTES

1 Maria Heimer and Joakim Palme, "Rethinking Child Policy Post–UN Convention on the Rights of the Child: Vulnerable Children's Welfare in Sweden," *Journal of Social Policy* 45, no. 3 (2015): 435–452.

2 Garton Kamchedzera, *A Commentary on the United Nations Convention on the Rights of the Child, Article 5: The Child's Right to Appropriate Direction and Guidance* (Leiden: Brill | Nijhoff, 2012); Noam Peleg, "International Children's Rights Law: General Principles," in *International Human Rights of Children*, ed. Ursula Kilkelly and Ton Liefaard (Singapore: Springer, 2019), 135–157.

3 United Nations Children's Fund (UNICEF), *The State of the World's Children 2021: On My Mind: Promoting, Protecting and Caring for Children's Mental Health* (New York: UNICEF, 2021), www.unicef.org.

4 Judith Diers, "Why the World Needs to Get Serious about Adolescents: A View from UNICEF," *Journal of Research on Adolescence* 23, no. 2 (2013): 214–222; Martin D. Ruck, Daniel P. Keating, Elizabeth M. Saewyc, Felton Earls, and Asher Ben-Arieh, "The United Nations Convention on the Rights of the Child: Its Relevance for Adolescents," *Journal of Research on Adolescence* 26, no. 1 (2014): 16–29.
5 UN Committee on the Rights of the Child, *General Comment No. 20: On the Implementation of the Rights of the Child during Adolescence*, CRC/C/GC/20 (2016).
6 Ruck et al., "United Nations Convention on the Rights of the Child."
7 Isabelle D. Cherney and Yee L. Shing, "Children's Nurturance and Self-Determination Rights: A Cross-Cultural Perspective," *Journal of Social Issues* 64, no. 4 (2008): 835–856.
8 Shelly Lundberg, Jennifer L. Romich, and Kwok Ping Tsang, "Decision-Making by Children," *Review of Economics of the Household* 7, no. 1 (2008): 1–30; Laurence Steinberg, Nina S. Mounts, Susie D. Lamborn, and Sanford M. Dornbusch, "Authoritative Parenting and Adolescent Adjustment across Varied Ecological Niches," *Journal of Research on Adolescence* 1, no. 1 (1990): 19–36.
9 Cherney and Shing, "Children's Nurturance and Self-Determination Rights."
10 UN Committee on the Rights of the Child, *General Comment No. 20*, para. 10.
11 Carl M. Rogers and Lawrence S. Wrightsman, "Attitudes toward Children's Rights: Nurturance or Self-Determination?," *Journal of Social Issues* 34, no. 2 (1978): 59–68; Martin D. Ruck, Rona Abramovitch, and Daniel P. Keating, "Children's and Adolescents' Understanding of Rights: Balancing Nurturance and Self-Determination," *Child Development* 69, no. 2 (1998): 404–417; Janet Mariet Bone, "Understanding of Nurturance and Self-Determination Rights in Maltreated Children and Youth" (PhD diss., University of Toronto, 2013); Michele Peterson-Badali and Martin D. Ruck, "Studying Children's Perspectives on Self-Determination and Nurturance Rights: Issues and Challenges," *Journal of Social Issues* 64, no. 4 (2008): 749–769.
12 Peterson-Badali and Ruck, "Studying Children's Perspectives."
13 Esperenza Ochaita and M. Ángeles Espinosa, "Children's Participation in Family and School Life: A Psychological and Developmental Approach," *International Journal of Children's Rights* 5 (1997): 280.
14 UN Committee on the Rights of the Child, *General Comment No. 20*.
15 Noam Peleg, "Developing the Right to Development," *International Journal of Children's Rights* 25, no. 2 (2017): 380–395.
16 Jonathan Todres, Charlene Choi, and Joseph Wright, "A Rights-Based Approach to Youth Participation in the United States," *Temple Law Review* 95, no. 3 (2023): 411–555.
17 UN Committee on the Rights of the Child, *General Comment No. 20*, para. 23.
18 Ibid., para. 45.
19 Ibid., para. 24.

20 Ibid., para. 45; Hava Rachel Gordon, "Gendered Paths to Teenage Political Participation: Parental Power, Civic Mobility, and Youth Activism," *Gender & Society* 22, no. 1 (2008): 31–55.
21 UN Committee on the Rights of the Child, *General Comment No. 20*, para. 45.
22 Ruck et al., "United Nations Convention on the Rights of the Child."
23 UN Committee on the Rights of the Child, *General Comment No. 20*, para. 15.
24 Ibid., para. 16.
25 Ibid., para. 17.
26 Yalda T. Uhls, Nicole B. Ellison, and Kaveri Subrahmanyam, "Benefits and Costs of Social Media in Adolescence," *Pediatrics* 140, no. 2 (2017): S67–70.
27 UN Committee on the Rights of the Child, *General Comment No. 20*.
28 Ibid., para. 32.
29 Petronella Grootens-Wiegers, Irma M. Hein, Jos M. van den Broek, and Martine C. de Vries, "Medical Decision-Making in Children and Adolescents: Developmental and Neuroscientific Aspects," *BMC Pediatrics* 17 (2017): 120; UN Committee on the Rights of the Child, *General Comment No. 12: The Right of the Child to Be Heard*, CRC/C/GC/12 (2009); Laura Lundy, "In Defence of Tokenism? Implementing Children's Right to Participate in Collective Decision-Making," *Childhood* 25, no. 3 (2018): 340–354.
30 UN Committee on the Rights of the Child, *General Comment No. 12*, para. 81.
31 Todres, Choi, and Wright, "Rights-Based Assessment of Youth Participation."
32 Christina McMellon and E. Kay M. Tisdall, "Children and Young People's Participation Rights: Looking Backwards and Moving Forwards," *International Journal of Children's Rights* 28, no. 1 (2020): 157–182; Johanna Wyn, "Generation and Class: Young People's New, Diverse Patterns of Life and Their Implications for Recognising Participation in Civic Society," *International Journal of Children's Rights* 15, no. 1 (2007): 165–179.
33 Fridays for Future, home page, accessed November 17, 2023, https://fridaysforfuture.org; March for Our Lives, home page, accessed November 17, 2023, https://marchforourlives.com; me too, home page, accessed November 17, 2023, https://metoomvmt.org.
34 Gordon, "Gendered Paths to Teenage Political Participation."
35 Constance Flanagan and Nakesha Faison, *Youth Civic Development: Implications of Research for Social Policy and Programs* (Ann Arbor: Society for Research in Child Development, 2001); Shawn Ginwright, Pedro Noguera, and Julio Cammarota, *Beyond Resistance! Youth Activism and Community Change* (New York: Routledge, 2006); Gordon, "Gendered Paths to Teenage Political Participation."
36 UN Committee on the Rights of the Child, *General Comment No. 12*.
37 Christophe Bahuet and AnnaMaria Oltorp, "Urgent Need to Protect Young Climate Activists," Climate Promise, United Nations Development Programme, June 12, 2022. https://climatepromise.undp.org; Aoife Daly and Laura Lundy, *Children's Rights & Climate Justice* (Strasbourg: European Network of Ombudspersons for Children, 2022); Zahra Hirji, "Teenage Girls Are Leading the Climate Movement:

And Getting Attacked for It," *BuzzFeed News*, September 25, 2019, www.buzzfeednews.com.

38 Rajiv Gupta, Arunima Gupta, and Dharmender Nehra, "Going Forward with #MeToo Movement: Towards a Safer Work Environment," *Journal of Psychosexual Health* 1, no. 2 (2019): 174–179.

39 Katharina Eckstein, Peter Noack, and Burkhard Gniewos, "Attitudes toward Political Engagement and Willingness to Participate in Politics: Trajectories throughout Adolescence," *Journal of Adolescence* 35, no. 3 (2011): 485–495; Bryony Hoskins, Jan Germen Janmaat, and Gabriella Melis, "Tackling Inequalities in Political Socialisation: A Systematic Analysis of Access to and Mitigation Effects of Learning Citizenship at School," *Social Science Research* 68 (2017): 88–101; Brian D. Christens and Ben Kirshner, "Taking Stock of Youth Organizing: An Interdisciplinary Perspective," *New Directions for Child and Adolescent Development* 134 (2011): 27–41.

40 UN Committee on the Rights of the Child, *General Comment No. 12*, para. 114.

41 Hoskins et al., "Tackling Inequalities in Political Socialisation."

42 Ibid.

43 UNESCO Institute for Statistics, *New Methodology Shows That 258 Million Children, Adolescents and Youth Are Out of School*, Fact Sheet No. 56 (Montreal: UNESCO Institute for Statistics, September 2019), http://uis.unesco.org.

44 Linn C. Lorgen and Marit Ursin, "A Children's Election—Dilemmas of Children's Political Participation," *Children & Society* 35, no. 3 (2020): 333–347; Barnas Valg 2023, "Forside | Barnas Valg," accessed November 17, 2023, https://barnasvalg.reddbarna.no.

45 UN Committee on the Rights of the Child, *General Comment No. 20*, para. 85.

46 International Labour Organization (ILO), Minimum Age Convention, art. 2 (June 26, 1973), C138.

47 ILO, Worst Forms of Child Labour Convention, art. 1 (June 17, 1999), C182; Yoshie Noguchi, "ILO Convention No. 182 on the Worst Forms of Child Labour and the Convention on the Rights of the Child," *International Journal of Children's Rights* 10, no. 4 (2002): 355–369; Gurchathen Sanghera, "Child Labor, International Law, and Multinational Enterprises," in Kilkelly and Liefaard, *International Human Rights of Children*, 455–486.

48 ILO and UNICEF, *Child Labour: Global Estimates 2020, Trends and the Road Forward* (New York: ILO and UNICEF, 2021), https://data.unicef.org.

49 Alhassan Abdullah, Inès Huynh, Clifton R. Emery, and Lucy P. Jordan, "Social Norms and Family Child Labor: A Systematic Literature Review," *International Journal of Environmental Research and Public Health* 19, no. 7 (2022): 4082.

50 Jo Becker, "'I Must Work to Eat': Covid-19, Poverty, and Child Labor in Ghana, Nepal, and Uganda," Human Rights Watch, May 26, 2021, www.hrw.org.

51 UN Committee on the Rights of the Child, *General Comment No. 20*, para. 85.

52 Mélanie Jacquemin, "Can the Language of Rights Get Hold of the Complex Realities of Child Domestic Work? The Case of Young Domestic Workers in Abidjan, Ivory Coast," *Childhood* 13, no. 3 (2006): 389–406.

53 ILO, *Child Domestic Work: Global Estimates 2012* (Geneva: International Programme on the Elimination of Child Labour and ILO, 2012), www.ilo.org.

54 Adriana Lleras-Muney, "Were Compulsory Attendance and Child Labor Laws Effective? An Analysis from 1915 to 1939," *Journal of Law and Economics* 45, no. 2 (2002): 401–435.

55 UN Committee on the Rights of the Child, *General Comment No. 20*, para. 85.

56 Breen Creighton, "Combating Child Labour: The Role of International Labour Standards," *Comparative Labor Law and Policy Journal* 18 (1997): 362–396; Sanghera, "Child Labor, International Law, and Multinational Enterprises"; Lee Swepston, "Child Labour: Its Regulation by ILO Standards and National Legislation," *International Labour Review* 121, no. 5 (1982): 577–594.

57 UN Committee on the Rights of the Child, *General Comment No. 20*, para. 73.

58 Rebecca J. Guerin, Audrey A. Reichard, Susan Derk, Kitty J. Hendricks, Lauren M. Menger-Ogle, and Andrea H, Okun, "Nonfatal Occupational Injuries to Younger Workers—United States, 2012–2018," *Morbidity and Mortality Weekly Report* 69, no. 35 (2020): 1204–1209; Kurt Rasmussen, Claus D. Hansen, Kent J. Nielsen, and Johan H. Andersen, "Incidence of Work Injuries amongst Danish Adolescents and Their Association with Work Environment Factors," *American Journal of Industrial Medicine* 54, no. 2 (2010): 143–152.

59 See UN Committee on the Rights of the Child, *General Comment No. 20*.

60 Rasmussen et al., "Incidence of Work Injuries amongst Danish Adolescents."

61 Tabetha Bennett, "Child Entertainers and Their Limited Protections: A Call for an Interstate Compact," *Child & Family Law Journal*, 9 no. 1 (2021): 131–158.

62 International Federation of Actors (FIA), *FIA Child Performer Toolkit* (Brussels: FIA, 2016), https://fia-actors.com.

63 Marina A. Masterson, "When Play Becomes Work: Child Labor Laws in the Era of 'Kidfluencers,'" *University of Pennsylvania Law Review* 169 (2021): 577–607.

64 Ibid.; Ana Saragoza, "The Kids Are Alright? The Need for Kidfluencer Protections," *American University Journal of Gender, Social Policy & the Law* 28, no. 4 (2020): 575–602; Grace Greene, "Instagram Lookalikes and Celebrity Influencers: Rethinking the Right to Publicity in the Social Media Age," *University of Pennsylvania Law Review* 168 (2020): 186.

65 Masterson, "When Play Becomes Work"; Bennett, "Child Entertainers and Their Limited Protections."

66 Masterson, "When Play Becomes Work"; Bennett, "Child Entertainers and Their Limited Protections."

67 LOI n° 2020-1266 du 19 octobre 2020 visant à encadrer l'exploitation commerciale de l'image d'enfants de moins de seize ans sur les plateformes en ligne; "France Passes New Law to Protect Child Influencers," *BBC News*, October 7, 2020, www.bbc.com.

68 Sonia Livingstone, John Carr, and Jasmina Byrne, "One in Three: Internet Governance and Children's Rights" (GCIG Paper No. 22, Centre for International

Governance Innovation and the Royal Institute of International Affairs, Ontario, November 2, 2015), www.cigionline.org.

69 Candice Odgers, "Smartphones Are Bad for Some Teens, Not All," *Nature* 554, no. 7693 (2018): 432–434.

70 UN Committee on the Rights of the Child, *General Comment No. 25: Children's Rights in Relation to the Digital Environment*, para. 19, CRC/C/GC/25 (2021).

71 Ibid., para. 19.

72 Mia Bloom and Chelsea Daymon, "Assessing the Future Threat: ISIS's Virtual Caliphate," *Orbis* 62, no. 3 (2018): 372–388; Esther Calvete, Izaskun Orue, Ana Estévez, Lourdes Villardón, and Patricia Padilla, "Cyberbullying in Adolescents: Modalities and Aggressors' Profile," *Computers in Human Behavior*, 26, no. 5 (2010): 1128–1135; Eric W. Owens, Richard J. Behun, Jill C. Manning, and Rory C. Reid, "The Impact of Internet Pornography on Adolescents: A Review of the Research," *Sexual Addiction & Compulsivity* 19, nos. 1–2 (2012): 99–122.

73 World Childhood Foundation, End Violence Against Children, ITU, UNESCO, UNICEF, UNODC, WeProtect Global Alliance, and WHO, *COVID-19 and Its Implications for Protecting Children Online* (New York: UNICEF, April 2020), www.unicef.org.

74 Lucía Magis-Weinberg, Ahna Ballonoff Suleiman, and Ronald E. Dahl, "Context, Development, and Digital Media: Implications for Very Young Adolescents in LMICs," *Frontiers in Psychology* 12 (2021): 632–713.

75 UN Committee on the Rights of the Child, *General Comment No. 25*, para. 81.

76 Dan Milmo, "2021 Was Worst Year on Record for Online Child Sexual Abuse, Says IWF," *The Guardian*, January 13, 2022, www.theguardian.com.

77 Yara Barrense-Dias, André Berchtold, Joan-Carles Surís, and Christina Akre, "Sexting and the Definition Issue," *Journal of Adolescent Health* 61, no. 5 (2017): 544–554; Karen Cooper, Ethel Quayle, Linda Jonsson, and Carl Göran Svedin, "Adolescents and Self-Taken Sexual Images: A Review of the Literature," *Computers in Human Behavior*, 55 no. 3 (2016): 706–716; Marie-Pier Giroux, "The Phenomenon of Self-Generated Sexual Content among Adolescents" (LLM thesis, Leiden University, 2021), 34.

78 Susannah Stern, "Sexual Selves on the World Wide Web: Adolescent Girls' Home Pages as Sites for Sexual Self-Expression," in *Sexual Teens, Sexual Media*, ed. Jane Brown, Jeanne Steele, and Kim Walsh-Childers (Mahwah, NJ: Lawrence Erlbaum, 2002), 265–285; David Buckingham and Sara Bragg, *Young People, Sex and the Media* (Basingstoke, UK: Palgrave Macmillan, 2004); Sonia Livingstone and Anke Görzig, "'Sexting': The Exchange of Sexual Messages Online among European Youth," in *Children, Risk and Safety on the Internet*, ed. Sonia Livingstone, Leslie Haddon, and Anke Görzig (Bristol, UK: Bristol University Press, Policy, 2012), 151–164; Jane Brown, Carolyn Tucker Halpern, and Kelly Laden L'Engle, "Mass Media as a Sexual Super Peer for Early Maturing Girls," *Journal of Adolescent Health* 36, no. 5 (2005): 420–427; Lars Loof, "Sexual Behaviour, Adolescents and Problematic Content," in *Understanding and Preventing Online Sexual Exploita-*

tion of Children, ed. Ethel Quayle and Kurt Ribisl (Abingdon, UK: Routledge, 2012).

79 Cami Goray and Schoenebeck Sarita, "Youths' Perceptions of Data Collection in Online Advertising and Social Media," *Proceedings of the ACM on Human-Computer Interaction* 6, no. CSCW2 (2022): 1–27.

80 EU Science Hub, "Examining Artificial Intelligence Technologies through the Lens of Children's Rights," June 22, 2022, https://joint-research-centre.ec.europa.eu.

81 Office of the High Commissioner for Human Rights (OHCHR), *Guiding Principles on Business and Human Rights: Implementing the United Nations "Protect, Respect and Remedy" Framework* (New York and Geneva: UN, 2012) www.ohchr.org.

82 UN Committee on the Rights of the Child, *General Comment No. 25*; UN Committee on the Rights of the Child, *General Comment No. 16: State Obligations Regarding the Impact of the Business Sector on Children's Rights*, CRC/C/GC/16 (2013).

83 "Meta Restricts Advertisers' Access to Teenagers' Data on Facebook and Instagram," *Irish News*, January 10, 2023, www.irishnews.com.

84 UN Committee on the Rights of the Child, *General Comment No. 25*, para. 38.

85 Eva Lievens, Sonia Livingstone, Sharon McLaughlin, Brian O'Neill, and Valerie Verdoodt, "Children's Rights and Digital Technologies," in Kilkelly and Liefaard, *International Human Rights of Children*, 487–513.

86 UN Committee on the Rights of the Child, *General Comment No. 20*.

87 Ibid., para. 47.

88 UN Committee on the Rights of the Child, *General Comment No. 25*, para. 94.

89 UN Committee on the Rights of the Child, *General Comment No. 20*, para. 59.

90 UN Committee on the Rights of the Child, *General Comment No. 25*, para. 104.

91 Lievens et al., "Children's Rights and Digital Technologies."

92 Martina Chapman, *Mapping of Media Literacy Practices and Actions in EU-28* (Strasbourg: European Audiovisual Observatory, 2016); Lievens, et al., "Children's Rights and Digital Technologies."

93 Se-Hoon Jeong, Hyunyi Cho, and Yoori Hwang, "Media Literacy Interventions: A Meta-analytic Review," *Journal of Communication* 62, no. 3 (2012): 454–472.

94 UN Committee on the Rights of the Child, *General Comment No. 25*, para. 84.

95 UN Committee on the Rights of the Child, *General Comment No. 20*.

96 Western Sydney University and London School of Economics and Political Science, "Our Rights in a Digital World," February 8, 2021, https://5rightsfoundation.com.

97 UNICEF, *How Many Children and Young People Have Internet Access at Home?* (New York: UNICEF, 2020), 1, www.unicef.org.

98 Ibid., 2.

99 UN Committee on the Rights of the Child, *General Comment No. 25*, para. 9.

100 Giovanni de Girolamo, Jessica Dagani, R. Purcell, and Angelo Cocchi, "Age of Onset of Mental Disorders and Use of Mental Health Services: Needs, Opportunities and Obstacles," *Epidemiology and Psychiatric Sciences* 21, no. 1 (2011): 47–57.

101 Myron L. Belfer, "Child and Adolescent Mental Disorders: The Magnitude of the Problem across the Globe," *Journal of Child Psychology and Psychiatry* 49, no. 3 (2008): 226–236; Benjamin N. Shain, "Suicide and Suicide Attempts in Adolescents," *Pediatrics* 120, no. 3 (2007): 669–676; World Health Organization, "Global Health Estimates: Life Expectancy and Leading Causes of Death and Disability," accessed November 17, 2023, www.who.int.

102 Nicole Racine, Brae Anne McArthur, Jessica E. Cooke, Rachel Eirich, Jenney Zhu, and Sheri Madigan, "Global Prevalence of Depressive and Anxiety Symptoms in Children and Adolescents during COVID-19: A Meta-analysis," *JAMA Pediatrics* 175, no. 11 (2021): 1142–1150.

103 Office of the Surgeon General, *Protecting Youth Mental Health: The U.S. Surgeon General's Advisory* 9 (Washington, DC: US Department of Health and Human Services, 2021); Paddy Ssentongo, Claudio Fronterre, Anna E. Ssentongo, Shailesh Advani, Emily S. Heilbrunn, Joshua P. Hazelton, John S. Oh, Jennifer S. McCall-Hosenfeld, and Vernon M. Chinchilli, "Gun Violence Incidence during the COVID-19 Pandemic Is Higher than Before the Pandemic in the United States," *Scientific Reports* 11, no. 1 (2021): 206–254; Office of the Surgeon General, *Confronting Health Misinformation: The U.S. Surgeon General's Advisory on Building a Healthy Information Environment* (Washington, DC: US Department of Health and Human Services, 2021), www.hhs.gov; WHO, UN, UNICEF, UNDP, UNESCO, UNAIDS, ITU, UN Global Pulse, and IFRC, "Managing the COVID-19 Infodemic: Promoting Healthy Behaviours and Mitigating the Harm from Misinformation and Disinformation," WHO, September 23, 2020, www.who.int; Wendy. M. Johnston and Graham C. Davey, "The Psychological Impact of Negative TV News Bulletins: The Catastrophizing of Personal Worries," *British Journal of Psychology* 88, no. 1 (2011): 85–91; Li Duan, Xiaojun Shao, Yuan Wang, Yinglin Huang, Junxiao Miao, Xueping Yang, and Gang Zhu, "An Investigation of Mental Health Status of Children and Adolescents in China during the Outbreak of COVID-19," *Journal of Affective Disorders* 275 (2020): 112–118.

104 UNICEF, *State of the World's Children 2021.*

105 Kaite Buston, "Adolescents with Mental Health Problems: What Do They Say about Health Services?," *Journal of Adolescence* 25, no. 2 (2002): 231–242.

106 Natalie Divin, Patrick Harper, Emma Curran, Dagmar Corry, and Gerard Leavey, "Help-Seeking Measures and Their Use in Adolescents: A Systematic Review," *Adolescent Research Review* 3, no. 1 (2018): 113–122.

107 Buston, "Adolescents with Mental Health Problems."

108 Clare Lamb and Margaret Murphy, "The Divide between Child and Adult Mental Health Services: Points for Debate," *British Journal of Psychiatry* 202, no. s54 (2013): s41–44.

109 UN Committee on the Rights of the Child, *General Comment No. 20.*

110 UNICEF, *State of the World's Children 2021.*

111 Western Sydney University and London School of Economics and Political Science, "Our Rights in a Digital World."

112 Mario Alvarez-Jimenez, Simon Rice, Simon D'Alfonso, Steven Leicester, Sarah Bendall, Ingrid Pryor, Penni Russon, et al., "A Novel Multimodal Digital Service (Moderated Online Social Therapy+) for Help-Seeking Young People Experiencing Mental Ill-Health: Pilot Evaluation within a National Youth E-Mental Health Service," *Journal of Medical Internet Research* 22, no. 8 (2020): e17155; Gloria Hongyee Chan, "A Comparative Analysis of Online, Offline, and Integrated Counseling among Hidden Youth in Hong Kong," *Children and Youth Services Review* 114 (2020): 105042.

113 UN Committee on the Rights of the Child, *General Comment No. 20.*

114 Buston, "Adolescents with Mental Health Problems."

115 UN Committee on the Rights of the Child, *General Comment No. 20.*

116 Richard G. Wight, Amanda L. Botticello, and Carol S. Aneshensel, "Socioeconomic Context, Social Support, and Adolescent Mental Health: A Multilevel Investigation," *Journal of Youth and Adolescence* 35, no. 1 (2006): 109–120.

117 UN Committee on the Rights of the Child, *General Comment No. 20.*

PART IV

Toward an Integrated Approach

10

Insights from Children and Youth

CHARLENE CHOI, JONATHAN TODRES, AND CLARA PAUL

I. Introduction

Children's rights initiatives are frequently undertaken *for* young people but are much less often done *with* young people. In both law and policy discourses and research initiatives, children's voices and insights are typically undervalued. As this book has explored how children's rights are operationalized at different stages of children's development, it is critical that we hear from young people themselves as to their views on their rights, the rights of their peers, and the opportunities and challenges associated with realizing their rights at various stages of childhood. Input from children and youth—from all communities—is vital both to the rights-based approach and to good development research. Therefore, this chapter focuses on young people's views and explores how we might incorporate them in the broader conversation about the interconnections between children's rights and children's development.

Due to a variety of factors, from the growing support for children's rights globally to the technology revolution and globalization, young people are increasingly aware of the challenges that they, their communities, and the globe face now and in the future. Millions of young people are already engaged in research, protest, organizing, and various forms of speech, expression, and assembly on a mass scale.[1] Their expression can help us understand better how they see their own rights and the rights of their peers and others. It can also inform research on children's rights and development. In addition, given the dramatic and ongoing changes to the world, young people's lived experiences offer unique insights into the experience of growing up in the twenty-first century. For example, young people are the only individuals alive today who understand what it was like to navigate school during a global pandemic. This lived experience provides vital insights into children's development.

It is essential, therefore, that any project that seeks to build bridges between the disciplines of children's rights and child development recognize the value of young people's views and incorporate them into this dialogue. Understanding the need for guidance and feedback from young people in this project, this chapter takes a step toward incorporating children's perspectives, drawing on children's voices and views expressed through research involving young people. In doing so, we hope both to show illustrative examples of the value of children's views and insights—beyond the children's rights law mandate to listen to children—and to contribute to efforts that seek to further normalize the idea that research and programs about or for young people must be developed and implemented with young people. We believe that the fields of children's rights and child and adolescent development can find common cause through rights-respecting child participatory research that improves the quality of our knowledge base about children and youth, their rights, and their healthy development.

The next section of this chapter outlines the two foundational justifications for children's participation: the legal mandate under children's rights law and the benefits of incorporating children's views. Children's participation in decision-making processes is important both as a right and for developmental reasons, and it also provides broader benefits to communities. The third section provides illustrative examples of how youth participation can inform research on how to implement children's rights and understanding of children's capacities in early childhood, middle childhood, and adolescence. Then, in the fourth section, we briefly look forward and identify key considerations to enhancing efforts to ensure the meaningful participation of young people in co-implementing developmental research projects and operationalizing the rights of children at different stages of childhood.

II. The Rationale for Engaging Young People

Children's insights are critical to considerations of equity in any project for or about children, and children's rights cannot be fully implemented without the participation of children. There are two central reasons for supporting their meaningful participation and leadership. The first is that children have a right to be heard. The second is that children's insights are particularly valuable because involving them produces better outcomes. This section explicates these two reasons.

A. The Right to Be Heard

Children's participation rights have been the topic of robust discussion by advocates across the globe for years, and much has been written on what they are, what they mean, how far they reach, and how they can be applied.[2] Due to near-universal support for and ratification of the UN Convention on the Rights of the Child (CRC), the core of children's participation rights stems from Article 12, which provides that "States Parties shall assure to the child who is capable of forming his or her own views the right to express those views freely in all matters affecting the child, the views of the child being given due weight in accordance with the age and maturity of the child."[3] The UN Committee on the Rights of the Child (Committee)—the body that monitors states' implementation of the CRC—has elucidated that the right to be heard comprises the following elements: (1) states parties have a clear obligation to ensure children's participation rights; (2) children must be afforded the freedom to express their views without pressure; (3) Article 12 rights extend to all children who have the capacity to form a view; (4) these rights must be applied meaningfully—that is, giving due weight to children's views—and in accordance with the developmental capacities of that child; and (5) these rights apply in all matters affecting the child.[4]

First, states parties have an obligation to ensure children's participation rights.[5] There are a variety of ways that the state can support children's participation in decisions that affect their lives. Policy makers, researchers, and other stakeholders can engage children and youth through three primary modes of participation: consultative, collaborative, and youth-led initiatives.[6] What is critical is that states recognize their legal obligation to facilitate child and youth participation and that they ensure that young people's participation is not tokenistic.[7]

Second, children must be afforded the freedom to express their participation rights.[8] The Committee's guidance states that this freedom requires choice with regard to whether the child wants to exercise their right to be heard, without pressure and without manipulation or undue influence.[9]

Third, children's participation rights extend to every child who is capable of forming their own views.[10] The Committee has been explicit that there is no minimum age for "capability," and this provision has been further explicated to define that capability begins at the ability to form a view, not the ability to express it.[11]

Fourth, participation must be developmentally appropriate.[12] A child's capability to form a view is the conceptual entry point to the dynamic nature of children's participation rights. While their right remains constant, the weight given to their views grows as the child develops and matures. Participation must be meaningful. The Committee has stated that meaningful participation does not mean that decision-makers should merely listen to children, but they should sensitize their interactions with children and the decisions they make on their behalf.[13]

Last, these rights apply to "all matters affecting the child."[14] This means that "children [should] have meaningful opportunities to participate in *all* decisions that affect their lives."[15] The Committee has given many examples of settings and situations where the right to be heard may be implemented, such as in the family, in health care, in education, in sports, in states of emergency, and at local and international convenings.[16] And we assert that children's participation rights must extend to research, where decisions are made that can shape discourses and policies that affect the lives of children and youth in all these settings.

B. Children's Insights in Research: Opportunities and Risks

> We need people to listen to us, our experiences of discrimination and oppression, rather than meet us with defensiveness and shut us down. We need to learn about other perspectives. Listen.
>
> —child in Ireland[17]

In addition to being legally mandated, children's participation can provide a range of benefits. Collaborating with young people can "lead to consideration of a broader range of ideas, help weed out ineffective

[ones], and secure greater buy-in among young people with respect to those policies [or processes] that are adopted."[18] Young people have unique insights, given their lived experience in this rapidly changing world. They are among the portion of the population who are growing up in an era of changing socialization, through increased interaction with and dependence on social media and technology such as smartphones. Further, if we want to understand children's experiences, we must recognize that as they grow into adolescence, they spend an increasing amount of time away from adults. Thus, young people have insights into their own lives and the lives of their peers that adults simply do not have access to.

Creating space for children to be heard can also improve outcomes. First, listening to children in research design and implementation can greatly improve the quality of analysis about them. Child participation can often improve the research questions and agenda by making them more relevant and authentic to children's perspectives and realities. Similar benefits can accrue in the policy arena if young people are incorporated meaningfully into the design, implementation, and evaluation of research that aims to inform law and policy development. Second, the process of participation also has immediate and longer-term benefits for children. Engaging with, and supporting the participation of, children in research can help with the development of a range of skills, including civic engagement, leadership, communication, and organizational skills. For example, children working on a child-led project in Croatia explored the extent to which children living in the care system participated in decision-making processes.[19] Young people commented that their participation in focus groups had positive effects on their development: "Participation is a very important process in our lives"; "We learnt new methods of research [and] we improved our communication skills."[20] Even more important, participation can build a concept of self and self-esteem among children and adolescents.[21] A sixteen-year-old working on a project with the Greek Children's Ombudsman shared that, by participating in the research project, she "discovered elements of [her]self" and concluded that the experience had been "a life lesson."[22] Young people's participation benefits children, their families and communities, and the nation. As beautifully put by an eleven-year-old child who participated in a project on the participation of refugee children in the Netherlands, "I love this life where children get attention for their opinions."[23]

III. Child Participation Has Reshaped Research and Our Understanding of Children's Capacities

Child participation has the potential to contribute significantly to any project that aims to better operationalize rights at different stages of childhood. In this section, we draw on illustrative examples of research projects that shed light on young people's views and the various ways they can contribute to the understanding of their own capacities and inform the implementation of children's rights in developmentally appropriate ways.

A. Children's Insights Have Expanded Scholarly Understanding of Early Childhood Capacities

Studies show that even very young children can appreciate and apply rights-based concepts. For example, in a Canadian early childhood program (ages four to five), young children understood that interrupting a classmate when they were speaking overstepped that classmate's rights in the group.[24] "After learning that all children have the right to be heard, one young boy who was frustrated by his classmates' interruptions yelled, 'You're hurting my right to be listened to!' 'Instantly,' the teachers reported, 'the group quieted and, without any further adult intervention, the conversation morphed from chaotic chattering into an exchange of ideas.'"[25] In this anecdote, it is evident that this group of young children had the capacity to understand their rights as well as the rights of others.[26]

In another example, Ireland's Ombudsman for Children gathered insights of children under six years old in its report to the UN Committee on the Rights of the Child. Early services providers worked with young children to find out what they liked, did not like, and wanted to see changed, to share with the Committee what mattered to these and other young children. One child shared that they do not like "not being listened to."[27] When children were asked what they wanted changed, some asked for the end of COVID-19, highlighting that they were aware of the negative effects from COVID-19 restrictions.[28] They also wished to have more of the things that they enjoyed, but not only in relation to themselves. Some statements from children included (1) "Everyone needs a home"; (2) "Get a playground in every village"; and (3) "Kids to be happy. My family to be safe. Kids to make more friends."[29] These statements indicate children's capability to understand many fundamental children's rights, such as the rights to have basic needs met, to play, and to be free from violence.

As seen in the preceding examples, attentive adults and multigenerational approaches are necessary and important in fostering a young child's rights and capabilities throughout development and especially during early childhood. A review of children's rights education in two Swedish preschools identified an array of teaching objectives including empowering young children to feel safe at school to learn, to receive care, to be able to influence their day and their needs, to be seen, to be listened to, to play, and to understand their own worth.[30] These teaching objectives are implemented in the teacher's daily interactions with the children. For example, when a child (age two and a half years) showed his agency by expressing that he wanted to know the names of colors in English, the teacher listened to him and encouraged his learning.[31] Or, in an interaction between two babies (one and a half and two and a half years old), the older toddler did not understand the younger toddler's actions. Before a conflict arose, the preschool teacher intervened, listened to the older toddler, and interpreted the younger toddler's actions for the older toddler to promote understanding.[32] Similarly, when conducting research with a group of children (ages birth to three years) in Spain, teachers found that sometimes the children would interrupt each other. The teacher asked a question to a specific child, but another child would answer instead. Here, the teacher intervened and asked the second child to let the first one answer, to ensure that they would have the opportunity to share their ideas.[33] Especially at ages when very young children are developing their capabilities to engage with themselves and with others, researchers need to take care to "presume that the child has the capacity to form his or her own views" while providing safe opportunities to learn and participate in a healthy environment.[34]

Adults supporting children in research processes should also ensure that they engage in the necessary dialogue to fully understand the children's opinions. A more in-depth dialogue with children may offer a new interpretation of their words.[35] For example, in the same study in Spain aimed at listening to children under three years old to improve everyday school life, a teacher shared, "When we took them out on the walks, they didn't like the tyres. I was quite surprised. How could this be possible? Later, when we showed them the photos and asked again, what they were really telling us was that they wanted to be able to take them somewhere else. They understood that the tyres had to be here and they wanted to take them to where the motorcycles are, with the balls . . . to a larger area, to roll them, . . . and that was not allowed. 'I don't like them' has evolved into 'I don't like them because I can't move them.'"[36]

Early childhood scholarship with this expanded understanding of capacities may yield profound impacts on built environments for families. Finland's early childhood programs have been particularly proactive in finding meaningful ways to incorporate interviews with young children in town planning. The city of Oulu's Well-Being Daycare and School gathers insights to understand the experiences of three- to six-year-olds and incorporates these experiences in its operating model.[37] In another Finnish city, Lappeenranta, the early childhood education department is surveying preprimary school children through mind maps (drawings with words added by teachers) to gather insights on what the children "think are important and what things they would like to improve."[38] These insights will be utilized to inform future urban planning projects, affirming not only the viability of researchers to incorporate the voices of very young children in community decisions but also that children have the capacities to participate in research when engaged in developmentally appropriate ways.[39]

Overall, as these examples illustrate, there are important opportunities to engage young children and learn from their insights in ways that can inform research on children's rights and early childhood development. Research "can be designed in ways that allow for very young children to express their views" utilizing consultative or collaborative methods.[40] Yet young children's expressions in settings such as schools are often "heard as noise more than voice, operating in ways that err from the available script, which is to be still and silent."[41] Children's rights law—especially Article 12 of the CRC—aims to counter the traditional notion that children should be "seen and not heard" and provides a different starting point, one in which children have the right to participate in such research, if they want to. The obligation then is on researchers and other adults to navigate ethical, logistical, and other issues to enable young children to participate in developmentally appropriate ways.

B. Children's Insights Have Expanded Our Understanding of Life Satisfaction and Self-Concept in Middle Childhood

As detailed earlier in the book (see chapter 4 on middle childhood), children's capacities to exercise their rights mature as they grow and develop. Children's awareness of their rights helps support their healthy development. Indeed, their agency to exercise these rights increases their sense of well-being. The International Survey of Children's Well-Being—Wave 2 (ISoCWB) included insights from over fifty-four thousand children (eight, ten, and twelve years old) from sixteen countries across Africa, Asia, Latin America, Europe, and the Middle East. In it, children reported that the more opportunities they had to exercise their rights and the more they agreed that adults respected their rights, "the more they were satisfied with the freedom in their lives and with being listened to."[42] In other words, children in middle childhood reported that their participation rights are critical because the impact of being listened to and having those views considered by their peers and/or adults influenced how satisfied they were with their life.[43] This analysis of the survey data sought to find the relationships between children's awareness of their own rights, being given the power to act on those rights, the effect of being heard, and life satisfaction.[44] This survey follows an earlier study that linked children's life satisfaction with the freedom of being able to make decisions within their family and decisions at school.[45] The growing evidence shows that rights awareness is linked to children's self-report of increased life satisfaction, and increased agency to freely participate is positively correlated with happiness.[46] Indeed, the right to participate is slowly beginning to be recognized as a prerequisite to well-being.[47]

Researchers have learned the value that some children place on their rights and what factors are important to their agency to exercise these rights in their daily lives.[48] For example, this agency should not be taken out of context of a child's right to a safe and secure home.[49] As one child puts it, "Children should not be sad. . . . We should be loved and taken care of. As a child, I have the right to be loved and to be happy."[50] Early experiences of home are central to being human; and this is central because middle childhood is an important time for growing understanding of the self in the context of others.[51] This self-concept begins early in life and is a necessary precursor to healthy identity formation, exploration, and development in adolescence and early adulthood.[52] In the words of a boy in middle childhood, "'Cause like normally I can just picture myself just walking through the forest with my mum and dad and sometimes maybe my granny and granddad. And just feel happy, and then again throwing pinecones at my brothers (laughing)" (town school, boy in the ten- to twelve-year-old group).[53] The child here demonstrates that his healthy peer and multigenerational attachments are a nexus for his happiness and well-being.

Finally, young people's involvement in research can test and affirm theoretical frameworks about children and their rights. For example, many researchers and caregivers have voiced the importance of the surrounding environment as critical for a growing child.[54] A girl in middle childhood reports, "When I go to my friend's house there's like, a woods there and we normally build dens and stuff. And also my mum, my dad, my brother and sister, I normally go walking with them and it would be really like, luxurious except for when we get spiked with plants (laughing)" (town school, girl in the ten- to twelve-year-old group).[55] She intermingles the importance of playing with her friends with spending time with her siblings and caregivers. Safe and stable neighborhoods may extend beyond primary attachments to inanimate attachments, such as built or natural environments. Another child reflects, "I have a field next door to my house and it's a fairy fort, so sometimes I go over there and just sit down on the rocks and climb on it. . . . It kind of just feels nice, sometimes there's this wind blowing and the grass is kind of just . . . I like the sound of the grass. And sometimes up in the shed there's a bird that sits on the window and starts singing every morning" (rural school, girl in the ten- to twelve-year-old group).[56]

Likewise, the National Children's Bureau (UK) worked with groups of children across England to gather their experiences, thoughts, and opinions on health care, in order to inform the development of the new

National Institute for Health and Care Excellence Guideline on babies', children's, and young people's experiences of health.[57] Some of the findings of this research confirmed the value of children's participation, their sense of emerging autonomy, and the importance of providing adequate support to children in the exercise of their rights. The study found that 44 percent of the children (aged seven to fourteen) agreed with the statement "I like to make my own decisions about my health," while 36 percent were in the middle, and 7 percent disagreed. However, this did not mean that they wanted to make their decisions alone or unsupported. More than half agreed with the statement "I want my parents or carers to help me make decisions about my health," and only 17 percent disagreed.[58] Children (aged five to fourteen) in Ireland also shared how they thought their participation in health-care decisions should take place. They recommended that doctors "should know how to talk to children."[59] They highlighted that young people should be prepared for procedures: "if you know what they are going to do, then I think you . . . feel less scared."[60] Children were able to offer insights on important characteristics of good doctors, such as someone who "explains things to children, tells them what's wrong with them," and is "kind and funny."[61] This highlights that children in middle childhood have a growing sense of their self—they want to have a say in decisions affecting them, while acknowledging that they can benefit from adults' support. While scholars have theorized frameworks on childhood, direct participation by children on matters that affect them puts theory to action.

Conversely, direct participation also teaches researchers where we have failed young people. For example, displacement or disturbance of a safe home causes significant disruption in a child's life. In juxtaposition to the agency and life satisfaction expressed in the preceding examples, consider the insights of Callum (aged twelve), in England, who was evacuated from a flood: "We live on the ground floor. . . . We lost everything." Callum explained to the researchers that on the day of the flood, his father "opened the door . . . and there was all this water sort of coming down": "Then we stayed for a little bit, then it went up more, and then it went to the top step and Dad said 'we need to go now. When I say now, I mean *now*.'"[62] Maggie Mort and colleagues explained how after Callum and his family evacuated abruptly to his grandparents' house, Callum experienced many challenges, including difficulty sleeping, as he had to sleep in a small room filled with all of his family's belongings. Callum told the researchers, "I could barely move in my room. I couldn't sort of get to sleep. . . . I was so scared like [of it] falling down on me, . . . all my stuff, Mum's stuff, everything in the kitchen, all the stuff [from] all the rooms."[63]

In addition, Callum's new bus journey was totally strange to him, as previously he had always walked to school, and he found the new journey "very stressful and claustrophobic": "I got sort of upset in school sometimes, because like I just couldn't stand going on the bus"; "I was like, I can't do this."[64] His family did not receive a bus pass to help with the cost of Callum's transportation to and from school (£2.50 per day), and as Callum explained, this added further stress because he had to pay the bus fare and keep money safe for his return home each day.[65]

Eight months after the flood, Callum and his family were able to return to their home, which he described as having become a "ghost town."[66] Callum's displacement from home and the compounded risks, hardship, and costs incurred as a result caused "severe stress" and anxiety that "undermine[d] his health and wellbeing."[67]

Displacement across the world occurs from "drought across many regions of the world, multiple forest fires, devastating floods. . . . In 2020, nearly 10 million children were displaced in the aftermath of weather-related shocks alone."[68] At the end of 2021, "36.5 million children were displaced from their homes," and this number is only increasing.[69] Although children are often portrayed by media as the face of disasters, their agency is often dismissed.[70] Yet, as Callum's story and insights show, children—when listened to—clearly articulate what matters to them, what concerns they have (for themselves, their families, and their communities), and what rights of theirs are in jeopardy. And, as demonstrated by the millions of young people who are participating in, and leading, the climate movement, young people readily understand threats to their rights and well-being and frequently respond with purpose. There is a sense of responsibility, even in young children, to maintain the places they call home. Children can also be forced out of their homes because of economic reasons. An eleven-year-old boy shares about the housing crisis in the country where he lives (Ireland), "My family have rented in the same place for years and are now being asked to move because they are selling the house. I cried, I don't know where I am going to live. Things are very expensive and my mam sometimes has little money."[71]

Disturbance of a safe and stable home does not always occur by displacement. As one child urges, "Please, don't let the children to be exposed to violence. . . . We don't want to be scared and exposed to violence. Adults should know about our rights and they should not shout at us."[72] In the words of another child, "We should live in a society in which I can easily live and defend my rights. . . . Children have this right."[73] Children are telling us that we have violated their rights. Developmental research should be focused less on whether children should participate in matters that affect their lives and more on how to listen appropriately to young people and to implement their rights and remedy those domains in which we have failed them.

C. Adolescents' Participation Has Informed Research and Demonstrated the Potential of Research Collaborations Co-led by Youth

As children grow and mature, their capacities evolve, and they can play more significant roles in research. Adolescents can, and have, participated in research projects in various capacities, from being consulted on research to co-designing and leading research initiatives.[74]

The *United Nations Global Study on Children Deprived of Their Liberty* was a groundbreaking research project not only because of its in-depth analysis of challenges children face in detention but also because it included consultations with young people in the context of a large-scale global research project.[75] The study included the participation of 274 children and youth from ages ten to twenty-four years old from twenty-two countries in Central Asia, Europe, Latin America, Northern Africa and the Middle East, sub-Saharan Africa, South Asia, and Southeast Asia.[76] Their participation offered important insights into both the services that are, or should be, offered to children and adolescents and how young people from diverse communities experience their rights in these services. For example, on accessing information about detention upon arrival at a detention facility, one adolescent in detention explained that there was "no information about rights given, length of stay, rules": "Rules [are] only mentioned when I get in trouble."[77] In addition, some youth expressed concern for their physical safety and well-being, while others reported, "We are safe here physically, . . . but we have stress all time."[78] Adolescents' input into this study was critical on a number of issues, as the study's author explains in part: children "demonstrated an acute awareness of the social and emotional 'gaps' that they experienced when being away from their families and their communities."[79] These are vital research findings that shed light on what is needed for children's healthy development and how, and to what extent, children experience their rights in detention. Consultations with children and youth have also been a part of other global research projects, such as the 2019 report *Faith and Children's Rights: A Multi-religious Study on the Convention on the Rights of the Child*, which included consultations with more than one hundred youth of diverse backgrounds from seven countries (Brazil, Bosnia and Herzegovina, India, Panama, Sri Lanka, Tanzania, and Uruguay) to inform the research outcomes.[80]

Beyond global studies, there is growing recognition at the national level of the importance of consulting youth in research affecting their lives. For example, in the United States, the Board on Children, Youth, and Families of the National Academies of Sciences, Engineering, and Medicine has begun incorporating consultations with youth in the studies it has convened in recent years, marking a change from earlier practice.[81] As Erin Fox and colleagues explain, while involving young people in research can add complexity to the research process, "meaningfully incorporating youth perspectives makes research more effective in that outcomes respond to the real needs of young people."[82] Or as one fourteen-year-old female participant articulated, "All these programs are formed by adults, and I think it's really important that those adults don't assume they know what kids want those programs to be."[83]

Other research is meeting young people where they are by taking advantage of youth-friendly technology platforms to give adolescents opportunities to participate in, and contribute to, research on issues affecting their lives. For example, MyVoice uses text messaging to collaborate with youth in designing research questions and rapidly conducting surveys of approximately one thousand youth from diverse communities across the United States on a variety of issues affecting their development and well-being.[84] MyVoice has facilitated youth input on a breadth of research questions on issues such as youth mental health and social media, LGBTQ+ issues, vaping and tobacco laws, the impact of political elections, and other matters affecting their lives.[85]

In addition to consultative processes, there are growing opportunities for co-designing research with young people, which not only can strengthen the research but also has the potential to cultivate the social responsibility and moral development of children. "Developmental scholarship situates social responsibility as interwoven with values (e.g., benevolence), the relational self (e.g., connection to others), emotions (e.g., empathy), and sociocognitive skills (e.g., moral reasoning, justice)."[86] Co-designed and co-led research can then serve as the foundation for advocacy initiatives that shape policy development on issues affecting children and youth.

As the examples that follow show, adolescents have been active participants in the co-creation of a variety of research projects exploring their experiences in schools. Out of this research, adolescents then worked in effective youth-adult partnerships with educators and the community to create a space for true youth voice and power in their school district. These examples of young people's involvement in education show how participatory research can lead to healthy identity exploration and positive moral development, as well as help identify opportunities to better support young people's healthy development.

In fact, research that genuinely listens to young people reveals that, contrary to many popular narratives critical of adolescents, youth ennui toward their secondary schools can demonstrate a level of awareness about the institution of education and what students think school ought to teach. A teenager in secondary school describes, "The key word to kind of sum it [education] up is it needs to be more holistic, and enabling [*sic*] students with a set of skills [and] knowledge, instead of the memory game, that they have skills to apply to it and to get rid of the rote-learning. If I had one word I would rip out of a dictionary, it would be rote learning because I hates it so much."[87] This research participant reveals that young people know that their learning should be more dynamic, but the pedagogy falls short. Another secondary school student in the same study added, "I don't know if this is the same for everyone, but I feel like in my school, and maybe in some schools, the focus is kind of more on just doing well in the [exit exam]. . . . The school has just been focusing on spewing out high points every year, you know, instead of like help us develop as full people."[88] These quotes indicate a marked departure from the CRC's right to quality education. The Committee on the Rights of the Child has emphasized that "education should be child friendly, inspiring and motivating [for] the individual child."[89] Although the aims of education ought to support the full development of a child's personality and abilities and respect their parents' and their own values, research incorporating adolescents' views has shown that in the eyes of young people, many secondary schools have become more a race toward achieving a score on a standardized test than the fulfillment of any right to quality education. Such insights from young people can help set the stage for more effective advocacy and policy development.

In another example, adolescents participated in the co-creation of research on young people's (aged eleven to nineteen) experiences, views, and preferences related to school-based sexual health and school nursing in England in 2015. This research followed a participatory process, involving young people from the outset in the design and execution of the research. The youth participants "helped inform the recruitment materials, the data collection methods, the analytical foci and outputs and reporting formats from the study."[90] One of the findings of the research was that the adolescents had poor awareness or knowledge of the school nurse: "I don't even know who she is"; "I think there are a couple of school nurses but I'm not sure when or what they specialise in or if they specialise in something."[91] This means that they are less likely to access these services: "I think in that situation you wouldn't go to the school nurse, you just wouldn't feel comfortable, because we don't know who she is like properly. . . . Our school nurse is literally just there, we're not feeling well, can you call our parents to come and pick us up. That is all I've ever had to do with the school nurse."[92] Adolescents also highlighted that they were anxious about privacy, discretion, and confidentiality.[93] In addition to providing valuable insights on adolescents' views on school-based sexual health and school nursing, this research also illustrates that adolescents know the issues that are important to them and that participatory research is critical to identify what children want and need.

In the gap between children's rights aspirations for what educational settings should be and what they are, research involving adolescents can inform the work of youth-adult partnerships that aim to address education policy issues. For example, a student organizing effort in East Side Union High School District (ESUHSD) in San Jose, California, that lasted for more than a decade led to numerous student policy improvements supportive of youth empowerment. Lupe Navarro, a student leader, states on the power of lived experience and the dangers of tokenism, "When you have student voice, you have voices from people who are experiencing education firsthand. The problem is not whether you have their voices or not, but whether you listen and value their voices enough to really consider and act on what they're saying. If you don't, now you've made it worse."[94] In other words, how Lupe's rights are implemented is important to her. It is not enough for her simply to know her rights; it is also important that she is afforded the space to exercise them and the power to have her views thoughtfully considered.

The organizing efforts of these students were supported by school administrative leaders and other decision-makers. "We started by saying, 'We will do something that we have never done: develop an understanding of what that interaction [between adults and youth] can be, come up with processes for these interactions, and then expand to other school sites once we have modeled it as a district,'" reported Glenn Vander Zee, the district superintendent.[95] Together, they have been able to adopt a bilingual certification program for the district, organize a student-led campaign for "access to high quality courses and [to] have a chance to work towards four-year university eligibility," organize in a statewide Student Voice Campaign, engage in participatory budgeting for high school allocation of funds, campaign for the passage of a "relationship-centered schools" resolution, establish student representatives to the school district's Board of Trustees, establish a Student Governing Board, campaign for the passage of resolutions to eliminate police resource officers, and design graduation requirements for an Ethnic Studies framework.[96]

The efforts at ESUHSD are also particularly illuminating because they demonstrate that the shift away from traditional views of child expression toward the right to be heard is, at its core, a shift away from fear to hope. Superintendent Vander Zee further states, "One of our fears in all of this was that if you lift up student voice, somehow it's going to be anti- what you're about as a district: anti-adult, anti-educator. What we've learned from this is that it's completely not true. . . . You can lift up student voice, and our students will grab on to the mission, and vision, and where we want to go. 'We're in! We want that too.'"[97] These multigenerational activities support young people's development by giving them opportunities to engage and interact in developmentally appropriate ways. They also highlight that adolescents can be key partners in developing agendas for research, carrying out that research, helping to translate that research into policy initiatives, and then evaluating the impact of those policy changes.

In short, adolescents have shown that at all levels (from the local to the global) and across all types of activities (from research to policy development), they can play meaningful roles in advancing collective understanding of children's rights and children's development. Perhaps no more obvious example of youth capabilities can be found than in the climate change movement, where numerous initiatives and organizations are being led by young people.[98] Adolescents'—and younger children's—social responsibility and collective critical consciousness show the potential of young people as partners and co-collaborators in dialogues and research on children's rights and child development. For example, in a study on attitudes toward solidarity among upper secondary school students in Sweden, some students articulated a "deep respect for life as the basic motive for solidarity."[99] Young people are taking seriously the issues confronting their communities and the globe, and their insights are vital to advancing research on the rights and healthy development of children and adolescents.

Research, projects, and programs in each of the three stages of childhood demonstrate the important insights that young people have, their interest in and concerns about their rights and the rights of others, and their willingness to partner with peers and adults to improve their communities and the globe. Children's participation materializes in different ways at each stage of childhood, but the interest in being heard is consistent. We believe that these examples highlight the need for more empirical work on collaboration with young people to realize their rights and on the implementation of children's rights in development research.

IV. What Is Needed to Incorporate Young People in Understanding How to Implement and Operationalize Rights at Different Stages

This book asserts that both children's rights research and child development research would benefit from further integration of the two fields' agendas. As the two disciplines build bridges to each other and draw on their respective strengths to advance interdisciplinary research that can support and strengthen child well-being and rights implementation, such connections must also support, and draw on, children's participation—and this participation should include children from all communities, including historically marginalized ones. Doing so will lead to a better understanding of how to implement and operationalize rights at different stages of childhood.

Achieving meaningful participation from young people will require addressing and overcoming several key barriers to ensure developmentally appropriate pathways for participation by children at all stages of development. These barriers include a lack of inherent knowledge about what research is and its processes, power imbalances between adults and children, consent issues, and remuneration difficulties.[100] Careful consideration by adults and guardians to overcome these and other barriers and to support the safe and meaningful participation of young people as co-researchers is necessary for effective research that involves children and adolescents. Such careful consideration needs to be paid especially when engaging very young children, so as not to tokenize or misinterpret their views and interests.[101] At an age when very young children may not be able to express themselves fully through verbal communication, there are also both well-established and promising practices in utilizing photography, mind maps, and other nonverbal modalities, educational action research methods, and arts-based educational research methods so that creative communication techniques may also be employed to better understand a child's perspective.[102] In all, ensuring meaningful participation from young people at each stage of childhood requires a considerable amount of forethought in the design and implementation of a research agenda, and particular attention is needed when including the perspectives of children in early childhood. Engaging young people from these early design stages would be ideal for the incorporation of their thoughts, ideas, and concerns. Finally, consideration must be given to ensuring that any research involving children and youth draws its participants from diverse communities, to ensure that young people from historically minoritized communities and children with disabilities have their voices heard and their participants rights ensured.[103]

Many community-based participatory researchers have long been co-designing interview questions and research agendas with young people in middle childhood and adolescence, and the surveys and focus groups are implemented together in dyads of young and older researchers.[104] Other researchers have sought to implement children and young people's advisory groups that work alongside adult researchers to help in deciding on themes for the research and trial/pilot research methods and to contribute to the analysis of data.[105] Laura Lundy and Leslie McEvoy conducted capacity-building activities with children from their Children's Researcher Advisory Groups (aged ten to twelve) and gathered their feedback from the approach that was used.[106] For one project, 87 percent of the children responded that the capacity-building sessions had assisted them in understanding the research questions more fully. For example, one child commented, "It gave you a chance to think seriously about it. We talked about the issues and it went into detail so I got a better understanding."[107]

Analysis of any research data may also require youth feedback or review, and this analysis and feedback may be structured formally through Youth Advisory Boards or more informally through staffing of a research team with young people. From co-design of research agendas to implementation and evaluation of the research, young people can and should be involved in every step of the research process. As noted earlier, for example, MyVoice has surveyed thousands of youth participants on more than one hundred topics such as the impact of social media on youth well-being and coping strategies during COVID-19.[108] Another example of positive collaborations is seen in research mapping children's perceptions and use of their neighborhood in Denver, Colorado, providing insights into the impact of neighborhood built environment on obesity outcomes.[109] The Youth-Led Participatory Action Research (YPAR) approaches taken in these projects emerge from a critical epistemological framework that recognizes the knowledge, insights, and experiences of children as the primary stakeholders as equally valuable to that of "expert" knowledge.[110]

Overall, the research to date involving young people offers several key lessons. First, despite the complexities of research and other partnerships involving children (including the vulnerability of young people and associated risks), it is possible to effectively collaborate with children of all ages. Second, we must move past any mind-set of minimum ages. Children of all ages can contribute in developmentally appropriate ways to the benefit of the child and all those who stand to benefit from the resulting research (recognizing that Article 12's right to be heard gives children the option to refrain from expressing their views as well). The burden for developmentally appropriate contribution is on the principal researcher to ensure the safe and ethical implementation of participatory practices. Third, and equally important, children have a role to play in all domains—that is, all sectors of society—and at every stage in the process: design, implementation, monitoring, and evaluation. To the extent that this chapter makes the case for involving young people, the other chapters of the book work in conjunction with this one to show how adults can engage young people on their rights in developmentally appropriate ways. Future scholarship that strives to harness the collective power of both children's rights and child development science should co-design research agendas about children with children from the start.

V. Conclusion

Children's insights are essential to any research agenda that aims to better understand and improve children's lives. No research agenda should be conducted on children, as the population impacted by such scholarship, by any proxy without the insights of children themselves. Moreover, involving children from diverse communities and partnering with them provides value relevant to both fields, as their participation helps fulfill their rights and contributes positively to their healthy development. This chapter has not only provided illustrative examples of the importance of youth participation but also highlighted that a number of researchers and organizations have already created pathways for children of all ages to play a meaningful role in research on children's rights and development. The hope here is that others can build on this foundational work and that youth participation becomes the norm in research, policy development, and any other area shaping the lives of young people, today and in the future.

NOTES

1 Laelia Benoit, Isaiah Thomas, and Andrés Martin, "Ecological Awareness, Anxiety, and Actions among Youth and Their Parents—A Qualitative Study of Newspaper Narratives," *Child and Adolescent Mental Health* 27, no. 1 (2022): 47–58; Scott Neuman and Bill Chappell, "Young People Lead Millions to Protest Global Inaction on Climate Change," *NPR*, September 20, 2019, www.npr.org.

2 Laura Lundy, "United Nations Convention on the Rights of the Child and Child Well-Being," in *Handbook of Child Well-Being: Theories, Methods and Policies in Global Perspective*, ed. Āšēr Ben-Aryē, Ferran Casas, and Ivar Frones (New York: Springer, 2014), 2439–2462; Piia-Kaisa af Ursin and Leena Haanpää, "A Comparative Study on Children's Rights Awareness in 16 Countries," *Child Indicators Research* 11, no. 5 (2018): 1425–1443; Jonathan Todres, Charlene Choi, and Joseph Wright, "A Rights-Based Assessment of Youth Participation in the United States," *Temple Law Review* 95, no. 3 (2023): 411–455.

3 UN Convention on the Rights of the Child, art. 12(1) (November 20, 1989), 1577 U.N.T.S. 3 (hereafter CRC).

4 UN Committee on the Rights of the Child, *General Comment No. 12 (2009): The Right of the Child to Be Heard*, CRC/C/GC/12 (July 20, 2009).

5 Ibid., para. 19.

6 United Nations Children's Fund (UNICEF), *Engaged and Heard! Guidelines on Adolescent Participation and Civic Engagement* (New York: UNICEF, 2020), 11.

7 Laura Lundy, "'Voice Is Not Enough': Conceptualizing Article 12 of the United Nations Convention on the Rights of the Child," *British Educational Research Journal* 33, no. 6 (2007): 927–942; Todres, Choi, and Wright, "Rights-Based Assessment of Youth Participation."

8 UN Committee on the Rights of the Child, *General Comment No. 12*, paras 22–25.

9 Ibid.

10 Ibid., paras 20–21.

11 Lundy, "Voice Is Not Enough"; Jonathan Todres, "Children's Right to Participate: Insights from the Story of Malala," in *Literary Cultures and Twenty-First-Century Childhoods*, ed. Nathalie op de Beeck (Cham, Switzerland: Palgrave Macmillan, 2020), 25–40.

12 UN Committee on the Rights of the Child, *General Comment No. 12*.

13 UN Committee on the Rights of the Child, *General Comment No. 5 (2003): General Measures of Implementation of the Convention on the Rights of the Child*, CRC/GC/2003/5 (November 27, 2003).

14 UN Committee on the Rights of the Child, *General Comment No. 12*, paras. 26–27.

15 Todres, Choi, and Wright, "Rights-Based Assessment of Youth Participation," 418.

16 UN Committee on the Rights of the Child, *General Comment No. 12*.

17 Ombudsman for Children, *Pieces of Us: A Children's Report to the UN Committee on the Rights of the Child* (Dublin: Ombudsman for Children, 2022), 158.

18 Todres, Choi, and Wright, "Rights-Based Assessment of Youth Participation," 433; see also Joining Forces, "Children's Right to Be Heard: We're Talking; Are You Listening?" (policy brief, Joining Forces, January 2021); Jennifer E. Blakeslee and Janet S. Walker, "Assessing the Meaningful Inclusion of Youth Voice in Policy and Practice: State of the Science" (Research and Training Center for Pathways to Positive Futures, Portland State University, Portland, OR, 2018), 1–2; Jessica Shakesprere, Mica O'Brien, and Eona Harrison, *Youth Engagement in Collective Impact Initiatives: Lessons from Promise Neighborhoods* (New York: Urban Institute, 2020), 6–7.

19 European Commission, Directorate-General for Justice and Consumers, *Evaluation of Legislation, Policy and Practice on Child Participation in the European Union (EU)* (Brussels: European Commission, 2015), 156.

20 Ibid.

21 Anne C. Dailey and Laura A. Rosenbury, "The New Law of the Child," *Yale Law Journal* 127, no. 6 (2018): 1448–1537.

22 European Commission, Directorate-General for Justice and Consumers, *Evaluation of Legislation, Policy and Practice*, 156.

23 Ibid., 153.

24 Pamela Wallberg and Maria Kahn, "The Rights Project: How Rights Education Transformed a Classroom," *Journal of Childhood Studies* 36 (2011): 31–35.

25 Ibid., 34.

26 Ann Quennerstedt, ed., *Teaching Children's Human Rights in Early Childhood Education and School: Educational Aims, Content and Processes*, Reports in Education 21 (Örebro, Sweden: Örebro University, School of Humanities, Education and Social Sciences, 2019).

27 Ombudsman for Children, *Pieces of Us*, 14.

28 Ibid., 41.

29 Ibid., 43–45.

30 Britt Tellgren, "Teaching about and through Children's Human Rights in Early Childhood Education," in Quennerstedt, *Teaching Children's Human Rights*, 39.

31 Ibid., 43.

32 Ibid., 42.

33 Noelia Ceballos and Teresa Susinos, "Do My Words Convey What Children Are Saying? Researching School Life with Very Young Children: Dilemmas for 'Authentic Listening,'" *European Early Childhood Education Research Journal* 30, no. 1 (2022): 81–95.

34 UN Committee on the Rights of the Child, *General Comment No. 12*, paras. 20 and 21; see also Laura Lundy, Lesley McEvoy, and Bronagh Byrne, "Working with Young Children as Co-researchers: An Approach Informed by the United Nations

Convention on the Rights of the Child," *Early Education & Development* 22, no. 5 (2011): 714–736.

35 Ceballos and Susinos, "Do My Words Convey What Children Are Saying?," 91.

36 Ibid.

37 UNICEF, *Effective, Representative, and Inclusive Child Participation at the Local Level: A Study on Child and Youth Councils in UNICEF National Committee Countries* (New York: UNICEF, 2022), 27.

38 Ibid., 52; see also UNICEF Finland, "A Guide to Listening to Children's Views," accessed November 17, 2023, www.lapsiystavallinenkunta.fi.

39 UNICEF, *Effective, Representative, and Inclusive Child Participation*, 52.

40 Ibid., 22–23, 92.

41 Perpetua Kirby and Rebecca Webb, "Taking Part, Joining In, and Being Heard? Ethnographic Explorations of Children's Participation," in *The Oxford Handbook of Children's Rights Law*, ed. Jonathan Todres and Shani King (New York: Oxford University Press, 2020), 486.

42 Hanita Kosher and Asher Ben-Arieh, "What Children Think about Their Rights and Their Well-Being: A Cross-National Comparison, *American Journal of Orthopsychiatry* 87, no. 3 (2017): 269.

43 Ibid.

44 Ibid., 260–263.

45 Jonathan Bradshaw Antonia Keung, Gwyther Rees, and Haridhan Goswami, "Children's Subjective Well-Being: International Comparative Perspectives," *Children and Youth Services Review* 33, no. 4 (2011): 548–556.

46 Kosher and Asher, "What Children Think about Their Rights and Their Well-Being," 256; Ronald Inglehart, Roberto Foa, Christopher Peterson, and Christian Welzel, "Development, Freedom, and Rising Happiness: A Global Perspective (1981–2007)," *Perspectives on Psychological Science* 3, no. 4 (2008): 264–285.

47 Juliana E. Karras, Martin D. Ruck, Michele Peterson-Badali, and Christine Emuka, "Being and Becoming: Centering the Morality of Social Responsibility through Children's Right to Participate in Society," in *Handbook of Moral Development*, ed. Melanie Killen and Judith G. Smetana (New York: Routledge, 2022), 119.

48 Ibid., 118.

49 Urie Bronfenbrenner, "Ecological Models of Human Development," *International Encyclopedia of Education* 3, no. 2 (1994): 37–43.

50 Erdem Hareket and Selma Yel, "Which Perceptions Do We Have Related to Our Rights as Child? Child Rights from the Perspective of Primary School Students," *Journal of Education and Learning* 6, no. 3 (2017): 340–349.

51 Laura Wray-Lake and Amy K. Syvertsen, "The Developmental Roots of Social Responsibility in Childhood and Adolescence," *New Directions for Child and Adolescent Development* 2011, no. 134 (2011): 11–25.

52 Ibid.

53 Ursula Kilkelly, Helen Lynch, Alice Moore, Angela O'Connell, and Sarah C. Field, *Children and the Outdoors: Contact with the Outdoors and Natural Heritage*

among Children Aged 5 to 12: Current Trends, Benefits, Barriers and Research Requirements (Kilkenny, UK: Heritage Council, 2016), 44.

54 Katherine Covell and R. Brian Howe, *The Challenge of Children's Rights for Canada* (Waterloo, ON: Wilfrid Laurier University Press, 2001).

55 Kilkelly et al., *Children and the Outdoors*, 44.

56 Ibid., 35.

57 National Children's Bureau, *"Being Listened to Is Better than Anything": Children and Young People's Opinions and Experiences of Healthcare* (London: National Children's Bureau, 2001), 7.

58 Ibid., 24.

59 Ursula Kilkelly and Mary Donnely, *The Child's Right to Be Heard in the Healthcare Setting: Perspectives of Children, Parents and Health Professionals* (Dublin: Office of the Minister for Children, 2006), 43.

60 Ibid., 44.

61 Ibid.

62 Maggie Mort, Marion Walker, Alison Lloyd Williams, and Amanda Bingley, "Displacement: Critical Insights from Flood-Affected Children," *Health & Place* 52 (2018): 152.

63 Ibid.

64 Ibid., 152–153.

65 Ibid., 153.

66 Ibid.

67 Ibid.

68 End Violence Against Children, "Guiding Policy to Protect the Millions of Children Displaced by Climate Change," accessed November 11, 2023, www.end-violence.org.

69 Ibid.

70 Jonathan Todres, "A Child Rights–Based Approach to Reconstruction in Haiti," *Intercultural Human Rights Law Review* 6 (2011): 43–85.

71 Ombudsman for Children, *Pieces of Us*, 13.

72 Hareket and Yel, "Which Perceptions Do We Have," 344.

73 Ibid., 345.

74 UNICEF, *Engaged and Heard*; UNICEF, *Effective, Representative, and Inclusive Child Participation.*

75 Manfred Nowak, *United Nations Global Study on Children Deprived of Their Liberty* (Geneva: United Nations, 2019), www.ohchr.org.

76 Ibid., 30.

77 Ibid., 96.

78 Ibid., 95

79 Ibid., 111.

80 Akila Aggoune, Savitri Goonesekere, Janet Nelson, Rebeca Rios-Kohn, and Jonathan Todres, *Faith and Children's Rights: A Multi-religious Study on the Convention on the Rights of the Child* (New York: Arigatou International, 2019).

81 Erin G. Fox, Nicole F. Kahn, and Gabrielle Battle, "When Youth Are Experts in the Field," *Issues in Science & Technology*, May 3, 2022, https://issues.org.

82 Ibid.

83 Ibid.

84 MyVoice, "About Us," accessed November 17, 2023, https://hearmyvoicenow.org; Melissa DeJonckheere, Lauren P. Nichols, Michelle H. Moniz, Kendrin R. Sonneville, V. G. Vinod Vydiswaran, Xinyan Zhao, Timothy C. Guetterman, and Tammy Chang, "MyVoice National Text Message Survey of Youth Aged 14 to 24 Years: Study Protocol," *JMIR Research Protocol* 6, no. 12 (2017): e247; Kendrin R. Sonneville, Lakshman Mulpuri, Ivana Khreizat, Lauren P. Nichols, Melissa A. Plegue, and Tammy Chang, "Youth Preferences for Weight-Related Conversations," *Health Communication* 35, no. 11 (2020): 1328–1333.

85 Jane Harness, Kate Fitzgerald, Humayra Sullivan, and Ellen Selkie, "Youth Insight about Social Media Effects on Well/Ill-Being and Self-Modulating Efforts," *Journal of Adolescent Health* 71, no. 3 (2022): 324–333; Halley P. Crissman, Christina Czuhajewski, Michelle H. Moniz, Missy Plegue, and Tammy Chang, "Youth Perspectives Regarding the Regulating of Bathroom Use by Transgender Individuals," *Journal of Homosexuality* 67, no. 14 (2020): 2034–2049; MyVoice, "Research: Vaping and Tobacco Laws," accessed November 17, 2023, https://hearmyvoicenow.org; Melissa DeJonckheere and Tammy Chang, "It's Not Just You—Politics Is Stressing Out America's Youth," *The Conversation*, February 13, 2018, https://theconversation.com.

86 Karras et al., "Being and Becoming," 122; see also Wray-Lake and Syvertsen, "Developmental Roots of Social Responsibility."

87 Ombudsman for Children, *Pieces of Us*, 52.

88 Ibid.

89 UN Committee on the Rights of the Child, *General Comment No. 1 (2001): Article 29 (1)—The Aims of Education*, para. 12, CRC/GC/2001/1 (April 17, 2001).

90 Kay Aranda, Lester Coleman, Nigel S. Sherriff, Chris Cocking, Laetitia Zeeman, and Liz Cunningham, "Listening for Commissioning: A Participatory Study Exploring Young People's Experiences, Views and Preferences of School-Based Sexual Health and School Nursing," *Journal of Clinical Nursing* 27 (2017): 377.

91 Ibid., 380–381.

92 Ibid., 381.

93 Ibid.

94 Miguel Casar, Conor Sasner, Felicia Graham, and Joseph Bishop, *"Nothing about Us without Us": A Local Control Funding Formula (LCFF) Case Study on East Side Union High School District* (Los Angeles: Center for the Transformation of Schools, School of Education and Information Studies, University of California, Los Angeles. 2022), 9.

95 Ibid., 11.

96 Ibid., 42.

97 Ibid., 23.

98 Nathan Grossman, dir., *I Am Greta* (B-Reel Films, 2020); Giulia Gasparri, Omnia El Omrani, Rachael Hinton, David Imbago, Heeta Lakhani, Anshu Mohan, William Yeung, and Flavia Bustreo, "Children, Adolescents, and Youth Pioneering a Human Rights-Based Approach to Climate Change," *Health and Human Rights* 23, no. 2 (2021): 95–108; Jennifer McRuer and Margarita Zethelius, "The Difference Biocultural 'Place' Makes to Community Efforts towards Sustainable Development: Youth Participatory Action Research in a Marine Protected Area of Colombia," *International Review of Education* 63 (2017): 847–870; Robin Happel, "Inside the Youth Campaign to Bring Climate Change to the World's Highest Court," *The Nation*, April 26, 2023, www.thenation.com; Todres, Choi, and Wright, "Rights-Based Assessment of Youth Participation," 440.

99 Tomas Torbjörnsson and Lena Molin, "In School We Have Not Time for the Future: Voices of Swedish Upper Secondary School Students about Solidarity and the Future," *International Research in Geographical and Environmental Education* 24, no. 4 (2015): 344.

100 Caroline Bradbury-Jones, Louise Isham, and Julie Taylor, "The Complexities and Contradictions in Participatory Research with Vulnerable Children and Young People: A Qualitative Systematic Review," *Social Science & Medicine* 215 (2018): 80–91.

101 Laura Lundy, Lesley McEvoy, and Bronagh Byrne, "Working with Young Children as Co-researchers: An Approach Informed by the United Nations Convention on the Rights of the Child," *Early Education & Development* 22, no. 5 (2011): 714–736.

102 Alison Clark and Peter Moss, *Spaces to Play: More Listening to Young Children Using the Mosaic Approach* (London: National Children's Bureau, 2005); Craig Mertler, *Action Research: Improving Schools and Empowering Educators*, 6th ed. (Thousand Oaks, CA: Sage, 2019); Caralyn Blaisdell, Lorna Arnott, Kate Wall, and Carol Robinson "Look Who's Talking: Using Creative, Playful Arts-Based Methods in Research with Young Children," *Journal of Early Childhood Research* 17, no. 1 (2019): 14–31.

103 Todres, Choi, and Wright, "Rights-Based Assessment of Youth Participation," 444.

104 Linda A. Camino, "Youth-Adult Partnerships: Entering New Territory in Community Work and Research," *Applied Developmental Science* 4, no. S1 (2000): 11–20.

105 Deirdre Horgan, "Child Participatory Research Methods: Attempts to Go 'Deeper,'" *Childhood* 24, no. 2 (2017): 245–259.

106 Laura Lundy and Leslie McEvoy, "Children's Rights and Research Processes: Assisting Children to (In)formed Views," *Childhood* 19, no. 1 (2012): 134.

107 Ibid.

108 Jennifer Abbasi, "Surgeon General Sounds the Alarm on Social Media Use and Youth Mental Health Crisis," *JAMA* 330, no. 1 (2023): 11–12; Eric A. Waselewski, Marika E. Waselewski, and Tammy Chang, "Needs and Coping Behaviors of Youth in the US during COVID-19," *Journal of Adolescent Health* 67, no. 5 (2020): 649–652.

109 Pamela Wridt, "A Qualitative GIS Approach to Mapping Urban Neighborhoods with Children to Promote Physical Activity and Child-Friendly Community Planning," *Environment and Planning B: Planning and Design* 37, no. 1 (2010): 129–147.

110 Karras et al., "Being and Becoming," 128; Emily J. Ozer, "Youth-Led Participatory Action Research, Equity and Justice," *Developmental Science: Theoretical and Methodological Issues* 50 (2016): 189–207.

Conclusion

Realizing Children's Rights through an Integrated Approach: Themes and Opportunities

JONATHAN TODRES AND URSULA KILKELLY

I. Introduction

Over the past few decades, research has led to greater understanding of children's experiences of their rights, identifying gaps and barriers to the implementation of the UN Convention on the Rights of the Child (CRC) and wider international children's rights law. While this body of research is multidisciplinary, coming from legal, education, and psychology perspectives, for instance, there has been relatively little interdisciplinary research bringing disciplines together to expand the understanding of children's rights. In addition, studies of the relationship between child development and children's rights are rare, and there have been few attempts to explore children's rights by taking account of children's distinctive ages and stages of development. Acknowledging the richness of such an approach, this collection has sought to address this gap by bringing together, for the first time, the fields of child development and children's rights around the main stages of development: early, middle, and late childhood or adolescence. In doing so, the focus of the collection has been to explore different disciplinary perspectives on these developmental stages, bringing together research and analysis from developmental psychology and children's rights scholars to advance interdisciplinary understanding of children's rights. By adopting a structured approach, this book has strived to enable comparisons between the literature on child development and children's rights on the three distinct stages of childhood, by drawing out the themes that cut across these three stages, in order to enrich our understanding of how children's rights are interpreted and applied at different stages of childhood. This concluding chapter thus aims to bring together the most prominent themes emerging from this research process, and in building a bridge or bridges between the different disciplines and perspectives, it endeavors to further support the book's aims of advancing a more nuanced understanding of children's rights across childhood in support of greater protection of their rights.

The merits of multiple disciplinary perspectives are well known and include, as Caralyn Blaisdell and E. Kay M. Tisdall suggest in chapter 3, the value of questioning "knowledge production, that of other disciplines as well as our own." And yet there are challenges with this approach too, as we have learned through this project. For example, while we expected the two fields to use different language, we learned during the editorial process that they can also mean different things even when using the same terminology. For instance, in children's rights discourse, "identity" is used to refer to a broad array of traits and characteristics and, in this sense, can apply from the beginning of life. However, developmental science typically uses "identity" in a much more defined manner, referring to the process of identity formation that occurs primarily in adolescence. Learning about and understanding these different perspectives, including the meaning and use of language, is thus an ongoing process, facilitated by dialogue that bridges disciplines centered around a common theme. We also found common ground across the stages of childhood insofar as authors at each stage referred to the stage under their examination as the "most overlooked" or "the least well researched" stage. While, on the one hand, they cannot all be correct, nonetheless this perspective reinforced that there remain gaps in our knowledge at each stage of childhood that are revealed through interdisciplinary analyses. As such, this theme served to underpin the importance of this project, vindicating its aim to create an interdisciplinary space for the exploration of children's rights from a developmental perspective.

In this respect, this chapter seeks to advance the dialogue on what these different perspectives say about children's rights in early childhood, middle childhood, and adolescence. It takes account of the different disciplinary expertise of the authors in this collection, bringing them together in what we believe to be the first integrated, thematic analysis of children's rights and child development. While the aim of this chapter is to identify common ground, we also seek to identify the divergent and distinctive features of the two disciplinary perspectives and the childhood stages, in order to expand cross-cutting perspectives on a range of children's rights issues. The chapter considers, in turn, a number of key themes that have been revealed through this interdisciplinary analysis of children's rights. It then briefly identifies significant issues that must be accounted for to forge a more integrated approach to children's rights and child development that enhances the well-being of all children.

II. Key Issues Revealed through Integrating Rights and Development

A. Change

There is little doubt that change is constant throughout childhood. As the analysis in each part of this book makes clear, children's development begins at the prenatal stage and continues right through childhood (and into early adulthood), such that children experience continuous and enormous flux from biological, emotional, and physical perspectives throughout all childhood stages. Although the pace of change in early and late childhood is well recognized, Josephine Grant highlights in chapter 4 that even middle childhood—while more slow paced—is nonetheless a period of change of great significance.

Indeed, independent of each other, the authors invariably referred to every stage under consideration as "critical" to the child's development, with references to the "rapid growth, learning, and potential," as Joanna Williams describes it in chapter 7, throughout each stage. These claims would appear to reflect the nature of childhood itself, as a dynamic and fast-paced period of change for children. It is a salient reminder, from both children's rights and child development perspectives, that the childhood years are so critical precisely because of the constant development that defines them.

Article 5 of the CRC recognizes childhood as a stage of continuous development, and its articulation of the concept of evolving capacity seeks to capture the dynamic nature of childhood from a children's rights perspective. Relatedly, Article 6, which is recognized as one of the General Principles of the CRC—along with Article 2 (nondiscrimination),

Article 3 (best interests of the child), and Article 12 (the child's right to be heard)—establishes that states have a duty to "ensure to the maximum extent possible the survival and development of the child."[1] At the same time, and compared with the extent to which change emerges throughout the child development research, relatively little account is taken elsewhere in the CRC or in children's rights literature of the intensely dynamic nature of children's development *or* its impact on their exercise of their rights as they develop. We know, however, that the dynamic, developmental, and rapidly changing nature of childhood both bears on children's exercise of their rights *and* imposes an urgency in the implementation and enforcement of children's rights. In the former respect, the fast pace of children's development means that law and policy reinforcing the protection of their rights need to remain adaptable and flexible to the implications for their rights of the change children are experiencing. Apart from impacting on their behavior at particularly acute times, the fast-paced nature of children's development demands frameworks that take account of the child's rapidly evolving circumstances.[2] Separately, the fact that childhood is a period of rapid change and growth also means that even relatively brief periods of interference with, or denials of, children's rights, such as short-term disruptions to education or health care, can have lifelong consequences.[3] As several authors have explored in their contributions, the COVID-19 pandemic taught us this harsh lesson, as schooling and children's engagement with their wider worlds were interrupted, with lasting detrimental impacts especially on vulnerable children.

For these reasons, therefore, it is important to take account of the changing nature of childhood—and the pace and impact of that change—as we undertake research to better understand children's rights. Moreover, as discussed in the third section of this chapter, states also need to ensure that law and policy are framed in a responsive way that takes account of the scientific evidence of change in child development, as well as the individual, familial, community, and societal factors that shape it.

B. Ages and Rights

The relationship between age and stages of development is not something on which either child development research or children's rights law has achieved consensus. We recognize, for instance, that development-based age ranges do not align with the definition of the child in the CRC, which defines a child as every human being below the age of eighteen and deems that childhood ends at age eighteen, unless states parties determine otherwise.[4] Perhaps not surprisingly, then, the process of delineating the age range of each stage of childhood for the purposes of this collection revealed complexities and challenges. During the drafting and exchange of the chapters among the authors, it emerged that ages and age categories are not uniformly applied and that the role that age plays in the interpretation and application of children's rights is inconsistent and ambiguous at best. In addition, the age ranges used to delineate the different stages of childhood overlap with one another—early childhood with middle childhood, and middle childhood with adolescence, for instance. In this volume, the development science authors considered the age-defined stages of childhood as follows: early childhood as zero to eight years; middle childhood as from approximately age six to age twelve; and adolescence starting around ten years old and reaching into one's early to midtwenties. They did so reflecting on the scholarly literature in their respective stage-based subfield of study. Although there was consensus—among both child development and children's rights authors—that the lines between stages of development are blurred, perhaps the more interesting question is what the overlapping ranges mean for children's enjoyment of their rights. What is also important is what reference points or evidence states use in choosing to include age limits in law and policy that seek to protect or indeed to limit the rights of the child.

At the same time, it is an important point that the CRC makes no reference to childhood's developmental stages in the context of the exercise of children's rights, although, of course, it references the child's right to development in Article 6. The only express references to age in the CRC are found in Article 12, which establishes that the weight given to children's views must be consistent with their age and maturity, and Article 40(3), which requires states parties to establish a "minimum age below which children shall be presumed not to have the capacity to infringe the penal law." Neither provision identifies which age is relevant for these purposes, noting that both age *and* maturity are important for the purposes of giving weight to children's views in Article 12.[5] Even the UN Committee on the Rights of the Child (Committee) has had difficulty settling on an age with respect to criminal responsibility—recommending twelve years in its General Comment in 2007 and raising that to fourteen years, in light of development science, in its revised General Comment in 2019.[6]

Overall, it is clear that international legal standards and the children's rights literature do not cohere on the question of age and age ranges, revealing a conceptual gap in the consideration of age in the children's rights scholarship. As Aoife Daly and Amy Walsh highlight in chapter 5, for instance, the Committee's approach toward the ages and stages of childhood is confusing given its tendency to focus either on early childhood or on adolescence, remaining largely silent on middle childhood. This approach raises important questions about what the Committee considers middle childhood to be and where middle childhood sits as a developmental category under the CRC. While there may be benefits to the Committee's flexible approach, there seems to be a disconnect between an approach that suggests middle childhood to be so fluid as to depend on the individual child's development, on the one hand, and the persuasive evidence, as explained by Grant, which indicates recognition of middle childhood as a much more distinct phase of development, on the other.

Looking to the very foundational years of life reveals additional challenges, as the development science makes clear. The decision not to extend the CRC formally to include the period before birth is well understood; given the highly politicized nature of questions around when life begins, the drafters of the CRC deliberately left that question to individual countries to determine that for themselves.[7] At the same time, it is nonetheless clear from the child development literature that what occurs in utero is critical to children's healthy development. As Iheoma U. Iruka indicates in chapter 1, development begins before the child is born, highlighting the significance for children's development of maternal health and factors relating to pregnancy and birth. Although references are made to the importance of prenatal and postnatal health care for mothers in Article 24 of the CRC, it is perhaps surprising that there has been so little focus on the full range of the child's rights, beyond the right to life, during this period and also relatively little integrated analysis of women's and children's rights in this respect.[8]

With regard to the age of majority, the drafters of the CRC—who undertook their work from 1979 to 1989—can perhaps be commended for setting the bar at eighteen years, with the caveat that it can be set earlier by national law, given the importance of late childhood as a developmental phase for older teenagers.[9] At the same time, more recent developmental science suggests that younger adults have much in common with those under eighteen, posing a question as to whether using age eighteen as the end of childhood should now be reviewed. For instance, Williams highlights the absence of a contemporary evidence base for the application of the age of eighteen years as a cutoff for the CRC's protections, noting the now-significant body of research on the risks young people face well into their twenties, as a result of their developmental stage. In this sense, it is a fair assessment that this book perpetuates the myth that childhood comes to a logical conclusion at eighteen years of age. Furthermore, this approach does not just disadvantage young people over eighteen years who are denied the protections of the CRC and other children's rights law. As Williams notes, the focus on the "narrow age band between sixteen and the early twenties has obscured more detailed, nuanced discussions about the capacity of younger adolescents." She notes that "cognitively, an adolescent's logical reasoning and capacity for abstract thinking are similar to those of an adult by age sixteen; however, continuing neurobiological maturation is associated with marked development of social processing, decision-making, and self-regulation through the midtwenties." This clearly makes the age eighteen cutoff even more arbitrary; it is, similar to any bright-line rule, simultaneously both over- and underinclusive.[10]

Yanghee Lee and Sangwon Kim also note, in their discussion of self-determination in chapter 9, that adolescent children can be prevented by adults from exercising their own rights through measures aimed at protecting them from harm. The question, as yet unanswered, is whether children under eighteen can ever be expected, and thus entitled, to exercise their own rights with full autonomy. Lee and Kim call for a more sophisticated analysis here, suggesting that the right to protection is best served by promoting adolescents' "individual autonomy and active construction of their own development."[11] Extension of the right to vote to children—not included in the CRC—is one means advocated by Lee and Kim to further empower children, and development science indicates that, at a minimum, sixteen- and seventeen-year-olds have similar capacity to vote as adults do.[12] Otherwise, they note that states regularly prioritize problem-focused services and supports rather than taking steps to support children's capacity to exercise their rights.

Overall, there are significant inconsistencies in the use of ages, with respect to either protection or responsibility, across jurisdictions and areas of life. The analysis presented throughout this book points to the critical opportunities that exist for deeper and more complex analyses of children's rights that take account of both age-related questions and the stages of development.

C. Maturity and Rights

A similar theme emerging from this collection is that the relationship between the child's "maturity" and the exercise of their rights merits further, more nuanced analysis. Express references in the CRC to the concept of "maturity" are limited to Article 12, which establishes two key ideas: first, that every child has a right to be heard on matters that affect their lives; and second, that the child's views must be given due weight in line with their age and maturity.[13] Beyond Article 12, however, there is very little consideration in the children's rights literature of the concept of maturity, and interestingly, where it is discussed, it is presented in a singularly positive light: maturity is seen as a good thing that enables children to take on greater responsibility for the exercise of their rights. As Article 5 represents, for instance, evolving capacity—arguably a proxy for maturity—enables children to take on the exercise of their rights, with appropriate direction and guidance provided by parents and extended family.[14]

However, fewer scholars draw attention to the fact that increased maturity does not *just* bring with it greater capacity to exercise rights; it also, inevitably, brings greater responsibility for children. In this volume, several authors, including Noam Peleg and Sheila Varadan in chapter 6, highlight the ultimate representation of this concept in youth justice, where children as young as ten can be expected to take the full weight of criminal responsibility when they come into conflict with the law. Moreover, as Stephanie Rap discusses in chapter 8, while the minimum age of criminal responsibility "protects children under the age from being held criminally liable, it neither protects nor empowers the children, usually adolescents, who fall above that age." Development science has much to contribute here, including helping to illuminate the approach to the concept of a minimum age of criminal responsibility. As Grant highlights, common law originally framed the age of responsibility as the "age of reason" (which it set at seven years), reflecting the view of this as a time when "the charming inaccuracies of early childhood" are turned toward more "systematic, rational thought." As she explains, the transition from the pretend play of early years is met in middle childhood with a "reality" that arrives through cognitive advancement. This can be countered by more recent advances in developmental psychology that underpin the case for adolescents, and even young adults, to be found less culpable for risk-taking behaviors on the basis of their stage of development. The willingness of lawmakers to take account of this evidence is weak, although the continued analysis of these issues is important nonetheless, and drawing together children's rights and child development science can forge a pathway toward a more developmentally responsive approach to maturity.[15]

Speaking to responsibilization more generally, a developmental frame on children's rights highlights the potential incoherence of rights discourse in places. This ambiguity is revealed during middle childhood—a time of increasing responsibility—under scrutiny by Daly and Walsh, while Rap notes, perhaps ironically, that even during adolescence, the extent to which children are entitled to influence decisions on matters that affect them—including consent to medical treatment—remains variable and, in some instances, highly contested. As Peleg and Varadan note with respect to children in middle childhood and the digital world, even when children have capacity to exercise their rights, protection can dominate the approach of caregivers and policy makers. They note the backlash of paternalism unleashed by heightened parental anxiety over children's safety and well-being online. As the various analyses of these issues in this volume make clear, the evolution of children's rights from the early childhood focus on protection toward greater autonomy in the exercise of rights is far from a linear path. Even a child with fully evolved capacity can have no guarantee that their autonomy will be recognized in law and policy that may contain exclusions based on age.

Although deeper analysis is required to conclude whether there is, in this area, a genuine disconnect in the concept of childhood at the heart of the CRC versus that in the development literature—or whether that reflects, in part, inherent differences between law and science, as noted in the introduction to this volume—the CRC's relationship with the stages of childhood does appear ambiguous. Daly and Walsh note the appearance of a linear approach in the CRC, with adulthood as a destination, highlighting the neglect of the middle stage. Yet this is such a vital stage of child development for a whole range of reasons, not least the attitudes formed by children's experiences at this stage. For example, as Grant explains, research demonstrates how children in middle childhood rationalize unequal distribution of favors, citing a desire to address group disadvantage, when those in early childhood typically do not. This highlights the significance of this period of a child's life not only for the child's development but also for its relevance to the learning process that leads to greater protection of the rights of others. As Grant notes, children at this stage "start navigating institutions on their own," becoming "increasingly aware of where they might fit in a world stratified by gender, race, and money." Thus, in middle childhood, as in other stages, evolving capacities from a rights perspective prompt questions about when children legally can have a say in decision-making processes and exercise more autonomy. But, as development science shows, the concept of evolving capacities is not merely about when and to what extent children can act "like adults," but rather, it is important for children's own development. As Williams, notes, for example, it is important for adolescents to have "safe and satisfying ways to explore the world and take healthy risks to test out new ideas and experiences." Children's rights law, thus, must give greater consideration to how law and policy can support healthy exercise of children's evolving capacities, and much can be learned in this respect from integrating child development with children's rights through an interdisciplinary research process.

D. Parenting and Children's Rights

It is well known that although children are rights holders under the CRC, parents have a pivotal role to play in enabling them to exercise their rights. This is recognized, along with the role of parents as caregivers, in Articles 3, 5, and 18, for instance. Viewed from a development perspective, the importance to the fulfillment of the child's rights of the *quality of parenting* comes into focus. Even if the child's right to development has expression in Article 6 of the CRC, the importance of quality parenting to child development appears understated in the children's rights literature.[16] Yet as Iruka states in relation to early childhood, parents are "critical in developing children's emotional regulation by helping them monitor, understand, and provide strategies for recognition and management." In chapter 2, Meredith Johnson Harbach similarly makes clear that "the role of parents and caregivers in children's survival and development is especially consequential in early childhood," when "parents' responsibilities are most extensive" and parenting "most demanding." Although Article 27 of the CRC recognizes the right of the child to a standard of living adequate for the child's development, it places the responsibility on parents to secure the "conditions of living necessary for the child's development." Notwithstanding the Article 18 requirement on states parties to support parents in their child-rearing responsibilities, this structure seems to fall short of ensuring the quality parenting that children truly need.

Despite numerous references to parents in the CRC, there is little in it or in the children's rights literature that addresses the particular importance of parenting, especially quality parenting, in early childhood. While Article 2 of the CRC prohibits discrimination in the enjoyment of CRC rights on the basis of the parents' status, there is no recognition in the CRC of the extent to which variable parenting styles can impact on children's enjoyment of their rights. In this regard, Grant makes the important point with respect to middle childhood that the focus on "optimal parenting styles" obscures the value of strategies that do not follow the approaches of "well-to-do parents in industrialized economies," noting that the perception of "harsh parenting" as "deficient or harmful for children" may miss their adaptation to dangerous environments. As she notes, "If we neglect the different risks that families face, we risk framing parenting strategies that are downstream of external threats as problematic rather than responsive." This point has significant implications for the way in which families are "policed," for instance, impacting how, and to what extent, they experience their rights in the child welfare and youth justice contexts.

As Harbach notes, Article 18(1) of the CRC provides that parents and caregivers have the primary responsibility for the upbringing and development of the child and that the best interests of the child will be their basic concern. She notes, interestingly, "By definition, the right to have one's best interests assessed by others in a variety of contexts is a right that children cannot exercise themselves. Instead, this right must be respected and carried out by adults: parents, guardians, private and public institutions, courts, administrative and legislative bodies." This is recognized, to some extent, in Article 3(3) of the CRC, which requires states parties to ensure that "the institutions, services and facilities responsible for the care or protection of children shall conform with the standards established by competent authorities, particularly in the areas of safety, health, in the number and suitability of their staff, as well as competent supervision." But no similar provision prescribes the importance of quality parenting to children, and there is little in the children's rights literature on this point. Here, too, child development adds important perspective. Reflecting the requirement under Article 18(2) of the CRC that states must support parents in the upbringing of their children, Grant notes, with respect to middle childhood, that children need parenting that provides "right-sized opportunities to explore, to contribute to the family, and to develop personal responsibility." Given the significance of developmental research highlighting the enormity of influence of parents and caregivers on the child's development, and in turn on children's enjoyment of their rights, Article 18 arguably sets the bar too low by failing to elaborate *how* parents are to exercise their responsibility. This is similarly clear from Harbach's analysis of the child's right to protection from harm, which reveals a negative rather than a positive obligations approach, requiring state intervention only *after* harm has occurred rather than earlier in the form of positive supports for families, although this is an approach that the Committee has been keen to highlight.

Overall, the development literature makes clear that the realization of children's rights across the stages of childhood depends significantly on parental support that is bolstered by state investment in and support of families. Taking the development science into account, the enormously positive and protective impact of parenting (and a positive child-parent relationship) on a child's development is worthy of much greater attention from a children's rights perspective. Although law may not be able to mandate parental affection, development science, as Iruka explains, is clear that children who enjoy parental affection, and the attachment and sense of security that go with that, do better. The Committee has recognized the important role parents play and stressed the duty on the state to provide adequate support to parents in child rearing. Blaisdell and Tisdall comment on the thirty-three references to "parents" in the CRC, reiterating Michael Freeman's view of the CRC as a parent's charter.[17] Perhaps this is where the developmental approach is most salient in helping to frame the instrumental nature of parental responsibility to the fulfillment of the child's right to development. Viewed from this perspective, it would appear a gap that there is still no dedicated General Comment in this area—a subject to be treated with great care, given, as Blaisdell and Tisdall remark, that in some cases, children's rights can be most at risk in their families.

E. Relationships, Connection, and Community

Extending outward from the importance of parenting in supporting children's development rights, it is clear that at almost every stage of a child's development, the child's environment—including their other relationships and their sense of belonging—is crucial. In early childhood, for instance, Iruka explains that in a variety of ways, "relationships with others" help children go "from dependence to independence," as the literature highlights the significance of "attachment" to the child's healthy development. Similarly, as Grant discusses with respect to the stage of middle childhood, "development is a continual interaction between self and other," as she notes the continuing importance of interactive play in middle childhood, even if children "become more selective about their playmates" during this phase.

Noting adolescence as an important period for identity formation, Williams explains how young people are agents in this process, selecting "the environments and people they want to be around." According to Rap, this highlights that the CRC is insufficiently adapted to "adolescents' realities." In particular, as she regretfully notes, "the CRC does not contain provisions explicitly aimed at protecting peer relationships," which are so important to children during the adolescent phase of childhood (nor does the CRC expressly address siblings). As Williams explains, "Peer groups provide a space for youth to practice social skills, like communication, conflict resolution, and cooperative learning. In step with physical, neurobiological, psychosocial, and contextual shifts (e.g., transition to secondary schools), peer-group 'cliques' often become more prevalent in early adolescence." Weighing up comparative influences of parents and peers, Grant observes that "children in middle childhood learn moral decision-making in play with peers," highlighting the importance of these relationships to children especially as they develop. Significantly, Blaisdell and Tisdall draw children's rights themes together with the concept of "relationality," noting the importance of multiple intersections and interdependencies in the context of early childhood, where power and vulnerability collide. And yet, this interaction between the self and the "other" that Grant references importantly includes peer relationships, references to which are entirely absent from the CRC, as well as the wider community, which is equally poorly represented in the CRC.

Williams notes the significance for the adolescent child of the environment outside the family. As Lee and Kim note, however, adolescents' expansion of their "scope of life by interacting with different people, including in the digital environment, outside the boundaries of their homes" can be said, ironically, to place them at greater risk—reducing the likelihood of their rights being protected. The internet clearly presents a new, wider landscape to children in middle childhood too. As Peleg and Varadan explain, "With the advent of the internet and the increasing accessibility of mobile devices, the location of social interactions has begun to shift from physical spaces to online platforms." They highlight that "combining the real world and the virtual one (with the help of augmented reality apps), children are now able to exercise greater agency in seeking out peers and obtaining direct, unmitigated, and unfiltered access to the outside world." As children and youth face a rapidly changing and expanding world through developmental stages, it is critical that children's rights are informed by the science of child development and what is known about how best to support healthy development in these domains. As part of this, greater attention should be given to the diversity of relationships in children's lives and their impact on children's developing identity and the realization of their rights.

F. Situating Children's Rights in Their Wider Context

The CRC recognizes children as individual rights holders, entitled to respect and dignity and to enjoy their rights as individuals in their own right. At the same time, the centrality of the individual in the CRC, as well as in wider human rights law, downplays the importance of the broader context within which children's rights are realized. Williams observes that Global North contexts tend to "emphasize individuality," a focus that is embedded in the foundations of human rights law. As this volume demonstrates, communities are largely absent from studies of children's enjoyment of their rights, and yet they play an integral role in children's development. The child development perspective presented here sharpens our understanding of the importance to children's lives of the wider context in which their rights are protected and enjoyed, including the family, community, and broader society. In this regard, the development literature also brings to the fore the interrelated nature of rights, a concept that is generally accepted but inadequately accounted for in international human rights law.

At the most basic level, as noted earlier in this chapter, the healthy development of children is dependent on the health and well-being of mothers, as development begins prior to birth. In this way, children's rights and women's rights are interrelated (vertical relationships among rights).[18] As Iruka notes, maternal mortality remains high in numerous parts of the world, threatening children's rights and also prompting us to think differently about what is needed to ensure children's rights and healthy development. Specifically, it demands that much greater attention be given not just to the rights of children who are without parental care (under Article 20 of the CRC) but also to preventing the loss of this parental care in the first instance. Although the Committee has addressed the issue of neonatal mortality, as Harbach highlights, it has yet to address the issue of parental loss and its impact on the child in any substantive way, preferring instead to focus on maternal health and its relationship to children's development.

At the same time, the rights of children are not connected only to the rights of mothers, or even parents. Harbach emphasizes that, "especially in early childhood, realizing children's rights requires engagement with the domains and environments in which they are embedded:

families, schools, communities, institutions, and religious and cultural systems." Grant and Williams highlight the importance of culture and young people's experience with and support from cultural systems. Yet, cultural rights are often last in the priority of civil, political, economic, social, and cultural rights and, as a category, receive comparatively little analysis in children's rights scholarship. This jars with its importance in the developmental research; as Grant writes, for instance, middle childhood is critical in part because it is when children "bulk up on cultural know-how."

At all stages of childhood, the different domains that intersect with children's lives, and the adults that play prominent roles in their lives, have a significant impact on the realization of their rights. For individual children, it is also clear in both the children's rights and the development literature that children's rights in one area have a material impact on their rights in another—for example, their capacity to realize their right to education is affected by the status of their health rights and their right to housing (horizontal relationships among rights).[19] While the idea that rights are interrelated and interdependent is broadly accepted in children's rights, the interrelated nature of rights has arguably been underaccounted for in law and policy aimed at securing the rights of the child.[20] Many law-based interventions are sector specific and fall short of providing necessary supports for marginalized children, who often simultaneously confront needs across multiple domains. Although intersectionality discourse has highlighted this dynamic as it relates to other populations, law and policy continue to account inadequately for the interrelated nature of rights in children's lives.[21] In this important respect, development science offers informative models, such as the socioecological model, which help elucidate not only the individual factors that shape children's development and well-being but also the relationship, community, and societal factors that have a vital impact on their enjoyment of their rights. In doing so, development science can partner with children's rights to inform law and policy developments so that they better account for the interrelated and interdependent nature of rights.

G. Inequality, Poverty, and Other Structural Barriers

Many of the chapters in this volume discuss how institutional, structural, and systemic issues shape children's development and the realization of their rights. As the development chapters lay bare, barriers of poverty and inequality impact on children's development at all stages of childhood, with multiple, complex effects that play out in different ways. As Iruka outlines with respect to early childhood, poverty can impact the quality of education young children receive, the resources parents have to create a safe and nurturing environment, and children's chances of timely access to quality health care. Extensive research has established the devastating impact that poverty has on early childhood, with effects that stretch into adulthood.[22] Moreover, as Grant indicates, extreme poverty poses an existential threat that "squeezes out middle childhood." In countries like Brazil, where poverty combines with entrenched inequality, she notes, "middle childhood is a privilege of the rich." In addition to the adverse outcomes, poverty is known to cause psychological stress, as children in middle childhood become increasingly aware, as Grant explains, that they live in "a world stratified by gender, race, and money." Nor are the harmful impacts of poverty confined to early or middle childhood; Williams emphasizes that the "promise of [adolescence] is severely curtailed by economic, social, and structural disadvantage." A potent and consistent theme throughout all stages of childhood, therefore, is that persistent inequality, structural racism, other entrenched forms of discrimination, and additional systemic barriers impact heavily, and in some instances devastatingly, on children's development.

For many children at all stages of development, the effects on their development of living in poverty are compounded by racism and discrimination. As Iruka writes, "Similar to the complex and compounding nature of poverty on children's early development, racism and systemic inequities have been found to negatively impact the optimal health and social and emotional development of children during this critical period." Social, economic, and institutional structures cause this disadvantage to fall disproportionately on those who are already vulnerable, meaning that some children are much more heavily burdened by rights violations and barriers to their healthy development as a result of persistent inequalities, entrenched discrimination, and other systemic issues.

In addition, in both middle and late childhood, children's increasing awareness of their identity—their ethnicity, race, or culture—affects their self-view. As Williams explains, "throughout adolescence, youth from historically marginalized ethnic, racial, or cultural groups increasingly believe that society holds negative views about their group." Blaisdell and Tisdall, in their discussion of vulnerability, neocolonialism, and the "racialized" children, note, however, that even "young children's lives are intertwined with political contexts."

These structural and systemic issues present enormous challenges for children's rights law. Poverty, racism, gender-based discrimination, and other inequities all heighten the risk of harm, exploitation, and other rights violations of marginalized children. While Harbach addresses poverty and inequality in early childhood, and Lee and Kim's chapter calls for a focus on poverty to reinforce adolescents' right to protection from economic exploitation, for example, a much more comprehensive effort is required in children's rights to confront the root causes of harm to children at all stages of development. The CRC contains multiple provisions that address children's right to enjoy their rights without discrimination (Article 2), as well as other provisions addressing poverty, including the "right to an adequate standard of living" (Article 27), the right to social security and state benefits (Article 26), and the right to "institutions, facilities and services for the care of children" (Article 18(3)). Children's rights scholars are well aware of the impact of these factors on children's rights, as discussion elsewhere in this chapter illustrates. As this collection shows, development research not only supports the importance of specific socioeconomic rights that are so critical to children's development but also makes the case for more focused attention on the interrelated and interdependent nature of rights. Ultimately, in their efforts to implement the CRC, states need to develop more comprehensive, integrated responses to the multiple threats to children's rights and healthy development, particularly for children who experience intersectional discrimination or who confront multiple rights violations simultaneously. What this interdisciplinary analysis also shows, therefore, is how critical it is in all areas—research, policy development and implementation, service provision, and evaluation—that we confront and address the impact of systemic issues on children's rights and development.

H. Participation: Applied with Ambiguity

Although this collection makes clear that comparisons across the developmental stages of childhood can focus on many aspects of children's rights, Article 12 of the CRC is perhaps an ideal case study from a child development perspective, given that its terms indicate a developmentally appropriate application. According to Article 12, every child capable of forming a view has the right to express their views, and the weight given to those views depends on the age and maturity of the child.

Despite the clarity of the provision from a children's rights perspective, when viewed through the developmental stages of childhood, participation is far from clear-cut. Analysis in this volume raises questions about the extent to which participation rights can or should reflect children's developmental needs at different stages. As Rap notes, for instance, even in the adolescent stage of childhood, when almost full weight could be considered to apply to children's views, not every child experiences the full protection of their participation rights. One of the challenges in this context is the dependence on "age *and* maturity" in Article 12, which means that neither criterion alone can be used to determine the weight to be attached to the child's views. Although the adolescent is arguably more likely to have their views taken into account than the younger child, Rap gives examples of "matters that affect" children on which adolescents' views are rarely deemed to carry weight. This is a far cry from the view posited by Lee and Kim, who argue that participation "requires viewing children and adolescents as active agents in their own right" and as "legitimate political actors, with a right to participate in public decision-making." Moreover, Rap notes that while children can expect to enjoy greater participation rights with the emergence of the digital space, ironically, this environment is one where the child's participation rights may be diminished in favor of their protection. In this context, she welcomes that the rights to access information and digital literacy—so essential to ensure that the child safely navigates the online environment and yet understandably missing from the CRC, given that it was drafted prior to the digital age—have been addressed, more recently, in the Committee's General Comment on the digital environment.[23]

The importance of accessing information and support to enable children's greater participation rights also emerges from both the development and the children's rights literature. In this respect, Blaisdell and Tisdall emphasize "the importance of scaffolding young children's participation, through information and support," while articulating the importance of the developmental stage to the form and manner of participation. Teasing out how best to implement a child's Article 12 rights amid the complexity of early childhood (as illustrated by Iruka) highlights the value of interdisciplinary perspectives. Harbach highlights that the "evolving capacities" concept is "central to the realization of [children's] participation rights. Rather than acting as a limitation, however, this qualification requires states to ascertain the child's ability to form an autonomous opinion to the maximum extent, with a presumption that a child has the capacity to form views and the right to express them."

Daly and Walsh highlight the particular relevance to children in middle childhood of participation rights, given that during this stage of their development, children begin to engage in the process of public debate, with some countries seeking to equip children for this. This public engagement has occurred at national and international levels, with recent involvement of children in climate advocacy, for example, illustrated also by Peleg and Varadan. Ambiguity around the application of Article 12 also arises from the different expectations that apply to children in middle childhood—in family proceedings, for example, children can be deemed too immature to contribute their views, despite being deemed mature enough to have responsibility in the criminal justice context. It is at this stage, most likely, that processes or "formal measurements" are used to determine a child's capacity, with Daly and Walsh noting that because the child's capacity is commonly underestimated during middle childhood, this accentuates the importance of a rights-based approach, given that all children capable of forming a view have a right to express that view in line with Article 12.

As a number of chapters in this volume make clear, the tension between protecting children and recognizing their autonomy often spurs calls to, and results in policies that, restrict young people's participation in public spaces, the digital environment, and the political domain. This tension between protection and participation rights is illuminated when viewed from a development perspective. On the children's rights side, the Committee has elaborated on the relationship between Article 3, the best interests of the child principle, and Article 12, the right to a say in matters that affect the child, highlighting the interconnected nature of these concepts. Although parents clearly have a responsibility under Article 5 of the CRC to guide children in the exercise of their rights, little guidance exists as to how they are expected to strike the appropriate balance between protection and autonomy in this context. Grant notes that, ideally, it is the role of parents to maintain a "productive tension between autonomy and protection."

The complexity of this role is highlighted, however, in other stages of childhood, when, perhaps in unexpected ways, children's acquired autonomy places them in greater need of protection, including during adolescence. As Lee and Kim's analysis shows, as children engage more outside the home and in public spaces including online spaces, the risks to their rights—both protection and participation—can increase. This can mean, ironically, that for children who have the maturity and capacity to exercise their own rights, even in the advanced stage of childhood, other obstacles to realizing their rights persist. In middle childhood, too, parents must navigate children's emerging autonomy, giving rise to greater focus on protection rights than might be expected. As Peleg and Varadan illustrate, for instance, during middle childhood, children's entry into the digital world—often without parents' knowledge, consent, or capacity to influence or control what children do online or what information technology companies collect about their children—creates particular challenges for the exercise of parental responsibility under Articles 5 and 18. They reflect how, especially in the digital age, navigating this complex period of evolving capacity and parental responsibility can present new challenges during middle childhood. They note, for example, "In the context of children's online lives, where access to information and privacy will have a direct bearing on how a child is able to freely express and test out thoughts and ideas, it will fall on parents and those adults closest to the child to both enable and safeguard this process in a way that allows children to explore a diverse sense of self and belonging in the broader world."

Throughout this volume, the importance of listening to children and enabling their meaningful participation in decisions that affect them emerges as an important theme from both the development and the children's rights perspectives. Writing from a children's rights perspective, Peleg and Varadan note that this process may "hold the key to ensuring that the CRC remains relevant and responsive to the challenges and issues facing children today." Similarly, viewed through a developmental lens, Grant highlights the value of participation to children's subjective well-being, drawing attention to the benefit, as well as the right, of children's participation. While such common ground is very important, what also emerges from the analysis is the added merit of exposing participation rights to the rigor of interdisciplinary scrutiny. It is remarkable, perhaps, that even participation rights—about which so much has already been written—can yield new layers of understanding when viewed through a lens in which child development and children's rights are integrated.

III. A Way Forward: Interweaving Rights, Development, and the Views of Young People

The key tenet of this book is that considering children's rights from the perspective of child development enables evidence from development psychology to be brought to bear on the understanding, analysis, and application of children's rights. We also believe that development research can be enriched by a focus on the legal frameworks within which children's rights are implemented. To reap the many benefits that such an approach offers, it is important to explore ways in which the two fields can be mutually supportive. In this section, therefore, we look briefly at the three pillars of this project—children's rights, child development, and children's perspectives—in order to offer some ideas for further collaborative research. We begin with children themselves.

A. The Role of Children and Youth

As Article 12 of the CRC makes clear, children have a right to a say in all matters that affect them. This applies to research and to the development of law and policy, which can benefit enormously from children's lived experiences of their rights and the law, policies, programs, and institutions that regulate their lives, as Choi, Todres, and Paul demonstrate in chapter 10. Ensuring that children and youth have opportunities to participate in a rights-compliant manner is thus essential to any strategy that seeks to build bridges between children's rights and child development.

The movement to secure the rights of all children and youth has long sought to confront the deep-seated adult practice of devaluing or ignoring children and their views—pushing back against the age-old adage that children should be "seen and not heard." As Blaisdell and Tisdall explain, "'traditional' constructions of childhood" have "tended to depict children and childhood (and especially young children and early childhood) as vulnerable, dependent, incompetent, and innocent." By contrast, recognizing children as rights holders brings with it an entitlement that children's views are taken seriously and that their participation in matters that affect them is secured. And, importantly, this applies and must be extended to all children, not merely children who are especially articulate or from privileged backgrounds. As varied contributions to this volume show, the broad-based participation of children in decision-making has significant developmental—and wider—benefits.

Although children's rights analysis accepts the legal principle, set out in the CRC, that children have a right to a say in matters that affect them, child development helps us understand why it is important both to the child and to the efficacy of processes and programs that support the child's development. Research on child development, as this volume shows, can also help to educate policy makers and others about the capacity of children to participate in developmentally appropriate ways. It is evident from the development chapters how important capacity is, and we see from the children's rights chapters too that it is a complex concept that is not easily or uniformly applied at the different stages of childhood. However, too often in the rights context, children's capacity is inappropriately treated as a threshold requirement to access not just their right to participate but their rights at all. Development science shows how rather than viewing capacity as a limitation, we can improve our understanding of the supports that children need at different stages of development to contribute in meaningful ways to their communities.

In other contexts, most notably social justice movements around issues such as climate change, gun violence, immigration, and more, young people are making their voices heard and emerging as leaders of movements that can help secure children's rights.[24] Williams notes that adolescents need "avenues to develop a sense of meaning and purpose by contributing to peers, families, and communities." Children of all ages, not just adolescents, are assuming the role of human rights defenders contributing to debates on the pressing issues of the day, holding adults to account. Both child development and children's rights arguably raise important questions about potential limitations in this context, as the question of protection from harm emerges often to limit children's civil and political participation. Perhaps ultimately this raises the issue of the voting age. Quoting the Committee on the Rights of the Child, which has recommended that states "adopt policies to increase opportunities for political participation, which is instrumental in the development of active citizenship," Rap argues that "one way to do so is to lower the voting age below the age of eighteen."[25] While pathways to civic engagement are vital, we emphasize here that from a rights perspective, children must have "space, voice, audience, and influence" in the research domain and, in particular, in any research on children's rights or children's development.[26] As is clear from Choi, Todres, and Paul's chapter, the children's rights research community has much to share with its counterparts in child development from the experience of rights-based participation in research.

B. The Role of Child Development Science

As the discussion in this chapter and throughout the book reveals, there is a tremendous amount to be learned from child development science that could be brought to bear on the implementation and application of children's rights law. It is clear from this volume that the rapidly evolving nature of the research process continues to illuminate our understanding of child development and of children's rights as development science grows and the CRC evolves from the 1980s world in which it was drafted. As Lee and Kim note, for instance, there was less scientific understanding of adolescent development at that time, although the Committee has in its General Comments demonstrated how to take account of the shifting science, for example, by revising its approach to the minimum age of criminal responsibility, based, in part, on changes in the understanding of brain development.[27] Similarly, there is growing recognition that the CRC's silence on early childhood education and preschool does not reflect what we now understand about the critical nature of early childhood development, and efforts are under way to address that gap in children's rights law.[28]

Among the benefits of child development research is that it helps elevate selected rights that are often overlooked in human rights discourses, despite pronouncements that all rights are equal and indivisible.[29] In this volume, Grant highlights the importance of play, which, like the right to culture, is often relegated to the margins. Article 31, which recognizes children's right to play, rest, and leisure (all taking on their own meaning at each developmental stage), can be seen as a "luxury" that is often underplayed from a rights point of view.[30] What we learn from the science of child development, however, is that play is vital to a child's healthy development—suggesting a link with Article 6 to reinforce Article 31—and is foundational to the development of an array of skills children need throughout life.[31] Thus, taking the learning from development science and meaningfully integrating it in rights analyses could help elevate the right to play and promote greater efforts by states toward its implementation.[32]

Emerging science must continue to inform our dynamic understanding of the exercise and application of children's rights, even as we recognize limitations in the science.[33] According to Williams, "pubertal changes have followed a secular trend, happening at earlier ages in most places around the world now than they did 150 years ago." This makes it important that policy approaches linked to specific developmental stages are regularly reviewed and evaluated. Indeed, this tension between the ever-evolving nature of science and law's need to make determinations at fixed points in time—adopting new legislation or issuing judicial opinions—is not limited to issues affecting children. But given the dynamic, time-sensitive nature of childhood, it is critical that stronger connections be forged between development research and the evaluation of law and policy on children's rights. Law not only must rely on the best available evidence at the time but also must be structured to allow for consistent evaluation and updating to ensure that it keeps up with our scientific knowledge of children's development.

As we have already noted earlier, child development research views children in their wider worlds, viewed against a range of variables and domains: relational, cultural, geographical, and economic. Scientific evidence reinforces the arbitrariness of age-based rules, suggesting that a challenge to the use of bright-line rules could well have merit from a development perspective. The CRC is largely silent on the use of age limits, offering a flexibility that allows emerging science to be taken into account. At the same time, as Rap notes, the approach of the Committee on the Rights of the Child is confusing insofar as it advocates the use of ages in certain contexts, in order to promote rather than to limit greater participation in decision-making. Her call for an approach that is based on sound developmental science resonates loudly here.

While there are many common approaches flowing through the pages of the book, dissonance between development science and children's rights can also be found. Williams notes, for instance, that the different perceptions of childhood, dependent on culture, as well as the biases inherent in research, can create a very confused landscape especially for adolescence. At the same time, it is clear that the preconceived ideas about children in early childhood being more worthy of protection, with those in middle childhood struggling to have their views taken into account, are unfounded in the developmental science, even if, as Williams notes, physical appearances can be deceiving with respect to emotional and wider maturity especially for adolescents. Similarly, Rap notes how media coverage can create a "biased and stereotyped image" of older children or of children from certain backgrounds (especially minoritized children), which states can then use to justify seeking to adopt more punitive approaches, including toward children in conflict with the law and those impacted by trafficking and sexual exploitation. Overall, however, it is clear that a greater focus on the evidence of child development science can promote a more positive, rights-based approach, requiring an approach that reflects children as rights holders, supported to exercise those rights in line with their evolving capacity, with protection and participation/autonomy rights taking on different meaning at each developmental stage. What is evident from this volume, therefore, is the need for evidence-based approaches to implementing and operationalizing children's rights, drawing on our growing and evolving understanding of the development stages of childhood. Recognizing that interdisciplinary analysis offers scope for critical as well as deeper analysis, it is hoped that this collection goes some way toward forging such an approach.

C. The Role of Children's Rights Law

Ultimately, this volume aims to bring a more nuanced approach to children's rights law and its application across the various stages of childhood, and while we address research and researchers throughout this chapter, our observations are equally applicable to law and policy makers. Development science has already revealed much about, and will continue to inform, our understanding of how children's rights operate in practice. These insights raise important questions about the nature of children's rights, given that it simultaneously emerges out of the liberal tradition of rights built on the autonomous individual and yet operates differently, given the developmental nature of childhood. Children, especially young children, need parents, caregivers, and others to help them realize their rights. As Harbach notes, quoting the Committee, "parents and other caregivers will be the 'major conduit through which young children are able to realize their rights.'"[34] At other ages and stages of development, children are still vulnerable and not fully autonomous, but they need to be given greater support and space to exercise their rights on their own. Blaisdell and Tisdall emphasize the universality of vulnerability. These ideas challenge children's rights, and the human rights movement more broadly, to make rights meaningful and relevant to children at each stage of development.

Relatedly, the present and future are both at play with children and their rights in ways that are different from discourses about the rights of adults, because of the developmental nature of childhood. As Peleg and Varadan note, "Children's present and future privacy interests can be impacted in multiple ways by their online engagement." Among other things, this could mean that we need to think about new rights, such as the right to be forgotten in the digital context, that will enable children to explore and develop in diverse, creative ways, without the burden of future opportunities being unjustly curtailed.

The world is changing rapidly, and its impacts on children's rights will continue to require understanding and rigorous research from multiple perspectives. Climate change, poverty, war and conflict, artificial intelligence, and other existential threats present enormous challenges to the implementation and enjoyment of children's rights. Peleg and Varadan write, "This new way of being a child in middle childhood, however, gives rise to a different set of questions, which relate to agency; privacy, including information sharing and surveillance; and rights." The broader point also holds true: the rapid and dramatic changes to the world will require adaptation and further development of children's rights law. Such adaptation and further development of children's rights law is likely to be most successful if it draws on rigorous interdisciplinary research combining insights from child development that show how best to ensure the fulfillment of every child's rights. Law and policy, as with research, must engage with children's rights, be informed by the science of child development, and take account of the views of children and young people themselves if its potential to support the development of rights-bearing children is to be realized.

IV. Conclusion

This chapter highlights some of the issues that emerge when children's rights and child development discourses are brought together. Drawing on all the chapters in this collection, we point to the need for a wider discussion about the relationship between developmental stages and children's rights. On the one hand, as noted in the introduction to this volume, there is an inherent tension between law's need to be broad and inclusive when recognizing rights holders and extending protections to children, and child development science's need to be precise and cautious in its conclusions, appropriately acknowledging limitations in existing research. At the same time, and conversely, child development literature recognizes that every child is unique and that development and maturation occur differently in every child, suggesting that, among other things, blurred lines between stages of development reflect the realities of children. And sometimes that flexibility pushes up against law's need for bright-line rules, to ensure greater clarity ex ante.[35]

As we seek to forge connections between children's rights and child development, we inevitably have to make some initial generalizations. It is stating the obvious to say that many children do not live at the mean, but rather children's lived experiences are incredibly varied and diverse; and so too is their development. It is also important to acknowledge that while many children are born into extreme poverty or conflict, others live lives full of opportunity. Notwithstanding this diversity, to advance this discourse between the fields, we have to start with what each field knows generally to be true, and thus some generalizations are necessary. As we do this, we need to be cognizant of not only our own personal assumptions and biases but also where the research on which we base our conclusions derives from. As Blaisdell and Tisdall note, certain views of a "good early childhood" privilege "individualized ways of being and learning" that are dominant in Global North perspectives, "rarely acknowledging other ways of knowing and doing in early childhood." This reinforces our call for greater interdisciplinarity in the field of children's rights, so that each field can be open to learning from the other and questioning its own assumptions.

The very important role played by structural, cultural, and systemic contexts including disadvantage is highlighted by all. Williams highlights that their influence in "promoting or curtailing opportunities for thriving can be difficult to pinpoint," while at the same time, she notes that "leaving them out allows for narratives about the role of the individual or of a particular group as the central cause of their own success or demise to prevail." While the multiplicity and complexity of interconnected factors is difficult to clearly decipher, what is apparent, as Williams succinctly suggests, is that "experiences and settings matter a great deal." Where this "context" and the biases it reinforces can be found in the children's rights discourse merits further examination.

Ultimately, there is much in common between development and children's rights. Grant mentions learning fairness as a foundation for human rights principles, quoting studies, for instance, that show how eleven-year-olds understand equity by focusing on the redistribution of resources. This reflects the worldwide consultation with children undertaken for the Committee on the Rights of the Child's General Comment on public budgeting for the realization of children's rights.[36] This volume also indicates multiple other instances when rights protections are positively correlated to children's subjective well-being in childhood, and whether in development or play, protection or participation, there is common ground to be found between development and rights perspectives. What both disciplines also share is an understanding of how incomplete the analysis of children's lives can be, without their participation in this process. As Williams highlights, "Our understanding of adolescent development and the implications of the science for adolescents' rights will remain incomplete until the voices of young people themselves are more meaningfully integrated." It is perhaps in this common approach to our research—where children are involved in our research as a right—that we can find a shared purpose and a foundation on which an integrated approach to children's rights and healthy child development can be built.

NOTES

1 UN Convention on the Rights of the Child, art. 6(2), 1577 U.N.T.S. 3 (November 20, 1989) (hereafter CRC). Although Article 6 is one of the General Principles of the CRC, it receives significantly less attention by the Committee on the Rights of the Child. See, e.g., Charlotte Alexander and Jonathan Todres, "Evaluating the Implementation of Human Rights Law: A Data Analytics Research Agenda," *University of Pennsylvania Journal of International Law* 43, no. 1 (2021): 1–77.

2 Kristin Henning, *The Rage of Innocence: How America Criminalizes Black Youth* (New York: Pantheon Books, 2021).

3 Jonathan Todres and Shani M. King, "Children's Rights in the Twenty-First Century: Challenges and Opportunities," in *The Oxford Handbook of Children's Rights Law*, ed. Jonathan Todres and Shani M. King (New York: Oxford University Press, 2020), 719–728.

4 CRC, art. 1.

5 UN Committee on the Rights of the Child, *General Comment No. 12: The Right of the Child to Be Heard*, paras. 28–32, CRC/C/GC/12 (2009).

6 UN Committee on the Rights of the Child, *General Comment No. 24 on Children's Rights in the Child Justice System*, paras. 21–22, CRC/C/GC/24 (2019); UN Committee on the Rights of the Child, *General Comment No. 10: Children's Rights in Juvenile Justice*, paras. 32–33, CRC/C/GC/10 (2007).

7 Jonathan Todres and Louise Howe, "What the U.N. Convention on the Rights of the Child Says (and Doesn't Say) about Abortion and Family Planning," in *The U.N. Convention on the Rights of the Child: An Analysis of Treaty Provisions and the Implications of U.S. Ratification*, ed. Jonathan Todres, Mark Wojcik, and Cris Revaz (Leiden: Brill, 2006), 163–175.

8 On the interrelated nature of women's rights and children's rights, see Jonathan Todres, "Children's Rights and Women's Rights: Interrelated and Interdependent," in *Handbook of Children's Rights: Global and Multidisciplinary Perspectives*, ed. Martin Ruck, Michele Peterson-Badali, and Michael Freeman (New York: Routledge, 2016).

9 CRC, art. 1.

10 Jonathan Todres, "Confronting Categorical Exclusions Based on Age: The Rights of Children and Youth," *Harvard Human Rights Journal* 36 (2023): 283–298.

11 Esperenza Ochaita and M. Ángeles Espinosa, "Children's Participation in Family and School Life: A Psychological and Developmental Approach," *International Journal of Children's Rights* 5 (1997): 280.

12 See Hiroharu Saito, "Equal Protection for Children: Toward the Childist Legal Studies," *New Mexico Law Review* 50, no. 2 (2020): 262–264; Daniel Hart and Robert Atkins, "American Sixteen- and Seventeen-Year-Olds Are Ready to Vote," *Annals of the American Academy of Political and Social Science* 633, no. 1 (2011): 208; Benjamin Oosterhoff, Laura Wray-Lake, and Daniel Hart, "Reconsidering the Minimum Voting Age in the United States," *Perspectives on Psychological Science* 17, no. 2 (2022): 445.

13 UN Committee on the Right of the Child, *General Comment 12*, paras. 20–21; Laura Lundy, "'Voice Is Not Enough': Conceptualizing Article 12 of the United Nations Convention on the Rights of the Child," *British Educational Research Journal* 33, no. 6 (2007): 935–938; David Archard and Marit Skivenes, "Balancing a Child's Best Interests and a Child's Views," *International Journal of Children's Rights*. 17, no. 1 (2009): 1–21.

14 Sheila Varadan, "The Principle of Evolving Capacities under the UN Convention on the Rights of the Child," *International Journal of Children's Rights* 27, no. 2 (2019): 306–338.

15 Claire McDiarmid, "An Age of Complexity: Children and Criminal Responsibility in Law," *Youth Justice* 13, no. 2 (2013): 145–160.

16 Noam Peleg, *The Child's Right to Development* (Cambridge: Cambridge University Press, 2019).

17 Michael Freeman, *A Magna Carta for Children? Rethinking Children's Rights* (Cambridge: Cambridge University Press, 2020).

18 See Todres, "Children's Rights and Women's Rights."

19 Ibid.

20 International Commission of Jurists, *Maastricht Guidelines on Economic, Social, and Cultural Rights* (Maastricht: United Nations, 1997); UN General Assembly, *Indivisibility and Interdependence of Economic, Social, Cultural, Civil and Political Rights*, A/Res/41/117 (December 4, 1986).

21 See Kimberlé Crenshaw, "Mapping the Margins: Intersectionality, Identity Politics, and Violence against Women of Color," *Stanford Law Review* 43 (1991): 1241–1299.

22 See Gary W. Evans, "Childhood Poverty and Adult Psychological Well-Being." *Proceedings of the National Academy of Sciences of the United States of America* 113, no. 52 (2016): 14949–14952; National Academies of Sciences, Engineering, and Medicine, *A Roadmap to Reducing Child Poverty* (Washington, DC: National Academies Press, 2019); Matt Repka, "Enduring Damage: The Effects of Childhood Poverty on Adult Health," *Chicago Policy Review*, November 27, 2013, https://chicagopolicyreview.org.

23 UN Committee on the Rights of the Child, *General Comment No. 25 on Children's Rights in Relation to the Digital Environment*, CRC/C/GC/25 (2021).

24 Jonathan Todres, Charlene Choi, and Joseph Wright, "A Rights-Based Assessment of Youth Participation in the United States," *Temple Law Review* 95, no. 3 (2023): 411–455; Charisa Smith, "Youth Visions and Empowerment: Reconstruction through Revolution," *Rutgers University Law Review* 75 (2023): 825–895.

25 UN Committee on the Rights of the Child, *General Comment No. 20: On the Implementation of the Rights of the Child during Adolescence*, para. 24, CRC/C/GC/20 (2016).

26 Lundy, "Voice in Not Enough," 932–933.

27 UN Committee on the Right of the Child, *General Comment No. 24*.

28 Bede Sheppard, "It's Time to Expand the Right to Education," *Nordic Journal of Human Rights* 40, no. 1 (2022): 96–117.

29 United Nations, *Children's Rights Mainstreaming: Guidance Note of the Secretary-General* (Geneva: United Nations, 2023), 4.

30 Ciara Davey and Laura Lundy, "Towards Greater Recognition of the Right to Play: An Analysis of Article 31 of the UNCRC," *Children and Society* 25, no. 1 (2011): 3–14.

31 Kenneth R. Ginsburg, "The Importance of Play in Promoting Healthy Child Development and Maintaining Strong Parent-Child Bonds," *Pediatrics* 119 (2007): 182–191.

32 UN Committee on the Rights of the Child, *General Comment No. 17 on the Right of the Child to Rest, Leisure, Play, Recreational Activities, Cultural Life and the Arts (Art. 31)*, CRC/C/GC/17 (2013).

33 See Catherine E. Draper, Lisa M. Barnett, Caylee J. Cook, Jorge A. Cuartas, Steven J. Howard, Dana C. McCoy, Rebecca Merkley, et al., "Publishing Child Development Research from Around the World: An Unfair Playing Field Resulting in Most of the World's Child Population Under-represented in Research," *Infant and Child Development* 32, no. 6 (2022): e2375; Christia Spears Brown, Rashmita S. Mistry, and Tiffany Yip, "Moving from the Margins to the Mainstream: Equity and Justice as Key Considerations for Developmental Science," *Child Development Perspectives* 13, no. 4 (2019): 235–240; Stephanie J. Rowley and Tissyana C. Camacho, "Increasing Diversity in Cognitive Developmental Research: Issues and Solutions," *Journal of Cognition and Development* 16, no. 5 (2015): 683–692.

34 UN Committee on the Rights of the Child, *General Comment No. 7: Implementing Child Rights in Early Education*, para. 16, CRC/C/GC/7 (November 1, 2005).

35 Todres, "Confronting Categorical Exclusions Based on Age."

36 UN Committee on the Rights of the Child, *General Comment No. 19 on Public Budgeting for the Realization of Children's Rights (Art. 4)*, paras. 8 and 50, CRC/C/GC/19 (2016).

ACKNOWLEDGMENTS

We would like to thank the contributing authors for their willingness to participate in this project, which required an openness to new ideas and cross-disciplinary critique of one's work. Forging new ground required that all the authors embrace a process that often evolved in real time, and we are grateful that they did. Thank you also to Clara Platter and the editorial team at NYU Press for supporting this project. We also want to thank Nancy E. Dowd and Robin Lenhardt, editors of the Family, Law, and Society Series of NYU Press, for their valuable early feedback as we were developing the book concept. A special thank you to Clara Paul, who not only coauthored one of the chapters but also provided important research support on several other chapters. We also want to thank Cody A. Choi and Jessi B. Bartholomew (both GSU College of Law, JD, 2024) for their excellent editorial assistance. Throughout the development of this book, we had numerous conversations with researchers and professionals across many disciplines, and we are so appreciative of the support and encouragement they gave to this project. Finally, we would like to thank our families: Alison, Benjamin, and Desmond; and Cathal and Evan and the Kilkelly clan. As with every other thing in life, this project was made possible and more enjoyable because of them.

ABOUT THE CONTRIBUTORS

Jonathan Todres is Distinguished University Professor and Professor of Law at Georgia State University College of Law. He is a leading expert on children's rights. His research focuses, in particular, on the implementation of children's rights law, human rights education, human trafficking, and youth participation. His recent books include *The Oxford Handbook of Children's Rights Law* (2020, with Shani King), *Preventing Child Trafficking: A Public Health Approach* (2019, with Angela Diaz), and *Human Rights in Children's Literature: Imagination and the Narrative of Law* (2016, with Sarah Higinbotham). He serves as a regular adviser to nongovernmental organizations working to address various children's rights issues. He is chair of the Board on Children, Youth, and Families of the National Academies of Sciences, Engineering, and Medicine. He is a past chair of both the Section on International Human Rights and the Section on Children and the Law of the Association of American Law Schools and has served in various leadership roles in the American Bar Association's Section of International Law. In 2018, he served as a Fulbright Scholar in residence at University College Cork in Ireland. He is a Life Fellow of the American Bar Foundation. He holds a JD from Columbia Law School and a BA (International Development) from Clark University, and he served as a US Peace Corps volunteer in Thailand.

Ursula Kilkelly is Professor of Law at the School of Law, University College Cork, Ireland. She is a leading expert on international children's rights and youth justice, having published multiple journal articles, monographs, and edited collections with a host of distinguished collaborators and publishers on subjects of legal implementation of children's rights, access to justice, health care, and youth detention. Her latest books include *National Human Rights Institutions for Children* (2021, with Emily Logan), *Advancing Children's Rights in Detention: A*

Model for International Reform (2022, with Pat Bergin), and *Children in Conflict with the Law, Rights, Research and Progressive Youth Justice* (2023, with Louise Forde, Katharina Swirak, and Sharon Lambert). She is Editor, with Stefaan Pleysier of KU Leuven, of *Youth Justice*, the leading journal in the field. She lectures on children's rights at UCC and around the world, and in 2022–2023, she held the Rotating Chair in the Enforcement of Children's Rights at Leiden University, the Netherlands. She is also a rights activist and leader and has significant experience in the implementation of children's rights in challenging settings like detention, through a decade-long appointment to the Board of Ireland's national detention facility, Oberstown. She also advises national governments, international bodies, and nongovernmental organizations on children's rights issues.

Caralyn Blaisdell is Senior Lecturer in Teacher Education at Queen Margaret University. She is an experienced early years pedagogue, having worked in corporate, Reggio Emilia–inspired, and Froebelian early years settings in the United States and Scotland. Her research focuses on two main strands. First, she explores children's rights in early childhood, particularly participation rights and listening to very young children. Second, she works on outdoor learning in the early years, particularly young children's experiences and relationships with land and place. She approaches both strands from a relational perspective, looking at how young children's lives and experiences are shaped by intergenerational relationships, attitudes toward childhood, policy/practice trends, and relationships of power. Her research has been supported by funding from the Froebel Trust, the Scottish Funding Council, and Starcatchers, Scotland's Arts and Early Years organization. Recent publications include papers in the *European Early Childhood Education Research Journal*, *Emotion, Space and Society*, and *Policy Futures in Education*.

Charlene Choi translates child health policy for multicenter research as the Principal Policy and Sustainability Analyst for the UCLA David Geffen School of Medicine's Medicine-Pediatrics Division. She works on statewide and federal projects in over thirty-five communities for the California Department of Public Health, UCLA Center for Healthier Children, Families, and Communities, and the UCSF Center for Child and Community Health. She has previously led the strategic and financial development of community-based organizations, safety-net clinics, coalitions, and programs from Port-au-Prince to Los Angeles, and she is also passionate about the implementation of health and human rights in the United States. She holds a Juris Doctor from the University of Washington School of Law and a Bachelor of Arts from the University of California, Los Angeles.

AOIFE DALY is a professor specializing in human rights law at the School of Law, University College Cork. Her research focuses on human-rights-based approaches and children's rights in areas that include environmental rights, children's cognitive development, and access to justice. She is also author of the globally celebrated *Children, Autonomy and the Courts: Beyond the Right to be Heard* (2018) and *A Commentary on the UNCRC, Article 15: The Right to Freedom of Association and to Freedom of Peaceful Assembly*. In 2023, she secured a European Research Council Consolidator Grant to build a team to carry out a large-scale research study on child/youth climate justice—inside and outside the courts—around the world. In 2020–2022, she was an Early Career Fellow of the Independent Social Research Foundation, researching the intersection of children's rights, law, and "competence." This fellowship funded her work on this chapter and other publications including "Assessing Children's Capacity: Reconceptualising Our Understanding through the UN Convention on the Rights of the Child" (*International Journal of Children's Rights*, 2020).

JOSEPHINE GRANT is an educational psychologist. She teaches at Georgia State University in the College of Education and Human Development, where her courses aim to bridge child development and classroom practices. Her research explores how implementation values like fidelity and fit are applied to social-emotional learning programs in schools. She has developed curricula for diverse settings, including an "anger lab" for women mandated to treatment for substance abuse. Relevant to children's rights, she helped to develop a curriculum for twelve- and thirteen-year-olds at risk for sexual exploitation. The multiyear project, sponsored by the GSU Center for School Safety, School

Climate, and Classroom Management, was informed by the children themselves. Subsequent publications provided a window into the often-ambiguous language and mixed motives that operate in exploitive relationships. Outside of academia, she has worked as a developmental consultant in elementary and middle schools in Georgia.

MEREDITH JOHNSON HARBACH is Professor of Law at the University of Richmond School of Law, where she teaches courses in family law, children and the law, civil procedure, and reproductive justice. Her recent scholarship has analyzed and critiqued the state's relationship to families and children through the lens of the United States' child-care law and policy. She has also written on children's rights, feminist legal theory, and reproductive justice. Her work has appeared in the *Washington and Lee Law Review*, *Yale Journal of Law and Feminism*, *Utah Law Review*, *Yale Law and Policy Review*, in books, and in other legal academic publications. She has been quoted in the *New York Times* and written opinion pieces for the *Richmond Times Dispatch* and the *Daily Press*. She has been a Visiting Scholar with the Vulnerability and the Human Condition Initiative at Emory Law School. She formerly served as Chair of the American Association of Law School's Section on Children and the Law and is also a former member of the Virginia Council on Women, where she was Chair of the Women's Healthcare Initiative.

IHEOMA U. IRUKA is Research Professor in the Department of Public Policy and Founding Director of the Equity Research Action Coalition at Frank Porter Graham Child Development Institute at the University of North Carolina–Chapel Hill. She is leading projects and initiatives focused on ensuring that minoritized children and children from low-income households thrive through the intersection of antibias, antiracist, and culturally grounded research, program, and policy. She has authored over eighty books and papers and has given over three hundred talks addressing systemic inequities and advancing research and action on the well-being of children and families. She serves on numerous national and local boards and committees, including the National Academies of Sciences, Engineering, and Medicine, the American Psychological Association's Board of Educational Affairs, the National Science Foundation, and the Lancet Commission on Racism and Child Health. In addition to being on the National Advisory Committee for the US Census Bureau and a Census Advisor for the National Urban League, she is the recipient of the 2022 American Psychological Association Mid-Career Award for Outstanding Contributions to Benefit Children, Youth, and Families and the 2023 Association of University Centers on Disabilities Leadership for All Award. She is also a 2023 APA Fellow.

Sangwon Kim serves as Assistant Professor in the Department of Psychology and Child Studies at Hanshin University in Osan, Korea. She received her PhD from the Department of Child Psychology and Education at Sungkyunkwan University. During her stay as a visiting scholar at the Kempe Center for the Prevention and Treatment of Child Abuse and Neglect, University of Colorado, she was involved in the revision of the ISPCAN child abuse screening tool (ICAST). She served as an adjunct professor at Sungkyunkwan University and also was a visiting scholar at the Family Translation Research Group at New York University. In this capacity, she engaged in various projects investigating the mechanisms of interpersonal violence among teens, intimate partners, and at-risk military couples. She has published extensively in leading peer-reviewed scientific international and South Korean journals. Her primary research interests are violence against children, family/peer/community relationships, social capital, posttraumatic growth, child rights, implementation of the Convention on the Rights of the Child, and a child-friendly environment. Much of her work has focused on investigating mechanisms that lead to violence, with the aim of applying these findings to enhance social, educational, and therapeutic programs.

Yanghee Lee is Professor Emeritus of Child Psychology and Education at Sungkyunkwan University in Seoul, Korea. She was elected to the Board of Governors at East-West Center in 2023. She is the former UN Special Rapporteur on Human Rights in Myanmar. She served as a member (2003–2013) and chairperson (2007–2011) of the UN Committee on the Rights of the Child. She has also served as chairperson of the Meeting of Chairpersons of Treaty Bodies (2010–2011). Nationally, she serves on the Advisory Committee of the National Human Rights Commission of Korea. She is the founding President of the International Child Rights Center. In 2009, she received the Order of Civil Merit, the highest recognition given to a civilian, for her work in human rights. Regionally, she actively takes part in Asia Pacific debates and actively participates in ASEAN Human Rights Dialogues in areas of children and armed conflict and human rights within the context of migration. Internationally, she is recognized for her work as a member and chairperson of the UN Committee on the Rights of the Child. She has taken an active role in the process of strengthening the treaty body system, including the Dublin process. Her efforts in reopening the discussions on the need for a communications procedure for children, which ultimately led to the adoption of a third Optional Protocol to the Convention on the Rights of the Child, have been recognized. She earned a BS degree from Georgetown University and an MED and PhD from the University of Missouri–Columbia. She has published numerous articles and books on human rights and children's rights.

CLARA PAUL is a children's rights researcher and advocate. At present, she is undertaking a PhD in criminology at Keele University, aimed at understanding the experiences and perceptions of children who have been "criminally exploited," funded through an ESRC CASE studentship. Prior to this, she worked as a researcher in the School of Law, University College Cork, focusing on the implementation of children's rights, children's access to justice, independent children's rights institutions, and children in conflict with the law. She also worked as Program Manager at the nongovernmental organization Stichting KidsRights and as Policy Officer in the Council of Europe Children's Rights Division. She is a graduate of University Paris Nanterre and Leiden University, where she specialized in international children's rights.

NOAM PELEG is Senior Lecturer at the Faculty of Law and Justice, University of New South Wales, Sydney. His work focuses on international children's rights law and its intersection with human rights law, family law, and childhood studies. His book *The Child's Right to Development* was published in 2019. He is Book Review Editor and a member of the editorial board of the *International Journal of Children's Rights*. In 2020, he was Visiting Professor at Columbia Law School (New York). Before moving to academia, he practiced in a number of human rights NGOs, specializing in representing children in courts.

STEPHANIE RAP is a researcher at the research group Forensic Child and Youth Care, University of Amsterdam. She holds master's degrees in pedagogical sciences and criminology and a PhD degree from Utrecht University. Her research interest lies in the field of the effective participation of children in (judicial) procedures and decision-making. She studied child participation in diverse procedures and settings, such as in youth justice, child care and protection, and asylum procedures. She is a member of the editorial board of a journal on youth and children's rights (*Tijdschrift voor Jeugd en Kinderrechten*). In addition to her academic work, she is working as Senior Advisor at the Dutch Council for the Administration of Criminal Justice and Protection of Juveniles.

E. KAY M. TISDALL is Professor of Childhood Policy at the University of Edinburgh. She is part of Childhood and Youth Studies at Moray House School of Education and Sport. Her policy, academic, and teaching work is centered around children's human rights. She undertakes collaborative research with children, young people, and adults on such areas as children affected by domestic abuse, family law, inclusive pedagogy for young children, young people's mental health, and children's participation and activism. She is involved in a number of partnership projects, with teams in countries including Brazil, Canada, Colombia, Eswatini, Palestine, and South Africa, funded by such organizations as the Global Challenges Research Fund, the European Commission, UK Research and Innovations, and the Canadian Social Sciences and Humanities Research Council. Publications include the coauthored book *Critical Childhood Studies* (2023) and articles in journals such as *Childhood*, *Children & Society*, the *International Journal of Human Rights*, and the *International Journal of Children's Rights*.

SHEILA VARADAN is Assistant Professor of Children's Rights at Leiden University in the Netherlands. Her work focuses on the role of parents (and other caregivers) in supporting their children's exercise of rights under international human rights law. She has published on children's rights to decision-making in medical research and the evolving capacities of the child. Prior to her doctoral studies, she worked as a human rights lawyer for fifteen years in Southeast Asia. She worked on projects related to human rights, access to justice, and child sexual exploitation, with international humanitarian aid organizations, international nongovernmental organizations, and UN agencies. She successfully defended her PhD, titled *Article 5 of the UN Convention on the Rights of the Child: Parental Guidance and the Evolving Capacities of the Child*, in June 2022 at Leiden University.

AMY WALSH is a practicing Barrister based in Dublin, Ireland. She has a particular interest in the areas of criminal law, European arrest warrant (EAW) law, coronial law, child law, family law, financial services law, and regulatory law. She has acted in a number of High Court matters and is currently on the legal team for the state in the *Stardust Fire Inquests*. She holds a first-class master's degree in literature, which focused on critical theory, and an LLM in criminology and criminal justice. She has held legal research assistant positions in both University College Cork and Trinity College Dublin in the areas of the Convention on the Rights of the Child and Prison Law and has held lecturing positions in areas including criminology. In 2022, she authored an article titled "Reform of Victim Testimony in Sexual Offence Trials" for the *Irish Criminal Law Journal*. She is passionate about researching and advocating for the rights of victims of sexual crime and children in the criminal justice system.

JOANNA WILLIAMS is Associate Professor in the Department of School Psychology at Rutgers University. Her scholarship centers on issues of race, identity, and relationships during the adolescent period and includes a focus on racially and ethnically diverse school settings. She is also Senior Director of Research for Search Institute, a nonprofit organization that promotes positive youth development and advances equity through applied research and collaborative partnerships with youth-serving organizations. She codirects the National Scientific Council on Adolescence. She is also a member of the National Academies of Science, Engineering, and Medicine's (NASEM's) Board on Children, Youth, and Families and served on the NASEM committee for the 2019 consensus study *The Promise of Adolescence: Realizing Opportunity for All Youth*. She was a recipient of a William T. Grant Scholars Award and is past Chair of the Black Caucus of the Society for Research on Child Development. She serves on the editorial boards for *Journal of Youth and Adolescence* and *Applied Developmental Science* and is an associate editor for *Developmental Psychology*.

INDEX

www.ingramcontent.com/pod-product-compliance
Ingram Content Group UK Ltd.
Pitfield, Milton Keynes, MK11 3LW, UK
UKHW031824260325
456724UK00003B/4/J

9 781479 825486